AGAINST THE ODDS:

Major Donald E. Keyhoe and His Battle
to End UFO Secrecy

A Biography by Linda C. Powell

Anomalist Books
Charlottesville, Virginia

An Original Publication of Anomalist Books

Against the Odds:
Major Donald E. Keyhoe and His Battle to End UFO Secrecy
Copyright © 2023 by Linda C. Powell
ISBN: 978-1-949501-32-2
Second Edition

Cover image: Donald E. Keyhoe, courtesy of the Mary Evans Picture Library
(maryevans.com)
Book design: Seale Studios

Anomalist Books
3445 Seminole Trail #247
Charlottesville, VA 22911

Contents

This work is dedicated to
Major Donald E. Keyhoe,
Richard H. Hall,
James E. McDonald,
and Gordon Lore

Donald E. Keyhoe (Mary Evans Picture Library)

Introduction

From where did the widespread belief come that UFOs represent extraterrestrial technology and that the government is hiding this truth from us? The man perhaps most responsible for these twin pillars of current UFO belief is Donald E. Keyhoe.

He was a 51-year-old retired Marine Major when his own investigation of a famous 1948 alleged flying saucer case led him to believe that the US Air Force and the CIA knew the Earth was under surveillance by beings from other worlds and were keeping it secret from the public. For the next twenty-one years, he devoted himself, at great personal cost, to exposing what he believed was an official cover-up of alien visitations. Through his highly-placed contacts in the military and secret informants in the Pentagon, he became the first nationally and internationally-known figure to truly challenge the official view that UFO reports belonged only in the domain of "kooks and fuzzy thinkers." Moreover, he was determined to bring about Congressional Hearings which, he hoped, would result in official action to end the cover-up. To facilitate these aims, Keyhoe became head of what was soon to be the world's most powerful civilian UFO organization, the National Investigations Committee on Aerial Phenomena (NICAP).

In this, the first biography of Donald Keyhoe, his public and private life before and during his time as the world's best-known UFO advocate is revealed, based largely on his own accounts taken from his books, letters, articles, and recordings, together with extensive use of the recorded or written words of key individuals. These sources tell us a great deal about not only his own actions and feelings, but also of those who worked with and against him.

Seventy-five years have passed since Keyhoe quietly began to take an interest in the saucers and to turn his life toward writing about and investigating their existence, thereby establishing the shape of civilian UFO research in our own time. Today, in the third decade of the 21st century, the status quo against which he battled continues to hold sway, exemplified when we learned in 2017 that the Pentagon had been secretly investigating the UFO phenomenon. This brought a glimmer of hope for the fabled "disclosure," which Keyhoe so fervently pursued, but it was another false dawn, like so many he'd experienced. History continues to repeat itself.

Keyhoe never doubted that someday, the real story would "break wide open" and he would be vindicated in his firm conviction that Earth was being observed by people from other worlds and that perhaps there was a terrible truth, hidden from the public for fear of panic.

After the greater part of a century, we are still waiting to know if he was right.

Prologue

From a mile away and a thousand feet in the air, Charles Augustus Lindbergh could already see the crowd of fifty-thousand people swarming across the sparse, 350-acre airfield at Hartford, Connecticut. They were excited, almost feverish, when the shining wings of the *Spirit of St. Louis* came skimming down out of the sky."[1] Few of them had ever seen "Lucky Lindy" in the flesh and the thrill of watching the most famous aviator in the world landing in their midst was an historic moment they would never forget.

Even fewer knew that their hero's visit, just ten weeks after his record transatlantic solo flight in May 1927, was coordinated and managed by a retired former Marine, Donald Edward Keyhoe. This 30-year-old, quiet-spoken man was deeply honored by, and profoundly conscious of, the responsibility given to him.

The "Lone Eagle" had been preceded only minutes earlier by a Fairchild FC2 monoplane, which carried his support team, led by Keyhoe. They should have arrived half an hour earlier to check that arrangements were in place, but had been delayed by unforeseen problems. As their plane made its hasty descent, Keyhoe was relieved that the star of the show hadn't yet arrived. Looking out of the window, he observed the milling multitude on the ground and "wondered what Lindbergh's thoughts would be on seeing this demonstration of the continued interest in him."

Thanks in large part to Donald Keyhoe, his idol was landing at the first stop on a unique, 48-state air tour to "promote interest in aviation" and "to show people that aviation can come through on time."[2] He had been chosen to work with Lindbergh only two weeks earlier, due to his experience the previous year, when he performed a similar function for a shorter US air tour by pilot Floyd Bennett who, with Richard Byrd, claimed in May 1926 to have made the first flight over the North Pole.[3]

The "mad uproar of a city gone wild,"which erupted when the *Spirit of St. Louis* touched down, left Keyhoe no time to study his hero's reactions to the "rapid series of greetings, photographs, welcoming by the committee, and other ceremonies" that followed his landing. This pandemonium would be repeated almost daily for the next three months, during which Keyhoe's admiration for Lindy, now the world's biggest celebrity, would only increase.

Two decades later his own name would become internationally famous in connection with other aerial craft of a type which neither he, nor Lindbergh, could then even dream.

Chapter 1: Roots

Donald Keyhoe could lay no claim to patrician or ivy-league roots, but his upbringing was nonetheless one to which a great many Americans aspired at the turn of the twentieth century and beyond.

His ancestral roots through both parents—Calvin Grant Keyhoe and Georgina May Cherry—went back to the colonial settlers of Maine, New Hampshire, and Pennsylvania, and the Keyhoes and the Cherrys, not yet acquainted, moved gradually west into Ohio, where they remained for several years before moving to Iowa.

Calvin Grant was born in Ohio in 1866 and eleven years later arrived in Ottumwa with his parents, Ephraim and Milvina, and his five older siblings. The city had undergone rapid development since it was staked in 1843, at which time it had little more than a cluster of log houses and a jail. By the time the Keyhoes arrived, it had become an ideal place for young, ambitious, patriotic families, who were filled with the spirit of expansion and of building a new nation in their own image.

In 1895 in Keokuk, Iowa, Grant (who had discarded his first name) married May Cherry (she also preferred her middle name), daughter of James and Laura Cherry. The couple settled in Ottumwa, first at West Fifth Street, where Donald Edward was born in 1897, and soon after moved to nearby West Woodland Avenue, one of many up-and-coming new neighborhoods in the rapidly-developing city of 20,000, where they were among working and lower middle-class residents—teachers, plasterers, clerks, and laborers. By the time little Don was only three years old and his sister, Lucy Katherine, was but eight months, his parents were already doing well; though they did not own their home, they were among very few residents who kept a live-in servant.[4]

Grant had been a mailman since 1890 and was known locally as "the whistling mail carrier," a position he held for nineteen years, which eventually made him "the oldest man on the force" and who was reputed to be highly popular with colleagues and the public. Moreover, he and his brothers, Harry, Horton, and Edgar, had lost no time in establishing themselves in Ottumwa's economy and politics. In 1888, only eleven years after the family had arrived, the brothers had founded the Union Iron Works, and Grant later became President of the local branch of the National Association of Letter Carriers and a member of the Ottumwa Civil Service Board. Keyhoe's uncle, Harry Parker Keyhoe, was treasurer and secretary of the Union Ironworks and would be elected Alderman of the city in 1903, a position he held until 1907. Uncle Horton was foreman at the iron works, and uncle Edgar owned a grocery store on West Fifth Street. None of this gained the Keyhoes spectacular wealth, but they enjoyed status and financial security and were integral to Ottumwa's municipal functions.

Grant, in addition to his role as Whistling Postman, possessed a prize-winning baritone voice, with which he gave solo performances and also sang with a male quartet, The Ottumwas, whose members included his friend, the local undertaker, Frank Daggett. His grandfather was wealthy William Daggett, who was "vice president of the Ottumwa Railway, Electric Light and Steam Company, president of the Equitable Loan Association, vice president of the Iowa National Bank, and a director of the Ottumwa Opera House Company."[5]

Don Keyhoe's mother was perpetually occupied with civic duties and activities common to genteel middle-class women of her era. The Keyhoes and the Cherrys were committed Episcopalians, which led May to become active in the Home Missionary Society, for which she was among Iowa's delegates at their annual meets, and her daughter, Katherine (she also preferred her middle name), would devote her life to missionary work in India and in her home country, until her senior years.

But Keyhoe's family were not merely ordinary folk who achieved stability and comfort entirely due to their personal virtues; they were part of a social and political circle that took care of its own. Grant Keyhoe, like his father, was a Mason and a Republican, with friends in the right places. Among the most influential in Ottumwa was Frank Nimocks, a "staunch Republican," who held several important positions, including that of GOP chairman for Wapello County, and he frequently placed fellow Masons and the party faithful in positions of influence in the city. It was this association which led, in 1909, to Grant being appointed as Deputy to Nimocks, who had been selected as Postmaster by "a considerable majority" thanks in part to his ability as a "political organizer."

Grant, of whom it was written, "There is no better nor more favorably known man in the city of Ottumwa," could now hang up his well-worn shoes and enjoy a rise in both status and income and perhaps hoped to rise further—his father and grandfather had both been postmasters. But although his new appointment was hailed as a demonstration of Nimocks' sound and unbiased

2

judgement, meted out to a deserving, high-mileage mailman, it was noted, without any apparent irony, that "[F]rom his position as carrier he was barred from any strong demonstrations of party interests, but the Republicans of the county have always felt that in Mr. Keyhoe they had a partisan to be depended upon."[6]

All this informs us that Don Keyhoe was raised in a family that was by no means unimportant or obscure. They were rooted in their Republican and Episcopalian beliefs and were among Ottumwa's leading citizens. The Keyhoes were employers, manufacturers, merchants, and politicians, and though small in influence nationally, they were a vital component, not only of their own city, but also of American society at the dawn of the twentieth century. Keyhoe's family, his hometown, and its people, epitomized a way of life, a moral code, and a set of patriotic ambitions that would come to represent American Values. Indeed, by 1953, when Keyhoe had become a national figure, his hometown was specifically held up as "a living example of everything the American people stand for…the crossroads of the nation…[a citadel] of the way of life we treasure."[7]

While little Don's parents were constantly busy with social and civic matters, he followed the social and educational route of children of his class and era. In pre-school, at age three, he was voted "Handsomest Boy Under Six Years," in a competition which awarded prizes for "prettiest baby" and for "fattest baby," but his formal education began at Ottumwa's Lincoln School.[8] In this large, church-like brick and stone edifice, classes often exceeded forty pupils, but he was among some Keyhoe cousins and also the children of his father's close circle, which reinforced the bonds of family, community, and social position. Don's education here encompassed not only literacy and numeracy, but also dainty activities, popular at the time. In May of 1903, a "Nature Afternoon" was held at the school where, in a classroom "prettily decorated with flowers gathered by the little ones," visitors were entertained by a program of entertainment provided by the children, including Don, who gave his rendition of the song, "Crow Calculations."[9]

Before the end of the decade however, his education was interrupted when maternal grandparents James and Laura Cherry moved to Colorado. James, suffering from a lung complaint, had retired from Seither and Moore, the large plumbing company he had helped to establish in Keokuk, and in 1908 he took his doctor's advice to move to dryer climes. Following an affectionate send-off by their neighbors, he and Laura embarked with enthusiasm on their new life in the tiny town of Granada in Prowers County, where James, perhaps hoping to draw on his early experience as a gardener, had purchased a claim of 160 acres to try his hand at dry-farming.[10] This method of cultivation used techniques that prevented moisture-loss from the arid soil, and for at least a short time Don's father lent a hand, while retaining his employment as Assistant Postmaster in Ottumwa, and had purchased his own plot of land nearby. This was no doubt a difficult time for the family; Don, with his sister and his mother, lived with the Cherrys, while Grant lodged in Ottumwa— almost 700 miles distant—with his brother Horton and his family. But, despite the Cherry's hopes for health and happiness in Colorado, their adventure was short-lived. In 1911 they returned to Keokuk where Seither and Moore announced that James had returned "to look after the affairs of their office and plumbing rooms."

Once again settled in Ottumwa, 15-year-old Don worked for his father at the Post Office as Special Messenger, which entailed delivering by hand urgent mail as soon as it arrived (a fee was charged for this service).[11] It was an important and busy occupation, for the Post Office at this time handled thousands of items per day but employed only one Special Messenger.

This job was in addition to his studies at Ottumwa High School (OHS), in which he had enrolled on the family's return from Colorado and whose somewhat severe elevation belied the slightly progressive nature of the education it provided.[12] Though pupils were educated with the intention of fitting them for traditional gender roles, the OHS was nonetheless a wholesome environment and encouraged students of both sexes to participate in many of the same activities. They were expected to dress smartly, join clubs, and engage in activities that would develop their character and provide them with the intellectual and social tools needed for their eventual lives as productive citizens. Membership of school clubs was encouraged and Don joined several. He was a member of the McKinley Debating Society, which in his final year studied the no doubt scintillating textbook *Essentials of Argument and Exposition*, and he was also a member of the Dramatic Club, the Commercial Club, and the Athletic Association.

Though this co-ed environment was genteel and innocent by today's standards, it was nonetheless prone to the rigors and excitements of children who were becoming young adults. Girls had certainly become of interest to Don, and by the time he graduated in 1915 ("much to the surprise of faculty and self," he later said), he was described as "a rare courtier," and had acquired a reputation as something of a pugnacious Romeo. Of note were his implied rendezvous at the local soda fountain with one Edith Shepherd, and later, his delivery of a black eye to the school Lothario, which seemed to garner some approval from his fellow students.[13]

But whatever his romantic aspirations, his mind now was turning toward life after graduation. He was in his eighteenth year and had decided on the path he would take. He would not follow his ancestors into the position of postmaster, nor would he follow his uncles into politics, manufacturing, or commerce. He wanted to become a United States Marine.

Chapter 2: Service

April 17, 1916, was a big day for Donald Keyhoe, for it was one that he fully expected, even at the age of eighteen, would set the course for the rest of his life. Today, he would sit the exam for entry to the United States Naval Academy (USNA) at Annapolis, Maryland.

He'd been working up to this day since his final year at Ottumwa High School, when he submitted his preliminary application to the Academy, followed by a request for nomination from his local Congressman, C. W. Ramseyer. Each Congressman was permitted to nominate three candidates from his own district, and on February 5th Keyhoe was informed that he had been selected, along with two of his schoolmates from Ottumwa High: Lloyd Harvey Carter, the son of the city's mayor, and Walter Aloysius Wachtler, son of the local barber.

A week later Don and Walter departed Ottumwa to attend Werntz's Preparatory School at Annapolis, one of many private establishments near the Academy that provided tuition for USNA hopefuls (the Academy had not yet founded its own prep school).[14] The exam was notoriously difficult, and it was considered essential to spend weeks preparing specially for it. Fees at "'Werntz' War College" were at the high end—about $79—and not every boy's family could afford this non-refundable expense.

The school was founded by "Professor" Robert Lincoln Werntz, himself a former USNA graduate (class of 1884) who, at the time of Keyhoe's attendance, was aged sixty, and with his brother had been running the school for over thirty years. Despite its reputation as the best of the prep schools and its close proximity—just three minutes stroll—to the distinguished Annapolis, it occupied a dingy third floor above a grocery store at 44 Maryland Avenue. Werntz, a colorful character who had a "whiny, squeaky voice," was rumored to own most of the property in Annapolis, thanks to his high tuition fees, which some considered to be his "racket" and he was frequently mentioned in the local press in connection with property deals and various lawsuits arising from them, which added to his murky reputation. Moreover, he was a noted eccentric. A former cadet recalled:

He nursed a permanent sore in the palm of one hand with

Vaseline from a small jar … One day somebody put red-hot cayenne pepper in the jar, with obvious effect [and he] said to his class, "Gentlemen, there are two kinds of sons-of-bitches in this world. One is the common ordinary son-of-a-bitch, and then there is the low down dirty son-of-a-bitch, and that's the son-of-a-bitch that put cayenne pepper in my Vaseline."[15]

He took in only thirty candidates at a time, and his school was as unconventional as its principal: the boys did not call him "sir," but addressed him as "Bobby," there was neither discipline nor rules, and it was left to each student to decide whether or not he wished to attend lessons. Mornings typically began with crap games played amid a haze of blue Calabash smoke, which was then the pipe of choice among fashionable young men, but although the school resembled a den of iniquity, it had a high rate of success. Keyhoe and his fellow students knew full well the purpose of their time at the "college" and the prospect of returning home a failure to parents who were $79 dollars lighter no doubt created enthusiasm. Consequently, when the bell for class sounded, the boys applied themselves fully—no mean feat, for the teaching methods used by Werntz and his staff required students to commit everything to memory, as per the demands of the USNA entry exam. For further inspiration, many boys would be permitted to visit the grounds of the Academy and take in its tranquil splendor, which served to reinforce their goal. In addition, Werntz would give individual attention to some boys or small groups, in the form of visits to a submarine or other vessel and "for a consideration" would provide extra tuition to give more "steam" to their rate of learning.[16] Overall, the students were in good and experienced hands, but the decision to work hard was left entirely to themselves.

After two months of crap games, pipe smoke (which may have given Don the life-long habit of heavy smoking), and intense study under the singular "War College" method, he returned to Ottumwa, ready to sit the "notorious four-day mental marathon" that would define his future.

The required exam subjects were English Grammar, Geography, US History, Algebra, and Plane Geometry. The only leeway permitted in the marking of these subjects was in English, where spelling errors would not necessarily count against a candidate who had scored well in the other subjects. The highest mark attainable was 4.00, which equated to 100%, the lowest pass mark was 2.5 (= 62.5%), and if Keyhoe failed this exam he would be unlikely to be offered a resit. Failure would label him a "bilger," i.e., "one weighed in the Academic balance and found wanting."[17]

On May 20, 1916, the three nominees were informed of their results. Carter had fallen short of the minimum mark and was rejected, but Wachtler had scored 3.4 and Keyhoe had scored 3.2, which was well-above the minimum 2.5 required: he was not going to be a bilger. So, in the first week of June, he returned to Annapolis to undergo a medical examination, and with this final hurdle accomplished, on July 11th he began his new life as a Midshipman of the Fourth Class.

Before his admission to the Academy, he was required to deposit with the Midshipmen's Storekeeper $291.84 to cover the cost of uniforms, other clothing, textbooks, and various academic materials. This amount was not refundable, but the items became his personal property and, like all cadets, he paid for his own travel expenses from home to Annapolis, and these were later refunded to his parents. His pay was $600 per annum plus 30 cents per day for food, which allowed him to live to an acceptable, if basic, standard. He was not permitted to receive additional money from home.

However, his acceptance at Annapolis did not mean that his future there was assured. It was only the first step on a grueling journey that many found extremely difficult and that some failed. Each cadet underwent a continuous program of marked assessment throughout the year and it was imperative not to be marked overall below 2.5 and be rated "un-sat" (unsatisfactory). This would result in dismissal and end his prospects as a Marine.

Keyhoe (soon nicknamed "Don" or "Deko") was one of 800 cadets that year, all of them housed in the single, enormous dormitory facility, Bancroft Hall, segregated according to Class (Fourth Class men were new cadets and therefore at the lowest rank). Two midshipmen shared each "suite," which comprised two small bedrooms, a study, and a shower bath. These suites were "severely plain in furnishings, and no ornaments" were permitted.[18]

In a closed environment filled with young boys on the brink of manhood, discipline and adherence to rules was essential, and to that end, penalties—demerits—were imposed upon cadets for infractions of the numerous rules. Each started their academic year with a clean sheet, but demerits were imposed up to a maximum of 300, which when reached would result in instant dismissal from the Academy. Some infractions, for example, "Bed, lying upon at unauthorized time," would impose only 5 demerits, but others would inflict 50, reflecting the severity of the transgression. "Civilian clothing, unauthorized wearing or possession of (1st offense)" was among this category, but discretionary "special" demerits up to 300 could be imposed for some second offenses or for major first-time infractions, such as assault.

Among Keyhoe's fellow cadets in 1916 were Roscoe "Rosquito" Henry Hillenkoetter, Delmer "Dead Shot" Stater Fahrney, and Calvin "Stormy" Mathews Bolster. Missouri-born Hillenkoetter, by coincidence, was the son of a mail-carrier and his personal motto, perhaps with tongue-in-cheek, was, "Letters first: all other duties next." Oklahoma-born Fahrney was the son of a carpenter and had a reputation for rough-housing ("not a night passes without a bang-up tussle"), and once during infantry drill he "started to shoot up the twelfth company with blank cartridges," but his most frequent cause of demerits was for "glass in door smashed." In contrast, Ohio-born Bolster, son of a bookkeeper, went through his training with a clean sheet and a shy disposition.[19] These three young men from ordinary, mid-west working-class backgrounds would go on to distinguished military and government service, but the bonds they formed at Annapolis would bring them together with Keyhoe more than forty years later to challenge the credibility of what by then had become the biggest military airpower on Earth: The United States Air Force.

Keyhoe's first year as a "Plebe" (a term soon to be replaced by "freshman") required a full-time commitment to his studies, and in order to counter any distractions, new cadets were confined almost entirely to the Academy grounds. They were not permitted to attend any functions, nor allowed any leave, and almost every minute of their day was mapped out. Keyhoe's day began at 6 am, when he would shower, tidy his room and locker for inspection, put on his uniform, and take breakfast in the mess hall. By 8 am, he was ready at attention outside in his section of ten cadets to march away to his first lesson. His classroom timetable was made up of mechanical drawing, algebra and logarithms, geometry, and modern languages (Spanish and French), and also included instruction in seamanship, ordnance, and marine engineering.

Evenings brought him no respite, for they were filled with swimming lessons, gymnasium practice, and even singing lessons, the latter meant to develop a midshipman's voice for issuing commands at sea. His physical development was further enhanced by compulsory training to row a Cutter, a notoriously heavy craft, and to handle a boat under sail. And amid all this were the basics of drilling, marching, and parade. His day did not finish until 9:30 pm, after which some personal time was permitted, and "Middies" could socialize in their dormitories until "Taps" sounded and the lights were put out. Some relief might be obtained for a Plebe who had maintained good conduct for sufficient time: he could have the privilege of going into the town on Saturday afternoon but was limited to where and with whom he could visit, and he must always be in uniform.

If Keyhoe felt homesick during his first year, it appears not to have negatively affected his training; after only two months, he wrote to his parents to tell them he had "won his honor badge as sharpshooter," which placed him second to the rank of expert rifleman, one of the academy's "highest honors." This no doubt delighted his family, but for Keyhoe it would almost certainly have exposed him to hazing by older cadets, because his achievement was published in his local paper.[20] Annapolis was not exempt from the *Lord of the Flies* mentality of young male society, and any excuse for older cadets to subject Plebes to indignity was quickly taken up. A boy's hometown newspaper was nicknamed the "Bazoo" at the Academy, and any Plebe found to have been mentioned favorably in his local Bazoo could expect some degrading punishment, from Third Class Men in particular.

During his first year, Keyhoe lived almost exclusively within the grounds of the Academy, where a variety of physical, educational, and cultural activities were scheduled to develop his mind and body, much like high school. Sports dominated, but Keyhoe (who favored "Mexican Athletics," i.e., not interested in physical exercise) restricted himself to membership of the Mandolin Club, a large group dedicated to performing tunes played on the then-popular instrument and for which he became noted among his fellow cadets:

> Did someone mention September leave? Then Keyhoe's around. The prospects of that month's leave, twanging a mandolin, a long and spirited hop fest, these are the attractions that keep "Don" among the living from one leave's end to the next.

After his first year, he was permitted to venture outside the grounds, and, minus his mandolin, he would make many Saturday night visits to watch comedy at the Republic Theater, a cinema house on Main St, about ten minutes' walk from the Academy. However, his apparent former reputation as a "rare courtier," if it continued, was not obvious to his fellow cadets, who considered him to be a "Red Mike," i.e., shy around girls. His high school reputation as a scrapper, though, seems to have been maintained until his graduation, by which time he was sharing room 33 at Bancroft Hall with fellow cadet, Eugene Willard Kiefer:

> [S]ounds of scuffling were heard emanating from room 33, followed by, "Yuh stuck your finger in my eye, didn't yuh?"
>
> "Yea-a. An' I'll do better next time," [T]he ground deck turned out en masse expecting to see murder done. But by the end of the year all the comment it ever called forth was, "Oh, that's Kiefer and Keyhoe breaking up housekeeping again."[21]

Life at Annapolis was intense, rigorous, and challenging for these young cadets, many of whom had never before been away from home. The short-term rewards were the comradeship and the sense of belonging to a privileged institution, and also no doubt the welcome approbation of their families. But the long-term rewards held the promise of an honorable career in defense of their country, at a time when America was reluctantly becoming entangled in Europe's deadly disagreements. When Keyhoe became a cadet, the US was resisting participation in The Great War, raging by then for two bloody years and with no end in sight, but its entry to the conflict in 1917 laid bare the nation's paucity of military might and in particular its lack of airpower. The US had done important aerial work before 1914, but of necessity European nations had surged ahead in military aviation and America lagged significantly behind:

> When the United States entered the first World War on 6 April 1917, Marine aviation consisted of only 6 Marine officers designated naval aviators, 1 warrant officer, and 45 enlisted men ... [T]he Marines finally got their own field in April 1918 ... at Miami ... In World War 1 a total of 282 officers and 2,180 enlisted men served in Marine aviation. ...[The Marine pilots who served in France] faced a most perplexing problem—no aircraft [and] it was not until 23 September they [were] received.[22]

Less than two months later, the War was over. By February 1919, "Marine air began demobilizing" the station at Miami, and by summer it was disbanded. Its remaining personnel "were transferred to Parris Island and Quantico" and by 1920, pilot numbers were reduced to sixty-seven and further again the next year, to only forty-three.[23]

This was a rather stark and unpromising outlook for Keyhoe and his fellow cadets. The prospects for those who yearned for a career as flyers seemed to be shrinking, and the government, despite the lack of military power the war in Europe had exposed, showed little interest in further expansion of its armed forces. At the time of Keyhoe's graduation in June of 1919, a "desperate struggle to persuade Congress to maintain at least their prewar personnel strength with the required bases, facilities, and equipment" was fomenting, led by the nation's first Marine aviator, the noted and influential Alfred A. Cunningham. He fully recognized and understood the vital role that Marine aviation ought to play in the nation's defenses, but his logic was met with apathy. He lamented that:

> One of the greatest handicaps which Marine Corps aviation must now overcome is a combination of doubt as to usefulness, lack of sympathy, and a feeling on the part of some line officers that aviators and aviation enlisted men are not real Marines.[24]

Thus, Keyhoe and his comrades were caught in something of a limbo. Marine aviation seemed to have no future, and when the War was over, it was left in a neglected state, with its potential disregarded and its young cadets largely given over to the increasingly outdated technology of military ballooning. And so, following his "shore leave" after graduation, Keyhoe transferred briefly to the recently-built Marine Barracks at Quantico, for officer instruction. From there, on January 12, 1920, he joined the Naval Air Training Station at Pensacola, Florida, where, despite the uncertainty that surrounded the future of Marine aviation, he looked to begin a new and important phase of his military career.

* * *

"It is a thrilling adventure, this free ballooning," recalled Keyhoe. "When you are riding the wind below a tiny gas bag you'll find plenty of thrills before you come to earth… Up to the moment that the basket is on the ground, standing still, there is always a chance that anything might happen."[25]

Pensacola Naval Air Station was almost new when Second Lieutenant Keyhoe arrived there to begin his training as a balloon pilot, though it was far from certain where his career as a Marine was headed.

> In the years following World War I, aviation training slowed. From the 12-month flight course, an average of 100 pilots were graduating yearly. This was before the day of aviation cadets, and the majority of the students included in the flight-training program were Annapolis graduates. Thus, Naval Air Station Pensacola became known as the "Annapolis of the Air."[26]

At this time, balloons, both free and tethered, were largely used for military observation, and America still expected, even after The Great War and the innovations that followed from the Wright Brothers' achievements, that these devices would eventually develop into wide-scale aerial transportation and delivery:

> The necessity for lighter-than-aircraft for the Navy is now fully realized by strategists, and work to provide our Navy with lighter-than-aircraft is being pushed by those in authority … The work done by the German Zeppilins [*sic*] in patrolling and scouting over the North Sea, and the effect of the British lack of rigids, has brought this necessity home.[27]

Powered flight was still a dangerous, seat-of-the-pants adventure, with a high casualty rate, for which pilots needed nerves of steel, but Ballooning, for all its silent gracefulness, was certainly not for the faint-hearted. Years later, Keyhoe would describe his experiences: "I have made about 25 balloon flights and on 24 of them came down in trees."[28]

He was making light of these incidents and evidently as a young cadet had accepted the risks involved as a normal, even exciting part of his training, but the dangers were real. Balloons were subject to unpredictable and uncontrollable natural forces, which might cost the crew their lives. Once aloft, the balloon could not be maneuvered and was at the mercy of wind currents and air temperatures. Floating over forests, desert, or water, or through clouds or fog, would either send the balloon soaring at high speed or plummeting to Earth. An experienced pilot knew largely what to expect, but his control was reactive, rather than proactive, and his fast judgement and actions made the difference between a successful landing or a fatal crash.

Weather conditions were not the only peril. In remote areas, moonshiners, fearing Revenue men, would take pot shots at any balloon, but sometimes locals would open fire just for the enjoyment of it. Keyhoe recalled one incident when he and his crew were lost with only "a vague idea that we were somewhere in Alabama." Descending to 600 feet, the pilot called to a group of men on the ground to ask where they were, and the reply was made in gunshots. Don and the crew immediately began to heave out bags of ballast, which sent the balloon soaring to an ear-popping 1500 ft and then to 8000 ft. He rather enjoyed it: "I was glad that we had been a target for by this time we had climbed above a huge mass of billowy, white cumulus clouds that entirely hid the Earth. It was like a vast snowbank, but much more beautiful."

Despite the enchanting view, the crew still had no idea where they were and had to descend through the clouds, which entailed more perilous tactics. The pilot had to "valve down," i.e., release hydrogen from the balloon, but when they hit the cooler air below the clouds, the remaining gas shrank and they sank faster. Keyhoe and the crew frantically poured out sand from the ballast bags, but "at 100 feet we headed straight into a tree. We dropped hastily below the basket's edge and not a second too soon, for a jagged limb poked itself straight through the space where we had stood."

Now stuck high in the tree with the bag aloft, the pilot intended to valve down further, but then the Sun emerged and warmed the gas. Suddenly the balloon jerked up, broke the intruding limb, and with its helpless crew was whisked away in a strong wind, eventually making a hard landing in a plowed field, from where Don and the crew, mercifully uninjured, trudged to find the nearest railway station and make their long journey back to base.[29]

Despite the perils and inconveniences of his training, there was some relief. Keyhoe's parents were doing well enough to have a second home in the new settlement of Valparaiso, on Bayshore Drive, about a two-hour drive from Pensacola. This beautiful, unspoiled location, overlooking Boggy Bayou, which joins with the Gulf of Mexico, was envisaged as a model community of some six thousand, a population figure it would never achieve, but it was rapidly becoming fashionable with a small number of the emerging middle-class who could own property purely for leisure. Electricity supplies were not yet fully laid-on and roads still under construction, but property-building was well underway. Calvin and May's holiday home was still incomplete in February 1920 when Don visited them and stayed at the Bayshore Hotel, but by late autumn, his parents evidently planned to spend much time there, as daughter Katherine, now almost twenty, had taken a teaching post at the school.[30]

New Year's Eve 1920 marked what had been a good year for Don Keyhoe, and to close it, he joined several hundred military and civilian attendees for a glittering dinner-dance at the San Carlos Hotel in Pensacola, where he escorted Miss Clara Moreno, niece of the city's judge.[31] He was now twenty-three, in full vigor and approaching the end of his training. Whatever the uncertainties about the future of Marine Aviation, it was still an exciting time to be a young American, and within weeks he had a new posting far away from home, which held the promise of a challenging, but important forward step in his career.

* * *

On January 24, 1921, the USS *Jason*, a navy collier, left the Navy Yard at Philadelphia and set off on a fifty-three-day voyage to the Pacific island of Guam. It was loaded with planes, artillery, and US Marines, including Second Lieutenant Donald Keyhoe, one of the nine officers and ninety enlisted men aboard who would be the first Marine Flight on the island. In response to the increasing strategic importance of the location, a small Marine detachment had been deployed there at Sumay since 1920, equipped with anti-aircraft guns, but the island lacked an airfield and personnel facilities. Keyhoe's unit, designated Flight L, Fourth Squadron, was tasked with its construction three miles away at Orote Point, a narrow peninsula on the west coast:

> Since no air facility then existed on Guam, the unit's first mission was to build an airfield and seaplane base ... to build up the island's defenses. To this end, the flight embarked with every spare piece of air station equipment the Navy and Marine Corps could gather from the East Coast. For aircraft, the flight received N-9s and HS-2Ls, along with the giant F-5L ...[32]

When they arrived on March 17th, any excitement the men felt at being "the first Marine aviators ever to serve west of San Francisco" was surely tempered by the conditions they found there: rudimentary buildings, tent accommodation, lots of mud, heat, humidity, "Guam Eagles" (i.e., large, winged cockroaches), and mosquitoes that carried Dengue Fever, which over the coming months did the rounds and laid-low many of the new arrivals. The condition was not fatal but very unpleasant. Symptoms would start with headache, joint, abdomen and eyeball pain, then a fever kicked in about the third day, which lasted for up to forty-eight hours, after which it got worse. Sufferers could then look forward to a second fever, a whole-body rash, intense itching, and "excruciating pains." It became particularly troublesome in April that year, when temperatures reached 84 degrees Fahrenheit and rainfall nearly six inches, which was a boon to the mosquitoes. The only remedy prescribed was "to bed immediately, cold applications to head, heat to feet. Rubbing with liniments [for pain]."

Of necessity therefore, the usual clear divisions between ranks and their assigned duties were blurred by the depletion of men. Keyhoe, though now a Naval Aviator, took on the extra duty of Quartermaster, until he himself became sick on May 14th and at one point took over as Commander of the Flight, while his fellow Second Lieutenants also had other duties, including Ration Survey Officer and Morale Officer. Regardless of the conditions however, work had to begin without delay:

> [T]he nine officers and ninety enlisted men of Flight L quickly constructed equipment and maintenance shops, a large hangar, and quarters. In addition to their flying duty, pilots completed navigational instruction and recurrent line training.[33]

Initially they were assisted in the construction work by Guamanians, ("a population of 14,000 natives happy and contented under the American Government"), but at the end of 1921 funding ran out and the Marines had to continue the work unaided.[34]

On the island, Keyhoe found at least one familiar face—Bill "Clabber" Onley, a fellow Annapolis graduate, who was now the editor of a short-lived, somewhat twee publication, *The Guam Newsletter*, "a paper devoted to the interests, development and progress of Guam," which covered almost all the island's news. Bill, who was a noted romantic in his youth, had married his sweetheart, Alma, the day before his graduation, and the couple were now stationed on the island. Years later, in Virginia, they would be Keyhoe's next-door neighbors.

Sickness aside, the delights of this South Sea island, which had "always held a charm for young men in search of adventure," was lost on some of the enlisted men, evidenced by the high incidence of punishment administered for a variety of infractions: use of foul and obscene language, failure to obey orders, neglect of kit and weapons, and even assault of a civilian worker.[35] The better-behaved Keyhoe meanwhile was juggling his various roles and responsibilities with time in and out of hospital, sometimes for one day, occasionally for longer, but almost all those in the unit were incapacitated by illness at some point.

Despite the fracas and the flies, the station was sufficiently completed and on September 19th, almost six months to the day after the men had arrived, the first recorded flight took to the air at 08:35, simply noted in the log as "N-9 2335 launched," and airplane testing could now begin.

Among the craft Keyhoe tested was "the largest and most modern petrol plane in the Marines' inventory in the early Twenties," the F-5L. This 7-ton twin-engine seaplane, with a wingspan of 103 feet, was heavy to lift off from the water, difficult to maneuver in flight, and was no luxury ride. Constructed largely of wood and wire, it could hold a crew of four, who were seated on bare planking and exposed to the elements. Its maximum speed was 90 mph and maximum climb was 2600 feet, but on February 4, 1922, Keyhoe took it more than three times higher, to 8,600 ft—at the time a perilous voyage into the unknown in what was, even allowing for its modernity, little better than a garden shed with wings.

By spring of 1922, Flight-L, despite the island's challenging conditions, had made impressive progress, and although work on the station was continuing, gradually "the unit settled down to routine training and the collection of meteorological data," along with "practice flights, photographic, radio and night flying. [Also] Instruction and practice in aerial gunnery and bombing … in preparation for the semiannual bombing practice."[36]

Keyhoe, in addition to his other duties, was now also the unit's Radio and Survey Officer, though he continued to make test flights in the station's two F5Ls. But that number would be dramatically halved on May 17, 1922, when he took one up for a night-flying test. "The lights failed to show the water," he could not see the dark Pacific beneath him, and he crashed into the waves.[37]

He was rescued and rushed to the hospital at Agana, the island's capital. Though he survived the terrifying crash, he had severed his right ulnar nerve, paralyzing his right hand. Following several weeks of treatment, on June 12th he was sent back to the States on board the USS *Beaver*, where he was admitted to the Naval Hospital at Mare Island, California.

After a sea voyage of five weeks, he now had to endure a lengthy recovery, which he hoped would be complete and allow him to return to service. It was not to be.

Chapter 3: Changes

Over the next year, Don was transferred to several different naval hospitals and by 1923 was receiving treatment at the Naval Hospital in Washington, D.C., his service having been extended until November 1925, but during this period it was undoubtedly becoming clear to him that he could not hope to continue active service in the Marines.[38] Moreover, he had now acquired a wife.

It was perhaps something of a surprise to Keyhoe's staunch Episcopalian family when, on October 10, 1923, he married an equally staunch Catholic, Margaret Theresa Bishop. She was the daughter of Joseph Eustace Bishop and Mary Cecelia (*née* Cook) and was exactly two years older than Don, born June 20, 1895 in Washington, D.C.

Their engagement had been announced on September 23rd, just seventeen days before their wedding, which was a quiet affair held at the bride's home in Mount Pleasant, Maryland. There were few guests, just a "small company of intimate friends and relatives" and the ceremony, conducted by Monsignor Gavan of the Church of The Sacred Heart, was followed by an "informal reception." The low-key nuptials were due to "illness in the family." Whose illness isn't known, but it appears that none of Keyhoe's family attended the wedding, though a schoolfriend from Ottumwa High, Missouri-born Vernal Brown, stood as best man and his wife, Clara, played the piano and sang. Don had been Vernal's best man less than a year before.[39]

How Don and Margaret met or why they married in apparent haste isn't clear, but unless it was a fevered love-match that drew them inexorably to the altar despite their religious differences, it may be that a child was expected and they were obliged to follow convention regardless of all else.[40] If the latter was the case, the child presumably did not survive, but whatever the reason for their union, it can be inferred that Keyhoe was no longer the "Red Mike" of his Annapolis years.[41]

Aside from their religions, the couple had at least the appearance of being well-suited. They had been raised in similar, close-knit communities of which their families were respected members, their standards of education up to high school were comparable (allowing for gender differences), and each of them possessed an artistic temperament. Don would soon take his first steps as a writer, and Margaret, since childhood, had been involved in local theatre, an interest she would continue throughout her life.

Her senior education was at the McKinley Manual Training High School in D.C., which provided vocational education for both sexes. Here she learned to type, and this led to her employment as a typist in the War Department, where Keyhoe had many contacts and was perhaps where the couple met. Margaret's younger sister, Emilie, was also employed there as a typist, but would later become a music teacher.

The girls' artistic inclinations were a reflection of their father's own. Massachusetts-born Joseph Bishop worked for more than thirty years as Chief Photographer at the Army War College of the War Department in D.C. He had been a photographer prior to settling in the city in 1875 and took up a post at the National Photographic Galleries on Pennsylvania Avenue, where he would later establish his own business, before joining the War Department. He retired in 1926 and his health declined until he died in 1929, but he left behind a large body of photographic work known as the Joseph E. Bishop Collection, which today is held by The Historical Society of Washington, D.C. and is a valuable resource for researchers of the city's history.[42]

On their return from honeymoon on November 15th, Lieutenant and Mrs. Donald Keyhoe took up residence in a newly-built apartment block at 1826 Vernon Street in the District of Columbia, a good address for a young couple, but their financial situation held some uncertainty. Though Keyhoe retained hopes of a full recovery and of staying in the Marines, he had rather suddenly become a married man and perhaps expected to be a father in the very near future, but his injury was still troublesome. If he retired from the Service, he would have a pension, but he was only twenty-six and needed an income. He received a base-rate monthly salary of $131, plus allowances for rent and subsistence, which would have taken him to around a high school teacher's earnings.[43] Small wonder then, that with a wife in tow and his ongoing and increasingly doubtful recovery, he was motivated to find other sources of income. He lost no time in pursuing a new course that would supplement his finances and take advantage of his Marine training. He turned to writing about his great passion: aviation.

While he was still on honeymoon, one of the Capital's leading newspapers, *The Sunday Star*, had published his first article, "Washington Flyers Make History" which was an informative and praiseful piece on the speed records recently achieved by noted rival pilots Harold J. Brow and Alford "Al" J. Williams (259 mph and 266.59 mph, respectively).[44] This article typified the writing style Keyhoe would use throughout his life. It was an easy-to-read combination of personal knowledge, interviews, and detailed facts linked to relevant events, which both informed the reader and demonstrated that he had researched his subject thoroughly.[45]

Freelance writing was far more lucrative in the early 20th century than it is today, and between about 1925 and 1935, a very small number of writers might earn as much as a dollar per word, though such munificence was not the norm, generally being reserved for specially-commissioned contributions from famous persons. Keyhoe's pay was unlikely to have been more than a few cents per word for this first article, even though *The Sunday Star* was a major newspaper, but it was a tentative beginning to a new and for many years, very profitable career.

At this time, few Americans had experienced flight, and it was not yet recognized as the wonder of the age, so Keyhoe, wittingly or not, was tapping into what was soon to become of vital interest to the nation. The main claim to fame for airplanes ("ships") was for "Barnstorming," during which daring young men in their flying machines gave death-defying aerobatic displays to the public. But by 1925 the government had introduced safety regulations that greatly reduced the numbers of these flyers. Some—among them Charles Lindbergh—became contracted to deliver air mail, which re-purposed their talents and their planes for the greater good. The government's decision to regulate flight safety and to place it under the governance of the Department of Commerce soon proved to be a turning point in Keyhoe's life.

His albeit inactive Marine career and his entry into freelance writing evidently made him a good candidate to be appointed editor of *Leatherneck*, the Marine Corps own magazine.[46] The December 5, 1923, edition announced:

> With the printing of this issue Lieut. Donald E. Keyhoe becomes the Editor of THE LEATHERNECK. It is hoped that the friendly relations between the former Editor and the readers of this publication will continue with his successor.

He kicked off 1924 with a piece for *The Sunday Star*, titled "Flying Disasters," which detailed several ghastly incidents in which balloonists had perished, including some from the Pensacola NAS. This was rather a "filler," lacking any current aviation news, but highlighted the dangers of flight, a subject close to his heart and one that would remain so throughout his life. His time with *Leatherneck*, however, was soon curtailed. In April 1924, it announced that "2d Lieutenant Donald E Keyhoe has been forced to give up his duties as editor on account of being ordered to the US Naval Hospital, Washington DC, for treatment."

He remained in the hospital for the rest of 1924 until, in January 1925, he was "retired from active service and placed on the retired list," with the rank of First Lieutenant.[47] His right hand remained paralyzed, and at the age of twenty-six, he would now have to pursue a career very different to the one he had hoped for only three years earlier.

* * *

Keyhoe's injury, though serious enough to end his active Service, evidently did not constrain him as a writer, for commencing in 1925, he began to produce articles and adventure stories at a pace.[48] In January, however, he published a piece rather different from most that would follow: a biography of his father-in-law. In it he extolled Joseph Bishop's photographic work and his sense of humor. Mr. Bishop, the piece noted, was also a prize-winning "connoisseur of flowers" and "an authority on the subject of mushrooms."

Familial ties appeared to be strengthened further at this time, when Don and Margaret spent several weeks with his family in Ottumwa, then travelled on to stay with hers in Ohio. On February 1st they returned to Washington, D.C., at their new address, the Lonsdale Apartments at 2138 California Street. Keyhoe continued to write, but before long the imperative to succeed was no doubt stoked by the news that Margaret was expecting a child, due in November.

April saw the publication of his first foray into fiction, one which perhaps indicated his state of mind at this juncture. "The Grim Passenger" was printed in *Weird Tales*, a popular glossy, which published works by writers including Lovecraft and Poe, but gave space to new up-and-comers.[49] This story was based on two major events in recent years: the Titanic disaster in 1912 and the discovery of Tutankhamen's tomb in 1922, from which Keyhoe created, in the formal style of English writers of the period, a tale of a mummy's curse sending the doomed liner to the bottom of the sea.

By summer, he was evidently making the best of his new situation, for he had now unwittingly made an important career move: he transferred to the United States Coast and Geodetic Survey (C&GS), writing editorials for their newsletter and publishing press articles about their activities. He was well-placed for this new assignment. The C&GS had historic ties to the Navy and had spent much of its long existence in a state of flux, but in 1913 it became part of the newly-established Department of Commerce. In 1917, it was re-organized along military lines, with half of its officers drawn from the Services, including the Marines. Keyhoe, unable to serve actively, could now utilize his experience and talents in an affiliated position, and by December he was appointed editor of the C&GS's *Bulletin*.[50]

After all the disappointments and difficulties since his crash in Guam, Keyhoe's life appeared to be back on track. He had been married now for just over two years, was settled in the nation's capital, and against the odds, had overcome his disability and begun a new career.

On November 16th, his son, Joseph Grant Keyhoe, was born, but this event, instead of adding to his fulfillment, brought about the immediate collapse of his marriage.

Chapter 4:
Home and Away

In January 1926, Donald Keyhoe moved out of his marital home. His reason, later stated in court by his wife, was "because the baby cried."[51] Whether that was the sole cause, or whether it was the final aggravation in an already unhappy marriage, isn't recorded, but the break-up seems not to have slowed his forward motion; indeed, it appears to have given him momentum.

In the January edition of *Weird Tales,* he published a fictional yarn, "The Mystery Under The Sea," which had several personal tags, telling of the heroic men of Flight L on Guam, who had to fend off attacks from a giant cuttlefish, and the story also mentioned "flying boat 3591," which was the F-5L he had test-piloted on the island in 1922.[52] Whether this tale suggested any psychological yearning by Keyhoe to escape the tentacles of marriage and return to his thrilling life as a test pilot is open to consideration, but in addition to publishing other articles, both fiction and non-fiction, he now threw himself into his work at the C&GS with full enthusiasm. As a result, his life was shifting in a rather dynamic direction, one which fitted nicely with his need to stay away from his wife. This came about by a rapid series of fortunate and connected events at the highest levels in Washington, D.C.

Although Herbert Hoover's single-term presidency—yet to come—would later be viewed largely as a failure, his term as Secretary of the Department of Commerce (1921-1929) was something of a triumph and it's thanks to his time there that civil aviation would undergo swift development, creating new, nationwide opportunities for travel and commerce.

The future of aeronautics was a hot topic in 1926, generating as much excitement and interest as manned space-flight would thirty years later. It was given a significant boost, first by the creation of the Air Commerce Act in May, and second by the founding of The Daniel Guggenheim Fund for the Promotion of Aeronautics, in June. The Guggenheims were among several fabulously wealthy philanthropic families of the era and had allocated to their fund $2.5 million (about $36 million today). Daniel and his son Harry, a former WWI pilot, were deeply committed to the advancement of air safety and civil aviation. They recognized the importance and urgency of the issue:

> There are indications of a great change in the last few months
> which has given an impetus to plans for developing Amer-
> ican civil aeronautics that is bound to produce permanent
> results. The extent of our country, its physical characteris-
> tics and its intimate contact with Canada, Mexico and the
> West Indies are such as to make air service highly desirable.
> The success of the trans-continental air mail operated by the
> Post Office Department and the general approval which has
> greeted its operations indicate that the choice of a method for
> developing civil aeronautics in the United States is the ques-
> tion demanding immediate solution. There is every reason to
> hope that before the end of the present year, civil aviation in
> the United States will have taken a long step forward toward
> a position of permanent security.[53]

Under the new Act, the C&GS was given responsibility for creating airways maps, and this put Keyhoe in the right place at the right time. His service background, up-to-date knowledge of aviation developments, experience as a test pilot, and his current editorial position, all underpinned his value at this time. The latter point was clearly of importance to the Guggenheim Fund, which noted: "The bulletins of such organizations as Chambers of Commerce are particularly responsive to aeronautic material because this is a topic which is of vital concern to their own interest."[54]

Keyhoe's immediate boss was Chicago-born lawyer William Patterson McCracken. Only nine years Don's senior, he was already accomplished and had a deep passion for aviation, inspired by his own flight training after army enlistment, which led to becoming a flight instructor in WWI. After the war, he resumed his career as a lawyer and specialized in aviation cases. His rise was swift, and in the 1920s he occupied many important positions, including that of Assistant Attorney General of Illinois, but his greatest influence and the bulk of his work was in aeronautics. In 1926, President Coolidge, who understood the need for rapid development of civil aviation, selected McCracken to be Assistant Secretary to Herbert Hoover.

Now, Keyhoe found himself working closely with a man whose zeal for aviation matched his own and who was committed both personally and professionally to the development of air safety and commercial aviation. "Bill" was a smiling, genial, high-powered fellow, who was evidently impressed with the C&GS editor, for he gave Keyhoe an assignment that would set him on an exciting and significant phase of his life.[55] He was selected to be aide and tour manager for pilot Floyd Bennett, one of the two men who claimed to have made the first successful flight over the North Pole on May 9, 1926, in Edsel Ford's giant Fokker Trimotor, the *Josephine Ford*.

Named for Edsel's daughter, the plane had already flown 17,000 miles when he financed its polar flight, with Bennett as pilot and noted aviator Richard Byrd as navigator.[56] Ford now made it available to the Department of Commerce, but Byrd was unavailable for the US tour, so Bennett agreed to be pilot and Don was among key personnel assigned to him for this, the first air journey of its kind, whose aim was to create awareness of, and enthusiasm for, the possibilities of commercial aviation.

Scheduled to begin in October 1926, the tour would be financed by the Guggenheim Fund and though the terrain it would cover was tame compared to the rigors Bennett and Byrd had endured in the Arctic wilderness, its significance was far greater. In the adventurous spirit of the age, flying across the almost-unknown polar region was potentially fatal and consequently had the luster of heroism and derring-do, but its achievement had demonstrated mainly that man and machine could boldly go where no airplane had gone before, over terrain that would never be encountered in everyday life. The most crucial and more relevant test was to establish whether or not aircraft were safe and reliable for civil use across America's vast expanse. If that were not proven, then flight offered no meaningful function for the daily lives of Americans, nor for the nation's economy. It was up to Keyhoe to organize and manage the tour, while liaising with the press, to ensure a smooth, trouble-free trip and good publicity.

The *Josephine Ford* tour of America was not, therefore, a journey of discovery, but a public relations endeavor and of necessity was planned to be achieved only within existing limitations. Among the issues fundamental to the expansion of civil aviation was the lack of accurate maps, which now fell to the C&GS to furnish. Their report a year after the tour observed that:

> There are extensive areas crossed by certain of these routes which have never been mapped, and there does not exist at the present time information of sufficient accuracy and completeness ... [D]ifficulty ... is further increased by the fact that these routes cross mountainous areas ...[57]

These cartographical deficits dictated the journey of the *Josephine Ford*—it was not out to prove endurance, but reliability, hence it would fly only already established air mail routes, such as they were. These "airways" formed a loop, beginning in New York, passing under the Great Lakes to Chicago, and keeping an almost straight line through Salt Lake City to San Francisco, from where it split north to Seattle and south through Los Angeles, with smaller branches to Phoenix and Tucson. There was no route across New Mexico, so flights to Texas departed from Chicago, which served as a national hub, from where additional routes to the southern states were either proposed or under development.

On October 7th, able only to rely on very basic maps of these airways, Keyhoe climbed aboard the newly-painted red Fokker in Washington, D.C. Ceremoniously piloting the first take off was Richard Byrd, who relinquished the controls to Floyd Bennett when they landed in New York. This inaugural short flight carried a dozen people, representing the various interests of the trip, including McCraken, but on departure to Albany, only the flight and support crew remained aboard: Keyhoe, Bennett, John D. McFail (chief mechanic), noted polar aviator Bernt Balcher (assistant pilot), and Milburn John Kusterer (tour arranger).

The *Josephine Ford*, despite being large and heavy, was significantly more comfortable than the hefty, drafty crates Keyhoe had experienced in his Marine test pilot days. For the Fokker's polar expedition, the crew of two had squeezed in among aerial and photographic equipment and made-do with only the pilot's seat and a fold-down seat in the rear, but for the tour, the cabin had been refurbished to accommodate passengers in comfort. With soft seating, large windows, and a heater, it approached luxury and made what would have been an arduous 8,600-mile journey rather pleasant. Indeed, it was something of a jaunt.

"We had a very enjoyable trip," said Keyhoe, when they spoke to reporters in Salt Lake City in front of a modest crowd of two hundred onlookers. "With a basket of sandwiches and a jug of coffee, we made out fine. To pass the time we took moving pictures of the mountains as we came along and played cards."[58] The only difficulty the crew experienced was the irony of a forced overnight stay in Cheyenne, Wyoming, thanks to a heavy snowstorm, which even the former polar-penetrator could not overcome.

Some cities gave the *Josephine Ford* a large, enthusiastic turnout, accompanied by parades, luncheons, dinners, and much accolade, while others were able to scrape up only a few dozen or low hundreds of spectators. Moreover, something of the prestige which ought to have been accorded to

Floyd Bennett during the tour seems to have been deflected by the downplaying of his role in the earlier polar flight; the press then and later either omitted to mention him, or referred to him variously as navigator or mechanic. In reality, without his skill at piloting the plane and his ability to endure as much as his commander, the trip would not have succeeded; rather like a librettist, his contribution was disregarded in favor of the composer. Indeed, during the early part of the goodwill tour with Keyhoe, most of the press reported that Byrd was the pilot and Bennett was often left out entirely. Despite these gaffes and snubs, he was generous in his own summation, giving credit for the success of the polar flight to Byrd's navigational skills and apparently disregarding the numerous reporting errors during the tour with Keyhoe, which left him unacknowledged.

Whatever Bennett may privately have thought about how his contributions had been frequently overlooked made no difference to the success of the US tour. When it ended, back in Washington, D.C., on November 23, 1926, it had accomplished its mission and had safely, on time, and in comfort transported passengers across a large part of America and returned them safely home. An estimated three million people had seen the plane and many thousands had heard or read about its success. Keyhoe had fulfilled his duty to the Department of Commerce in its aim to show how easy commercial flight could be. He extolled the ease and comfort the plane had afforded, telling how, during the last leg of the journey, some passengers were asleep or reading the paper. It was more comfortable than a train, he remarked.

Don had now been part of an important, if somewhat under-reported event in aviation history. Back on the ground, however, he still had a wife, and in December, just a few weeks after the completion of the Bennett tour, he returned to the marital home. Whether or not this was a mutual desire to mend fences isn't known, but whatever the state of his and Margaret's relationship, any reconciliation was soon to be interrupted by a far greater assignment, of which he had no inkling, but would prove to be one of the most noteworthy and exciting experiences of his life.

Chapter 5:
Flying with Lindbergh

On June 28, 1927, eight days after his thirtieth birthday, Donald Keyhoe was summoned to see MacCracken, who gave him an assignment that left him "dazed ... with an odd sense of reality."

MacCracken told him, "You will be Colonel Lindbergh's aide."[59]

The world was clamoring to get even a glimpse of "Lucky Lindy," the handsome, taciturn, intensely private hero, who would have no truck with publicity on anything other than aviation. Now, Keyhoe had been chosen, above all men in America, to be his personal companion for three months, during his forthcoming historic air tour of the United States.

Charles Lindbergh, a twenty-five-year-old mail-pilot and former US Army Air Service pilot, had made his famous transatlantic flight overnight during May 20-21, 1927. He had departed Mitchel Field in New York as a determined but largely unknown hopeful for the Orteig Prize and had landed in Paris as the most famous man on the planet.

Lindbergh had been not the first, but the 77th person, to fly the Atlantic, though he was the first to make the trip solo and this somehow created a public and political frenzy of delight, engendering a blaze of international glory and American pride, which would not be seen again on such a scale until the first Moon landing in 1969. His feat had certainly needed both guts and a nerveless self-confidence, but his personal disposition and his experience as a mail-pilot had tested these characteristics fully; there was no other group of flyers from which to draw a man better suited for a potentially fatal journey.

Keyhoe was still a cadet when the first air mail flight had been made only nine years earlier, from Washington to New York, with President Woodrow Wilson in attendance to witness the inaugural event. It had not gone well. The plane was unable to set off because someone had forgotten to put gas in the tank. Forty-five minutes later, now with fuel and in front of an annoyed President, the pilot set off in the wrong direction and had to land to get his bearings, but on doing so, he crashed, uninjured, in a field twenty miles away. The mail, also uninjured, was sent on its way by road.

This embarrassing set-back was only a minor blip, and aircraft design, safety, and reliability underwent constant improvements thanks to the derring-do of these mail pilots, whose needs instigated many essential changes, including the addition of lights on their aircraft and beacons on airfields. Yet, despite rapid advancements, planes were far from safe, a fact brought home to Keyhoe just a month before Lindbergh would make his famous flight.

On April 18, 1927, he put on his Marine's uniform to take part in an event that was a somber reminder of the dangers of aviation. He and five other uniformed reserve aviators from the Department of Commerce served as pallbearers for John L. Hosch, a 26-year-old inspector in the air regulations division.[60] He had joined the Department in October the previous year, where he worked as an examiner of civilian aircraft to assess their air-worthiness for government license. On April 13th, Hosch, with McCracken's administrative assistant, Homer R. Sands, age 31, took off from Washington's Bolling Field in their capacity as Army Reserve aviators to make a practice flight in a Curtiss JN "Jenny." No-one knew what went wrong, but the plane took a sudden sharp right turn, went into a tail-spin from 200 feet—too low for their parachutes—and crashed with such force that the engine was buried in the ground. Sands died immediately, and Hosch lingered in the hospital for three days but died from head injuries.

Two months later however, catastrophe was far from Keyhoe's mind. On receiving the dizzying news from McCracken, followed by a few minutes briefing, he returned to his office in the Aeronautics Branch, scarcely able to believe the privilege bestowed upon him:

> Aide to Colonel Charles A. Lindbergh! The words had a magic sound, and an even more magic meaning. I remembered Annapolis classmates and comrades in the Marine Corp who had been thrilled on being ordered to the staffs of high ranking officers. But not one of them had had so enviable an assignment as mine. To fly day after day with the man who had crossed the Atlantic alone would in itself be a glorious experience. But to live within the same walls with him, to see beyond the world hero and to know him as a friend … such was the promise held out by that simple word "aide."[61]

Although for Keyhoe, the honor of this assignment and the expectations it created within him were felt in intensely personal terms, its political and social significance was immense. Thanks to Lindbergh, America could now lay claim to an aeronautical achievement of international renown, and it was essential to ride the giant wave of excitement and pride that had almost overwhelmed its citizens. But if this era of fervent expansion and growth was to fulfill its potential, the nation must open up its skies and quickly. Their newest hero was a perfect poster-boy for this ambition, for he fully understood the importance of aviation, was far-sighted about its possibilities, and was wholly committed to its development.

Consequently, following many earlier discussions with Hoover, the Guggenheims, and McCracken, Lindbergh had agreed that if his transatlantic flight was achieved, he would make a unique 48-state tour of the US, and like the Bennett tour the previous year, it would be paid for by the Guggenheim Fund. A successful Lindbergh tour, coming so soon after his Atlantic crossing and taking in every state in the nation, would give extra impetus to develop new aerial technologies, expand communications and travel, create jobs to build infrastructure, and crucially, whip up enthusiasm for aviation in a public that thus-far saw flyers merely as entertaining barnstormers and their "ships" as curiosities that would never catch on. If the tour were not a success, it would serve to justify that view, and such an opportunity might never occur again. At stake, therefore, was not only the prestige of the most celebrated aviator of the time, but also the very future of commercial aviation in America, and vital parts of this responsibility had just been placed on Keyhoe's shoulders. If he should fail, the reputation, perhaps even the life, of the world's most famous man might be lost, along with all that the government hoped for from the tour.

Don had no time to absorb the enormity of his impending task: within twenty-four hours he was sent to meet his hero at Mitchel Field, where his initial sense of unreality following McCracken's pronouncement was quickly replaced with a manly appreciation of Lindbergh's "keen blue eyes…the warmth of his spontaneous flashing smile … his firm grasp …"[62]

The dazzling Lindbergh got straight down to business, shunning the suggestion that he had any special needs to be met during the trip and "in ten minutes the tour had been roughly planned … without waste of words." He would fly his famous, custom-built *Spirit of St. Louis*, and the Department of Commerce would provide support staff with a red-painted Fairchild FC2 monoplane and also a pilot to accompany him, since Keyhoe's own "flying had … not included extensive cross country work."[63] Lindy requested they recruit Phil Love, his Army friend and fellow mail pilot who had made his deliveries for him while he crossed the Atlantic. Unlike the Bennett tour, Lindbergh would not follow the regular routes that avoided mountainous terrain because it would be quicker to fly straight over these areas, despite the perils such rarely-attempted shortcuts entailed. Each of the forty-eight states would be visited and a strict schedule would be adhered to, even if it meant disappointing some cities: "we want to show people that aviation can come through on time," insisted Lindbergh.

Initially accompanying them was mechanic Ted Sorenson, who would service both aircraft, though he was soon after replaced by English-born Cecil Charles "Doc" Maidment. Milburn Kusterer, previously of the Bennett tour, would be the Guggenheim Foundation's representative and serve as Lindbergh's Advance Man on the ground. He would travel a week ahead of the party and try to ensure that necessary arrangements at each destination were in place, keeping in touch with Keyhoe by mail or phone.

The meeting over, the group went outside, where Don got a hint of what to expect over the next three months as he watched his hero swamped by hundreds of photographers, autograph hunters, and general onlookers, all wanting "to get close enough to touch this famous youth."

The Lone Eagle had intended to immediately set off for St. Louis, but he delayed in order to try out a new Army training plane. After working his way through the throng, he settled into the cockpit, then roared into the sky, executing rolls, loops, and spins, while Keyhoe looked on and listened to the comments of yearning admirers on the ground. Among them was a woman who thought Lindbergh should no longer fly. "He means too much to the world now," she lamented. "He ought to realize that now."

Major Thomas Lanphier, who was commanding officer of the First Pursuit Group and "an intimate friend" of Lindbergh's, was nearby, waiting to fly with him to St. Louis. He told the woman, "That's the only chance he has to be alone."[64]

* * *

"I was waiting on a balcony overlooking Port Washington," Keyhoe recalled. This balcony happened to be at the staggeringly opulent home of Harry Guggenheim where on July 13th he had arrived with Kusterer to meet his hero for the second time.

This Long Island property sat on a private wooded estate of 300 acres on which stood four palatial dwellings, all built by the Guggenheims since the turn of the century and each a pastiche of old European style, including a castle. Thirty-seven-year-old Harry and his wife, Florence, lived in the

50,000-square-foot Tudoresque Hempstead House, which had within its splendid walls an aviary, a palm court, and a billiard room with a gold-leaf ceiling.[65]

Lindbergh was not staying in this house but was living temporarily in *Falaise*, which stood in isolation on the shoreline of the estate, overlooking Long Island Sound, about half an hour by road from where he had set off on his famous flight just eight weeks earlier. *Falaise* was smaller than Hempstead House but no less impressive. Constructed of red brick in the lofty, arched style of a 13th-century French manor house and completely private, it was perhaps the only place where Lindy could have peace and seclusion. He'd been invited to stay there in order to finish—or rather to rewrite—his autobiography, *We*, a highly-anticipated account of his recent achievement.[66] It had already been hastily ghostwritten by a former *New York Times* reporter, Carlyle MacDonald, but Lindbergh disliked it and the publishing deadline was looming, so he entirely rewrote it in just three weeks. *Falaise* was perfect for this arduous and ultimately record-breaking task.

During the two weeks since his first meeting with Lindbergh, Keyhoe had been unceasingly busy dealing with "a barrage of long-distance calls, telegrams, personal visits and insistent letters from hundreds of cities," each pleading their case to be included on the Lone Eagle's itinerary.[67] Today, the details must be finalized, for there would be no further opportunity to get together before the tour, due to start in only a week's time.

If the splendor of the Guggenheim home had made any impression on Keyhoe, it was eclipsed by Lindbergh himself, who, with his host, strolled in from their short fishing trip. Don recalled him at this meeting in smitten terms:

> He looked more like a boy as I saw him then, bronzed by exposure to the sun and comfortably attired in khaki trousers and a loose shirt. We sat down as Mr. Guggenheim joined us, the colonel disposing of his long legs by stretching them out lazily to the side.[68]

As before, the meeting was brief and to the point. Don brought Lindy up to date with the preparations he had so far completed. They pored over maps, addressed a few questions, and discussed contingency plans for potential difficulties. Guggenheim told Keyhoe, "as the Colonel's aide, you will have to be a sort of buffer and take all the knocks possible." At this, Don caught Lindbergh looking at him and wondered if his hero, standing 6' 2", had misgivings about how this much shorter man might withstand the rigors to come.[69]

A week later, his test would begin.

* * *

On July 20, 1927, Keyhoe and pilot Phil Love touched down hastily, late and embarrassed at Lindy's first stop, Brainard Field, Hartford, Connecticut, where their task was to make sure everything was ready for his arrival. They were thirty minutes behind schedule due to a change of course to avoid heavy rain, which was made worse when they discovered they had been following an incorrect map. When the Lone Eagle landed minutes later, the frenzy that was to surround them all for the next three months began, and it was as frightening as it was exhilarating.

(Left to right): Donald E. Keyhoe, Philip Love, Charles Lindbergh, C. C. Maidment, and Milburn Kusterer. (National Air and Space Museum, Smithsonian Institution)

For almost every one of the stops during the tour, Keyhoe and his team had to steer Lindbergh safely through "an all but violent public admiration," which screamed, roared, and clawed wildly about him, presenting unending opportunities for disaster. Prior to every arrival, Keyhoe would seek assurances from local organizers that crowds at their airfield would be kept back, and in some cases press notices would clearly state that "Lindbergh will not land at all if the field is not clear." His pleas often would be met with a confident assurance from the local committee that their people would behave themselves because they "weren't like that," but when the *Spirit of St. Louis* began its descent, the populace would nonetheless swarm like locusts onto the airfield. And frequently, the police who were tasked with keeping order would themselves become distracted by their own excitement and so pandemonium ensued. Even when the crowds were better behaved, the press would fill the void of stupidity: one reporter sauntered within three inches of the plane's propellor and was saved only by the Colonel's quick reaction, which prompted him to lean from the cockpit and give the fool a stern ticking-off. Later, when landing in San Francisco, Keyhoe watched in horror when three hundred schoolchildren ran directly toward the front of the plane—which had no brakes, nor any forward visibility due to its fuel tanks being in the nose of the plane—but Lindy, always on the alert for such madness, immediately took off again until the area was cleared.[70]

Even when the crowds were contained behind barriers, they were sometimes not positioned far enough back, and Lindbergh had to carefully calculate his approach down a narrow corridor of fevered flesh. During one such landing on a sloping site, an unexpected shift of wind direction sent his plane, with its slicing blade, speeding toward the crowd less than a hundred feet away. Keyhoe and Phil frantically raced after it hoping to grab a strut and turn the craft, but Lindbergh had reacted fast and disaster was very narrowly averted. These near-misses were a constant reminder to Keyhoe that everything Lindbergh represented to the world, and all that the tour promised for his country, could be trashed in a second.

Nonetheless, when the excitement and tension of each landing had passed and Lindbergh stepped out of the cockpit, Keyhoe would set about making hasty introductions to elated and awed local representatives. That done, the Lone Eagle, accompanied by Don, would be driven in an open car to a civic reception, followed by hundreds of vehicles that had brought thousands of onlookers to the airfield. In a *Wacky Races* frenzy, cars and trucks chased after him amid clouds of dust and fumes, with horns blaring, speeding recklessly through intersections to try and keep him in sight. The streets of each town or city were crammed with jostling, cheering spectators, their numbers sometimes swelled by the granting of a "Lindbergh Day" during which banks and businesses were closed. Kids on bicycles rode around and in between the police motorcycles and his open car, while paper streamers and ticker-tape snowed down on him from every window, flags waved, cameras clicked by the thousand, and each time his car slowed, the bellowing multitude would surge forward to try and touch him. He made each journey under a near constant rain of blows from the throng, which, in its enthusiasm "whacked him unmercifully on back, shoulders or head," leaving him bruised.[71] Sometimes if the car was slow enough, a hand would try to drag him into the crowd, so he learned to keep a foot hooked on some part of the interior to counter these attempts. And when physical contact couldn't be achieved, items would serve as proxy. Boxes of candy and numerous gifts were hurled into the car, often hitting him or others riding with him. On one occasion a model airplane was thrown at him, which he ducked, but it struck Keyhoe in the face giving him a deep cut, and moments later a jackknife was hurled into the car, slightly injuring Lindy.

When he wasn't dodging missiles, Keyhoe was deflecting anger and criticism from those places that wanted to be included on the tour, but were not, so when possible, he had to come up with compromise solutions. The timetable was king, and Lindbergh would stick to it no matter what, but if it wouldn't make him late, he agreed to circle over some towns to give the masses a glimpse of him and sometimes dropped a personally signed message to be devoured on the ground:

> Greetings: Because of the limited time and the extensive itinerary of the tour of the United States now in progress to encourage popular interest in aeronautics, it is impossible for the "Spirit of St. Louis" to land in your city. This message from the air, however, is sent you to express our sincere appreciation of your interest in the tour and in the promotion and expansion of commercial aeronautics in the United States. We feel that we will be amply repaid for all our efforts if each and every citizen in the United States cherishes an interest in flying and gives his earnest support to the air mail service and the establishment of airports and similar facilities. The concerted efforts of the citizens of the United States

in this direction will result in America's taking its rightful place within a very short time as the world leader in commercial flying. — Charles A. Lindbergh

One newspaper, from a town which had not been included on the tour, ran an extraordinary and excoriating column, accusing Don of deliberately depriving the masses of their Lindbergh. It was, the paper claimed, entirely due to "his manager, Mr. Keyhoe, whose chief aim in life seems to be to antagonize the public and impress it with his own importance." The piece claimed that Lindy had been "bossed" by Keyhoe and recommended that the hero should "refuse to go further until he is provided with a 'manager' instead of a river packet first mate." Keyhoe was "a stupid manager" who was destroying the good will "ten times faster" than it had been created by the Colonel, and at almost every stop on the tour, it was his fault that crowds were disappointed.[72] Whether or not Don ever saw the piece isn't known, but its bizarre, petulant rant was very far from the reality.

Throughout the tour, there were frequent requests for Lindbergh to bless or acknowledge something or other named in his honor. In Tucson, the locals had affectionately constructed from wicker, a full-scale model of the *Spirit of St. Louis*, which they displayed at the landing site, where Lindy dutifully inspected it, before being whisked away to local festivities.[73] The city of Moundsville, however, wanted him to crack a bottle over the nose of the "Lone Eagle," the first "ship" produced by their aircraft corporation, but Keyhoe had to turn it down; he told the dejected organizers that he daily received "hundreds of requests" but could not afford to set a precedent.[74] He was under constant pressure to offer up Lindbergh in some capacity and consequently, as Guggenheim had instructed him, had "to take all the knocks possible." This he did readily and without complaint.

Despite Keyhoe's best efforts, occasional scheduling errors arose because of his own mistakes, and he would have to work fast and diplomatically to put matters right. Columbus, Nebraska, was annoyed at him, because he had promised it would be included on the tour, but he hadn't realized it would take the flight a long way from its route and thereby screw up Lindbergh's rigid timetable. The city was dropped, which led to demands for Keyhoe to "live up to his promise," so he had to hastily negotiate with Lindy to put it back in the itinerary. At the next stop, Omaha, Nebraska, the Colonel was presented with a bouquet of flowers, which he immediately threw to the floor and stamped upon. Keyhoe was left to explain to the astonished City Commissioner that this apparent rudeness was due to a misunderstanding; Lindbergh had thought the flowers were from "some silly girl" and that only the day before, a bouquet had been thrown into his car that had hit him "squarely in the face"; hence he had developed a hostility to blossoms.[75]

Indeed, flowers were something of an issue throughout the tour. Lindbergh was daily showered with them during his open-car parades, more were thrust upon him at speeches, and an abundance would adorn the various hotel rooms where the group stayed. To alleviate the latter problem, the Colonel had Keyhoe arrange for these to be sent to local hospitals, but in one hotel, as soon as flowers were sent out, more were delivered. It turned out that the local florist, who was surely reveling at this upturn in business, was under instructions to ensure Lindy's room was kept permanently in bloom, so as fast as they were dispatched, they were replaced.

Occasionally there would be on-the-spot difficulties that Keyhoe had no opportunity to resolve. One city, in its adulation, put Lindbergh in a car with a raised seat bedecked with flowers, which rather suggested a throne in a beauty queen pageant. The Colonel drew the line at this and personally persuaded the disappointed committee chairman to let him sit in the back seat of the car.

Then came the speeches and the dining. On arrival at each public venue, the local worthies would laud the Lone Eagle, listen with rapture to his message about the importance of commercial aviation development, then sweep him and his team away to a civic reception. Evenings would be spent at a lavish dinner, attended by hundreds, but it would sometimes follow an equally lavish spread laid on for the Colonel at his hotel, served up shortly before his departure for the banquet. Despite this, and to his team's amazement, "Slim" would often do justice to the platter and then do the same at the banquet, which relieved Keyhoe of the need to placate offended organizers who had gone to great expense to feed their hero, only to find he had no appetite.

Even while dining, autographs were in constant demand, but there was insufficient time to eat and oblige and this caused offense, so again it was up to Keyhoe to smooth the waters. Often he would explain in advance to organizers that the Colonel was on a tight schedule, and if he signed every autograph and answered every question he would be both late and hungry. Most were receptive to this reasoning—indeed some small towns thoughtfully provided the team with generous lunch baskets so they could eat en route— though some felt spurned, having laid on a feast. Yet, despite these and many other problems, the team generally enjoyed the dining and socializing, though

Keyhoe later reflected that the feasting was more exhausting than the flying.

On top of banquet fatigue were the bogus visitors claiming to be Lindy's relatives, which turned out to be true in one case, much to Don's embarrassment, after having rejected a fellow who was indeed Lindbergh's uncle, John Cabot Lodge, the mayor of Detroit. And the press gave the Colonel a taste of what he could expect from them in the future when they installed a microphone on his hotel window ledge to snoop on his private time. Even his public time was prey to journalistic dirty deeds; at one function, despite a police presence at either end of the long dining table, a woman reporter had hidden under it and emerged with pencil and pad, believing that this bit of ingenuity would allow her to interview a surprised Lindbergh at his very plate.

Females were a frequent source of embarrassment and irritation during the tour, and Keyhoe found his hero's apparent shyness toward them to be one of his virtues—he seemed to be a Red Mike. Lindbergh was as yet unmarried and during the tour showed no interest whatsoever in the fairer sex, but the women of America, deprived only a year earlier of Rudolph Valentino, lost no time in latching onto the latest handsome hero and for many of them he had become a figure of romance and fevered desire. Girls in the crowds either screamed wildly or were lost for words when they saw him. They pestered Keyhoe to get his autograph, begged him for an introduction, and even sneaked into Lindy's hotel and hid in the closets of adjoining rooms, then waited until his door was unguarded and pressed their ears to it. Some, finding the door unlocked and the room empty, quite brazenly wandered about his suite looking through his drawers and toiletries, then fully expected that when he returned, their idol would be happy to shake their hands and answer all their questions. There was no hiding place.

Even his clothes were frequently stolen. The group's laundry would usually be returned minus various items because the adoring thieves, some with an eye to turning a profit, would filch something they hoped must have been worn by the Colonel, so in addition to all the other demands on their time, Keyhoe and the team had to hurriedly purchase replacement garments. Matters became so difficult that on one occasion, when Lindbergh took delivery of a new pair of shoes, he dumped the old ones out of his plane over the desert to prevent them being stolen and put on display.

In addition to the delirium on Lindbergh's arrivals and the hysteria and intrusion surrounding his presence in every location, there was the madness of getting him out of his hotel. Like latter-day roadies, Don and his team often had to create a distraction in the lobby to enable the star of the show to escape through a service entrance and into a waiting vehicle, or had to play decoy to a frenzy of reporters; they would pile into a car, pull down the shades, and speed off with the press in pursuit to enable the Colonel to make his getaway unobserved. But matters didn't always end when he departed because opportunistic hotel staff would rifle through the waste baskets in his rooms and sell the contents. It was up to Keyhoe to make sure absolutely nothing was left behind.

And there were the pranks. The public face of Lindbergh was sober, rarely smiling, and his conversation was restricted entirely to aviation, but Keyhoe felt profoundly privileged to see a side of his hero that none could have guessed existed: he loved to play practical jokes. Perhaps it was Don's experiences in the mean world of little boys and later the obligatory hazing of Annapolis that colored his view, but he treasured each of the many humiliations his hero inflicted upon him, often with the enthusiastic assistance of Phil Love, whose devotion to Lindy was total. At the start of the tour, Don sported a slender mustache and felt he cut rather a dash with it, but Lindbergh felt differently. The three amigos, Love, Maidment, and Kusterer, at the behest of their leader, forced Keyhoe into a corner of his room, and the Colonel wielded a razor, which left their victim minus mustache and with an "aggrieved state of mind." He was never able to exact revenge on his tormentor and came to regard this incident with great fondness, later regaling his audiences with it, boasting how he had been the "goat" of the pranks that Lindbergh "pulled" on his friends.

Don was constantly on alert for his idol's tomfoolery throughout the tour and with good reason. One morning he awoke to find Lindy had sewed up the sleeves, pants-legs, and pockets of his only suit, and on other occasions the Colonel regularly disposed of, or damaged, each of Keyhoe's hats (he was a committed hat-wearer), so time had to be spent obtaining new ones. This sartorial mischief, however, paled against Slim's attempted shenanigans during a visit to a copper mine in Butte, Montana. Lindbergh was "visibly disappointed" when the hoist engineer was prevented at the last moment from complying with his secret request to drop the cage and its occupants down a 2,800 ft shaft. "I wanted to give Kusterer a surprise," he lamented.

Phil Love's eager participation in Lindy's antics was not confined to terra firma. On many occasions when he was flying alongside the *Spirit of St. Louis*, while Keyhoe and the others were in the rear catching up on sleep, Lindy would signal Phil to suddenly send the plane into a nosedive, then jerk it back up to a fast ascent, tumbling the startled passengers and all their loose items like dice in a cup. "This performance never failed to amuse Lindbergh,"

Keyhoe recalled, even though it happened "rather too often." Phil, however, despite his ovine complicity, was not exempted from similar indignities. One time, Lindbergh had been sent a gift of toiletries that included perfume, with which he drenched Phil's coat, and the odor lingered strong at their next banquet. A guest seated with the Colonel thought the ladies were responsible for the almost overpowering fragrance, but fun-loving Lindy explained soberly that his party had used up the gift of perfume "in one night," leaving Don "extremely mortified" at the unspoken inference this cast upon him and the group. Yet, like a star-struck movie fan, he interpreted such humiliations as a sign of familiarity given to a privileged insider, rather than contemplating that perhaps his hero took sadistic joy in the degradation of his acolytes.

Even when away from his team, Lindbergh could not resist an opportunity to inflict humiliation on someone else. Occasionally he would take a solo break from the tour and spend a few hours flying alone, which his companions did not begrudge him, given the maniacal public interest in his every moment. He returned from one of these excursions boasting to Keyhoe how he had buzzed an isolated Indian village, his approach to it silenced thanks to the wind direction. He merrily recollected to Keyhoe how he had swooped down and sent the inhabitants "streaking for their huts, falling into them headfirst, all but one old fat squaw...she was scared to death...as I flew over her, and crawled on her hands and knees for the nearest tent." He continued to circle over the village for five minutes "but not one of them even peeked out. I suppose they thought I was some kind of a flying devil."[76]

But hi-jinks and low tricks aside, there was serious business to be done, and the schedule could not be allowed to slip, though as the tour progressed, changes had to be made to prevent delays. The initial practice of preceding Lindbergh to his destinations by half an hour was dropped because frequently he would be held back by unplanned demands on his time before take-off, so Keyhoe and Phil would stay on hand to field such interventions. Once he was in the air, they would deal with enquiries on the ground, then catch up with him and fly close, preceding him to the next destination by only minutes, while the Colonel circled above before touching down. This permitted the crowd a good look at the *Spirit of St. Louis* and gave its pilot time to assess the landing site.

It soon became evident to Keyhoe that Phil, despite his willing participation in Lindbergh's cruel japes, was the right choice to accompany the Colonel; his aviation skills were substantial and almost matched Lindbergh's own. The two had first met during their Army air service and their later experience as night mail pilots gave them an edge that proved crucial to the success of the tour. Weather conditions that would strike fear into other flyers were par for the course to these men, and they learned to cope with "blind flying," i.e., flying in low or zero visibility, even though it was sometimes fatal. Keyhoe considered it "the supreme test of any pilot." Airplanes did have instruments—compass, bank-and-turn indicator, altimeter, tachometer, and air-speed meter—but these often-inaccurate apparatuses were designed for daylight flying in good visibility. In low or zero visibility, even with lights on the aircraft and beacons on landing fields, a flyer had to interpret and combine their readings with poor-quality maps and a personal knowledge of the terrain. He would check them against each other in constant rotation, while outside the cockpit, the wingtips of his craft might be hidden in cloud or fog. In an age when streetlights were few, even a clear night offered little guidance from below.

Anxiety levels were therefore high when Lindbergh decided to stick to the schedule and fly to Portland, Maine, in a heavy fog. Keyhoe pleaded with him to change his mind:

> "Don't take any more chances than you have to, Slim," I begged, not realizing that I was saying his nickname for the first time, though I had envied Phil Love his easy use of it. "Your getting down safely is more important than the tour, any time."

Slim shrugged away these concerns and took off. He was determined to land at Portland's air field, though he could have landed elsewhere, but this would mean leaving the *Spirit of St. Louis* in an unguarded location, which he would not do. To increase Keyhoe's uneasiness, Phil climbed into his own plane to follow Lindy but insisted on flying alone because one of his instruments was playing-up and he wouldn't risk the life of a passenger. Keyhoe had to make his own way by car, which "plunged and skidded" on treacherous roads shrouded in fog.[77] Several anxious hours later, he learned that all was well, but Phil, in following his friend into the blind sky, had shown not only his mettle, but also his devotion to Lindbergh and to the success of the tour.

There was some relief from the demands and worries of the schedule when the group enjoyed a few rest days between destinations. Some were a busman's holiday, spent flying wherever they—or rather, the Colonel—wanted to go, others were spent aground as the guests of various businessmen or local worthies, yet even here the press would often intrude, hiding in bushes or peering over walls to snap pictures of Lindy swimming or relaxing in the grounds of private houses. Perhaps he tolerated this because, as he later told Keyhoe, he "expected public attention to wane" after the tour, and he would be able to go about in public unrecognized.[78]

On one special day, August 19th, business and pleasure combined for Keyhoe when he and the Lone Eagle flew over Ottumwa. The previous day, he'd sent word to his father that their home town would have an aerial visit during the Iowa schedule, and Lindy had requested, as he did with each destination, that to aid navigation, the name of the city be painted on some prominent roofs. The populace obliged and at about 1:30 pm, Lindy put on his show for Ottumwans, who cheered and waved from streets and rooftops amid the sound of factory and locomotive whistles. The silver wings of his "ship" reflected shafts of sunlight through the clouds as he circled around the city sky, flying within 200 feet over the Hotel Ottumwa, allowing citizens to see him clearly in the cabin of his plane, while Keyhoe, from the Fairchild, dropped a personal message for his father.[79]

Delightful and emotional though this surely was, perhaps the greatest highlight of the tour for Keyhoe was on September 30th in the skies over Oklahoma. For one glorious, exhilarating five-minute flight, Lindbergh allowed him to share the cockpit of the *Spirit of St. Louis*, a rare privilege exceeded by only one other person—automaker Henry Ford, who on August 11th, had taken his first ever flight and was allowed to briefly take the controls from Lindy, at Ford Airport, Detroit.[80]

On October 23rd, their 103-day tour ended where it had started, at Mitchel Field. During this last flight, taking off from Philadelphia, Don felt gloomy at the prospect of parting from his hero, whom he had come to regard as a friend. It was evident that the tour had been a total success, which Keyhoe attributed entirely to Lindbergh's many virtues, while regarding his own role then, and later, as insignificant. As he flew toward their final destination, he reflected for the first time on their achievement. He had flown 20,000 miles and the Colonel 22,000.[81] They had landed, on time, in each of the 48 states, taking direct routes that other flyers had feared and circumvented, thereby gaining knowledge of terrain vital to aerial mapping. This was a unique achievement to which history has given the barest recognition, leaving it as merely a footnote in Lindbergh's career, yet those miles were so successfully accomplished thanks in part to Keyhoe's commitment and involvement.

Whatever pressures he felt during this tour, he kept to himself, not least due to his admiration for the Colonel, who seemed to remain calm under all conditions and in this respect, set a perfect example to his aide. This calmness, this lack of reaction, led to some criticism of Lindbergh, which Keyhoe defended at the time and in the years to come. From his privileged insider perspective, he judged that Lindbergh possessed a natural modesty and restraint. He saw not an aloof egotist, nor a sadistic prankster, but a rather noble man, at times fun-loving, but always in control, and like a master chess player, always able to plan the next move. "I cannot recall a single incident in which his judgement proved unsound," Keyhoe later wrote. "We followed unhesitatingly where he led, knowing that his decision was sure to be the best."[82]

Lindbergh had certainly fulfilled his obligation to the Guggenheim Fund, raising the profile of flying beyond mere barnstorming entertainment or serving the plucky ambitions of record-breakers. He had shown that airplanes had the potential to expand and enrich the lives of US citizens and could play a vital role in national commerce. As a direct consequence of the tour, commercial aviation received a tremendous boost upon which it would rapidly build, creating jobs, infrastructure, new opportunities for business and travel, and ultimately, as the Guggenheim Fund had hoped, made America "the world leader in commercial flying."

No one had died, no one had been injured. A few people were disappointed, several millions were awestruck, and many florists were ecstatic. But perhaps no one was happier than Donald Keyhoe.

Chapter 6: Moving On

Now back to Earth in both literal and figurative senses, Keyhoe's thrilling three months spent cheek-by-jowl with the most famous man in the world was unlikely to endear him to the connubial domesticity he had earlier spurned, particularly as he was now occupied with the follow-up to his adventure.

He had so far released only a few press and magazine articles about the tour, because his main focus was the writing of his book, *Flying with Lindbergh*, published in October 1928, which tellingly was dedicated not to his wife, but to his mother. This fly-on-the-wall account of his time with the Lone Eagle was very well-received, even being hailed as "practically a sequel" to Lindy's *We*, and subsequently the Department of Commerce gave him a six-month leave of absence to embark on a speaking tour around the country. His subject matter during these engagements covered not only aviation development and the work of the Department, but he also gave audiences what they really wanted—the inside dish on Lindy. Keyhoe, at all times respectful to the Colonel, gave admiring examples of his serious-minded approach to the tour and mirthful accounts of his pranks, serving to both humanize his hero and to embed himself in the public mind as Slim's friend.

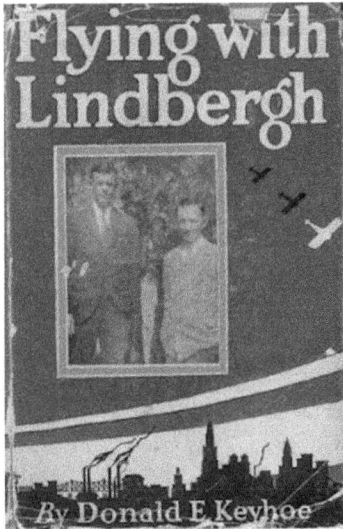

All this inevitably detracted from any reconciliation with his wife. In November, he left Margaret for good and moved into the YMCA in Washington, D.C. Soon after, he told her that he was "interested in another woman," following which, in February 1929 his wife sued him for maintenance and they formally separated.[83] She retained custody of their son but never remarried, while for his part Keyhoe continued to tour, giving talks mainly at

47

schools about his time with Lindbergh.

Even as the dust was still billowing from his marital woes, he was forging ahead with his writing career, notably in a nationally-syndicated adventure yarn, *The Sky Raider*, "A Thrilling Mystery Story of Life, Love and Danger in the Air Mail." Hailed as the first air adventure serial, it was given full-page treatment in many newspapers and often bannered on the front page. The hero was Dick Trent, a daring mail pilot, who braved the elements in gripping, cliff-hanger tales of "romance, adventure, mystery, devotion and death," while courting the attention of the beautiful Mary Rand, daughter of "Old Man Rand," the bushy-browed, gruff, "veteran of the air mail." Written in thirty "chapters," some newspapers published several at once, others only a daily extract running to a couple of columns, but *The Sky Raider* formed the blueprint for much of Keyhoe's fiction in the years to come. Still influenced by his recent experience, he gave Dick Trent clear elements of Lindbergh: he was a former Army Air Cadet turned mail pilot, with an innate calling to be a flyer, who had "that uncanny skill which seems instinctive and which men bring to the callings which they love." He flew little-known routes under conditions that only mail pilots dared attempt and possessed sterling, manly qualities: upright, honest, strong, wise, and decent—a natural hero.

The Sky Raider serial was unashamedly promoted as the work of former "flying ace" Keyhoe, the man that Lindbergh had "chosen" to accompany him on his US tour. Neither claim was true, but such inaccuracies, coupled with the success of *Flying with Lindbergh*, raised Keyhoe's profile sufficiently to underpin his status as a close associate of the Lone Eagle, perhaps influencing a minor, but widely reported incident.

Late in 1929, Keyhoe was rather surprised to receive from publishers Dorrance & Co of Philadelphia a request for more information regarding his forthcoming book, *We Fly*. Keyhoe wrote back informing them that there was no such book, which led to the discovery that he'd been impersonated by one Gerald R. Gage of Los Angeles. Gage, a mailman, no less, of seventeen years' service, either because he was obsessed with Lindbergh or just wanted to get rich, claimed to have previously written a book titled *Lucky Lindy* and wanted to build on its success.[84] He entered into correspondence with Dorrance & Co on letterhead notepaper bearing the names of both Lindbergh and Keyhoe and wrote variously under each of their names to promote the non-existent book. He then pitched a supposed second forthcoming book that would be Lindy's personal memoir, complete with childhood photographs, which, it later turned out, were his own. Dorrance & Co was taken in and began written negotiations with, they believed, Donald Keyhoe.

After Keyhoe's reply, the publisher made quick work of uncovering the scam, and Don "hurried to New York" to inform Lindbergh of the attempted fraud, but he was merely "quite amused at the man's audacity." Though Keyhoe insisted it was a serious matter, Slim's only action was to telephone various newspapers and put them straight on the story.[85]

Gage was sentenced the following January to two months in prison and two years' probation for defrauding the mails. He offered several explanations for his actions. He was at first defiant, calling the whole matter "a joke," then later said that he had impersonated Keyhoe because he felt that, as a mere postal worker, he wouldn't have enough credibility as a writer, and he didn't think it would be against the law. Still later he said he had been motivated by "hero worship" (perhaps the offer of $6,000 dollars for serialization in a national weekly played no part). "I guess I should have stuck to delivering mail," he lamented, but the incident marked the end of his postal career and he disappeared into obscurity, employed thereafter as a salesman.

Despite the crisis of Keyhoe's matrimonial collapse, by the end of 1929 he had been publishing new material about twice a month, including, somewhat inevitably, a piece on the virtues of air mail pilots and laudatory profiles of the admirable fellows who made up the Department of Commerce's Aeronautics Branch.[86]

After he and Margaret divorced, she settled into a new life as a single divorcee, but Don was ready to marry again. On August 18, 1930, twenty-six-year-old Helen Wood Gardner, a native of Round Hill, Virginia, became the new, adored and ultimately lifelong, Mrs. Donald Keyhoe.[87] She was the daughter of Robert Bennett Gardner, a farmer, born in Washington, D.C., and Julia Rust Wilson of Augusta, Virginia. Helen's maternal grandfather, Earnest Augustus Wilson, was an "engineer who built railroads" in Knoxville.[88] Now that Keyhoe's marital travails were behind him, this welcome change to his domestic life ushered in a happy and productive decade, and he was evidently spurred on to commit fully to his writing career.

In May 1931, the *Saturday Evening Post* published his lengthy and rather saccharine piece on Lindbergh, written after a privileged evening dining with "Slim" and his wife, the former Anne Morrow, at their temporary retreat in New Jersey, where Keyhoe also engaged playfully with their infant son, Charles Jr. They chatted about old times, new times, and the continuing intrusive harassment Lindbergh endured, a point which was reinforced when, after dark, Keyhoe saw through the window a "disheveled, wild-eyed" man watching them who ran away when he was spotted. Keyhoe alerted the couple and recommended they employ a guard, but Lindy pointed out that they had moved to this remote location to avoid that necessity and he wasn't worried.[89]

Despite this alarming trespass, Keyhoe came away with the feeling that all was right with his hero and his family, believing that the future for all three was bright and filled with promise. Only ten months later, baby Charles would be kidnapped and murdered, under circumstances that remain inadequately explained and which would savagely intensify media interest in his father.

By the time the Lindbergh piece was published, Keyhoe had significantly expanded on his earlier foray into fiction, for this was the era of the pulps and glossies. Lurid in color and content, but always entertaining, these magazines were the accessible, exciting, darkly-stimulating alternative to traditional books and magazines. Readers could lose themselves in these publications, which served up part-illustrated stories, blurring the boundaries between fantasy, crime, science-fiction, super heroes, and sex. Considered low-brow and cheap, they of course sold in their millions. Among the most widely-read were *Argosy*, *Sky Birds*, and *Weird Tales*, and Keyhoe wrote frequently for all of these. In this medium he let rip, with adjective-heavy, action-packed tales of fearless men overcoming terrifying odds, battling both human and supernatural enemies, with occasional death-rays, dinosaurs, and pterodactyls thrown in for added excitement.

From 1930 to late 1939, his non-fiction aviation pieces dwindled, but his output of pulps was prodigious, publishing new stories almost weekly. Mostly based on air adventure, they had sinister titles: "The Skeleton in the Sky," "Flying Fate," "The Flying Corpse," "Blood on the Joystick," and "The Masked Menace." He especially favored titles with "Drome"—another term for "aerodrome"—or "Devil" ("Dead Man's Drome," "The Drome of Dread," "The Devil's Holocaust," "The Devil-Dogs Decoy"), and his characters were larger-than-life men's men. They were daring, direct, and fearless, with names that inferred manly, adventurous, no-nonsense personalities: Lucky, Pug, Mack, Cyclone—oversized fellows who yelped, bawled, thundered, and of course smoked Camels. Their brutish, sinister, sadistic, and merciless foes were no match for the square-jawed, tough-but-fair American male, whose ruggedness was often tempered by romantic inclination to a pretty gal in need of rescue. These daring pilots valiantly swooped down on enemies in the sky amid showers of bullets, while their own injured aircraft plunged toward the Earth at each cliff-hanger ending; yet some piece of luck, bravery, or ingenuity would save them at the start of the next episode and they would live to fight another installment.

Perhaps inspired by his new and happy marriage, in 1932 Keyhoe dipped a toe deeper into romantic fiction with a syndicated piece, "The Queer Mrs. Farnstone." Running to about 3,000 words, its heroine, Carol, was a classy single gal who had agreed to a platonic six-month marriage with a stranger for which she was to be paid handsomely after they divorced. In the meantime, she was required to portray herself as something of a tart in front of her husband's friends to suit his own ends, but being unable to suppress her natural sophistication and high morals, mutual love ensued, resulting in bliss.[90]

Romance aside, Keyhoe's airborne fictional heroes were his mainstay and he developed characters who were more than just square-jawed and courageous: some had special powers. One of the longest-running was Captain Philip Strange, a.k.a. the "Brain-Devil," a WWI pilot and spy who was not only a scourge of the Germans, but also possessed ESP and he appeared in *Flying Aces* magazine almost every month from 1931 to 1939. Another specially-gifted pilot was Richard Knight (1936-1942), who had been blinded in WWI but was super-naturally able to see in the dark. Other characters during this period were short-lived: Dr. Yen Sin, Oriental bad-guy with a flair for sinister deeds in a fictional fog-shrouded Washington, D.C, lasted for only three episodes, while another heroic pilot also named Trent—Eric—flew for just twelve episodes, from 1940-1942.

These works would set in stone the style Keyhoe would use in his later non-fiction UFO writing and for which he would be often criticized by his detractors, but it served perfectly for the pulps and was certainly lucrative. Between 1935 and 1938, he and Helen, having spent their first married years residing in expensive hotel apartments, were living on and off in Palm Beach, Florida, while at the same time they had purchased a plot of land on Mount Vernon Boulevard in Lorton, Virginia, where they built their $35,000 home. He also kept an office in the Mills Buildings in the capital.[91] His income at this time was stated to be "over $5,000" (over $100,000 today).[92]

For the present, he was successful, increasingly wealthy, and at last, happily married. Soon however, he would largely put aside his dramatic fantasy-fiction tales of combat and begin to write about the terrors of real war.

* * *

By 1938, while the Keyhoes were settling into their new home, Europe knew it was headed for yet another bloody conflict, and Americans were once again resolute in their isolationism. But on October 30th that year, the nation's attention would be diverted from matters across the Atlantic by a small incident that caused a brief maelstrom at the time, and which Keyhoe, a successful writer of fiction, could not have imagined would be of great significance for him a decade later.

Radio was then the nation's most popular form of entertainment, and from the 1930s through to the advent of television in the late 1940s, families would cluster around their wirelesses, collectively feeding their imaginations from the smörgåsbord of aural delights on offer. Indeed, the medium was so popular that cinema audiences had become heavily depleted and could only be tempted to turn out if the movie were interrupted with a radio broadcast of a popular show, after which the film would resume. Consequently, on Halloween 1938, when Orson Welles broadcast his dramatized version of H. G. Wells' *War of the Worlds*, setting it in modern-day America in the form of a live news broadcast, it was assured of a large and receptive audience.

A generation earlier, Mars had become fixed in the public imagination as the most likely source of an enemy from another world when the British *Pearson's Magazine* had serialized H. G. Wells' tale of a Martian invasion (coincidentally, around the time of Keyhoe's birth in June 1897). It was immediately popular and unwittingly set the tone and standard for much of the space-based science-fiction that would be created during the twentieth-century. By March of 1938, the Flash Gordon serial *Trip to Mars* was already thrilling cinema audiences with its weekly cliffhanger portrayals of deadly rays coming from the Red Planet to destroy life on Earth, which was undoubtedly fiction except in the minds of its youngest audiences. The elevation of Mars to a genuine and present threat was due entirely to the Orson Welles broadcast.

Welles prefaced his play with a brief but perfectly clear explanation that the performance was an interpretation of a work of fiction. Unfortunately, many listeners missed his announcement and believed their country was being invaded by Martians. Thousands reacted in blind terror and many took to the streets in panic. While the number of listeners who reacted hysterically may have been exaggerated at the time, the scale of panic and its effect on US citizens was nonetheless significant and was widely reported in the media.

In 1940, a Princeton psychologist, Hadley Cantril, recognized the startling impact it had had and as part of the Radio Research Project, funded by Rockefeller, which sought to study the social effect of radio on the public, produced a report on the Welles broadcast. It found that about a million listeners became panic-stricken and many tried to flee from what they believed was a deadly invasion from the Red Planet. The report noted, however, that the popularity of radio, and the reliance upon it for informing the public, was an important factor in its collective response:

> On the evening of October 30, 1938, thousands of Americans became panic-stricken by a broadcast purported to describe an invasion of Martians which threatened our whole civilization. Probably never before have so many people in all walks of life and in all parts of the country become so suddenly and so intensely disturbed as they did on this night ... Long before the broadcast had ended, people all over the United States were praying, crying, fleeing frantically to escape death from the Martians. Some ran to rescue loved ones. Others telephoned farewells or warnings, hurried to inform neighbors, sought information from newspapers or radio stations, summoned ambulances and police cars. At least six million people heard the broadcast. At least a million of them were frightened or disturbed.[93]

It seems ridiculous to us now that such an effect could result from a radio play, but as the report also noted:

> The importance of radio's role in current national and international affairs is too well known to be recounted here. By its very nature radio is the medium par excellence for informing all segments of a population of current happenings, for arousing in them a common sense of fear or joy, and for exciting them to similar reactions directed toward a single objective.

The upshot of this unique and astonishing event was that it soon became firmly fixed in the public, military, and scientific mind that not only was Mars the most likely origin of an invasion from space, but also that the collective human psyche would experience a meltdown leading to the rapid collapse of ordered society if space beings were found to exist. This view would misinform, misdirect, and negatively influence the thinking of millions for decades to come.

The innovative rendering by Orson Welles of an almost forgotten classic tale would become an immovable obstacle for Keyhoe in his yet-to-come career, the nature of which he would surely have thought too far-fetched even for his own works of fiction.

Chapter 7:
From Pulp to Propaganda

The ideological paranoia that would come to shameful fruition in the McCarthy years had long and deep roots in America. By the mid-1930s, fear of foreign infiltration and its potential effect on democracy was increasing. Consequently, Donald Keyhoe's attention was now being deflected from his colorful pulps to matters of national security. Though he couldn't wield a sword against the enemy, he could still wield his pen, and he began to publish articles that warned citizens of the enemy within and speculated on the ramifications of US mobilization. As early as 1936, when Hitler's increasing despotism added to America's fears, publications addressing what might happen on "M-Day" (Mobilization-Day) first appeared, and in 1940 Keyhoe took a crack at it himself.

In July he published his pamphlet, *If War Comes: M-Day Plan. What Your Government Plans for You.*[94] Its publication coincided with economist Leo M. Cherne's similarly titled, *M-Day and What It Means to You.* Cherne, who later would briefly serve under Presidents Ford and Carter as Chair of the President's Intelligence Advisory Board, had already published *Adjusting Your Business to War*, which also dealt with the M-Day scenario. His recent speculations on the matter were largely factual, utilizing a sort of question-and-answer format, but Keyhoe's offering placed the subject in a fictional setting, creating characters, businesses, and situations whose reward or punishment would be meted out depending on their compliance with a rather Draconian government "plan," which he believed had been decided upon.

At this time, President Roosevelt was continuing to appease the majority isolationists, who remained tightly opposed to entering the European war that had begun in 1939, while his perpetually busy wife, Eleanor, was casting a critical eye over Keyhoe's *M-Day*. Starting in 1935, the First Lady had a syndicated and highly-popular six-days-a-week column *My Day*, which she utilized to draw attention to those issues that were of importance to her. She of course held no political power and her marriage to the President had long-since failed, but the couple had formed a remarkable working partnership, and she was a valuable asset to her husband, who generally had a high regard for her views and knowledge of political and social issues.

She was therefore well-placed to offer her opinion on Keyhoe's rather doom-laden, fictionalized predictions about the ramifications of "the plan" and on July 15th, wrote:

> I have recently been looking over a pamphlet ... by Donald Edward Keyhoe. It is very interesting, though the War Department says nothing of the kind has been worked out in such detail and, so far as they are concerned, the whole thing is still in the realm of discussion.
>
> My main objection to this plan is that, while the publication of such a plan may be of value in arousing the United States to the realization of the possibility of someday having to defend its own shores, the plan does not make clear that it is too late to undertake such mobilization when there is an attack.[95]

Though there was some praise for Keyhoe's *M-Day* among reviewers, there was plenty of criticism, perhaps best expressed in Mary-Carter Roberts' literary column in *The Sunday Star*. She considered Cherne's version "immeasurably superior" to Keyhoe's, which she felt addressed the possible infringements of civil liberties "only incidentally" with the means justifying the end.[96]

But this was not Don's first attempt at alerting his country to potential threats from beyond its shores. By 1938 he was publishing articles about the dangers of spies and their deadly, imported ideologies, which he co-authored with *Washington Post* journalist John "Jack" Jay Daly. Nine years' Keyhoe's senior, Daly became a noted reporter in the early 1920s and over the years developed close links in the White House.[97] He and Don wrote for some of the same national magazines and Washington newspapers, and evidently, from their separate and combined articles, they shared the same concerns on national security and social matters. They wrote several pieces for *Cosmopolitan* magazine, including one on the illegal abortion racket that was said to be flourishing in Washington, D.C.[98] Moreover, their writing styles were not dissimilar, evidenced by Daly's syndicated series *Secrets of the Civil Service*, which, if the cases he detailed were not known to be real, might be mistaken for fiction of the pulp variety. Most were word-by-word, gesture-by-gesture accounts of misdeeds that had come to the attention of the Treasury Department, but dramatized by Daly to create scenarios fit for an Edward G. Robinson movie rather than the factual reporting of rather mundane cases of counterfeiting.

Their similar use of colorful hyperbole served the two men well and certainly drew attention to their subjects, notably in Keyhoe and Daly's August 1938 *Cosmopolitan* article "Web Over Washington," which claimed that in the Capital there were 120,000 foreign spies and that infiltration into US intelligence was widespread. "To fight this horde America has only a skeleton force" and "our few agents cannot keep track of the ever-increasing thousands," they warned, concluding that this horde "may some day attempt to choke us to death." This information, reliable or not, was generally well-received and was certainly unsettling news to a nation that considered itself to be an impenetrable fortress.

Keyhoe and Daly's Washington links were on display in the October 1939 issue of *Cosmopolitan*, in which the two co-authored a sort of fly-on-the-wall report on the daily routine of President Roosevelt, detailing his activities in a gentlemanly and complimentary way. It of course made no mention of his disability, nor of the crisis unfolding in Europe, but threw in a few humorous anecdotes and extolled the warmth of his famous "fireside chats." Whether or not it chafed Keyhoe, a Republican, to write this way of a Democrat isn't known, but his patriotism presumably overrode partisanship. FDR was a president like no other before him, and it spoke to Keyhoe's status that he was permitted to publish a piece of this nature in a leading magazine.

That same month, Britain declared war on Germany, and though hostilities were delayed by an eerie, uneasy period when no war was evident (the "phoney war"), by spring of 1940 there was no doubt of its reality. Keyhoe's old Annapolis pal, Hillenkoetter, was now a Lieutenant Commander and an Embassy naval attaché in Paris when the first German air raid on the city struck on June 3rd. He was lunching across the street at the luxurious Hotel Crillon, when he and his companions heard the sirens. They dashed back to the Embassy and from its roof observed the first of more than a thousand bombs falling over the city and saw the smoke rising in the distance. Eleven days later, France surrendered, and Hillenkoetter himself was present, standing behind General Studnitz on the Place de la Concorde, while the occupying German 6th Army paraded past in triumph.[99]

By 1941, every country in Europe had either fallen to Hitler, declared neutrality, or had appeased him in some way, and Britain was in a lone, desperate struggle to remain free from subjugation. Whatever Keyhoe felt about America's continued isolationism, the current crisis gave him the opportunity to publish something of a blitzkrieg of articles during that year, warning of Nazi and Communist infiltration and their dirty deeds that threatened America. But also on his mind was the now-crucial subject of aviation development, and to that end he highlighted the efforts of the Royal Air Force, whose heroic young pilots were a vital factor in keeping the Germans at bay in aircraft whose speeds and altitudes far exceeded those he had experienced himself in his Marine days. His 8,600 feet altitude record in the F-5L over Guam was barely a playful leap compared to the 33,000 feet of modern aircraft that he anticipated would soon achieve 40,000 feet.

Keyhoe, of course, had never experienced aerial combat. It was one thing to be a test pilot but quite another to be in a kill-or-be-killed sky battle, and his own descriptions of such in his pulps of yore were works of extrapolated imagination, likely fed by accounts from WWI pilots. Now that a new war was raging, in which air power was emerging supreme, he could write of real and deadly air duels, albeit secondhand. On May 25, 1941, in *This Week*, a syndicated Sunday supplement, he quoted an RAF pilot who described the action above Dover using terms far different from the snarling, grunting, and barking of Keyhoe's rugged fictional heroes. In very cool, unintentionally comical, understated terms, the English pilot described how he fired bursts at "Jerry" from his "bus," which was "tricky work." After blacking out and regaining consciousness, he awoke to find he was twenty miles away "from all the fuss."[100] Such was the mettle of these young airmen upon whom Britain depended.

After the Pearl Harbor attack in December 1941, followed swiftly by Hitler's declaration of war on the US, isolationism was over, and though America would see no bombs or combat at home, its armed forces would see plenty of "fuss" overseas. Keyhoe was now in his mid-forties and his age and injury were against him, but within days he had rejoined the Marines and by spring 1943 was promoted from Captain to the rank of Major, serving in the training division of the Bureau of Aeronautics.[101] Though he couldn't see action in the field, he could serve his country from behind his typewriter, continuing to write articles on aviation and air combat.

His duties now were, essentially, propaganda and some of it he dispensed from a "secret" location on the top floor of the Navy building in the War Department (now the Eisenhower Executive Office Building) on 17th NW in Washington, D.C. In a room allegedly containing padlocked files, "some of the country's highest-priced writing brains" were specially selected to produce Navy training literature written "as interestingly as a novel." It was presumably during this period that he "was often brought into policy-decision sessions, and after a while was entrusted with a number of such decisions."[102]

Among Keyhoe's fellow writers beavering away with him were Izetta Winter Robb, a WAVE who would go on to be editor of *Naval Aviation News* for twenty-five years and Lawrence E. Watkin, famous then as author of the book *On Borrowed Time*, which in 1939 had been adapted as a film starring Lionel Barrymore. Also laboring at the keyboard was John Clarke Mattimore, a former Marine lieutenant, who would later create phone shopping.[103]

Each writer was separated by a partition from behind which, in their respective uniforms, they Typed For Victory, while occasionally fielding telephone calls from women staff elsewhere in the building, enquiring about lingerie and slacks; the office's internal number was the same as that of a local department store, so if it was erroneously dialed without "9" for an outside line, the call would go through to the writers who would sometimes prank and confuse the ladies with slightly personal questions about their dimensions.[104]

Keyhoe's mind, however, was not wholly occupied with office mischief or the daily grind. During June, he had been rubbing Hollywood elbows, specifically those of studio mogul Jack Warner who, during a trip to New York, had purchased his unpublished *Cosmopolitan* article, "Honeymoon Freight," which Warner intended to be a romantic vehicle for actors Dennis Morgan and Jane Wyman. With screen-adaptation by Francis Swann and produced by Alex Gottlieb, the film, still slated for production two years later, was never made.[105]

Amid movie-deals, lingerie japes, and patriotic typing, Keyhoe, aged forty-seven, once more became a father. On October 24, 1944, Helen, now almost forty-two, gave birth to non-identical twins, Caroline and Kathleen. Whether or not parenthood was planned at this point in their lives isn't known, but unlike the consequences of the child from Don's first marriage, he and his wife remained united as a couple and appeared to welcome their brand-new Keyhoes.

Less than six months later, on May 8, 1945, the war in Europe was over, followed by the Japanese surrender to the US on August 15th. On September 6th, Japan's foreign minister signed the documents of surrender, aboard the USS *Missouri*—of which Hillenkoetter would soon be commander—and the world could now, it hoped, enjoy lasting peace.

On the family front, that same month Don, Helen, and the twins traveled to his parents' current summer home near Montrose, Iowa, for Grant and May's golden wedding anniversary celebrations. The senior Keyhoes were living a happy retired life, seeing friends around the country, and traveling the world. Frequently they visited their daughter Katherine, who had been five years in charge of a girl's school in Balaghat, Madhya Pradesh, India, though at this time she was anxiously awaiting transport back to the US in order to join the family gathering.[106]

Keyhoe's military career was, of course, now ending, and he was "at home awaiting retirement," though still receiving treatment at Bethesda Naval Hospital, presumably for his hand injury.[107] Otherwise, it was largely business as usual, and back at the typewriter he wrote frequently about the Communist threat, a viable topic now that no more pretense of comradeship with Stalin needed to be maintained.

The emerging Cold War aside, Keyhoe's ardor for all things aviation was as strong as ever. By 1945 he was writing as "aviation expert" for *True: The Magazine for Men*, under editor "Bill" (Donald Ayres) Williams, for which Don reported mainly on air safety and on test flights he had made specially for the magazine. Even so, the devastating end to the war in Japan naturally remained fresh and relevant in his mind. In the November issue, "the greatest *TRUE* story ever printed" was published: "Adventure in the Desert, by Major Donald Edward Keyhoe," which told "The Story BEHIND The Story of The Atom Bomb," an alarming tale of how close the Germans and Japanese had come to developing atomic weapons during the war.

Keyhoe could certainly have continued on this course, writing about what-might-have-been during the war and what-was-to-come in aviation for as long as he could keep his subjects relevant and popular, until he eventually settled into a comfortable retirement. But that potential future changed in December 1948, when Bill Williams, aged 43, died suddenly from a heart attack. The following February, Bill was replaced by 36-year-old Chicago-born Ken Purdy, a noted automobile writer and previously editor of *Parade: The Sunday Picture Magazine*.

This unexpected change in staff would irrevocably alter the course of Donald Keyhoe's life. Nothing for him would ever be the same again.

Chapter 8:
The Shape of Things to Come

In the summer of 1947, Kenneth Arnold's sighting of disks over Mount Rainier and the startling press announcement of a crashed saucer near Roswell would later prove to be the most significant reports of their kind in the 20th century. These were followed by many other sightings, and coming less than nine years after Orson Welles' infamous broadcast, created a jolt in public awareness of possible invasion from space. Press interest nonetheless quickly receded and the events might well have been forgotten—indeed, the alleged crash at Roswell would not be heard of again for decades. And after all, there had been no death rays, nor alien machines stomping through America's cities, just things in the sky that were intriguing, not terrifying.

However, Arnold's credibility—he was clearly a responsible, sensible citizen, not prone to fantasy or hyperbole—gave encouragement to others to report their own sightings, some of which pre-dated his and the era of "flying saucers," a term created by the press (Arnold described the movement of the disks as similar to skimming a saucer over water) was born. Consequently, on September 23, 1947, Air Material Commander (AMC) Lt. General Nathan F. Twining issued what would become his famous memorandum, stating that "the phenomenon reported is something real and not fictitious or visionary," upon which so much emphasis would be placed in the years to come. The Mount Rainier sighting, having opened the saucer floodgates and potentially raising public awareness to an alarming level, also led to an order to establish Project Sign (aka, Project Saucer) on December 30, 1947. Located at Wright Field (later Wright-Patterson AFB) in Dayton, Ohio, the Technical Intelligence Division of AMC was "charged with the collection, investigation and interpretation of data relative to unidentified flying objects."[108]

But even before January 22, 1948, when the Project was launched, saucers were back in the news. On January 7th, Kentucky National Guard pilot Thomas Mantell had died when his plane crashed into a wooded area near Franklin, Kentucky. Within hours, the press carried reports that he'd been chasing a flying saucer (later, but not in the first press coverage, it was reported he'd described "something tremendous in size...metallic looking...") and this raised the stakes. Lurid tales of the condition of his body, or its absence from his plane, which itself was described as "shredded" or "disintegrated" or scattered widely, did the rounds (all were not true). As a result, saucers were suddenly not just a tantalizing oddity for which there might, after all, be Earthly explanations, nor might they be benign observers from another world passing through. They were, perhaps, deadly. The specter of Wells and Welles loomed again.

Before the dust settled on the Mantell incident, another two cases aroused special interest. The first occurred on July 23rd, when Eastern Airlines DC-3 pilots Captain Clarence S. Chiles and his First Officer, John B. Whitted, flying passengers from Houston, encountered a high-speed glowing craft in the skies over Montgomery, Alabama, "about one hundred feet long, cigar-shaped, and wingless... It was about twice the diameter of a B-29, with no protruding fins." Its description matched an object seen, not only four days earlier in The Hague, but also an hour before the Chiles-Whitted sighting at Robins Field (now Robins AFB) in Macon, Georgia. Combined with the solid reputations of the pilots, these additional sightings gave credible confirmation.

The second case involed a small, "fast maneuvering light" over Fargo, North Dakota, seen on October 1st by George Gorman, an Air National Guard pilot. At the end of a practice flight in his F51, he was preparing to land at Hector Airport, but his approach was deflected by the sighting and he gave chase, resulting in almost half-an-hour's "dogfight," as it would later be called. His pursuit of the object and his attempts to engage it were watched through binoculars by Civil Aeronautics Authority (CAA) personnel on the ground and witnessed by both pilot and passenger in a nearby private plane.

Before long, these three cases would become known as "the classics," and even today they continue to fascinate and intrigue, but Keyhoe could not have guessed how important they would become to him within a year.

He would later say that he had no interest in the saucers until 1949, but his own accounts, sprinkled unobtrusively throughout his writings, tell otherwise. Following the 1947 flurry of reports from around the nation, he was sufficiently curious to make enquiries to Captain Tom Brown of the press branch at the Pentagon, from whom he learned that the reports were being taken seriously. "Too many stories tally," said Brown, adding that pilots were ordered to "bring down" the disks if they could.[109]

At that time, it was easy for individuals to go directly to the Pentagon and ask for information. Broadcaster Frank Edwards—soon to become a key figure in Don's life—later commented that, before the 1952 mass sightings over Washington, D.C.,

> … you could go over to the Pentagon almost whenever you
> liked and go in to see General Sory Smith, or Major Dewey
> Fournet, or some of those other fellows who were level-head-
> ed and in positions of responsibility. You could go in and ask
> them questions, you could request to see sighting reports that
> had come in, you could generally look at the photographs,
> and if you asked about the movies that they had, they'd prob-
> ably let you see them.[110]

Though the 1947 sightings and the Pentagon response to them were
intriguing, Keyhoe's interest was significantly heightened after the Mantell
crash. On January 17, 1948, when he spotted an Associated Press item about
the case in *The New York Times*, he went again to the Pentagon, where "no one
in the Press Branch would admit knowing the details of the Mantell saucer
chase," but a security officer did concede that it was under investigation.[111]

As he left the building that day, he bumped into his old pal, Jack Daly,
who seemed similarly interested in the case and told Keyhoe he'd heard from
a reporter that around the time of the crash something "going like hell. Fast as
a jet [and] as big as a C-47 … [with] a reddish-orange exhaust streaming out
behind," had been sighted. After some further discussion, he promised to keep
Don informed and they parted.[112]

By the spring of 1949, Don had supposedly "half forgotten the disks."[113]
He was now approaching fifty-two, with an interesting, slightly notable
career behind him, no shortage of work to come in the future, and life was
pretty good for the Keyhoes. They now lived in a magnificent home in
Alexandria, Virginia, had a young family, holidays when it suited them, and
all underpinned by financial security. He seemed destined to continue on this
track for the rest of his life.

Though he was as busy as ever, his work output since the war had lacked
the innovation of his previous years. Now that peace had broken out, he
no longer needed to write rousing articles to remind his countrymen of the
technical advances and bravery of the armed forces, and his pulp fiction career
was in the past. He would write occasional fantasy tales in later years, but
he had effectively left the genre. Moreover, the tone and subject matter of
his post-war articles remained doom-laden and now were tinged with the
pessimism and cantankerousness of later life—warnings about the dangers
of picking up hitchhikers, dire laments about how the Commies had once

planned to turn Americans into slaves, and unhappy features on air crashes. Given his fervent patriotism and anti-communism, he might well have found himself a niche, writing only about the perceived growing Red Menace that would soon lead America down the frightening path of McCarthyism. But he would be irrevocably deflected from this potential fate by a brief telegram:

> NEW YORK, N. Y., MAY 9, 1949
> HAVE BEEN INVESTIGATING FLYING SAUCER
> MYSTERY. FIRST TIP HINTED GIGANTIC HOAX
> TO COVER UP OFFICIAL SECRET. BELIEVE IT MAY
> HAVE BEEN PLANTED TO HIDE REAL ANSWER.
> LOOKS LIKE TERRIFIC STORY. CAN YOU TAKE
> OVER WASHINGTON END?
> KEN W. PURDY, EDITOR, TRUE MAGAZINE

The next day in Purdy's office, Keyhoe rejected the assignment to investigate and write an article about the suspected cover-up. "As a pilot I'd been skeptical of the flying discs," he later wrote and considered the subject to be "all a lot of crap."[114]

In response, Purdy put him on the spot. "Well, I guess you don't want your job anymore," and he gave him an ultimatum. "If you don't do this we'll let you go, and find somebody else."[115]

Keyhoe was taken aback, but having already dipped a toe into investigating the saucers, he surely didn't think they were a pile of ordure. His initial reluctance to take up Purdy's assignment was, however, most likely rooted in practical matters:

> I thought it was nonsense. When I was first asked to inves-
> tigate this I said I'll do it and you pay me for it but I'm not
> going to have my name on it.[116]
>
> It had taken me more than twenty years to establish my-
> self with national magazines. If this article drew nothing but
> ridicule, it could set me back a long way.[117]

So, encouraged no doubt by Purdy's unexpected offer to show him the door and lose his position as one of *True*'s mainstays, he agreed to "take over" the Washington investigation. The two men now unruffled their feathers and got down to business.

"There's something damn queer going on," complained Ken and told

Keyhoe about a two-part article by Sidney Shallett of *The New York Times* that had appeared in the *Saturday Evening Post* on April 30th and May 7th. They were collectively rather a stinking composition, which thumbed its nose at "The Great Saucer Scare" and the sensible folk who had seen inexplicable things zipping around the sky. Shallett gave examples of high-ranking military fellows who had not been fooled for more than a moment by sightings that only hysterics would have reported as flying saucers. He trotted out the names of the mighty to support his contention; the illustrious General Vandenberg topped the list because he had easily resolved a sighting from his own cockpit by simply moving his head to disperse a reflection of light from the ground. In doing so "he could reproduce the saucer at will." The "tough-minded Strategic Air Command boss," Lt. General Curtis E. LeMay, and "retired Air Chief" General Carl Spaatz were among the fruit-salad brigade whose scorn for saucers and their observers was laid out for public placation. LeMay had "put his weather expert on the trail, and substantial proof was uncovered that one out of six of the current crop of reports could be traced to a certain type of aluminum-covered radar-target balloon." Failing to note the lack of explanation for the other five out of six sightings, Shallett extolled Spaatz' indignance "when he thinks of saucer hysteria" and of "the American people [who] are capable of getting so excited over something which doesn't exist."

Perhaps most egregious was the article's attempt at undermining sightings by pilots. It proclaimed that "both Air Force and Navy aero-medical experts have prepared volumes of research findings, spelling out in detail how vertigo, hypnosis and other sensory illusions affect pilots at high altitudes and extreme speeds. Vertigo or hypnosis sets in [and] the pilot can come down and practically tell you how many rivets were on the nose of that Martian space ship."

Shallett, according to Purdy, had been primed to write the article by Defense Secretary James Forrestal. For two months, "the Air Force flew him [Shallett] around, arranged interviews, supposedly gave him inside stuff" and cleared his write-up.[118] (Twelve days after Keyhoe's meeting with Purdy, Forrestal was found dead by apparent suicide, having thrown himself out of his hospital window, thereafter spawning ongoing conspiracy theories.) A few years later, an alternative explanation for Shallett's influence was offered by Air Force pilot Captain Edward J. Ruppelt, who by then had become a noted figure in the UFO world. He believed that control over the article was exercised by Harry Haberer, "a crack Air Force public relations man," and that Shallet had written it up "as it was told to him."[119] Haberer at the time was press section chief AMC, Wright-Patterson, until 1951 when he left to become public relations director at Bell Aircraft Corp in Fort Worth, Texas.[120]

With so much negativism already foisted on the public, Purdy told Keyhoe, "I might as well warn you, it's a tough story to crack," and he brought him up to date on what had so far been learned.

In March, he had assigned the investigation to (among others) a thirty-five-year-old freelance writer and friend of Ernest Hemingway, Sam Boal, a short, hard-drinking, heavy smoker, with several eccentricities (often parsimonious, he haggled over the cost of his mother's cremation and then had her ashes mailed to him cross-country in a small cardboard box).[121] Boal had been to the Pentagon and talked to Secretary of the Air Force Stuart Symington, who had rubbished the idea of saucers, though someone let slip to Boal that a photograph of a saucer taken over Harmon Field, Newfoundland, existed. When he enquired further, it was denied.[122] This and other similar occurrences had caused Purdy to smell a rat. Keyhoe, of course, as an old hand on aviation for *True* and with many contacts gained during his military and civilian career, including some acquired during his Lindbergh tour in 1927, was once more in the right place at the right time.

They discussed what the reported sightings might be—missiles or secret projects, theirs or ours—and Purdy said that none of the answers he had found "stacks up. But I'm positive one was deliberately planted when they found we were checking." Then he emphasized a report that he felt was important: "You've heard of the Mantell case?"

Keyhoe had, but his own earlier enquiries had brought no result. Purdy wanted him to "get the details of Mantell's radio report to Godman Tower" because the unreleased transcript held by Project Saucer (Sign) contained the pilot's description of "the thing he was chasing."

At the end of their meeting, he warned Keyhoe to "watch out for fake tips," contradictions, and other trip-hazards that might be thrown into his path. With this in mind and the scent of Air Force secrecy in his nostrils, Keyhoe immediately began asking questions at the Pentagon.

Among the first he spoke to there was Major Dewitt Richard Searles, a former WWII pilot who had flown combat missions in the Pacific theatre. After the war, he had earned a Bachelor's degree in journalism, which led to him becoming Chief of the Air Force Press Desk at the Pentagon. Keyhoe asked him what he personally thought about the saucers, to which he replied, "you can't ignore the testimony of competent pilots. We don't know the answers, but we're making a careful investigation."

Next, Keyhoe conferred with "about 100 pilots" and his old Annapolis pals, starting with Calvin Bolster, now an Admiral and director of the Office of Naval Research. "Cal" was puzzled and told him that if the sightings were caused by "special weapon programs," he would know about it. He could offer no answer to the sightings.[123]

Don then spoke to Delmer "Deadshot" Fahrney, former trigger-happy roughhouser, who appropriately had become known as "the father of guided missiles." He was soon to retire as Rear Admiral and his work left him well-placed to offer his thoughts on what pilots were seeing. He told Keyhoe: "We're years from anything like the saucers' performance" and pointed out that for the military to test them over inhabited areas would merit a court martial. As to Russia being the source, he ruled it out entirely, "no matter how many Nazi scientists they kidnapped."[124]

By the time the investigation (undertaken with others whom Keyhoe does not name) was completed, he was utterly convinced there was far more to the story of the saucers than the Air Force admitted. Something was being covered up, and it could only be that Earth was being observed by alien beings. The public were being kept in the dark, and Don, though entirely mindful of national security, believed he had sufficient evidence to expose the deceit without breaking the rules. Despite the risk to his reputation, he would have to follow through on Purdy's assignment and write the story:

> I had had six months of preparation, six months to go from complete skepticism to slow, final acceptance ... I was finally convinced it [interplanetary craft] was the only answer. But saying so under my own by-line was a lot different ... Yet the evidence all added up. Still a little uneasy, I decided to go ahead.[125]

By October, it became imperative to get the article out fast; Purdy had been tipped off that another publication, unnamed, was working on a similar exposé (it was the soon-to-be-famous sighting of three saucers by USN Commander Robert B. McLaughlin in spring 1949). It was now essential for *True* to get the jump on it, so he and Keyhoe got together and decided that the Mantell, Chiles-Whitted, and Gorman cases would feature prominently among others that demonstrated *True's* conclusion—the saucers were interplanetary and the AF knew it. However, against expectations, it appeared that there would be no challenge to its publication from the Air Force. When Keyhoe had visited the Pentagon in the first week of October, he informed the press relations people that *True* intended to publish "the space-travel answer," but there was no attempt to dissuade him. They reiterated that there were no security issues involved and that nothing affecting the safety of the nation had been found.[126]

Purdy was suspicious of the Air Force's reaction, or lack thereof. "I think we're being used as a trial balloon," he said, reasoning that the AF could simply prevent publication by making it a matter of "patriotic duty" to keep quiet "just the way they did about uranium and atomic experiments during the war."[127]

There was one other consideration for Keyhoe: were the visiting space craft from Mars? And if they were, could he say so? "Mars had been associated with the Orson Welles stampede," he reflected, so he decided it was in the public interest to shift the focus from the Red Planet with its bad reputation and relative closeness—averaging 140 million miles—to one which seemed less threatening by virtue of its distance: Wolf 359. At just under eight light-years away in the constellation of Leo, Keyhoe felt it would "have a comforting effect on any nervous readers."[128]

The story was tested out on the staff of *True*, some of whom didn't know about the investigation, and the feedback was positive. There was no reason to hold it back; it would go out in the January issue.

Keyhoe didn't know it then, but the publication of his article would not only set his life upon a new course but would also impact upon his family, his finances, his personal credibility, and would pitch him into a two-decade attritional battle with scientists, politicians, cultists, and the mightiest military air power on Earth—the United States Air Force.

Chapter 9: Lift-off

Christmas 1949 proved to be unique for Donald Keyhoe. He and his family had left by train for an overnight journey to Ottumwa on December 19th to spend the holiday with his mother, and it was the first time they would be without his father. Grant had passed away in August, aged 84, and if ever the Keyhoes needed to be together, it was surely now. But for Don, this holiday would be additionally unique, for it marked the start of a new, challenging, and disruptive way of life for him, his wife, and his daughters.

Before he arrived at his mother's home, the January issue of *True*, containing his article "The Flying Saucers Are Real," had already hit the stands. Despite its sensational claims, it attracted no attention until Frank Edwards, a popular radio newscaster for The Mutual Broadcasting System, read a copy, and he immediately proved to be another man in the right place at the right time.[129]

When he was a young pilot in the 1920s, Edwards became intrigued by saucer reports told to him by famous "bad-boy" aviator Bert Acosta, who recalled seeing "flying manhole covers" zipping around his plane. Over the next twenty-five years he heard similar tales from other credible sources and had been told in 1948 by "two Air Force intelligence men" that the saucers were an American secret development, which he was content to believe—but that was about to change.

On Christmas Day an advance copy of *True* was erroneously delivered to fellow Mutual announcer Gordon Graham who showed it to Edwards. He was galvanized by Keyhoe's article and he "wanted to use the story right away":

> After my network broadcast that night I [called] Purdy, and finally got him out of bed at his home .... He was unhappy about that and he was even less happy when he learned that I had come into possession of that advance copy.
>
> "Let you break it?" he snapped. "I don't see how I can do that; we've already made arrangements with Walter Winchell to give him first break on the story ...". Purdy knew, of course, that I could break the story without his consent. We finally agreed that I could go ahead the following night, providing I used not more than two hundred words of the text.

It was a good deal for both of us.[130]

Having successfully elbowed aside radio fish-wife Winchell, Edwards' show went out and others followed suit, including coverage by respected broadcaster Lowell Thomas, by then famous not only as an intrepid reporter and adventurer, but also as the man who brought to public attention T. E. Lawrence (Lawrence of Arabia). Immediately after the radio broadcasts, a news-quake erupted, which took Keyhoe by surprise. He called a Washington reporter whose beat included the Pentagon, from where he'd learned that the Air Force had underestimated the response to the *True* article. They were receiving a "barrage" of calls and wires and were now afraid of public hysteria breaking out.

For Keyhoe, Christmas was over. He and his family hastily packed their bags for the overnight journey home, but the Washington reporter phoned again and told him that the Air Force intended to deny "the whole thing" and were looking for some way to knock down the article.

The Air Force's "knocking down" didn't amount to much. It issued a statement that said its own findings lent "no support" to the idea of saucers originating from another planet, and that its study, Project Saucer, had now been closed down. This was a rather feeble and insufficient riposte to *True*'s sensational claims.

The following day, the story had been picked up around the nation, and during his homeward journey, Keyhoe read many of the press reports, some making the front pages. On arrival in Washington, he flew to New York to meet with Purdy, later recalling events in vivid terms:

> I found *True* in a turmoil. Long-distance calls were pouring in. Letters on flying saucers had swamped the mail room. Reporters were hounding Purdy for more information.[131]

The reader response was quickly analyzed and showed that "between 25 and 30 percent" were "completely convinced" by the interplanetary explanation, "less than 5 percent" ridiculed the article, and the rest were open in varying degrees to the possibility of visitors from other worlds. Moreover:

> Several confidential tips had come in when I arrived .... We were given evidence that Project Saucer was still in operation, since its true code name was not "Saucer" it could be continued without violating the Air Force press release. This same

information was received from a dozen sources within the next two weeks. We were also told that there had been 722 cases, instead of 375.

Keyhoe's informants were correct. Project Saucer was known internally as Project Sign but now had quietly been renamed Project Grudge. It was continuing investigations but with a change of personnel, and its focus now had essentially shifted from trying to find out whether the saucers were real and interplanetary, to proving they were neither. He hoped to get a copy of Project Saucer/Sign's recently released report and analyze it for himself.

Meanwhile, he was in demand. Up to that point, Kenneth Arnold had been the principal media figure in the pro-saucer world, but Keyhoe would soon be his equal. On January 6th, he kicked off his new life in the public eye when he appeared on a simulcast *We The People*, a talk-show hosted by Dan Seymour who, by coincidence, had played the part of the news reporter in Orson Welles' *War of the Worlds*. The show was scheduled to feature a couple who renewed their romance of fifty years earlier, "the zaniest movie-maker of all time," and Junius P. Shaw, the first US baby born on January 1, 1901.[132] But in an apparent change to the advertised guests, Keyhoe was now to appear with pilot George Gorman, whose aerial "dog-fight" had featured in the *True* article. The event proved to be flavored with a sour taste of what was to come. Don recalled:

> When I saw Gorman, before rehearsals, he seemed oddly constrained. I had a feeling that he had been warned about talking freely. During rehearsals, he changed his lines in the script. When the writers argued over a point, Gorman told them:
> "I can say only what was in my published report—nothing else."
> The day before the broadcast, a program official told me they had been told to include the Air Force denial in the script. That afternoon I learned that the Air Force planned to monitor the broadcast.[133]

Back in Washington, Don had now seen a copy of the Project Saucer report and read the press response to his *True* article, which had been given by Major Jerry Boggs, Project Saucer's intelligence officer, who served as liaison man between Wright Field and the Pentagon. Boggs explained away the three planks of the *True* article's platform: Mantell had been chasing the planet Venus; Chiles and Whitted had seen either an "extraordinary meteor," a fireball, or an exploding bolide; and Gorman had been dogfighting a weather balloon. "The answers he gave amazed me," Keyhoe later wrote, and when he met with Boggs, he learned nothing. The young Major, sphinx-like and inscrutable, was calm and unflinching, while maintaining his ridiculous denials.[134] "His manner, his voice carried conviction. He would have convinced anyone ..."[135]

Many were indeed convinced. The Air Force rebuttal was sufficient for some to entirely deride and dismiss Keyhoe's investigation, and it didn't take long for the insults to come. On January 12th, Jim Dan Hill, PhD, President of Superior State College, Wisconsin, wrote a sarcastic and obtuse piece, describing Keyhoe as a man "of very limited imagination," while lauding the Air Force's investigation for having resolved the saucer situation to its own and everyone else's satisfaction. He suggested that *True* should be renamed, "Remotely True—Maybe," and opined that Keyhoe "merits no congratulations," while demonstrating his own astounding ignorance by comparing him unfavorably with Edgar Allan Poe, Jules Verne, H. G. Wells, and Charles Fort.[136]

This was tame compared to later brick-bats, many of which hurt Keyhoe deeply. Nonetheless, he was so utterly fixed on his belief that the Air Force was withholding what it knew about interplanetary visitors, that he remained persistently optimistic about its eventual disclosure. He was convinced, however, that the cover-up was surely for the best of reasons: Don did not suffer from paranoia, but pronoia, a state in which a person suspects a benign conspiracy, something hidden for one's own good, and so for him, the matter ought to be easily dealt with. Since none of the sightings reported since 1947, nor Keyhoe's article, had sent Americans tearing around the streets in a wild, Wellesian panic, it was clear that the people could take it and a cover-up was unnecessary. Therefore, simply give the men in power "all information" (a term he frequently used), rationally presented with statistics backed up by credible witness accounts, and they would do the right thing: the truth would set everyone free.

Surely, such a strategy could not fail.

* * *

If the Arnold sighting had given birth to the saucer movement, Keyhoe's article slapped its behind and made it scream. The press continued to comment on it, the Air Force continued to dismiss it, and the public were divided in their opinion about it. But Don knew that the story couldn't be just a one-off; he and *True* were still receiving reports and these added fuel to his conviction that there was an Air Force cover-up. In spite of denial and derision from all sides, he realized there was a deep pool of genuine, sober interest, backed up by credible witness accounts. In order to strike while the iron was hot, he now began working on a book also titled *The Flying Saucers Are Real*, which would expand on the cases already highlighted in his article and feature some of the others to which he'd since been alerted.

True's pursuit of the saucers gained further momentum with the March 1950 issue. It had now obtained an exclusive on the story by USN Commander Robert Bright McLaughlin of three objects seen over White Sands Proving Ground, New Mexico, between April and June the previous year. McLaughlin, a 1934 graduate of Keyhoe's old alma mater at Annapolis, wrote a clear, rational, and detailed account of what he and others had seen, concluding that they were craft from another world. Ed Ruppelt would later write that McLaughlin's story "had been cleared by the military and was an absolute, 180-degree, direct contradiction to every press release that had been made by the military in the past two years." [137]

Meanwhile, Keyhoe had swiftly completed his book, and it was scheduled for release on June 5th by Fawcett Publications under their Gold Medal imprint. By May 22nd, some midwestern retailers had been sent "test" copies, but the following day they received a telegram:

> Urgent to withdraw from distribution all copies of "Flying Saucers Are Real" immediately until further notice.

Gold Medal's editor, Jim Bishop, explained that the recall was due to "government protest…on the grounds that the book made public "information vital to national defense" and said that officials had exerted "a lot of pressure" to prevent the book going on sale. He appeared steamed at this and insisted it would be published as scheduled "unless the defense department gets out a restraining order." According to press reports however, the DoD said it had "no interest" in the book and moreover had "never heard of the book in any way, manner, shape or form."[138]

Whatever the DoD's real position and whether or not this was a marketing ploy by Bishop, no further impediment materialized, and Keyhoe's book was released as planned. Like the article on which it was based, it drew both praise and ridicule, but nonetheless quickly sold half a million copies. In his usual dramatic style, Don gave vivid accounts of sightings and verbatim discussions about them, while taking issue with the Air Force because it "refused to admit" and "flatly denied" the existence of the saucers. Even allowing for his pronoia,

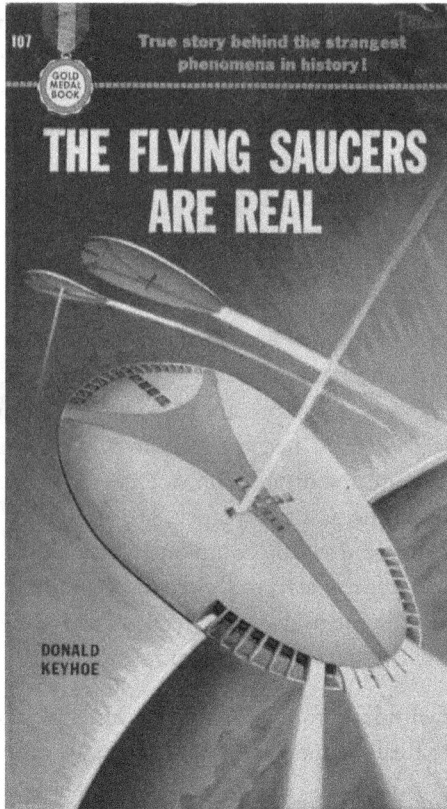

he rejected their debunking and in particular repeatedly held up the Mantell crash as a prime example of what he believed was a cover-up.

But only five months after *The Flying Saucers Are Real* hit the shelves, its status as the leading story of visitors from other worlds was undermined, thanks to the publication of a book with even more sensational claims.

Fifty-seven-year-old columnist and author Frank (Francis Joseph Xavier) Scully, a native of Long Island and graduate of Columbia University (journalism, 1917), followed up on two articles he had written for *Variety* in October and November 1949, in his regular feature, *Scully's Scrapbook*. In those pieces he wrote of having

> ... just spent a weekend with scientists who know all there
> is to know about flying saucers .... [I]n one afternoon these
> men convinced me they knew more about flying saucers
> than the surviving members of Mack Sennett's crockery that
> once functioned for entertainment ... [T]hese sages ... had
> checked on two of the disks which had landed here from an-
> other planet ... "The Mojave Desert got one and the Sahara
> got the other."

The saucers contained the charred, uniformed remains of little men, thought by the "scientists" who informed Scully, to have travelled from Venus. Their ship was made of unknown metals and had a central dome around which the perimeter rotated. On board was a supply of "heavy water" and their craft had many pushbuttons and controls that the scientists dared not activate for fear of explosion.

In September 1950, Scully published his book, *Behind the Flying Saucers*, which expanded on these articles. It received largely a similar response to Keyhoe's—some derided it, others believed it, and yet others sat on the fence. Two years later, *True* would publish its own investigation of Scully's claims and expose his association with the "sages," "Dr Gee" (GeBauer) and Silas Newton. They were imaginative con-men, seeking $800,000 for a device that could detect oil wells, which was in reality "a worthless piece of war surplus equipment" for which they had paid $4.50.[139]

For Keyhoe, Scully's book was the first high-profile hoax of many that would follow in the coming decades, and it served to muddy the waters of public and scientific interest in interplanetary visitors. Indeed, many reviewers and commentators could not distinguish between Keyhoe's and Scully's books, even after Scully was exposed as a likely pigeon for a pair of hucksters. Less discerning readers would accept both publications as the result of genuine investigation, while others would deride both as fantasy.

This conflation of the two approaches would forever after plague Don's life, for if his book had awoken Americans to the UFO experiences of credible witnesses, Scully's had lit a fire beneath the growing hoard of fools, charlatans, and New Age believers whose unceasing onslaught would become, for Don and other serious researchers, an invincible hydra.

One of the dirtiest attacks against saucerdom at this time came from journalist Bob Considine of Hearst Newspapers. Noted for his prodigiousness and the speed of his output, he no doubt easily and quickly penned a poisonous piece, "The Great Flying Saucer Hoax," which appeared in the January 1951 issue of *Cosmopolitan*. This was the fourth and final part of a series of rancid articles he had written on the subject, all previously syndicated in the press during November 1950. He poured scorn on saucer stories, notably in part three, where he described the Mantell case as "one of the feeble straws usually reached for by the amateur or professional true believer," but part four was a truly shameful offering, displaying the characteristics for which his employer—and to some extent, himself—were noted. He turned no stone in his blanket dismissal of any and all claims regarding saucer reality, choosing instead the childish resort of ridicule and insult. He asserted that all reports were made by demented screwballs, pranksters, and half-wits, implied that the sanity of all air personnel, including Commander McLaughlin, was flawed, and that "hapless" Kenneth Arnold had seen only an apparition. Even Orson Welles was given the treatment; Considine described him as a "bizarre hambone" and went on to groan about how the taxpayer was having to foot the bill for investigating all this fakery, foolishness, and nonsense.

In this one, odious article, he had managed to insult Americans both generally and specifically. Civilians and pilots who reported saucers, men who investigated them, and men who wrote about them were heaped together, drenched in his verbal gasoline, and set alight. It was shabby in the extreme, drawing plenty of criticism and even a couple of libel suits, but it made no difference to Considine's view, nor to others who shared it.

Considine had been stoked and primed to write these four articles by one Colonel Harold E Watson, a former test pilot and at the time chief of the Air Technical Intelligence Center (ATIC) in Dayton, Wright Patterson AFB, the unit charged with saucer investigation. During WWII, Watson and his team, known as "Watsons' Whizzers," had engaged in accessing enemy air materiel and technology from Europe. Post-war, this activity was divided into two teams and labelled Operation Lusty. Watson's Team One, focused on collecting enemy aircraft and weapons, which were taken back to the US for study. Perhaps having seen for himself the conventional nature of the enemy's planes and knowing the equally conventional nature of US aircraft, these duties served to underpin his denial of anything that fell outside that technology and led him to encourage Considine's foolish pronouncements. Whatever the reason, he would be described in the mid-1950s as "violently anti-saucer" and was known to "haul in writers who would plug him and debunk the UFOs."

The source that told of Watson's effect ("he completely snowed Bob Considine") was a young officer who, in a short time, would become a household-name in saucer circles and would play a vital and significant role in Keyhoe's life for the next several years: Captain Edward J Ruppelt.[140]

Chapter 10:
Friends, Flaps, and Flimflam

The first year of Donald Keyhoe's life as the nation's civilian "saucer expert" had been hectic and challenging, establishing the nature of his existence for the next two decades. He kicked off 1951 with a gouge into highfalutin flesh regarding the Mantell crash, rebutting the claims of physicist Dr. Urner Liddel, chief of nuclear research at the Office of Naval research. Quoted in the magazine *Look* in its issue of February 27th and titled "A Nuclear Physicist Exposes Flying Saucers," Liddel declared that the object of Mantell's pursuit had not been a saucer but a then-secret Skyhook balloon. In an example of the overkill response Keyhoe would make to such contentions in the future, he argued—in a four-page telegram—that this was not sufficient explanation for what had been seen, and moreover that the Skyhook was known about in 1947. He considered that Liddel was "attempting to foist a ready-made explanation for future sightings upon the American people" and went on to say, "If this constant smokescreen were designed to cover some super-secret American weapon, I would be the first to say 'Thank God.' But the 'saucers' are not an American device."[141]

Yet, while Keyhoe's life became given-over to saucer reports and to exposing official cover-ups thereof, the body charged with investigating the phenomenon—the US Air Force—was shirking its supposed responsibilities.

By mid-1951, the aptly-named Project Grudge had become something of a tumbleweed outfit, with "a lone investigator," James Rodgers, who had been appointed by the anti-saucer Colonel Watson and whose negative views on the subject he shared. Rodgers at this time had, in any case, little to do thanks not only to his reluctance to investigate, but also to a merciful paucity of sightings to occupy him; the skies had dried up. The neglect inflicted on the Project by the non-dynamic duo of Watson and Rodgers came to the attention of their boss, General Charles Cabell, director of Air Force Intelligence, who was angered at this laxity and disregard for their assignment. In short, Watson was made to jump to it, resulting in Rodgers' removal, and in August, intelligence officer Lieutenant Jerry Cummings was installed, albeit briefly, into what seemed a sleepy posting.[142]

During this short period, Cummings would occasionally be visited at the office by his friend, twenty-eight-year-old Captain Edward James Ruppelt, a decorated former wartime B-29 pilot, whose honors included two Distinguished Flying Crosses.[143] Ruppelt would tease his pal "about the poor state of the saucer business," but Jerry was unconcerned, as he was coming up for discharge within weeks.

But in September, just as Cummings' discharge was imminent, the quiet skies became busy again and an outbreak of sightings brought saucers whizzing back into focus. At ATIC on September 12th, "a teletype began chattering out a yard-long message from northern New Jersey. When it signed off, it looked as if the Garden State had been invaded by something out of H. G. Wells."[144] The incident was especially juicy, for it occurred at a New Jersey radar school while

> A student operator was giving a demonstration to a group of visiting brass … He had been picked [for this task] because he was the top man in his class … The operator spotted an object about 12,000 yards southeast of the station, flying low toward the north. He tried to lock on for automatic. He failed, tried again, failed again. He turned to the audience of VIPs, embarrassed.
>
> "It's going too fast for the set," he said. "That means it's going faster than a jet."
>
> A lot of very important eyebrows lifted. What flies faster than a jet?

To add further intrigue and excitement, "a dull silver disk like object" was sighted twenty-five minutes later over Point Pleasant by a jet trainer pilot, whose passenger was an Air Force major, and soon after the object was back on the radar school's instruments, "travelling slowly at 93,000 feet. They also could see it visually as a silver speck."[145] The following day, it was again picked up on radar:

> It would climb, level off, climb again, go into a dive. When it climbed, it went almost straight up.[146]

The report on these incidents generated "reams of raw data" for Grudge, but Cummings had little chance to examine it; on the 14th, his discharge was effective and someone would have to replace him. Ruppelt would later write:

> Up to this point. I had done the work I was assigned to and paid little attention to flying saucers. But the New Jersey outbreak fascinated me. Whatever had happened there was plainly a lot more than the occasional "saucer" story I'd read in the papers, where a Dakota farmer saw something zip over his barn, or a housewife saw six disks wobbling through the sky while she hung up her wash. My curiosity overcame the ancient rule that men in uniform have followed since Hannibal's day. I volunteered.[147]

He was, arguably, a shoo-in for the position since he had already impressed the brass with "work he did on a captured Korean/Soviet MiG jet. Because of the meticulous reports and files [he] kept," he was felt to be the right man for this job, which was in sore need of organization.[148] Moreover, an assignment which had about it the aura of crackpotism could scarcely be expected to have a long line of volunteers. He began his new job in November "with curiosity and no preconceptions," expecting that he would "solve the Jersey puzzle and then go back to my regular work."

Now that the lull was over, the Air Force, having since 1947 repeatedly declared that there was nothing to see here, quietly allowed the moribund Grudge to slip away, but didn't give up on the saucers. Behind the scenes, in 1952, USAF Lt. Col. Charles Cooke renamed it "Project Book," though he recalled later that, "Upstairs (at the Joint Chiefs of Staff level), somebody made it "Blue Book," a name "taken from the traditional college blue books which had all the answers to the examination questions."[149]

With a new name and a new broom to sweep the project clean of Grudge stains, there was an opportunity to bring order out of indifference. But Ruppelt could not have envisaged that this short assignment—fated to last less than two years—would turn him into a saucer-celebrity, forever fix his name in the pantheon of UFO researchers, and for years to come, exert a vast influence on the life of Donald Keyhoe.

* * *

Despite Keyhoe's increasing obsession with all things saucer, he still found time to expound on non-saucer matters. It had always pained him to hear the slurs inflicted on his hero, Lindbergh, by the late President Franklin Roosevelt, who had branded him a traitor and a suspected Nazi sympathizer. In the May 18, 1952, issue of *American Weekly*, he rebutted these accusations in his article, "The Riddle of Charles Lindbergh," pointing out:

> All the evidence [which would clear Lindbergh's name] is buried in government files—his confidential reports on the Nazi air force; his secret defense work, during and after the war; the private reports of ranking officers who knew that Slim was loyal. Lindbergh himself would never ask that these records be published. The last thing he would want is a new wave of adulation. His fear of hero worship is very real …[150]

Even the libelous Bob Considine wrote favorably of the piece, describing it as "a fascinating resumé" of Lindbergh, which was high praise indeed considering his previous appraisal of Keyhoe's work.

Everyday life occupied Don's mind, too. In the June 1952 issue of *Cosmopolitan*, he gave advice on how to survive a car crash. In "Train Your Reflexes to Save Your Life," he recommended that drivers should prepare mentally for such an event and work out in advance what to do if one should occur. "Drawing upon personal experiences," he described how he had once evaded collision with a convertible that had pulled out at high speed from behind a truck and a head-on crash was imminent.[151] Being self-primed for such an event, Keyhoe swerved off the road through a fence and came to a halt in a handy cornfield. He further recommended that injury might be lessened in the event of a rear-end collision, by slipping down into the seat, to take advantage of its cushioning effect.

Such psychological preparations were rather a good idea in Don's case, for he was a menace on the road, as his neighbors could attest, and it was no surprise to them that he had crashed his plane on Guam. At around 5' 5", he could barely see over the steering wheel of the Cadillacs he always drove, yet would tear at high speed through the local streets, much to the vexation of residents, not least because their children might be out at play, then further annoy them when he went to pick up the babysitter and park outside her house, honking the horn.

To add insult to aggravation, on one occasion Don approached a neighbor in Alexandria and asked if he could "fix" a speeding ticket he'd received. It was within the neighbor's ability to do this, being a well-connected fellow, but he felt that Keyhoe deserved his fine, so pretended he was unable to help.

In any case, the neighbor and his wife (along with almost all the neighbors) disliked the Keyhoes, but would occasionally get together with them as a foursome at Collingwood restaurant, noted for "terrible food" but excellent pecan pie, which was so good it made the ordeal of dining with Don and Helen worthwhile. The Keyhoes were additionally unpopular with the locals due to their "junkyard dog," Rascal, which was left out most of the time to "guard the garage." Even worse, Don's credibility was somewhat questioned, due to the "floodlights in the backyard affixed to the siding or roof of the house that were pointed up at the sky." According to the realtor who later sold the property, these were installed so that Keyhoe could "signal for/observe the flying saucers."

The animosity felt toward him appeared to be largely mutual. At some point, he'd learned to play the piano and provided a piano-tuning service for local residents, to one of whom, after completing the job, he gave a signed copy of one of his books in which he'd inscribed, "All the other neighbors are duds."[152]

Local tensions aside, badgering the Air Force was Keyhoe's day job, and the more cases he learned about, the more firmly he believed that a cover-up was in place. In this respect, a future ally was already at work, a young Wisconsin housewife named Coral Lorenzen, who, in July 1952, established America's first large-scale, nationally and internationally coordinated research group, the Aerial Phenomena Research Organization (APRO). Prior to this, she wrote columns for her local bazoo, the *Green Bay Press-Herald*, on a variety of topics, including barbershop quartets and the best places to vacation. But her deepest interest was in what she referred to as Unidentified Aerial Phenomena—UAP—a term that in our own time is set to replace the maligned acronym UFO.

Long curious about the idea of visitations from other worlds, Coral was "an amateur astronomer" who'd had her own sighting on June 10, 1947, when she "saw a light leave the ground south of Douglas, Arizona, and disappear among the stars."[153] This event spurred her on to commit herself to the study and investigation of such phenomena. In spring of 1952, she had written a series of articles for her bazoo, which detailed the best-known cases (Chiles-Whitted, Mantell, and Gorman), as well as looking at the history of sightings back to Ezekiel's Wheel. These articles were well-written and free of hyperbole, but in retrospect were naïve; she still had lots to learn. She praised Keyhoe's article in *True*, but also heaped accolades on Frank Scully and "Professor" George Adamski, who was soon to become the deepest thorn in the flesh of objective research. She felt that Scully would not "risk his reputation as a top-notch reporter" and referred to Adamski as "an astronomer of some note." Her favorable opinions about all three men would change entirely before long.

The popular press had also got in on the saucer-act. In early April, *Life* magazine published "Have We Visitors From Space?" Ruppelt later admitted that the Air Force had "unofficially inspired" the article, which was based on "the personal opinion of several very high-ranking officers in the Pentagon."[154] The piece began with a bold statement:

> The Air Force is now ready to concede that many saucer and fireball sightings still defy explanation; here LIFE offers some scientific evidence that there is a real case for interplanetary saucers.

This startling announcement was followed in mid-June by a piece in *Look* magazine, penned by the academically-festooned bombast, Dr. Donald Howard Menzel of Harvard University, whose facile solutions to saucer sightings were a convenient explanation used by those who didn't want to be bothered with the facts. Every sighting, no matter who had seen it or under what conditions, was, in his unshakeable opinion, due solely to natural phenomena. In his article "The Truth About Flying Saucers," Menzel brandished his obtuse pronouncements on their unreality—including how to make them in one's own kitchen—and claimed that "the Air Force has expressed a lively interest in" his work on the subject. This was not true.[155] *Look* followed this up on July 1st with "Hunt For The Flying Saucers," which asserted that the USAF was "launching a secret scientific search to discover once-and-for-all" what Americans were seeing in their skies.

Within days of its publication, Menzel's fatuous assertions were thrown into sharp relief when the famous Flap of Flaps occurred over Washington, D.C. Since early July, sightings had been made throughout the nation, but beginning on July 12th and climaxing during two weekends, the 19th and the 26th, fast-moving objects were seen on radar above the skies of the Capital and some were confirmed visually by ground observers and by jet pilots, who were scrambled to intercept.[156]

These events made for unsettling headlines, which prompted a packed 4 pm press conference at the Pentagon on July 29th. It was headed by General John A. Samford, who had replaced Cabell in November the previous year, and consequently the saucers were now in his lap. Keyhoe was among the throng and recalled, "I hadn't seen a bigger turn-out since the A-bomb story broke."[157]

Samford was assisted by several ATIC officers, including General Roger Ramey, whose connection to the Roswell case in 1947 had been forgotten, and also Captain Ed Ruppelt, now eight months at Project Blue Book. He had arrived in Washington from Dayton the previous afternoon with his pro-saucer boss, Major Dewey Fournet, who had replaced the inscrutable Jerry Boggs as Blue Book's liaison officer in the Pentagon. On route to their hotel, Ruppelt had spotted headlines proclaiming that a "saucer expert" was arriving in the Capital to address the sightings. He wondered who this expert might be and soon after discovered that it was himself.[158]

The conference got under way, during which Keyhoe noted what he felt to be extreme caution in the replies of Samford and the other officers to the increasingly specific questions from the press. He thought that Ramey, though polite, was skillfully evading pointed questions because he and all the other officers present were under orders to do so.[159] The result of such evasiveness was that nothing was admitted, many answers were open to interpretation, some were contradictory, and others bizarre (Samford occasionally drifted off into odd ramblings that bore no discernible connection to the questions asked); once again, it was a case of "nothing to see here."

It's perhaps worth noting, however, that Samford could have—yet did not—give a simple and reassuring explanation. Well-covered in the press for some weeks, Operation Signpost was a Continental Air Defense exercise that was carried out at the time of the Washington sightings:

> It was a joint SAC Air Defense Command operation where they were testing Strategic Air Command ability to penetrate targets or simulated targets and Air Defense ability to … detect and repel simulated attacks … and Washington was one of the area, regions that they were involved in … radar chaff was dropped on the Washington DC area …[160]

In fact, personnel participating in Operation Signpost were often named in their local bazoo in what seemed to be a matter of municipal pride, so there was certainly a readily-available cover for the sightings if such was needed. Keyhoe evidently didn't know of Operation Signpost either, which in itself is surprising since he was always up-to-date on what was happening in the skies, thanks not least to the clipping services he used—and it seems even stranger that the press, some of which might well have reported on the Operation, did not raise it as a possible explanation.

Also not revealed at the time was that the Washington sightings had been predicted, presumably by the CIA. Ruppelt later wrote:

> A few days prior to the [first weekend saucer] incident a scientist, from an agency that I can't name, and I were talking about the build-up of reports along the east coast of the United States. We talked for about two hours, and I was ready to leave when he said that he had one last comment to make—a prediction. From his study of the UFO reports that he was getting from Air Force Headquarters, and from discussions with his colleagues, he said that he thought that we were sitting right on top of a big keg full of loaded flying saucers. "Within the next few days," he told me, and I remember that he punctuated his slow, deliberate remarks by hitting the desk with his fist, "they're going to blow up and you're going to have the granddaddy of all UFO sightings. The sighting will occur in Washington or New York," he predicted, "probably Washington."[161]

Similarly odd was the unmentioned recent closure of the runways at Andrews and Bolling Air Force Bases for "runway repairs," which required interceptors to be relocated at New Castle, Delaware, roughly 100 miles northeast of DC, thereby delaying their arrival over the Capital during the flap.[162] None of these coinciding factors were revealed.

When the conference ended, reporters began to file out and were exchanging views on the information, or lack thereof, they had been given. Some were unconvinced by Samford et al., feeling they had "never heard so much and learned so little," but others were content that "it was on the level." Keyhoe was not among the latter group and as the room emptied, he managed to direct two questions to the General, both concerning temperature inversions, a well-known weather phenomenon in which, under certain conditions, warm air is layered above cool air beneath, sometimes causing radar blips. This had been offered at the conference as a possible answer to the sightings, though without specifics, and Keyhoe asked for details on what would be the temperature of such inversions to create the effects on radar. Samford didn't know, but in any case at that moment he was conveniently interrupted by someone else and the audience was over.

Despite the dissatisfaction Keyhoe felt about the conference, it gave him a consolation prize; he had his first meeting with fellow-Iowan, Ed Ruppelt, who admitted he had read Don's fiction work of years earlier and more lately had read his *Flying Saucers Are Real*—just in case they ever met each other.[163]

Don asked him the same two questions about temperature inversions which Samford had not answered, but Ruppelt gave him no enlightenment, so they "talked a little longer, on safer subjects." Keyhoe then drove to the airport for his flight to New York and pondered the statements at the press conference. His pronoia came to the fore again:

> Obviously they had acted for the good of the country, and I suddenly realized what an ordeal it must have been.[164]

Their ordeal, however, was less for the good of the country than for their own. What Keyhoe interpreted as a selfless intention to protect the public from learning that interplanetary craft had been buzzing America's Capital was in reality about protecting their own behinds and delivering up flimflam to the press. Ruppelt himself explained it four years later:

> The next day [the 29th] was one of confusion. After the first Washington sighting [the previous weekend] the prevailing air in the section of the Pentagon's fourth floor, which is occupied by Air Force Intelligence, could be described as excitement, but this day it was confusion. There was a maximum of talk and a minimum of action. Everyone agreed that both sightings should be thoroughly investigated, but nobody did anything. Major Fournet and I spent the entire morning "just leaving" for somewhere to investigate "something." Every time we would start to leave, something more pressing would come up ...
>
> General Samford made an honest effort to straighten out the Washington National Sightings, but the cards were stacked against him before he started. He had to hedge on many answers to questions from the press because he didn't know the answers. This hedging gave the impression that he was trying to cover up something more than just the fact that his people had fouled up in not fully investigating the sightings.
>
> Then he had brought in Captain Roy James from ATIC to handle all the queries about radar. James didn't do any

better because he'd just arrived in Washington that morning and didn't know very much more about the sightings than he'd read in the papers. Major Dewey Fournet and Lieutenant Holcomb, who had been at the airport during the sightings, were extremely conspicuous by their absence, especially since it was common knowledge among the press that they weren't convinced the UFO's [*sic*] picked up on radars were weather targets.

But somehow out of this chaotic situation came exactly the result that was intended—the press got off our backs. Captain James's answers about the possibility of the radar targets being caused by temperature inversions had been construed by the press to mean that this was the Air Force's answer, even though today the twin sightings are still carried as unknowns.[165]

Unaware of the headless-chicken mayhem behind the scenes and the Air Force's intention to close down press interest, Keyhoe arrived in New York where he checked into the luxurious Commodore Hotel (now the Grand Hyatt) and over the next twenty-four hours caught up with newspaper reports on the Pentagon conference. The press had snatched-up the temperature inversion theory like a football and slammed it down over the goal line: the saucers didn't exist, the Air Force had done its job, and all was right with the world. Keyhoe was dismayed, suspecting deception, but his pronoia again came to the fore. He speculated that perhaps the Air Force might have a serious angle to justify its debunking and that maybe he shouldn't be giving it such a hard time. There was only one way to find out. When he got back to Washington, he would ask them "squarely," and if they convinced him that there was really something behind their actions, then he would hold his peace.[166]

On return from New York a week later, he was put in the picture about how some pilots felt after Samford's conference: they were not happy. One TWA (Trans World Airlines) pilot told Keyhoe that many were "plenty sore" at the AF, and an Eastern Airline pilot wrote that, due to the conference, his captain would not now report a six-minute sighting of a disk seen by both crew and passengers.[167]

Such grievances strengthened Keyhoe's resolution to have a "frank talk" with the Air Force, and he spoke to one of his Defense Department contacts, who advised him to see Al (Albert) Chop, Public Information Officer at the

Pentagon's press desk, though he was currently unavailable: "I guess he's at home, resting up," his contact told Don. "He took it on the chin, the last week or two."

He was referring to Chop's role in providing information to the press during the July sightings over the Capital. Like Keyhoe, he had once thought UFOs were "a bunch of crap," but during his two years as the Pentagon's PIO (Public Information Officer), he had begun to feel differently. He'd not been much involved in the Washington sightings on the first weekend—he was home asleep at the time—but was up to his eyeballs in the second wave the next weekend. A midnight call from Washington National Airport alerted him to "these sightings on radar, and that there were a lot of press people there." After he had spent the night in the tower watching strange radar targets and heard one pilot say, "they're closing in on me. What shall I do?," he was no longer a skeptic. He recalled:

> I, in fact, was scared! . . . it scared me! It was frightening! And I think everybody in the room was very apprehensive! … I'm convinced they're solid objects. I am convinced that they are probably from another planet, from outer space somewhere. I always felt that way since that night.[168]

In the absence of Chop, Keyhoe took the opportunity to let off steam at PIO Colonel Boyd and two others who happened to be in his office at the time. He complained that his requests for ATIC reports had been turned down every time, that the press conference had been badly handled, and that as a result many people suspected a cover-up. Moreover, the Air Force claimed it wanted its pilots to submit UFO reports but made fools of them when they did. He threatened to write an article about these issues, pointing out that he didn't want to continue "sniping" at the Air Force, but his decision to publish would depend on whether or not it would give him a solid reason to keep quiet.

After a silence, Boyd insisted nothing was being held back, and then interestingly told Don, "You're the one person we'd like most to convince."[169]

Leaving a flea in Boyd's ear, Keyhoe went home and within an hour, his threat of publicizing his concerns had paid off. He was invited to meet Al Chop the next day.

Chapter 11: Lifting the Lid

Keyhoe was unaware of Chop's pro-saucer mindset when they sat down for what turned out to be a three-hour meeting. The two men were introduced by Lt. Col. DeWitt Searles, the officer Don had previously met, but whose one-time support for the interplanetary theory had evaporated, earning him the nickname "Death to the saucers" Searles. Despite this, Chop considered Searles to be "a very, very open-minded guy. And he didn't care what I thought … He was a hell of a nice guy to work with."[170]

"I've been instructed to help you," Chop told Keyhoe and they began the first of many dialogues they would have over the coming months. Don, typically suspicious, felt he was being "weighed carefully—not just my beliefs, but whether I could be trusted," while Chop gave away nothing of his own views, sticking with the party-line. He did, however, concede that "The Air Force doesn't deny they may be interplanetary," only that they had no physical evidence to support that hypothesis.

Keyhoe evidently made a sufficiently good impression for, to his surprise, Chop offered to help him obtain ATIC reports because his reputation was already—crucially—in good stead with Major Dewey Fournet. The two men had met sometime after the Washington sightings and Fournet later recalled:

> [H]e contacted me and said that he'd like to talk to me briefly if he could meet me, so I agreed. I'd go ahead and meet with him, because as I said I thought he could be [for] the government, [and] the public a big service, since he was well equipped to write about the [UFO] stuff with his background, and if he was dealing with facts, what we called the facts, it was more like it to come up with a good story for the public, for public consumption than if he had all this other stuff mixed up with it. So I talked to him and told him, OK, fine, look, and I described what my reasoning was for seeing it that he got fed all the stuff beforehand. And I said, I think you ought to go to it, but try to get the facts across to the

public, so I met him briefly that way.

… I had enough respect for Don and his background as a Marine officer, a Marine flying officer, were enough to tell me, well gee wiz, we'll bend over backwards to give him what I want him to get, which was the factual information rather than some of the trash that he'd picked up in one of his early books. So I thought he could be a big help to us to get some of this trash off display and not presented as factual stuff, instead deal with what we thought were the facts. I wasn't trying to brainwash him, I was just giving him good information, and he came in on that policy that we had enacted, that anybody can ask for a report based on a specific incident that he can describe to us, we'll release that information whatever is releasable in the report, and that's how he had got the stuff through Al Chop … [171]

Fournet's role was later recalled by Chop:

Dewey was more or less the guy I was working for in a way, not on paper. He had nothing to do with my position or anything, except the way they had set it up in his office, was that Dewey was my contact. If he didn't have the information, I could go to Ed Ruppelt. And that's the way it was. Ed Ruppelt and Dewey both know that the agreement was with the—we're going to handle the press. Was that they ask for information on a specific sighting, we give them everything we got, if we got anything! And if we didn't have anything, we couldn't give any information. [172]

A week later at the Pentagon, Chop came through on his promise to provide ATIC reports. Keyhoe expected to be given unimportant "watered-down reports that didn't prove anything" but was surprised to receive five juicy cases. The first was of a recent incident, the August 5th sighting at Oneida [Haneda] AFB, Japan, where tower operators and ground personnel saw "a dark circular shape," hovering near the tower before "it divided into three units, as if two other saucers had been launched from the first" and disappeared. The second, "barely a day old," concerned a radar pick-up from Congaree Air Base, of an object speeding at 4,000 mph over the skies of South Carolina. The other three reports, all from late July, included one seen over

Los Alamos just a few hours after Samford's conference.

Chop assured Keyhoe that the reports had been cleared and he could write about them, but under one condition. "Here it comes," thought Don, but Chop asked for his help merely in denying reports that pilots were shooting at the UFOs.[173]

He was happy to comply with this easy request, but was baffled as to why, with the Washington sightings still fresh in everyone's minds, the Air Force had so quickly changed its position from ludicrous denials to encouraging him "of all people" to write about cases that appeared to support the interplanetary theory.[174] What could be the reason?

For the present, he put that question aside. His immediate task was to set about disproving the inversion angle, so he spent the next two weeks getting an earful from aggrieved radar operators who felt insulted at the idea they couldn't recognize an inversion when they saw it. He checked with the Weather Bureau and, at a suggestion from Chop, interviewed Major Lewis S. Norman, Jr., of the Aircraft Control and Warning Branch, an interceptor pilot who had rather handily "made a special study of temperature inversions." Norman told him that this weather phenomenon "couldn't possibly explain the Washington sightings."[175]

Chop followed up with other cases, released under orders from Samford which reversed everything he and James had said in the conference. One case had a photo of a flying disk, captured on the gun camera of an F-86 jet interceptor on August 1st, near Wright-Patterson AFB. The ATIC analysis had a startling conclusion: it was not a balloon, nor a known aircraft, nor was it any meteorological phenomena. It was an "unknown."

Now confident that he had indeed disproved "the inversion angle," Keyhoe wrote "with Air Force help" another article for *True*.[176] The December issue ran "What Radar Tells About Flying Saucers," opening with a blunt statement:

> U.S. Air Force and civilian radar experts know enough about temperature inversion to be sure that it doesn't explain the strange objects they've seen on their scopes in Washington, and in other places.

The article also gave him an opportunity to kick "the Menzel theory in the teeth" by relating that the Air Force told him it had invited Menzel to "apply his theory to cases on record," but he hadn't done so.

This "kick in the teeth" ought to have either silenced Menzel or caused him to abandon his theory, but his opinions, in an obvious case of Denialism, only hardened and would never change. Like the UFO contactees, who by now had begun to stir, he would be the irritating gadfly, forever buzzing and biting at rational discourse.

Keyhoe, meanwhile, believed he finally understood why the Air Force had changed its stance from ridiculous denials, to allowing him, their main critic, access to information that supported his interplanetary theory. He concluded there were three groups, which he labelled A, B and C, who were "involved in UFO policy decisions." Group A wanted to release sightings reports to the public to "prepare" them for "the final solution—whatever it proved to be," but that he inferred meant support for the interplanetary theory. Groups B and C were what he referred to as "the silence groups," each with a different reason for not talking. Group B feared public panic and Group C simply chose to ignore or disbelieve sightings reports. Don's conclusion, however, was rejected by an "Intelligence officer" who said that the basis of Air Force denials was that it simply didn't know the answers.[177]

Nonetheless, as 1952 drew to a close, it appeared that Keyhoe had begun to prise the lid off the Air Force's can of worms. They had allowed him unprecedented access to their files, supported his radar article in *True*, given him a reliable go-to guy in the Pentagon Press Office, and helped him deliver a blow to Menzel's dentures. Moreover, he'd established contact with the young new officer in charge at the freshly-painted Blue Book, who was under the command of his pro-UFO benefactor, Dewey Fournet.

The year held one more gift for Keyhoe. Before Christmas, an old pal who was "a former service man whose contacts I'd often envied," leaked to him that the Air Force had "the Tremonton pictures," soon to be better known as the Utah, or the "U" pictures.[178] On July 2nd, Warrant Officer Delbert C. Newhouse, a Navy photographer, had filmed "a formation of round, bright objects going like a bat out of hell ... maneuvering in formation," an analysis of which, according to Don's contact, proved they were "machines of some kind, making speeds and turns no plane on earth could duplicate."[179]

Though this was the first Keyhoe had heard of the "U" pictures, the case was already known to the FBI, despite its oft-repeated denials of any interest in UFOs. In a memo dated October 27, 1952, Assistant Director A. H. Belmont was advised that:

> [S]ome military officials are seriously considering the possibility of interplanetary ships ... a small percentage of ex-

tremely creditable sightings have been unexplainable.

In reference to the Utah film, the memo reported:

> [T]he possibility of weather balloons, clouds or other explainable objects has been completely ruled out; and that they are at a complete loss to explain this most recent creditable sighting. The Air Technical Intelligence Center experts pointed out that they could not be optical illusions inasmuch as optical illusions could not be recorded on film.[180]

Chop was taken aback when Keyhoe told him what he'd heard about the "U" film, but nonetheless confirmed the information was correct, adding that analysis had so far showed no possibility of fraud. He asked Don to keep quiet about it, though talked tantalizingly of maybe showing the film to the press and gave his personal opinion that General Samford would not oppose revealing its existence to the public. It seemed that, at last, the Air Force was set to reveal a genuine, captured-on-film sighting that would eliminate any doubt as to the non-terrestrial origin of the saucers.

With this unexpected nugget, Keyhoe could look back on a remarkable year that seemed to have set the foundation for even better things to come in the next. Surely, the Air Force lid on the saucers would be blown off completely in 1953.

Chapter 12:
Elation and Deflation

Early in the new year, Keyhoe's optimism seemed justified when Chop said it was "definitely settled" that the Utah film would be shown to the press, but disappointing news soon followed. After a conference with Fournet's boss, Colonel William Adams at the Pentagon, Chop told Keyhoe that Dewey Fournet had been "put on inactive duty" and that the wording to accompany the Utah film had been altered to avoid any interplanetary conclusion. It now said that the objects were not conventional, "like aircraft, balloons, or birds," but offered no suggestions as to what they might otherwise be.

As usual, Keyhoe felt suspicious. Fournet's departure "sounds queer to me," he told Chop, and he suspected that the Utah film showing had something to do with it. Fournet's own later explanations for his departure are contradictory. In 1977 he said:

> Personally, I regret the fact that the government no longer associates itself with this subject, although I feel no remorse whatsoever over the burial of the USAF project because of the extremely negative path that it generally followed after 1953.[181]

In 1988 he said:

> I had promised myself when I walked out of the Air Force in 1953 I never wanted to hear about this [UFO] thing again, I had a bellyful...[182]

In 1997, he stated:

> I resigned my reserve commission when I was released from active duty with the Air Force in early 1953 ... this action by me had nothing whatsoever to do with my involvement with the UFO program.[183]

Whatever the reason, Fournet was out of the picture. He'd had little direct contact with Keyhoe —Al Chop had been the conduit—but the absence of his pro-saucer influence on Blue Book would ultimately prove detrimental to Air Force co-operation with Keyhoe and other researchers. It was a blow, followed soon after by another: Al Chop had resigned. "This hasn't anything to do with the saucers," he told Don who, typically, didn't believe him.

The two men got together at Chop's house that night where he reiterated his position and explained that he wanted to work in private industry. "It's the truth… I might have put it off a while—they wanted me to stay on. But the way this thing's worked out, I'm glad I'm going."

Keyhoe's suspicions were unfounded; Chop's resignation had indeed been made for wholly personal reasons. His wife Dolores longed to move to California, and Al was quite prepared to "give up a good job in the Pentagon to go live in California when the pay in California is not as good as it is in the east …" It turned out to be the right move; he was almost immediately hired by Douglas Aircraft, who paid him three thousand dollars more per year.[184]

The following day brought more disappointing news when Chop told Keyhoe that the Utah film would stay under wraps: "the whole thing's been killed," he said, "there won't be any public showing—you can take it from there."

This decision was not wholly popular behind the scenes, and Chop encouraged Keyhoe to keep trying to get the story out but asked him not to "give the whole Air Force a black eye." A similar plea was sent to Don, anonymously, though he recognized the handwriting as that of a "Defense official." The sender complained about the "human ostriches in the Air Force" who wouldn't examine the facts because they feared "something they don't want to face."[185]

Keyhoe knew that somewhere there had to be "an Air Force report that the saucers came from space," so he contacted "Brennard," one of his confidential informants who was for him what Deep Throat would later be for Bob Woodward's Watergate investigation. Brennard told him there had recently been a secret briefing, after which one of the officials attending, who used to think the saucers "were a joke," was now "convinced they were extraterrestrial."

His informant had been correct about the "secret briefing." Keyhoe had not yet learned that in January, the CIA had convened The Scientific Panel on Unidentified Flying Objects, later to be termed the Robertson Panel, because it was chaired by physicist Dr. Howard Percy Robertson, then Director of the Defense Department Weapons Evaluation Group.[186]

Creation of this panel was rooted in the Red paranoia that had set the military's Cold War nerves on edge and had become deeply embedded in the national psyche. But there were legitimate security concerns about how the Soviets might manipulate UFO sightings to create confusion, under cover of which an attack could be made on the US—an argument which Keyhoe himself often used in his efforts to bring an end to official secrecy about the saucers.

Director of Ohio State's McMillin Observatory, astronomer Dr. J. Allen Hynek, in the years before he became Ufology's poster-boy, had been the nearest "handy astronomer" to Dayton and had done a few months stint at Project Sign (Saucer) before returning to academia. In 1952, however, he found himself back in the saucer fold, working with Ruppelt and Blue Book. Hence, he merited a place at the Robertson Panel meeting as an Associate member. He later recalled that:

> The great "Washington flap" of 1952 and the tremendous wave of UFO reports that swamped the Blue Book office that summer was a true source of worry to the Air Force and to the government from two entirely different stand points. There was the question, "What are they?'" but the CIA was even more interested in the possibility that enemy agents might clog military communications with a barrage of false flying-saucer reports, thus camouflaging a real attack on the country.
>
> The second concern took overriding precedence. On December 4, 1952, the Intelligence Advisory Committee recommended that: "The Director of Central Intelligence will 'enlist the services of selected scientists to review and appraise the available evidence in the light of pertinent scientific theories ...'" But this was only the official reason, as is clearly indicated by the recommendations of the "selected scientists," convened under the chairmanship of Dr. H. P. Robertson, a noted physicist and relativity expert. The true purpose of the panel was to "defuse" a potentially explosive situation from the standpoint of national security. In short, in convening the panel, the CIA was fearful not of UFOs, but of UFO reports. So, under the guise of a symposium to review the physical nature of UFOs, the meetings of the scientists, who already subscribed to the "It can't be, therefore

it isn't" philosophy, got underway on January 14, 1953. I sat in on three of the five day-long meetings as an associate panel member.

The other question, "What are they?," was already being studied intensively at the Battelle Memorial Institute, in Columbus, Ohio. The rising tide of reports in 1952 had caused the Air Force to contract with Battelle, a most prestigious scientific institution, to study secretly all reports through the end of 1952 to determine primarily whether the "Unknowns" differed in basic characteristics from the "Knowns."[187]

The CIA couldn't wait for Battelle to complete its study, so it convened the panel in haste. The decision to establish "a panel of top scientists and engineers in the fields of astrophysics, nuclear energy, electronics, etc., to review this situation" had been taken on December 10, 1952, following which it was quickly arranged and, less than five weeks later, was underway. It convened from January 14th to 18th, and its panel members were: Luis W. Alvarez (University of California); Lloyd V. Berkner (Associated Universities, Inc); S. A. Goudsmit (Brookhaven National Laboratories), and Thornton Page (John Hopkins University). With Hynek was one other associate member, "aerospace specialist" with the consulting firm of Arthur D. Little Inc, Frederick Clark Durant, and among the interviewees were Ruppelt and Fournet. Durant, then aged 37, had by now "befriended" these two officers, and he was, according to Fournet, "on the CIA payroll."[188]

Following its "substantive scientific review," Durant penned its report—which has received plenty of comment and analysis over the decades—supporting the Air Force's view that witnesses were fools and the entire subject was a waste of time. Notoriously, among its conclusions was

> That the national security agencies take immediate steps to strip the Unidentified Flying Objects of the special status they have been given and the aura of mystery they have unfortunately acquired. We suggest that this aim may be achieved by an integrated program designed to reassure the public of the total lack of evidence of inimical forces behind the phenomena.

It also recommended that Blue Book be expanded and given necessary equipment and facilities to continue its study, in the hope of finding better reports than the "circumstantial" offerings it had reviewed:

> The investigative force of Project Blue Book should be qua-
> drupled in size, they wrote, and it should be staffed by spe-
> cially trained experts in the fields of electronics, meteorology,
> photography, physics, and other fields of science pertinent
> to UFO investigations. Every effort should be made to set
> up instruments in locations where UFO sightings are fre-
> quent, so that data could be measured and recorded during a
> sighting. In other locations around the country military and
> civilian scientists should be alerted and instructed to use ev-
> ery piece of available equipment that could be used to track
> UFO's.
>
> And lastly, they said that the American public should be
> told every detail of every phase of the UFO investigation—
> the details of the sightings, the official conclusions, and why
> the conclusions were made. This would serve a double pur-
> pose; it would dispel any of the mystery that security breeds
> and it would keep the Air Force on the ball—sloppy investi-
> gations and analyses would never occur.[189]

This was what the Project and the public surely needed, but it was not to
be. It became evident over the next year that none of these recommendations
were to be actioned. Coral Lorenzen, though also unaware of the Robertson
Panel, had been making her own enquiries in the weeks after it secretly met,
and she smelled a rat. By this time, Ed Ruppelt had left Blue Book, but she had
spoken to his recent replacement, Lt. Robert Olsson, who was accompanied
by Hynek. It was her opinion that Hynek specifically wanted to meet with
her, as he had rearranged his schedule to be in Milwaukee after he learned she
would be there, visiting family.[190] During a four-hour lunch meeting with the
two men at the Hotel Schroeder, Olsson told her:

> We are going to keep these reports (of saucers) out of the
> papers. We believe most of them are due to mass hysteria and
> the power of suggestion. If people are allowed to forget this
> matter, they'll quit seeing them.

This, she felt, showed that "arrangements had already been made."

* * *

The negligent, uninterested attitude of the Panel was confirmed almost exactly fifteen years later, on January 26, 1968. Dr. James E McDonald, atmospheric physicist at the University of Arizona, by that time had been deeply involved in UFO research for ten years. He met socially with Thornton Page, who made several admissions. He said that the Panel "never had any real interest in the subject," that the four-day meetings gave insufficient time for meaningful research, and that neither the CIA nor the Air Force were concerned that the subject had been merely skimmed over. The other panel members also were unconcerned. "What did they care?" he said.[191]

Page hadn't cared, either. He admitted that he had thought it was "a fringe subject, misidentifications, mass hysteria," though confessed that McDonald's interest in the field now made him feel differently.

But in 1953, and without details of the "secret briefing," Keyhoe immediately suspected (erroneously) that it had concluded the saucers were interplanetary, so he made a last attempt at getting something out of Chop. "Doesn't this [Brennard's information] prove there's a secret report?" he pressed, but Chop wouldn't violate security. He could admit that the previous year there had been a "detailed analysis of all the evidence" that came to a definite conclusion, but frustratingly, he wouldn't say what it was. This analysis was a motion study undertaken by Fournet and presented to the Panel, which examined the flight characteristics of UFOs and concluded that "the UFOs were interplanetary spaceships." The report at some point was "filed as an unfinished Air Force document."[192]

Chop couldn't breach security on the motion study, but he did have something to give Keyhoe.[193] Publisher Henry Holt & Company had earlier requested official confirmation from the Air Force that the cases Keyhoe cited in his new book, *Flying Saucers From Outer Space*, had been cleared. It had been provided in a letter, dated January 26, 1953, signed by Chop, a copy of which he now handed to Don:

> We in the Air Force recognize Major Keyhoe as a responsible, accurate reporter. His long association and cooperation with the Air Force, in our study of unidentified flying objects, qualifies him as a leading civilian authority on this

investigation.

... The Air Force, and its investigating agency, "Project Bluebook," are aware of Major Keyhoe's conclusion that the "Flying Saucers" are from another planet. The Air Force has never denied this possibility exists. Some of the personnel believe that there may be some strange natural phenomena completely unknown to us, but that if the apparently controlled maneuvers reported by many competent observers are correct, then the only remaining explanation is the interplanetary answer.[194]

Keyhoe was elated. "I've waited four years for this," he said. "I guess I don't have to ask what you believe, now." Chop gave him his personal opinion "as a private citizen":

[O]ne thing's absolutely certain. We're being watched by beings from outer space. You've been right from the very start.'[195]

This letter was a tremendous boost to Keyhoe. Though he interpreted it as justification for his conviction about saucer-reality, he still had to overcome Air Force resistance, and in that respect, he was dismayed a few months later to hear of two major obstacles that stood in his—and everybody else's—way.

In September, he first learned of Joint Army Navy Air Force Publication order JANAP 146 from Arthur Caperton, one of his Marine buddies from his days at Pensacola Naval Air Station, whose own rather interesting flying career had a small Lindbergh link; as a civilian pilot, he had flown a photographer 150 miles out to sea to take pictures of the Lone Eagle winging his record-breaking way toward Paris in May 1927.

By 1953, Caperton was a senior crash investigator for the Civil Aeronautics Board and inadvertently let slip to Keyhoe the existence of this order, which came under CIRVIS (Communication Instructions for Reporting Vital Intelligence Sightings). It specified procedures for both civilian and military pilots in the US and Canada for submitting sightings reports but prohibited them from revealing the existence of such reports.[196] Breaching this order, even by a non-pilot, could result in a fine of up to $10K and ten years in prison.

In December, Keyhoe learned from Frank Edwards of another obstacle, the recently created Air Force Regulation AFR 200-2. Don was investigating the incident of November 23rd in which pilot Lt. Felix Moncla, Jr., and

The astounding FACTS behind the greatest mystery of our age— by the recognized authority 25¢

FLYING SAUCERS FROM OUTER SPACE

Major Donald E. Keyhoe U.S. MARINE CORPS (Ret.)

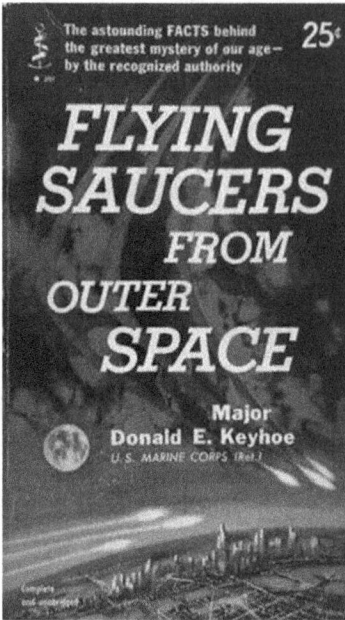

radar observer Lt. Robert L. Wilson, had disappeared over Lake Superior, after their F-89 jet was seen on radar merging with a blip caused by "an unknown machine." No traces of the men or their plane had been recovered, but the story had appeared in the press. Coral Lorenzen, who had recently begun corresponding with Keyhoe, had first alerted him to this case by letter, pointing out that the incident was the second within a few hours from Truax Field.

The other had occurred only five hours later, when pilot Lt. John W. Schmidt and his radar operator, Captain Glen E. Collins, crashed in their F-89 jet just outside of Madison, in what was thought to be a sacrificial effort to maneuver their plane away from a populated area before it went down. The bodies of Schmidt and Collins were found, but the remains of Moncla and Wilson were not, though according to one press report a salvage operation had succeeded in recovering parts of their plane from the "muddy hole" created when the F-89 had exploded on impact. It's likely, however, that the report had confused the two events and the recovered plane was that of Schmidt and Collins.[197]

Edwards told Keyhoe he'd heard that AFR 200-2 had been broken by "someone at Truax" AFB who had reported the Moncla incident and was concerned about the consequences of his loose lips. Don followed up and learned that AFR 200-2, like JANAP 146, was designed to keep UFO reports under wraps. It "took a firm public relations stance: it prohibited the release of *any* information about a sighting to the public except when the sighting was positively identified."[198]

Still unaware of the secret CIA Robertson Panel, Don couldn't know that both these "gagging" orders "reflected the Air Force's attempts to institute the …panel's desire to end public speculation about UFOs with the concomitant threat of increased reports."[199] The CIA, for its part, was interested in knowing just how much Keyhoe knew, as reported in a memo on December 8, 1953, from P. G. Strong, its Chief of Operations Staff, Office of Scientific Intelligence

(OSI), to the Assistant Director of Scientific Intelligence, giving his views on the Major's recent book, *Flying Saucers From Outer Space*:

 a. The book itself is highly readable, but the content is highly distorted and filled with so many half-truths and inferences that I feel certain the author is knowingly committing a perpetration. Prominent in the book is one Albert N. Chop, an Air Force (Reserve) Public Information Officer who was on duty at the Pentagon until recently ...Keyhoe makes extensive use of Chop's statements and implies that the Air Force is deliberately concealing positive conclusions from the public.

 b. CIA is mentioned several times on page 242 ... Keyhoe states here that a friend of his, with high level "contacts," told him about February 17, 1953, that:

 (1) CIA "people" advised the Air Force to put out a report debunking the saucers, tell the public the project was ended and then carry it on underground, Top Secret.

 (2) Some of the "intelligence boys" were mad as the devil at CIA for even suggesting the above action.

 c. CIA is supposed to have made these recommendations following a "secret high level briefing" There is no apparent knowledge of the CIA panel meetings although the Panel's recommendations might have been interpreted by a fanatical saucer "believer" as "debunking". However, there was certainly no recommendation that suggested hiding any information from the public.

 d. Therefore, Keyhoe, having built up a "case" for saucers being interplanetary, insists that the Air Force (and CIA) know the "truth" and are refusing to give the public the facts.

 e. I saw Dr Stefan T. Poscony [Possony, Chief, USAFOIN Special Study Group] recently. He was not aware of any particular concern in the Pentagon over Keyhoe's assertions. However, it might be wise to check directly with the officer who replaced Fournet in Current Intelligence. I believe his name is Smith. Part of his duties are to follow all reports of sightings of UFOs.

 f. As to the possibility of a security breach, it is difficult to say. I suspect that Chop heard of CIA's being briefed but that no leak occurred regarding the O/SI Panel.

2. It is believed that no security breach is involved and any investigation of this book would only serve to focus additional attention on an obvious bit of sensational science "fiction"... no further action ... by this office.[200]

Unaware of the CIA's dismissive review of his book and its internal denial of intent to hide "any information from the public," Keyhoe would thereafter decry JANAP 146 and AFR 200-2 as evidence of official determination to keep the public from knowing the truth about the saucers that he so fervently wanted to reveal, an endeavor that had by now become his full-time occupation. The negative Air Force decision about the Utah film and the loss of Chop and Fournet were deflating setbacks, but he still had one vital contact, whose support would be crucial to his cause: Captain Edward J. Ruppelt.

Chapter 13:
A Friend Among Foes

Since Donald Keyhoe's first dealings with Ed Ruppelt, he had come to hold this young officer in high regard and believed he had found an ally on the inside who was not afraid to counter the official Air Force line in cases where the evidence against it was compelling. During their most friendly years, the two men never wholly saw eye-to-eye on the origin of the saucers, but Keyhoe thought Ruppelt had at least a leg on the same side of the fence as himself, albeit keeping the other on the official side for reasons of duty.

Ruppelt was no stranger to the skies. His own military career certainly fit the profile of the "experienced observer," a term upon which he would later pour scorn. He himself had been followed by a foo-fighter during his wartime service, though he apparently accepted the theory that it was merely "a static electricity phenomenon." On another occasion, when returning to base after a particularly stressful mission, he'd mistakenly fired at the planet Venus, which perhaps for him and other pilots who had done the same, encouraged acceptance of what became the Air Force's go-to explanation for decades to come.[201]

When saucers hit the news in July 1947, Ruppelt was on vacation in Yellowstone:

> Within a few days after Arnold's sighting youngsters were tossing paper plates over our lodge at Yellowstone and yelling, "Saucer, saucer!" Some of the tourists started seeing things and would come in and tell about them, as if their vacation was complete. I read Arnold's story and shrugged it off.[202]

This apparent indifference toward the saucers evidently turned into sufficient curiosity for him to volunteer at Blue Book, though he could not have expected that his new posting would make him a household name in saucer circles.

As it was, Ruppelt now found himself up to his neck in the subject and, both during and after his less than two years on the Project, gained a popular reputation as a lone maverick, a beacon who was bravely helping to shed light on USAF secrecy. He's credited with bringing order out of the chaos of earlier UFO projects and also for creating the term Unidentified Flying Objects, though this is incorrect. It was used in the press as early as 1947 and again in 1948 and 1949, employed in the latter case to report Air Force rebuttals of Keyhoe's *True* article.[203]

The rather heroic image conferred upon Ruppelt by some was not universally held. His "friend" Fred Durant dismissed him in 2008, saying "As far as competence it was obvious he did not have professional competency above engineer."[204]

Hynek and his "colleague, confidante, and friend" Jenny Gluck (later, Zeidman) were less than wowed by the man or his Project.[205] The late Zeidman recollected her impressions of her monthly visits with Hynek to ATIC, which somewhat puncture the idea that Ruppelt, the noble crusader, had created an efficient, crack unit:

> The Blue Book facility ... consisted of three cramped, crummy little offices. The paint was peeling and the file cabinets were warped ... [a] US map with pins stuck in it, a sergeant gofer, a gum-cracking, beehive hairdoed secretary (a civilian) and a dried-out coffee pot on the window sill ... I never saw [Ruppelt] smile ... I remember him as a by-the-book sobersides. I don't recall a human side of him, even when we were having an informal lunch.[206]

Hynek was also unimpressed when he recalled his meetings with Ruppelt:

> That was in my debunking days, and he regarded me with a certain amount of suspicion. I was just one of these professors who were coming around. He never really took me into his confidence ...it was something of an ego trip for him. He was constantly in demand, briefing this general and that general. If I had to give an impression of [Ruppelt], it would be that he was sort of a weather vane ... He was extremely puzzled and one day he was in one direction and the next day his weather-vane had shifted to the other. He was trying to do the best job he could to debunk and yet he had this weird perception ... something was going on that was beyond him ...'[207]

Moreover, Hynek knew that Blue Book was not the high-powered, all-knowing, top-secret facility the Air Force successfully touted to the public:

> For many years the Blue Book operation had very low priority as far as the Air Force was concerned. And it was sloppy, just kid's stuff, actually. If there had been some way of bringing in the NICAP [National Investigations Committee on Aerial Phenomena] or APRO [Aerial Phenomena Research Organization] data ... the picture might have changed, but scientists were unaware that the amateurs were getting the good data they were.[208]

> [I]t was in certain respects "low man on the totem pole." The low rank of the officer in charge of Blue Book was a dead giveaway. A mere captain doesn't have much authority ... I saw extremely few reports at Project Blue Book that were marked Top Secret—and not too many that were labeled Secret—mostly they were classified as Confidential or Restricted.[209]

Ruppelt, however, felt that he and Blue Book were further up the totem:

> [Blue Book] had risen from the one-man operation to a project within a group, then to a group, and now it was a section. Neither Project Sign nor the old Project Grudge had been higher than the project-within-a-group level. The chief of a group normally calls for a lieutenant colonel, and since I was just a captain this caused some consternation in the ranks ... Colonel Donald Bower, who was my division chief, decided rank be damned, and I stayed on as chief of Project Blue Book. The location within the organizational chart is always indicative of the importance placed on a project.

Whatever Keyhoe's perception of Ruppelt's place in the hierarchy, he came to increasingly rely upon and respect the young captain, who seemed to be a straight-shooter, unafraid to tread confidently along a fine line between the Air Force's dogma and Don's insatiable need for information. Al Chop later recalled his own experience of Keyhoe's persistence, during the Ruppelt period:

> [He] spent 100% of his time worrying about, and study-

ing them, and asking questions about UFOs. While the rest of the press, maybe once in six months they say something about UFOs. But Don Keyhoe was at my desk three times a week!

And he used to bug the hell out of me! I'd come to work and he'd be in my chair! Waiting for me! ... He did spend 100% of his time on this. So you know, naturally he's going to get more information than somebody who's just taking a cursory look at it. I didn't favor him with anything. Except he was just a smart cookie, and subscribed to a [clipping service] ... any sighting in the United States, he had a hand, he was there! He had it, he had the information that would appear in the local press and he'd come and ask about it. Many times, I didn't have anything to give him. I would say, we never heard of it! Well evidently, he showed me this piece in the paper, and I'd say, "Well, call the paper. I don't have anything on it! I will ask Blue Book. I will call Ruppelt and see if he has anything on it. But frankly, this is first we heard of it!" That happened many times. He was there all the time. That was his number one project in life! [210]

Though Ruppelt's value to Keyhoe would remain high in the years to come, his tenure at Blue Book, and the apparent openness that accompanied it, was both short-lived and interrupted. Even before the Robertson Panel convened, he had already decided to move on, and post-Robertson it was evident to him that Blue Book, like its predecessor, was destined to become moribund. His former boss, Dewey Fournet, later said:

> Captain Ruppelt confided to me that he could see the negativism developing following the report by the CIA Scientific Panel in early 1953, and this was the main reason for his request to be reassigned from the project. [211]

Ruppelt himself wrote:

> In December of 1952 I'd asked for a transfer. I'd agreed to stay on as chief of Blue Book until the end of February so that a replacement could be obtained and be broken in. But no replacement showed up. And none showed up when

Lieutenant Rothstien's tour of active duty ended, when Lieutenant Andy Flues transferred to the Alaskan Air Command, or when others left.

When I left the UFO project for a two-month tour of temporary duty in Denver, Lieutenant Bob Olsson took over as chief. His staff consisted of Airman First Class Max Futch. Both men were old veterans of the UFO campaign of '52, but two people can do only so much. When I came back to ATIC in July 1953 and took over another job, Lieutenant Olsson was just getting out of the Air Force and Al/c Futch was now it. He said that he felt like the President of Antarctica on a non-expedition year.[212]

His decision to request a transfer, even before the CIA panel met, may have been instigated during the first week of December 1952. On the 9th, he received a call from the CIA to ask if he would be available to come to Washington for a meeting. Ruppelt was keen to do so. He "had a package of analyses and reports which he desired to have the Office of Scientific Intelligence study and was planning to hand-carry to Washington," but had been "running into a snag." This, he "intimated," was due to "his intention to specifically visit CIA ... By oblique references it was determined that Colonel Donald L. Bower (Chief Analysis Division) was blocking his trip."[213]

Whatever the reason for Ruppelt's transfer request, the Robertson Panel ensured that Blue Book was a dead duck, and in reality it had always been a lame duck, lacking adequate support and commitment from those in a position to provide it. The brief flowering it seemed to have under Ruppelt was left to wither and nothing like it would ever bloom again. He left the Air Force in August 1953 to take up a job with Northrop Aircraft Inc., as "senior engineer, Ordnance Project, Weapon Systems Analysis department."[214] Nonetheless, he and Don would continue to correspond on friendly terms for a few years to come, until Ruppelt contemptuously washed his hands of Keyhoe and the saucers for reasons that were never adequately explained. But before his apostasy, he would continue to support the Major and would make two notable written contributions to the cause in 1954 (an article in *True*) and 1956 (his book), with a notorious addition to the latter in 1959.

Although Ed had become a private citizen and Blue Book had become another Grudge, the saucers were still in business and Keyhoe's interest in them continued to deepen. He remained convinced that an Air Force cover-up was in place, and that any day now it would yield to his persistence and be persuaded to reveal "the truth about flying saucers."

Unfortunately for him, at the same time, others were developing their own pursuit of "the truth" about the saucers and their influence would have far-reaching consequences for Keyhoe and UFO research for decades to come.

Chapter 14:
A is for Adamski

As much as Keyhoe was a gadfly to the Air Force, he had his own swarm that buzzed unceasingly about him: the contactees.

> [This group] represented an entirely different type of UFO witness. They exhibited behavior consistent with the assertion that they fabricated hoaxes. They did not report their "experiences" to a reputable investigatory agency. Instead, they publicized them by writing books and articles, presenting lectures, and appearing on radio and television shows. Indeed, the contactees had no fear of ridicule and eagerly sought publicity. They often organized special flying saucer clubs based on their experiences and used the clubs to help publicize their stories. Also, their "experiences" often differed markedly from all other UFO observers, in that some contactees claimed to have taken a ride in a flying saucer and described the ride and the planets they visited in great detail. Moreover, most contactees reported that space people had charged them with a mission, which, they said, was why they had to seek publicity.[215]

Though the legion of pseudo-prophets had many contactee-celebrities whose influence eroded objective analysis, none would surpass their most famous and persistent advocate, George Adamski, a Polish-born café attendant with an interest in mysticism, who liked to give the impression that he was a professor working at the Palomar Observatory. He would go on to claim contact with beautiful Venusians and benevolent Saturnians, from whom he received wise messages for humanity, thereby setting a trend that gained rapid, global momentum.

In a 1954 letter to Ed Ruppelt, Keyhoe's feeling of helplessness in dealing with Adamski and his ilk, is revealed:

> The big trouble today is the crackpots who claim to have

ridden saucers and talked with spacemen or women. Unfortunately I have laid the groundwork for these phonies to succeed; I think I have built up a fairly logical case for the interplanetary answer, and people like Adamski ... can find plenty of readers who have been sold on the space-visitor answer, so they cash in without much trouble. In writing a new book on UFOs ... you have to be <u>stronger</u> than the fakers, one way or another. Either you have to attack them violently and raise so much hell it will get attention, or present something <u>new</u> which is important enough to appeal to the more intelligent citizens. I've been trying to decide what to do, if I write another book; that is, what to do about Adamski and the others. I'd rather ignore them, but I'm afraid I can't because I get hundreds of letters asking me if I believe the stories. I've got to answer the questions I get in fan mail, and a new book is easier than trying to handle them separately.[216]

Born 1891 in Bydgoszcz, Poland (then part of Germany), Adamski's rise had been slow and obscure. The son of an immigrant laborer, he arrived in America as a child and had an unremarkable younger life. At nineteen he was a "core maker" at a locomotive works, then a laborer at Yellowstone National Park, before serving two years as a cavalry private.[217] In 1920, aged 29, he was a house painter in Oregon and had been married for three years to Iowa-born Mary [Marie] Shimbersky, who was twelve years his senior (and whose existence would be almost unknown, even among his close circle). In 1930 he was calling himself a lecturer and by 1933 was advertising himself as "Professor" of The Royal Order of Tibet, a cult he had created and for which he intended, at that time, to build a monastery in Laguna Beach, California.[218]

By 1948 he had abandoned this idea and installed himself inland at the Palomar Café near the Mount Palomar Observatory where he kept three telescopes: a 15-, 10-, and 6-inch. (Astronomer Frank Halstead, later a NICAP adviser, visited him at this "observatory" in 1951 and "found it a fake, could not move."[219]) Thanks to the GI Bill of Rights, Adamski said he began his "career" in astronomy and intended to create a planetarium that would seat between 75 and 100 persons.[220] By the end of 1949, he had progressed from this ambition to serving refreshments at the café. Ruppelt, during his Blue Book incumbency, paid a visit:

I walked into the little restaurant at the foot of [Mount Palomar] one day in 1953. The four stool restaurant, with a few tables, where Adamski worked as a handyman, was crowded when I arrived and he was circulating around serving beer and picking up empty bottles. There was no doubt as to who he was because his fame had spread. To the dozen almost reverently spoken queries, "Are you Adamski?" he modestly nodded his head.

Small questions about the flying saucer photos for sale from convenient racks led to more questions and before long the good "professor" had taken a position in the middle of the room and was off and running. In his slightly broken English he told how he was the son of poor, Polish immigrants with hardly any formal education. To look at the man and to listen to his story you had an immediate urge to believe him. Maybe it was his appearance. He was dressed in well worn, but neat, overalls. He had slightly graying hair and the most honest pair of eyes I've ever seen. Or maybe it was the way he told his story. He spoke softly and naively, almost pathetically, giving the impression that "most people think I'm crazy, but honestly, I'm really not."

Whatever Adamski's mental condition, on December 1, 1949, before publication of Keyhoe's *The Flying Saucers Are Real* article, he claimed that the military knew more about the strange craft in Earth's skies than it was admitting. And while the *True* exposé was still hot from the presses, he was giving a talk, agreeing with Keyhoe's recent comment that the saucers "were not a joke."[221]

By April 1951, Adamski also didn't see the joke when he, posing not only as a "Professor "but now also as a one-time scientist at the Palomar Observatory, declared that eleven extremely handsome men from another world had landed in Scotland where they and their 4,000-foot-long ship were being studied by scientists. He boasted that "on the drawing board" was a spaceship, partly designed by himself, that could move at up to 300,000 miles per second.[222]

Such was the mind and the world of George Adamski, and vast numbers of Americans were awed by his many claims and swallowed them in toto. Keyhoe was not among them. In regard to one of Adamski's infamous tales of meetings with space beings, he wrote:

Adamski was amazed to see a round device, some 20 feet

in diameter, descend near him. Climbing out of the saucer, a man from space quietly stepped to the ground. The visitor was about 23 years old, with a tanned, ruddy face, greyish-green eyes, and long sandy hair which hung down his back and blew in the wind. He was wearing a brown Eisenhower jacket, ski pants, and reddish-brown shoes ...[223]

Setting aside Adamski's encounters with alien fashion-victims, his unremitting persistence and unflinching denials when his hoaxes were challenged or even fully exposed, hacked away at serious research. For the anti-saucer brigade, he, like his beautiful space folk, was heaven-sent, and he became a sort of umbrella under which all "believers," of whatever flavor, were herded by those determined to dismiss UFOs. This ignored an important difference between Adamski et al. and rational observers: the latter group could easily be silenced by ridicule, but Adamski and other contactees were strengthened by it, making them double-down on their claims all the harder and were therefore, in a way, invincible.

This disregard for disapprobation, along with the idea of being specially chosen to receive cosmic wisdom, was a common mindset among contactees. Like Biblical prophets, they spoke of catastrophes to come if mankind did not behave and of a golden age of peace if it did. Only *they* could communicate with superior, all-knowing heavenly beings and only *they* could be the conduit for downloading higher wisdom to foolish humanity. Hence, contactees and some Christians found common ground.

Adamski was not alone in these beliefs. He had competition, much of it from a group in which he was included, among them, other "Flying Georges." George Hunt Williamson, also a phony doctor who later identified himself as Dr. Michel d'Obrenovic, had been one of Adamski's acolytes and swore an affidavit that he had witnessed Adamski's desert encounter with a space being in November 1952, though he later recanted this.

That same year, George Van Tassel published his book, *I Rode in a Flying Saucer*, which told of his experiences with, of course, Venusians. In 1954, he organized the first Giant Rock Convention at a disused airfield near Yucca Flats, California, and later built a dome in the desert called "The Integratron: A Time Machine for basic research on rejuvenation, anti-gravity, time travel," that claimed to have brought back to life a lizard with a terminal head injury; "proof" of this miracle was provided in "before" and "after" pictures of the poor creature. It seemed not to have occurred to his followers that perhaps the pictures were presented in the wrong order. The Integratron is nowadays a tourist spot.

The third "Flying George," George King, operated from across The Pond, where he had founded the Aetherius Society in England, based on his claims of contact with peace-promoting space beings, which of course, included Venusians. His Society still exists.

There were many others thrown into the mix, most of them men, whose philosophies, like many Western cults of the 20th century, had shades of Christianity and/or sexual fantasy. The male space beings, like Jesus, were long-haired, wise, and spoke of peace, and the space women were beautiful, shapely, and sometimes keen to mate—indeed, how could they not be, coming from Venus? Prominent among these chosen prophets were "Dr." Frank Stranges, John Otto, Truman Bethurum, Gabriel Green, Reinhold O. Schmidt, and "Dr." Daniel Fry leading a long parade of self-made seers with self-bestowed titles and self-proclaimed special access to higher knowledge. Each had their own variations on Adamski's theme and vied for the top spot in the contactee charts, but they could never quite equal "A," as he was often referred to in correspondence, and his influence was wide and deep.

There were, of course, rumors that he was a fake. According to one Ray Stanford, who in the 1950s was a young contactee-enthusiast and budding ufologist (and later a NICAP member), Adamski not only showed him some of the models he had used as mock-ups for his photographs of Venusian spacecraft, but also confided to him that he had become involved in "this saucer crap" as a moneymaker due to the repeal of Prohibition. The Royal Order of Tibet had been a front for his bootlegging operation, taking advantage of the concession for alcohol to be purchased for religious ceremonial purposes. When Prohibition was repealed on December 5, 1933, this cut off his income stream and, perhaps sensing the gullibility of those who had attended his "religious" lectures, he was encouraged to try other flimflam, which he described as taking up the "saucer cup."[224]

Author Marc Hallett wrote that this account given to Stanford cannot have been correct because Adamski didn't found the Order until 1934, by which time Prohibition had ended.[225] However, as early as April 1932, the Royal Order of Tibet was in operation and advertising in the press, so it's certainly possible that Adamski had indeed jumped on the sacramental wine bandwagon, as many did at the time.[226] Coral and Jim Lorenzen's 1967 book, *Flying Saucer Occupants*, refers to Adamski's "own admission" that he was running a scam to cover his bootlegging.[227] A hint of this is perhaps suggested in the obituary of his co-author, Desmond Leslie, in which Adamski is referred to as a "philosopher and winemaker."[228]

In 1953, at the same time Keyhoe's *Flying Saucers From Outer Space* was published, Adamski delivered his most significant blow to objective research when, with Leslie's collaboration, *Flying Saucers Have Landed* was published. In this unsettlingly influential work, he told of a 1952 meeting in the California desert, "at a point ten and two-tenths miles from [the town of] Desert Center, on the road to Parker and Needles," where he spoke with the handsome, oddly-dressed space being to which Keyhoe later referred in his book.[229] His experience was vouched for by George Hunt Williamson—at this time still an acolyte—who had earlier been instructed by Adamski (while supposedly in a trance) to have ready a supply of Plaster of Paris for this desert trip. Williamson was wholly taken in by this display and provided the plaster with which, after Adamski's alleged solitary contact with the space brother in the desert, he made casts of hieroglyphic-imprinted alien "footprints" in the sand. (Williamson later recalled that Adamski that day had a box in his possession that he and the accompanying group of believers were utterly forbidden to open. He later thought this may well have contained the implements used to fake the footprints.)

Subsequent events would show that *Flying Saucers Have Landed* had a deeper influence than could be predicted at the time. Its writing and publication were in great part due to an elderly Washington widow, Clara Colcord John, who, in 1956, would be a major force behind the creation of the National Investigations Committee on Aerial Phenomena (NICAP) and whose advocacy of Adamski would irredeemably weaken the organization from its very first moment.

The book was gulped down greedily by vast numbers of cultists in the US and abroad, serving to establish Adamski as the leading intimate of the space brothers and making him the premiere saucer-celebrity on Earth. That image was further burnished when he followed up in 1955 with another book, *Inside the Space Ships*. For his followers, his reputation could not be tarnished under any circumstance; even his nonsensical responses during "lectures," or when being interviewed, didn't dent the adulation of his disciples. Unlike Keyhoe, he gave no details about the saucers that could be factually verified by official or credible sources. His technique was to shift from semi-logical explanations about the space-brothers' missions (e.g., warnings about the consequences of the atomic bomb), to rambling incohesion when asked for specifics on that or any other topic. In a 1954 radio program, a sympathetic interviewer asked

Adamski about evolution. He answered:

> I would say I think that when the Bible speaks where the
> firmament finally was burned away as the fog at that time
> cooling took place and naturally we find that that wasn't the
> beginning of so-called death of the earth. The surmise is that
> on the dying side, and I am inclined to believe that the earth
> itself is of that same side because if the history is true where
> the Bible says that one time there was a thousand year life
> span on this planet and now is only sixty-five year span—we
> have come down quite a time on this earth when life was
> longer than it is at this time, if the Bible is correct…
>
> Let us say now we have conceive the earth finally solid-
> ified and become a bald-headed earth—had nothing on it.
> Supposing a combustion takes place within due to compres-
> sion, which had to take place when the boiling post started,
> and then it had to escape … so the dinosaur had to come
> in—and the dinosaur did come in because he is a vegetarian
> and he ate up all the stuff … then naturally those dinosaurs
> vanished and other animals took place and they went along,
> right along. And the adjustment took place..[230]

This apparent level of media interest and tolerance for Adamski, as well
as the legion of other contactees who would be given air time over the years,
may in some cases not have been due to the host's gullibility or personal
beliefs, nor to the need for ratings. Arthur Campbell, who would later become
Director of NICAP's Kansas City affiliate, knew of at least one radio presenter
with another agenda: Lee Vogel, host of Kansas City's WHB radio program
Nightbeat. In 1959, Campbell wrote to Keyhoe:

> You mentioned about writing Mr. Vogel about the UFO
> censorship on his program. Things aren't quite what they
> seem. He was told that there would be no more UFO per-
> sonalities after my last appearance in November, but since
> that time, he has done Geo. Adamski, Dan Fry, Geo. Van
> Tassel, and Otis T. Carr on his program. They have all had
> a subject bordering on UFOs and drifted into the discussion
> of such. The policy is that of the station which is trying to
> appeal to the working man with "down to earth" topics. I do

not know whether you know this or not, but Mr. Vogel gets
5% of the gate of these speakers under the table. So naturally,
he has more than an ordinary interest in them.[231]

Keyhoe, for whatever reason, didn't expose this practice of contactee-kickbacks but nonetheless doggedly devoted enormous time and effort—which he could ill-afford—to battle against Adamski's influence, while trying to be fair-minded toward him and other contactees. He didn't deny that genuine contact might have occurred, but until adequate proof was shown, he would maintain polite rejection of such claims. It was therefore no doubt interesting to him whenever he received accounts supporting his conviction that Adamski was a huckster. One such came in 1959 from Ray E. Barnes of Phoenix, Arizona, enclosing a list of witnesses to the events he described, which had occurred the previous year.

Barnes was a contactee-advocate, secretary of a cult named The Christ Brotherhood and also editor of its publication, *The Search Lighter*. The group's President was Fry-follower and Adamski-admirer, Dr. Wallace Carey Halsey, cousin to Fleet Admiral William Halsey Jr., whose 1947 autobiography happened to have been co-authored by Col. Joseph Bryan III, a CIA agent and later a board member of NICAP.[232]

Wallace Halsey, a Bible scholar, believed in trance-mediumship with the Space Brothers and had been due to give one of his lectures in Davenport, Iowa in December 1958.[233] On arrival, he found himself double-booked with Adamski (who as per his usual demands had been "sponsored" to appear), so he agreed to reschedule his own lecture, permitting Adamski to take the stage, where he played to his own and Halsey's audience.

Contrary to expectations, Adamski said it was a "damn lie [that] the US Government and military authorities were with-holding information concerning UFO" and he could prove it. His proof was a photocopy of a recently passed bill in Congress which allocated $3 billion dollars for a project to study the phenomenon. President Eisenhower was to be the head and would remain in that role even after he left office. The project would be directed and operated by "a large group of prominent military personnel as well as a number of prominent scientists." The bill, which he read out in full, was HR 7843. Barnes later checked on this House Rule, which he said turned out to deal with "civil service pay deductions."[234] However, HR 7843, "A Bill to Create a Joint Committee on Extraterrestrial Exploration," was introduced on August 2, 1955, by Frank M. Karsten of Missouri, under the Special Committee on Space and Astronautics.[235] It would be composed of "9 senators and 9 members of the House of Representatives to study problems concerning extraterrestrial exploration and travel," though it appears not to have been implemented.

Adamski then stated that there was nothing spiritual about the saucers: "Well, get this, there's nothing to them, or anyone, or anything about them but cold, hard fact science," and he refuted the surprised audience's challenges that this was a "complete negation of his 1955 book, *Inside the Spaceships*."[236] Things didn't improve when many people walked out "due to his use of profanity and at times, lewd allusions," behavior that Barnes said Adamski had displayed before in Phoenix, with the same result.

The following day, Adamski met with Halsey and some of his group at a private dwelling, and being unable to out-do Halsey's knowledge of the Bible, he turned on him furiously. Barnes quoted him in his letter to Keyhoe:

> "You're trying to say spaceships got something to do with God, or the bible. You know what your bible is? Well, three hundred years ago King James and a bunch of yokels got together and wrote it up, or re-wrote it, so as to enslave people with the idea that they had to follow what it, or God, said. It's just a lot of flowery words to keep them scared into doing what the kings and aristocrats wanted them to do. There's nothing to it. Just flowery words, that's all."
>
> Then he, Geo. Adamski, shook his finger violently in Dr. Halsey's face and shouted "You want to know who God is? I'll Tell you! SATAN IS GOD—and DON'T YOU FORGET IT!"
>
> This is on tape, with many witnesses.

This extraordinary incident brought to Halsey's mind an earlier encounter he'd had with a disreputable fellow, also a food vendor on Mount Palomar, who Adamski called "my buddy." The lunchroom where this "buddy" worked displayed a picture of Christ, and when Halsey remarked "that's a beautiful painting of the Messiah," the man replied, angrily and emphatically, "THAT'S NOT CHRIST. THAT'S SATAN. WE WORSHIP SATAN!"

Barnes' letter offered Keyhoe a final interesting nugget. In April, he had been visiting one of the Brotherhood's members, Ralph Huffman, and asked him what he thought of Adamski. In reply, Huffman showed him a rare surviving copy of Adamski's booklet, *Wisdom of the Masters of the Far East*, published by his Royal Order of Tibet in the 1930s. He told Barnes, "Here are identically the same messages, only here they are stated as … Philosophies … Here is where he got his messages of the 'Masters.'"[237] He had recycled his earlier invented wisdom for an audience of more contemporary gullibility.

This is supported by Marc Hallett's *A Critical Appraisal of George Adamski*, in which he reproduces a page from one of these booklets, showing annotations by Adamski. The "Royal Order of Tibet" is crossed out and replaced with "the Space Brothers" and "Mastery" is replaced with both "Cosmic Brotherhood" and "Cosmic Consciousness." Adamski later published this amended version as material for his *Science of Life Study Course* and sold it with the helpful information that each copy gave unique vibrations to the individual, therefore it would serve no purpose to borrow someone else's.[238]

By the mid-1960s, NICAP found it necessary to produce an information sheet about Adamski and his Road to Venus, which it sent to correspondents as appropriate:

> Many of the themes and details of Adamski's allegedly factual claims since 1962 may be found in a 1949 book in the Library of Congress … entitled "Pioneers of Space; a trip to the Moon, Mars and Venus." In the foreword Adamski states the book is a work of fiction. The book describes Venusians "reputed to be proficient in mental telepathy," "ethereal" women and "radiant" men, all of whom reappear in his later allegedly factual books. A religious hierarchy of noble beings who inhabit the planets also appears first in the fiction book, later in the allegedly factual books.
>
> An earlier esoteric book (1936) by Adamski, also available at the Library of Congress … shows his past association with the mystical "Royal Order of Tibet." To religious questions, the book gives the answers of oriental mystical philosophy. Adamski's later allegedly factual books describe spacemen who expound oriental mystical philosophy to him as they sojourn through space.[239]

All these "New Age" prophets were buzzing away in the background, giving lectures, enthralling crowds, and being reported—sometimes uncritically—in the press, attracting far more interest and support than Keyhoe or any objective proponents of UFOs ever garnered. In an era when journalism was considered a respectable profession and academic qualifications conferred automatic veneration from the public, newspaper reports of pronouncements by "doctors" and "professors" carried weight. This encouragement led some readers to make no distinction between Keyhoe's documented objective approach, often supported by scientists, and the contactees' belief-based, subjective methodology that rode on the coat-tails of Christianity, thereby gaining credibility with many Americans and other Westerners.

Adamski, always the most prominent of the contactees, was viewed by objective researchers as either a fool or a charlatan, but one scientist believed he was neither. Chemical Engineer Dr. Leon Davidson had read his books and corresponded with him, asking pertinent questions about his claimed experiences with the beautiful, benevolent space beings. He concluded that Adamski was telling the truth as he genuinely perceived it to be, but the reality was that his evident susceptibility to the idea of off-world beings made him a suitable subject to be hoaxed and used by the CIA. In the Jan-Feb issue of *Flying Saucer Review*, Davidson published his theory, titled, "Why I Believe George Adamski."[240] He felt sure that Adamski's "space brothers" were Earthlings who were part of "an elaborately detailed 'interplanetary' explanation of the flying saucers" controlled by the CIA. The Agency had "maneuvered or created all UFO club activity, contactees, books, and so on to confound the Soviets about [American] technological capabilities."[241]

Adamski, of course, was always keen to boast about supposed official interest in his claims. Widely reported in the press, he said that two boffins visited him at his Palomar set-up in 1949 and asked him to "take pictures of the various objects in the sky." He identified these men as J. P. (Joseph Pease) Maxfield (MIT physics graduate, 1910) and G. L. (Gene Luther) Bloom (chemical engineer, B.S. Alabama Polytechnic, 1943) who at the time of their visit to Adamski were both with the Point Loma Navy Electronics Lab (NEL). Davidson confirmed the existence and employment of both men, but neither replied to his letters asking for information about their meeting at Palomar. Later, due to the actions of one Thomas Eickhoff (see Chapter 16), he felt sure that the CIA's involvement with Adamski was clear.

It's worth noting here that Dr. James McDonald followed up on the visit of Maxfield and Bloom. In short, the two men confirmed they had indeed visited Adamski at his "lunch place" after inspecting "some radiation monitoring equipment on the top of Mount Palomar at that time." An anomaly had been reported by a technician who "had an over-imaginative interest in UFOs," but it turned out to be a mundane aberration. At Adamski's lunch counter, the subject of UFOs arose, and though the two men couldn't recall the specifics, it was conveyed to McDonald that "there was probably some allusion to photographing flying saucers," and as they left, Bloom

> ... may have said something to the effect that if [Adamski] should get any photographs they would be interested in having a look at them, or something like that.

Maxfield later received "a couple of photographs taken with a Brownie camera" which showed only "wiggly images" caused by static electricity "off the velvet inside" of the camera. It was made clear to McDonald that neither of the NEL men gave any credibility to Adamski's pictures, nor had they indicated any official interest in his claims.

* * *

Despite the increasing influence of the contactees in the early 1950s, Keyhoe could have no inkling of how troublesome these New Age gurus would become just a few years hence, for he was intent on "getting the truth" out to the public and, as a private individual, could afford to keep his distance from them. Still afflicted by pronoia, he felt that reason would overcome the preachings of the cultist fringe, and he remained focused on persuading the Air Force that their policy of secrecy should be brought to a speedy end for the good of all. It was therefore undoubtedly a blow when, in addition to the increasing horde who shared or preached some version of Adamski's alleged beliefs, Keyhoe found that one of his most sober scientific allies was not immune to contactee contamination.

In 1950, he first met Canadian scientist Wilbert Smith, Superintendent of Radio Regulations Engineering with Canada's Department of Transport (DoT), for which he researched radio wave propagation. Smith had persuaded the DoT to allow him and a team of researchers to use its facilities for an unofficial study of "unidentified flying objects and physical principles which might appear to be involved" under the name of Project Magnet.

Smith speculated that magnetic fields were employed in saucer propulsion, and Keyhoe was highly interested in this theory, as it appeared to explain much about how the discs could achieve speeds and maneuvers entirely beyond the abilities of conventional aircraft. The two men would meet about twice a year, sometimes at Keyhoe's home, and would engage in long discussions on the subject; indeed, their first meeting spanned two weeks, when Smith was attending a scientific conference in Washington. They "covered every angle of the saucer problem...between his committee meetings and at nights."[242]

Though the magnetic field theory had lost much of its appeal in serious minds, Keyhoe's talks with Smith led him to feel it was worthy of reconsideration. He was additionally impressed with Smith's theory that the saucers glowed and changed color due to the speed at which a disc rotated because "it overheats from its movement through the magnetic field." Moreover, his logical thinking about the saucers was appealing. He wrote:

> I maintain that it takes only one black sheep to prove that all sheep are not white, and one unexplained saucer sighting should be enough to warrant establishing a serious scientific study group.[243]

Keyhoe liked Smith, who possessed the "cool detachment of a typical scientist" and had no doubt about the interplanetary origin of the discs. When he returned to Canada after his Washington trip, Smith penned his famous memo, dated November 21, 1950.[244] Smith wrote:

> I made discreet enquiries through the Canadian Embassy staff in Washington who were able to obtain for me the following information:
> a. The matter is the most highly classified subject in the United States Government, rating higher than even the H-bomb.
> b. Flying saucers exist.
> c. Their modus operandi is unknown but concentrated effort is being made by a small group headed by Doctor Vannevar Bush.
> d. The entire matter is considered by the United States authorities to be of tremendous significance.

Yet, within five years, even he, a man of hard science, had succumbed to the contactee message. The first indication came in January 1954 when Smith wrote to Keyhoe asking if he had read Adamski and Leslie's *Flying Saucers Have Landed*. "If true, it really is most astounding, but if it is a hoax it is an extremely clever one since quite a bit of it is scientifically quite correct and in line with our work."[245] In 1955, he wrote again, explaining that he hadn't been in touch with Keyhoe for some time,

> ...not at the request of the Canadian Government, who no

longer have anything to do with the saucer research, but at the request of the saucer people themselves. Certain officials in my government are aware of my contact with these people and are willing to let me play it my way. I am convinced that this will be in the best interests of the human race.

I have learned a great deal ... I have been shown glimpses of a philosophy and technology almost beyond comprehension. Nor am I alone, as there are quite a few people who have gained the confidence of these beings and are being instructed.[246]

Smith later expanded on his beliefs and said that after lengthy scientific study

...the inevitable conclusion was that it was all real enough, but that the alien science was definitely alien and possibly even forever beyond our comprehension. So another approach was tried, the philosophical, and here the answer was found in all its grandeur ... I began for the first time in my life to realize the basic one ness of the universe and all that is in it. Science, philosophy, religion, substance and energy are all facets of the same jewel. And before any one facet can be appreciated the form of the jewel must be perceived.

One of the most important things I had to realize is that we are not alone. The human race in the form of man extends throughout the universe and is incredibly ancient ... our civilization here on earth now is only one of many that have come and gone. This planet has been colonized many times by people from elsewhere and our present human race are blood brothers of these people ... [T]o orthodox thinkers this may seem strange, but not nearly so strange as our orthodox ideas on evolution. The question might be asked if these people are our brothers and are interested in our welfare why do they remain so aloof. The answer is available. There is a basic law of the universe which grants each and every individual independence and freedom of choice so that he may experience and learn from his experiences. No one has the right to interfere in the affairs of others. In fact our ten commandments are directives against interference.

If we disregard this law we must suffer the consequences
...these people from outside have a much greater knowledge
than we have and have means of perceiving the sequences
which must not be changed ... they are not permitted by
cosmic law to interfere ...[247]

In spite of his staggering adoption of contactee beliefs (Dr. James
McDonald said Smith had "gone off the deep end"), Keyhoe could not afford
to discard this man and ultimately had to take a careful middle course.[248] He
offered no criticism of his Adamski-like leanings, but generally agreed to differ
and keep faith with his rational, scientific theories.

Notwithstanding the wide and deep contactee contamination of UFO
research, there was still support from serious-minded folk who not only held
the cultists in contempt but were also committed to objective research and
evaluation.

One organization was especially prominent, and it would, until 1958, be
among Keyhoe's most ardent allies.

Chapter 15: APRO Accord

Coral and Jim Lorenzen looked as though they had stepped right out of a 1950s sci-fi movie. She was shapely and beautiful, in the mold of the General's daughter who would inevitably be kidnapped, screaming and fainting in the arms of the shambling, bug-eyed space creature. He was handsome, bespectacled, and looking every inch the heroic, brilliant young scientist, who would rescue her and the world from alien capture.

The reality was far more Earthly, though not wholly conventional. Coral Ethel Lightner and Leslie James Lorenzen—Jim—had married in Minnesota in 1943. Her father was Jewish and Jim's family were German. His parents disliked their daughter-in-law due, she believed, to her Jewish ancestry, even though she had been raised a Baptist and became a Unitarian, but this family tension took away nothing from the couple's devotion to each other.[249]

This devotion was perhaps no better expressed than in Jim's unfailing support of his wife's passion: her commitment to what she termed UAO (Unidentified Aerial Objects), or the aforementioned UAP, research. This had led, in July 1952, to the creation of APRO—the Aerial Phenomena Research Organization, which they (mainly, she) operated from each of the many homes they lived in over the following years, producing UFO bulletins for the organization's members. Coral was, as she liked to remind readers and correspondents, "the first publisher of a 'flying saucer' periodical, and a pioneer in UFO research."

She had certainly sensed the shape of things to come, for it was thanks in the greatest part to Keyhoe's influence that the 1950s would see a rapid blooming of saucer-interest groups in America and beyond. Coral recognized that national and international co-ordination of sightings reports, coupled with a commitment to sober analysis, was essential to discovering who or what was flitting about Earth's skies.

For Keyhoe, these organizations, which varied in size, quality, and beliefs, were the unexpected result of "the apparent brush-off by the Air Force" that caused "groups of reputable civilians" to undertake their own private investigations. According to Al Chop, the Air Force was "not against them ... but it gives the public the idea we're not taking the saucers seriously."[250]

By 1953, Don had become the most prominent figure in civilian UFO research and stood high in Coral's estimation. Prompted by a recent tussle between him and the Air Force, she opened up communication with the Major by letter on October 3, 1953:

> I and the members of this organization have followed with interest your opinions and policy regarding flying saucers. Your recent charges of duplicity by the Air Force regarding same are duly noted with some elation.[251]

She was referring to the challenge he'd issued that week to General Sory Smith, director of Air Force public information, who had followed the party-line and accused Keyhoe of misrepresenting "the Air Force analysis of the Utah flying-saucer pictures" in his newly-published book, *Flying Saucers From Outer Space*. As a result of his book's revelations, Keyhoe felt he had been "savagely denounced to the Pentagon press corps." The Utah film had not yet been seen by the public; the Air Force claimed it was worthless and had never been analyzed, but Don knew this was untrue. In his book, he had stated that the Air Force had indeed analyzed the film and concluded that, though it did not show birds or balloons nor any known aircraft, it couldn't be explained by any conventional answer. According to Ruppelt, the analysis was classified, but oddly its conclusions were not, and unknown to the Air Force, Keyhoe possessed a copy that confirmed the claims he had made. Strengthened by this hidden document, he sent a telegram to General Smith on October 1st and copied it to the wire services:

> On September 29, the Air Force publicly implied that I misrepresented the Air Force analysis of the Utah flying-saucer pictures. If this is true, then as a Marine Corps officer I should be subjected to disciplinary action … If my claims are incorrect, I suggest you ask that I be court-martialed for making false statements about the Air Force analysis.[252]

He would repeat this challenge on air in December, when he debated against *Time* magazine's science editor, Jonathan H. Leonard, on the radio program *America's Town Meeting*, broadcast from New York City. Titled "Flying saucers, Fact or Illusion?," Keyhoe and Leonard faced-off on the subject of Air Force secrecy, which Leonard utterly refuted, relying solely on recently received letters from the AF which denied such accusations. In contrast, Keyhoe produced cases and documents from his book that Leonard, in the manner which American nuclear physicist and ufologist Stanton Friedman would later describe as "don't bother me with the facts," simply blew off.[253] Of course, no court martial followed.

Coral was impressed with Don's chutzpah with respect of his challenge to General Smith, but feared it might backfire. She wrote:

> We want you to know that if there is any way we can be of any assistance we shall be only too happy to comply with any request. We have always looked upon you as our champion and are extremely happy that … there is one capable, intelligent man willing to fight for the truth with the strength of his own convictions and a fine backlog of facts and technical knowledge.[254]

The two would maintain their friendly, often lengthy, correspondence for several years, and Coral's high opinion of Keyhoe during this time was unwavering. She rarely missed an opportunity to plug him and his books in the *APRO Bulletin*:

> Congratulations, Mr. Keyhoe—you're doing a good job! … Keyhoe Scores Another Hit!! … We recognize Mr. Keyhoe as the outstanding civilian expert on saucers who has the ability to put his ideas, convictions and evidence down in a book in a very interesting, but all the same factual manner …[255]

She shared his scorn of contactee "crackpots" and, though acceding to the notion of a Creator, considered religion to be nonsense of the same flavor: "We've often wondered how the minds of those who believe in all that goes with religion, yet doubt the actuality of the existence of flying saucers, even when the evidence is at hand to inspect …"[256]

The "crackpots" had directly intervened shortly after Coral's first letter to Don, when he was being interviewed live on a popular morning radio chat show hosted by former model Jinx Falkenberg and her husband, Tex McCrary. It was broadcast from New York's Waldorf Astoria and Keyhoe was plugging his *Flying Saucers From Outer Space*. During their discussion, a call came in through the switchboard that triggered something of a panic, described by the press (optimistically) as the biggest since Orson Welles' 1938 broadcast. The caller, in a "thickly accented" voice, typically threatened mankind with annihilation if it continued to make war and atom bombs.

Jinx became too hysterical to deal with the call, turning it over to her husband, who unintentionally held the receiver close to the microphone, and as a consequence, the "space message" was heard by the show's audience, jamming the hotel's switchboard with frantic callers. The Major immediately denied he had any hand in the incident, McCrary did the same, and Keyhoe's publisher, Henry Holt & Co, also denied involvement, adding that it would never perform such a publicity stunt.[257]

Though the crackpots were ever-present, the business of serious investigation had to go on, and Don's efforts continued to win favor with Coral. By mid-1954, her increasing admiration for him led her to suggest they correspond on a first name basis ("I feel as though I know you to some extent and the formal title seems a little out of place"), and she extended keen invitations for him to give lectures in her local area and to stay at the Lorenzen home.[258] By January 1955, she declared effusively:

> APRO is definitely on the side of, and indorses [*sic*] the writings of Donald Keyhoe. For the first time we would like to state that of all the writers on the UFOs, Keyhoe is the most restrained, dedicated to facts, and worthy of the confidence put in him by so many people … Mr. Keyhoe is well-endowed with honesty, ethics and just plain guts.[259]

In December's *APRO Bulletin*, following the publication of Keyhoe's latest book, *The Flying Saucer Conspiracy*, her accolades went from lavish praise to full-on, gushing, over-the-top adulation:

> Mr. Keyhoe has done a magnificent job … If all the superlatives known to the artisans of literary review were to be employed in favor of "The Flying Saucer Conspiracy" I feel they would be insufficient for the portent of this book is beyond mere words. We may well find some day that it has had more profound effect on the lives of the people of the world than the reformation or the fall of the Roman Empire'.

For his part, Don kept a level head, though welcomed her support, and their letters to each other during these honeymoon years showed a mutual respect. Much of their content was of course on UFOs, and she shared his feelings about the "silence" group and Air Force secrecy, but there was also plenty of chatty, personal information exchanged. Keyhoe, perhaps feeling the mantle of authority and responsibility that Coral had bestowed upon him, was the more business-like of the two but always expressed his gratitude for her assistance and offered his sympathies for her numerous debilitating ailments and family difficulties. He confided to her some of his own:

> [T]hanks for everything, and keep up the good work. It's nice to know there is one honest organization to count on, against all the nuts and crooks who have jumped on the bandwagon … I'm sorry to hear your arthritis is still bad … [My] wife's been quite ill again, I've been sick myself, everything went wrong around this place—a pump trouble … hot water tank had to be replaced, same for some kitchen installations, car trouble …[260]

His replies to her letters were usually tardy, due to the high volume of correspondence he received. For a time, he had employed a secretary at his home, but she seemed to make matters worse and so the backlog grew to unmanageable proportions. Indeed, when he later took up the reins at NICAP, among his motivations was the prospect of having his outstanding mail dealt with by the organization's staff so that he could start afresh, but matters were only made worse and the problem would never be resolved. Consequently, many of his letters to Coral (and most other correspondents) began with an apology for the delay, which was often months-long, but she didn't seem to mind and knew something of the issue herself, having her own backlog often at her elbow.

Their main point of divergence was the matter of "little men" (not "little green men," a term rarely used at that time). Though Coral entirely dismissed the claims of Adamski et al., she felt there were some cases worthy of investigation. It was, and would remain for most of his saucer-life, Keyhoe's policy to leave these cases alone because too often the very nature of the people who claimed such contacts undermined the goal he had set himself—to bring UFOs into serious, official consideration through factual data. The contactee stories were entirely lacking in empirical evidence. Like religious adherents, no tangible proof was required, nor offered, to sustain their dogma.

He was, though, cautiously prepared to consider less outlandish claims from at least one trusted source: Coral. In August 1954, she wrote him about an experience she had had with a "strange light" and the reaction of a dog at the scene. Keyhoe responded:

> I don't think it's impossible that the glow you saw came from
> a UFO ... Why a UFO should be over your place I won't
> venture to guess. The obvious answer is, as you said, hard
> to believe—that "they" were aware of your UFO interest. It
> could be coincidence. The action of the dog is very interest-
> ing ...there have been several authentic reports of dogs being
> frightened by something or somebody, not identified.[261]

This was about as far as he dared to go in acknowledging that perhaps
the saucers had occupants, a subject he almost always dodged. He simply
could not afford to be tarred with the contactee brush. For the time being,
however, he and Coral were content to respect each other's slightly divergent
views about the "little men" and each regarded the other as an important and
credible adherent to the principles of objective research.

Their mutual admiration and collaboration, while it lasted, gave both
parties encouragement, support, and motivation to pursue their common aim
in the face of increasing intransigence and obfuscation from all sides.

Chapter 16: Biters Bit

Serious research was given a boost in January 1954, when the "Mars Committee," headed by astronomer Dr. Earl C. Slipher of the Lowell Observatory, announced it was ready to begin coordinated international observations of the Red Planet, which was due to make its closest approach to Earth in June. This study, led from the Lamont-Hussey Observatory in Bloemfontein, South Africa, hoped to find out more about the diameter of Mars, its "aerology" (i.e., geology), and whether or not there was plant life around its famous canals, which were then widely believed to exist.

The study presented opportunities for observations that might explain why an increase in UFO sightings seemed to occur when Mars was nearer the Earth. Keyhoe was excited at the prospect of a dedicated study at such an important time and was sure that this "astronomers patrol ...was certain to focus public attention on Mars just at the time when sightings were expected to increase." Typically, he colored the whole issue with conspiratorial speculations: "the silence group faced a new danger," he wrote darkly, and he was convinced that Dr. Slipher "worried the silence group" because it was rumored that "he, also, was convinced that Mars was inhabited."[262]

This Committee was naturally of interest to Coral. She informed *APRO Bulletin* readers about the Mars project and also reported on Keyhoe's recent April appearance on NBC's new talk/variety program, *The Betty White Show*. Though it often featured A-list celebrity guests—among them Vincent Price, movie-hunk Jeff Chandler, and comedy duo Martin and Lewis—it ran for only a year, but gave the Major a welcome opportunity to talk about the study and to promote interest in his favorite subject. He told saucer-enthusiast Betty:

> We expect a tremendous flurry [of flying saucer sightings] this summer when we near Mars ...They [the Mars Committee] expect to prove that there is actually life on Mars. I was told by some of them in Washington—one of the officials on the project—that the moment they find out any proof, it will be announced publicly. And I think that the Mars Committee is tied in with the government's plan gradually to tell the public what the saucers really are and where

they're from. I think that this summer you're going to hear some headline news.[263]

Betty's show also gave him a platform to air a new grievance against the Air Force that had inflamed him since the beginning of March. A report in *American Aviation* magazine said that the Pentagon "definitely attributes" recent UFO sightings to Keyhoe's *Flying Saucers from Outer Space*. Later the same day, he learned that Senator Francis Case (Republican, South Dakota) had written to Air Force Secretary Harold E. Talbott, asking if the claims in the book—that UFO reports were being withheld from the public—were true.

Brigadier General Joe Kelly (Director of Legislative Law) replied on Talbott's behalf, saying that no UFO information was withheld from the public, to which Keyhoe replied in the press with a counter-statement to this "attack" on him. More fuel was thrown on the fire when a Yale professor asked the Air Force if it had cleared the forty-one cases listed in Keyhoe's book, and if it had analyzed the Utah pictures. He received only a mimeographed reply, signed by First Lieutenant Robert C. White, stating that the Air Force chooses not to comment on the book but that it "was not submitted to the Air Force for authentication prior to publication."

Keyhoe wanted to tackle Kelly personally but couldn't get him on the phone, though he did get through to Lt. White and asked him if it was indeed true that all UFO reports were open to the public. "No-one can see those reports," said White, but denied Keyhoe's accusation that Senator Case had therefore been deliberately misled by Kelly's comments to the opposite. It had been an error, White said, but he fell silent when Keyhoe pointed out that Kelly, as a supposed expert on military law, ought to know better and he wanted a retraction. White said he didn't want to be dragged into the matter and that it was up to Kelly himself to decide if such a statement would be issued. Having thrown his comrade under the bus, he did at least admit that the cases in Keyhoe's book were obtained "on the level."

More dispute arose after Don spoke to Senator Case's press secretary and left with him a copy of the cancelled Utah pictures press release he'd had in his possession for some time. Senator Case then wrote to the Air Force for their comment on this document, but they denied knowledge of it and said they wanted to meet with him. Five days later, no meeting had been arranged and Keyhoe reckoned he and Case were getting the run around, at which point he decided to relate the incident on *The Betty White Show*.

He was still in touch with Ruppelt, who was about to publish a book-length feature, "What Our Air Force Found Out About UFOs," in *True* magazine, detailing his experiences with Blue Book. The day prior to Don's appearance on Betty White's program, the two men got together in Hollywood with Al Chop and Ruppelt's brother Jim at the Roosevelt Hotel. At this meeting, Ruppelt told Keyhoe about a 1953 visual and radar sighting of which, surprisingly, he was unaware. Two Air Force jets had pursued a UFO over Rapid City, South Dakota, and the case "shook a lot of skeptics." When Keyhoe asked Ruppelt to state what he believed, he answered: "All right, here's what I concluded in *True*. If the flying saucers exist, they're interplanetary."

A few years later Frank Halstead, by then one of NICAP's special advisers (astronomy) and a frequent correspondent, wrote to the Major, recalling an interview he'd had with Ruppelt in late May 1957, during which he asked what had been the most "realistic investigation" he had made at Blue Book (the inference being, which was the most convincing case for the interplanetary theory). Ruppelt cited the Rapid City incident, and Halstead felt that, "Throughout his talk he gave us the impression that there was no doubt in his mind, that he, personally believed the UFOs were space ships from outer space."[264] In 1963, Halstead repeated his recollections of this interview to Dick Hall (then NICAP's Assistant Director), with a little extra detail:

> When I asked Captain Ruppelt if he did accept this [the Rapid City incident] as proof, that the UFOs were space ships from outer space, what do you really think about it, he laughed and said, what do you think? Other investigations were mentioned, but none as clear cut as above.[265]

Whether Ruppelt really was leaning over the interplanetary side of the fence or was simply jerking Halstead's chain appears far from "clear cut," but for Keyhoe, his own 1954 discussion with Ruppelt about the Rapid City sighting was compelling and reinforced both his trust in his young friend and his feeling that Ed was coming round to the interplanetary theory.

Despite exposing the recent Kelly farce on Betty's show, Keyhoe received no response from the Air Force, leading him to send a lengthy, detailed telegram to Secretary Talbott, explaining the matter and asking why Kelly's statement had not been retracted.

Meanwhile, two days after his TV appearance, he wrote to Ruppelt, asking him to confirm in writing that he had arranged declassification of the documents cited in his new book and that ATIC's conclusions described therein, were correct:

> It was swell seeing you again, and I certainly appreciate your making that long trip to talk over the UFO situation ... I meant to ask you something, but forgot it Sunday [4th April]. I am going to make a talk in Cleveland [on] the 14th, and Al has—some time ago—given me a few statements I can use if necessary later to back up what I say. Mainly they refer to the fact that the ATIC reports listed in my book were [per Chop's request] declassified at Dayton ... last December 28th, you confirmed this ... however you asked me not to use your messages without your permission ... I'd greatly appreciate it if you could give me either an okay to quote from those messages, or else a new statement.[266]

Ruppelt quickly obliged, sending him the requested confirmation on April 11th (though it was received too late for the Cleveland talk). He added a P.S. to the covering letter, which indicates the nature of their relationship:

> I tried to make it sound as if we weren't especially friends since the AF seems to tie you and Al together like that. I thought it would hold more weight if people didn't say "Oh they are friends and he would say anything."[267]

The Kelly debacle ended three days later, not with a bang, but with a whimper. Air Force officers never visited the Senator, nor did Talbott ever reply to Keyhoe's telegram, though Case received a letter dated April 14, 1954, which made no apology, nor any admissions, and brushed off the matter as merely an unfortunate overlap of information due to an Air Force revision of UFO reports.[268]

* * *

Ruppelt's 134-page article, "What Our Air Force Found Out About UFOs," appeared in the May 1954 issue of *True* and featured his investigations of many famous cases, including the 1951 Lubbock Lights and the 1952 Sonny Desvergers story.[269] In typical "weathervane" fashion, he switched repeatedly between mocking the subject to coming within a hair's-breadth of admitting that UFOs were interplanetary. Readers who might have hoped for a definitive statement from this apparently authoritative source would not find it in his summing up, which he had already given to Keyhoe at their April meeting:

> My own opinion is that either the saucers are interplanetary or they do not exist. I do not believe that there is enough evidence at hand to choose between these alternatives. You can argue either case independently, and in the end you will have only an opinion.

Ruppelt added, in what might be interpreted as a dig at the Air Force—whose clearance he had not obtained for the article—his view that

> The job of Project Blue Book was fact-finding, not specu-lation. Our investigation of the saucer sightings was aimed at compiling as much data as we could, in the hope that it would provide the basis for analysis that would answer the seven-year mystery. The project failed in this attempt.

The article was given little coverage in the press, which noted mainly the lack of any conclusion by Ruppelt. Coral Lorenzen was unimpressed with it, finding "discrepancies in the logic" which she felt "knocked flat" some of his arguments, among them:

> ...where Ruppelt is summing up what he has learned, he makes this statement: "To my knowledge, the Air Force has not concealed any secret sensations about saucers." Those words are a qualification of the whole article. Does Capt. Ruppelt assume that he would know everything going on in the saucer investigation? The final analysis and deductions are handled by the top intelligence agency in this country, and would not be available to a mere captain in the Air Force. That agency is the Central Intelligence Agency ...[270]

Keyhoe wrote to Ruppelt in May and was complimentary, but nonetheless seemed to damn his friend with faint praise:

> Your TRUE piece was a good job, Ed. As you know, I dis-agree on some points, but I think you did a commendable

piece of writing and nobody can say you tried to whitewash the AF. I think you have changed your ideas somewhat since that was written, though.

He added that, aside from the usual saucer-related problems, "we had a car accident and my wife was injured—not too seriously, but enough so that we feared a concussion at first," from which we might speculate that Keyhoe's driving remained flawed. He continued the letter with further reflections on their April get-together and his appearance on *The Betty White Show*:

> I did feel let down [by Al Chop] since he'd said he would put it in writing about an Intelligence colonel helping him write the Utah pix release. Don't let him know I mentioned this—I'm telling you, so you'll know I doubly appreciated what you did [Ruppelt's written confirmation of April 11, 1954], since you're in the same boat, working for an aircraft company with Air Force contracts ... Maybe I'll get out that way again; if so, we might arrange a quiet meeting—I'd be glad to have your brother there, but not Al. He took up too much time that night griping about things, arguing with you ... Don't know whether you saw me on the Betty White show—hope you didn't. Some guy on the staff told me to keep looking back and forth, but not straight at either camera (they usually have you watch for the one with the red light on) and my wife said later I looked like a lost soul. Also, the make-up didn't disguise my hollow cheeks, as one or two make-up jobs had done, before. I probably shouldn't ever get in front of a camera.[271]

In reply, Ruppelt sympathized with Keyhoe's latest family calamity and was "glad you liked the *True* (Magazine) piece. I got quite a few favorable reactions. The 'lunatic fringe' that live under the rock out here weren't too happy, however ..."[272] Three months later, he admitted that the Air Force was also unhappy:

> I find that I got a rather violent reaction to the *True* piece from some quarters. They started screaming Security and yet they say nothing is classified.[273]

Though now embedded at Northrop, Ruppelt continued taking an interest in Blue Book and was being permitted access to its "people." After a 1954 visit to ATIC, he wrote to Keyhoe:

> They claim they have gotten the unknowns down to about 10% but from what I saw this was just due to a more skeptical attitude. The reports are just as good as the ones we got and their analysis procedures are a hell of a lot worse.[274]

These letters from Ruppelt can only have served to reinforce Keyhoe's faith in him and in his own conviction that there was more going on behind the scenes than the Air Force admitted. To that end, Don replied:

> I have heard from sources I think are reliable that there is a sort of "board of scientists" made up of some top men in various fields—astronomy, rockets, space travel plans, guided missile operations, physics, chemistry, magnetics, etc—and that these people all help analyze the important UFO sightings.[275]

* * *

Though the Kelly matter was settled, there was scarcely time for Keyhoe to draw breath before a similar tussle erupted and diverted yet more of his energy and attention. In early June, Lt. Colonel John O'Mara, Deputy Commander of Air Force Intelligence, based at Dayton, became another in the unending parade of USAF officers who, like Sideshow Bob from *The Simpsons*, would tread on rakes in every direction.

This latest farce had come about through the impetuous actions of one Thomas Eickhoff, a Cincinnati businessman and friend of Len Stringfield of Civilian Research, Interplanetary Flying Objects (CRIFO), who had become chafed about contactees Bethurum and Williamson. They were due in town to "peddle" their stories to the fee-paying public, and because, along with Adamski, they never produced the "facts" and "truth" on which their lectures and books claimed to be based, Eickhoff believed they were committing a fraud and it was a matter for the law. He wrote to the FBI in Cincinnati, which made a report to its feared and exalted Director, J. Edgar Hoover. He was a past master at dismissing cases, while maintaining the appearance of still being, as he once was, devoted wholly to his work. In reality Hoover and his lover, Deputy Director Clyde Tolson, had by now become a tetchy old couple who spent most of their working day dining out, but the public bought into the propaganda that portrayed them as a dynamic duo, righting every wrong. The case was, unsurprisingly, documented but not pursued, and the Bureau's response to Eickhoff was that Bethurum and Williamson "were only stating personal opinions which they were entitled to state."[276]

Eickhoff, through his lawyer, also took the matter to "a certain agency," ultimately, he said, prompting a peculiar response from CIA Director Alan Dulles, who said that there was a case to answer but that he would block any court testimony. Moreover, in regard to Adamski's book, because it dealt with UFOs, it was a matter of maximum security. The case was dropped.[277]

Undaunted, Eickhoff and his wife—by some unknown means—managed to have a lengthy meeting at the Dayton base with O'Mara (which surprised some officers there and "puzzled" Keyhoe, as he had been unable to achieve the same). According to Stringfield, Eickhoff had "barged" into O'Mara's office on June 7th and told him he would force a "showdown" over the matter of contactee fraudsters. O'Mara then claimed that Keyhoe's latest book was based on unauthorized material and that his work was fraudulent. Eickhoff reported this to Stringfield, who phoned O'Mara the next day, and he repeated his accusations. When questioned about the Utah film, he at first denied its existence, then admitted it did exist, but said it was Keyhoe's imagination that had interpreted the objects as space vehicles.

O'Mara then made some surprising admissions; the government had "over 1000" leading US scientists working on UFO projects. Among them, Drs. Clyde Tombaugh and Lincoln LaPaz were heading a UFO project at White Sands (which was rumored to be investigating artificial satellites orbiting Earth) and the Air Force was receiving 700 sightings reports weekly. This was counter to its recently claimed eighty-seven sightings, a figure that O'Mara told Stringfield represented "cases under special analysis" but wouldn't confirm that these were spaceships without checking first "in Washington." Strangely, when asked about the alleged artificial satellites under study, he "clammed up, stuttered" and said that the various scientific analyses were "contradictory."

Stringfield told O'Mara he would inform Keyhoe about his accusations of fraud, but the Lt. Colonel, apparently determined to tread on one last rake, said he had the proof "in Washington."

On receiving this news, Keyhoe became angry and threatened legal action against O'Mara if he didn't withdraw his remarks, though his distress was surely made worse by matters at home. Helen already had a heart condition but had recently been diagnosed with cancerous growths, requiring urgent surgery. Thanks to further tests conducted by "a highly reputable Washington surgeon," it was determined that the growths were benign; the Keyhoes had likely been the victims of shyster medics who were fee-splitting.[278] It was not until this new diagnosis was given some weeks later that Don was able to deal fully with the O'Mara situation, but during this unavoidable hiatus, Eickhoff had taken matters into his own hands and things quickly moved beyond Keyhoe's control.

In September, Stringfield again spoke to O'Mara, who embarked on yet more rake-treading. Now he said flying saucers *did* exist, he had not received any information that the mysterious Earth satellites were merely rocks (as had been reported in the press), and he didn't deny his earlier claim about 700 sightings per week. When Stringfield asked if his CRIFO newsletter "was slanted in the right direction" (i.e., pro saucer), O'Mara said "in effect" that it was.

The whole affair rumbled on until December, by which time O'Mara had, it seemed, been hauled over the coals by General Samford, who ordered him to write a letter of retraction and apology to Eickhoff, with copies to Stringfield and Keyhoe. He complied, claiming he had been misquoted and misunderstood:

> I did express to you that I might differ with Major Keyhoe's opinions but never that he was a liar and a fraud.[279]

Keyhoe was relieved that the issue was resolved without litigation, but Eickhoff's impatient actions had inadvertently set back his own agenda, which was to get "the best possible advantage out of O'Mara's" statements. There had been "conferences at the Pentagon, and long distance calls to O'Mara," and moreover, the incident had made the AF "more friendly [to Keyhoe] than they'd been for a long time," which made him feel hopeful that he would have more amenable access to General Samford and others. It was not to be. He informed Eickhoff:

> [T]he only thing I regret is that I was apparently on the point of getting an interview with someone in Intelligence. I was using the argument that you got one with O'Mara, and I should have one, too, especially since I'd been injured by O'Mara's statements … But after this thing came to a sudden head [they] told me that, after this incident, there would be absolutely no interviews on UFOs with any Intelligence

officer ...[280]

In compensation for this, Keyhoe was certain that General Samford had given O'Mara "a tough bawling out," and that his chances of promotion in the future were blighted by the whole affair.[281] To Eickhoff he wrote "I think he's hurt himself, in his Air Force career, enough to repay what he's done or tried to do to me."[282] To Stringfield, he indulged in a little gloating:

> I hope you and Mr. Eickhoff will be pleased that you finally forced O'Mara into a corner and made him squeal. You can know that he is a very unhappy man right now, due to your combined efforts.[283]

As 1954 drew to its end, a final discomfort was delivered to the Keyhoe family when it came down with a virus on Christmas Eve, but Don was still looking to the future. He had at last begun work on his next book, and his overall agenda was unchanged. He wrote again to Eickhoff:

> With the official orders proving the present cover-up, which I intend to publish, I don't see how the Air Force can remain silent.[284]

After months of derailments, Keyhoe was now back on track.

Chapter 17:
The Merry Widows

Due largely to Donald Keyhoe's influence, the 1950s saw the rise of "saucer clubs" across America, but they usually worked in isolation and some served only the contactees, who were largely ridiculed by the media and the Air Force. Consequently, the fragmentary, biased, and inefficient nature of these groups, whether "cultist" (subjective) or scientific (objective) in their aims, was serving only to hamper public understanding and investigation of the "problem" of the saucers. By early in the decade, it had become evident that a coordinated approach was needed to address this perplexing issue, but little meaningful action had been taken to bring it about. Despite APRO's work in this direction, the subject still lacked gravitas, organization, and recognition.

It was in this vacuum that NICAP—the National Investigations Committee on Aerial Phenomena—would eventually form, and it quickly became prominent, influential, and for thirteen years the main preoccupation of Keyhoe's life. But he was not its instigator.

The mantra of NICAP's formation, and the start of Keyhoe's tenure as Director, generally repeats that the organization was first founded in October 1956 by a scientist, Thomas Townsend Brown, known for gravity/propulsion research and for the Biefeld-Brown effect. He was quickly ousted due to fiscal mismanagement and "grandiose" plans for projects that he hoped to fund via NICAP. As a result he and Keyhoe had a heated exchange, following which Brown was shown the door, and thereafter, what became later regarded as "the real NICAP" began under Keyhoe's management. There is, however, very much more to the story than this brief account suggests, and it is inextricably—and to some extent, inexplicably—linked with the ambitions of two elderly widows who were devoted to the turbulent George Adamski.

Most "saucer clubs" varied from handfuls of locals gathering round a kitchen table to larger groups meeting in premises hired for the purpose. Some did little more than review among themselves the latest sightings reports and digest them along with tea and cakes, but others were more structured, inviting guest speakers and publishing newsletters. This latter variety was represented in Washington, D.C. by Iowa-born, Seventh Day Adventist, Mrs.

Clara Louise John (aka Mrs. Walton Colcord John). By the time the idea of what would become NICAP was mooted, she had been twice-widowed, the first time following the death of her husband Ray Leslie in 1924 and the second following the death of her husband Walton Colcord John, PhD, in 1942.[285]

As early as 1948, Clara John was publishing her own bi-monthly newsletter, *The Little Listening Post*. (a.k.a. *LLP*), which she described as "the only publication of its kind." It is "the News in Capsule" and watches everything on a far-out front—especially saucers."[286]

By the early 1950s, the *LLP* was widely read throughout the US and had overseas subscribers. She later formed The Flying Saucer Discussion Group, which would meet at either her townhouse on Illinois Avenue or in the local YWCA, and occasionally at the house she owned in rural Maryland.[287]

Clara John, however—who herself is almost worthy of a biography—was no bored senior looking for an interesting outlet in her declining years. Born in 1889, she had a background in article writing and scientific/spiritual research going back to at least 1918. After she was first widowed, she took up cudgels on behalf of Edison's rival inventor, Emile Berliner, even compiling evidence for Congress to persuade it to find in his favor for inventing the microphone. Her attempt was noted in *Time* (May 1928) and in the general press.

It was specifically due to her efforts that Frederic William Wile wrote his 1926 biography of Emile Berliner, best known for inventing the gramophone record, and he singled her out for praise:

> To Clara Louise Leslie, whose researches in the storehouse of Emile Berliner's papers, books and memories, paved the way to the construction of this narrative, the author's acknowledgements are here rendered. Her enthusiasm and zeal were incessant sources of helpfulness.[288]

Clara's parents, Willard and Anna Colcord, were noted members of their church. Willard, ("a trenchant writer, fluent speaker and fine musician") had taken his young family to Australia when he was a missionary preacher, and while out there Anna wrote a well-regarded early book on vegetarianism, *A Friend in The Kitchen: Or What To Cook and How To Cook It* (1899).[289]

The family returned to the US and settled in Battle Creek, Michigan, moving from there in 1904 to Takoma Park, Maryland, where Clara Colcord and Ray Leslie married in 1907. By 1925, the now-widowed Clara had moved to Washington, D.C., where on Christmas Eve 1929, she married fellow

Seventh Day Adventist Walton Colcord John, whom she may have known at Battle Creek prior to or during her first marriage.[290] At this time she was "a well known newspaperwoman" who had "a special column in *The Washington Post*" and she also wrote a syndicated column, *High Heeling Around Washington*, for the *Evening Star*, which pre-echoed the style and content of her *LLP* newsletter. Keyhoe, also writing for the *Star* at this time, would certainly have known of Clara.

This background of religion and writing informed her thinking, with the result that her "New Age" *LLP* newsletters ("watching phenomena and sleuthing on science") were eccentric, energetic, and eclectic, a multifarious hodge-podge—a blog of its time—in which the author's varied views and interests were aired. Her "followers" were her members, to whom she would mail her newsletters in the US and overseas ("$1 for four issues"). She was entirely convinced by the stories of Adamski and other contactees, and she enjoyed a correspondence with noted, well-connected, Adamski-ite Desmond Leslie (second cousin to Winston Churchill) and received visits from many notorious contactees, including Daniel Fry. He claimed scientific status that had led to him being at White Sands in 1950, from where he was given a ride in a flying saucer.

Notwithstanding Clara John's commitment to the cultists, she often praised Keyhoe's work in her *LLP* or plugged his books and interviews. It's evident that she also kept herself well up-to-date with saucer, military, and scientific news, much of it gleaned from print media. In her newsletter, she typed up selections under attention-grabbing often wry headings, sometimes supplemented by biblical excerpts, which she felt were related "to FS phenomena." Along with "saucerian" items, she reported on a great many topics, including the atomic bomb, postal rate increases, garden birds, juvenile delinquency, and fatherless turkeys.

Somewhat ahead of her time, she expressed concern about declining species, environmental damage, the plight of the world's poor, and even advocated the use and spread of birth control. But where the mystery of the sky was concerned, her evident intelligence and rationality would occasionally lapse into excruciating doggerel:

ODE TO OUR ROCKETS Oh Thor! Oh Atlas! Oh Jupiter! Oh Snark! Oh, when on the MOON we will we all disembark? Go Prowl the skies, Go feel out the way, Only mind you this—Just don't delay! Roar Up, Roar Out, go

defy the Unknown—but the SAUCERS Up There, They
call it HOME! You can split our skies, you can race, you can
Zoom, but to THEM you're no more than a Witch and a
Broom![291]

Despite the diverse content of these publications, they give a strong flavor
of her enthusiasm and her capacity for understanding the connections between
science, military, and individual approaches to the saucer "problem." She was
certainly a cultist, given her faith in Adamski et al., but she was excited by, and
curious about, the future of science and the possibility of both human space
flight and space visitors. Science and the "space brothers," she believed, were
heralds of a new "golden age" for mankind.

Clara prided herself on being the only American female member of the
British Interplanetary Society, which she had joined at the strenuous urging of
her mother, whom she said "had vision." In 1953, she received one of several
personal visits from Arthur C. Clarke, then Chairman of the Society, at which
time they discussed the idea of space stations, and he shared with her his
prediction that man would be on the moon by 1978. Against the expectations
of the time, Clara was a woman confident enough in her own opinions to
supplement those of the illustrious Clarke, and she pointed out that he was
conservative in this estimate. "Look at predictions in the past …twenty-five
years have often turned out to be five," she asserted and believed that, "we
need new frontiers. The world is getting too small."[292]

Among her wide range of correspondents was Ruppelt's "friend" and
member of the CIA's Robertson Panel, Fred C. Durant, who, when a young
man, had been a naval aviator, test pilot, and flight instructor. He'd been
inspired to follow this career path at the age of ten when he saw Lindbergh
fly over his Philadelphia home on the last leg of his US tour, though perhaps
was then unaware that the plane accompanying it carried Donald Keyhoe. In
1953 he became President of the International Astronautics Federation (IAF),
and the following year, just months after he had participated in the then-secret
Robertson Panel, he phoned Clara John and told her he was departing for
Innsbruck, where he was attending the IAF's fifth Congress. Why this sober-
minded scientist, who was among the chief debunkers on the Panel, would
be calling a New Age cultist and telling her of his plans, isn't known. He was
still corresponding with her in 1956, updating her on topics discussed at that
year's IAF Congress in Italy.

Her amicable relations with Durant and Clarke, and her positive mentions about Keyhoe, took nothing away from her devotion to Adamski, and she was instrumental in achieving publication of his first book, *The Flying Saucers Have Landed* (1953). She compiled the various pieces of his story and turned them into a volume that went, via its co-author, Desmond Leslie, to English saucer enthusiast Waveney Girvan of Werner Laurie, a London publishing house. Adamski gave her special mention in the foreword, acknowledging that without her "editing and helpful encouragement ...this book in its present form and at this time would have been impossible."[293]

Thus, thanks to Clara John, Adamski went on to achieve international fame and a decent living, becoming an irremovable thorn in the side of serious research and laying the foundation for the ridicule of the subject that plagued Keyhoe and NICAP and continues to prevail in our own time.

Clara John's interest in UFOs—somehow—linked her with secretive boffin Thomas Townsend Brown, head of the Townsend Brown Foundation, created in 1938 from a $500,000 bequest left to him by his father, Louis K. Brown. It was intended to be a "non-profit corporation" that would "maintain science laboratories, finance scientific expeditions, and award scholarships to individuals for meritorious endeavor in the fields of science."[294] Eight years earlier, Brown had enlisted in the Navy as apprentice seaman, stating that he wanted to "learn radio," an interest that would form part of his later scientific endeavors. [295]

By the mid-fifties he and Clara John "had been corresponding for several years," though on what isn't known, but some of it can be inferred from what survives of her letters to him.[296] The two evidently enjoyed a special relationship, which was not widely known outside their intimate circle. Some of that circle met on Halloween 1955 when Brown, accompanied by his school-age daughter, visited Clara John at her elegant country house in Maryland, where she played the perfect hostess to an all-male gathering, some in suits, others in uniform. Her knowledge of saucer sightings, Brown told his daughter, was because she had some very good "inside sources." Her group, he felt, was very interested in the subject, and he thought it might lead them to join something more formal than Clara's discussion meetings. He envisioned a national organization that would gather information about, and investigate, the saucers.

* * *

A month before Clara's meeting, another widow and contactee-fan, 53-year-old Gladys Rose Hackett (*née* Davis), also Iowa-born, had become Secretary of the new Civilian Research Society of Maryland (CRSM), formed in September 1955 in Baltimore. This club, like Clara John's, had unquestioning belief in contactee stories and was heavily Biblical in tone, but at the same time it appeared to recognize that there were scientific considerations to be made with respect to understanding the saucers. It briefly published the "Maryland Saucer 'Mag,'" of which only two issues appear to have survived.

Rose, as she later preferred to be known, had married widower Dutton Pioneer Hackett, a teacher, in Des Moines in 1924. The couple had three children and in 1948 moved to Seattle, where Rose worked as personnel manager for Field Enterprise, a division of World Books, which specialized in educational publications, but in 1951 Dutton died of a heart attack. By early 1955 Rose had left behind her adult children and a $4,500 per year salary and settled in Baltimore. There she worked as a secretary-typist with "secret security clearance" for VanZelm Associates, a company contracted by the US Air Force for the development of a "heavy bomber overrun barrier" (which was to be installed at Edwards AFB in late 1957).[297] Having made a solo, three thousand-mile "lock, stock and barrel" move, apparently just to take a clerical job, she quickly became acquainted with Clara John—indeed the speed of their association implies that Rose was a subscriber to the *LLP*—and during 1955 and 1956 she visited Clara at her home, as did "saucer researchers" Jim Moseley, Gray Barker, and astronomer Morris K. Jessup.[298] These latter three were already controversial figures in UFO research, though Jessup, despite being later judged as part of the lunatic fringe, quickly became disillusioned with the cultists, privately siding with Keyhoe's scientific, evidence-based approach to the saucers. Clara, presumably unaware of his waning enthusiasm, continued to associate with him and occasionally referred to him in her newsletter.

By this time, Rose Hackett was already giving mention in her own newsletter not only to Clara's group, but also to Keyhoe's work, citing it as a pivotal factor in the thinking of the CRSM's founder, Murray (Morris) Shockett, a Russian-born Baltimore storekeeper who had served in the US Army during WWII and heard tales of foo-fighters. When he read Keyhoe's 1950 book *The Flying Saucers Are Real*, it set him on a path that led him to establish the Society in September 1955.[299]

Within days of the CRSM's formation, Rose had written to Adamski, giving him her "good wishes" and enquiring as to his future lectures.[300] He sent her an encouraging reply, offering to "work with your group in any way possible for the greater understanding of the reality of present day events." He agreed with her view that "we have been given information which clears away much mystery that has existed for centuries regarding the Christian Bible and its records," and he thoughtfully enclosed a brochure which asserted that

> Prophecy will be fulfilled one way or the other: either the Kingdom of Heaven WILL be established on this earth, or the complete annihilation of earth's inhabitants will be inevitable.

As chief prophet of the space brethren, it might have been expected that Adamski would know which of these two outcomes would occur, but this lack of specifics did not take the edge off Rose's adulation.

Clara John's oar was in the CRSM's waters too. In July 1955, when Shockett first advertised for members, she had referred to him some of her own subscribers. Then in November she wrote to his group, forwarding a suggestion from John Otto (who claimed, in 1954, to have made radio contact with space beings) that it send someone over "to give a run-down about your new club" when the latter hoped to give one of his "saucer lectures" in Washington, D.C.[301] By the end of the year, she announced in her *LLP* that the CRSM was "now fully organized" and informed her readers that Keyhoe's latest book, *Flying Saucer Conspiracy*, the writing of which she had been plugging throughout the year, had been launched with a "big Washington press conference."[302]

For these two merry widows, the purpose of saucer clubs was to spread the contactee/Bible message, and inevitably when discussion turned to the need for a national organization, there was no doubt in their minds that such a body should fulfill this function. Their own plans appear to have been mooted as early as December 1955, as indicated by a letter to Clara from Rose in 1957, when the latter was firmly installed at NICAP: "We know that our work of two years ago was not in vain …"[303]

Their ideas merged with, or perhaps underpinned, Brown's own, bringing together this unlikely trio, which very soon would create a research organization like no other before it.

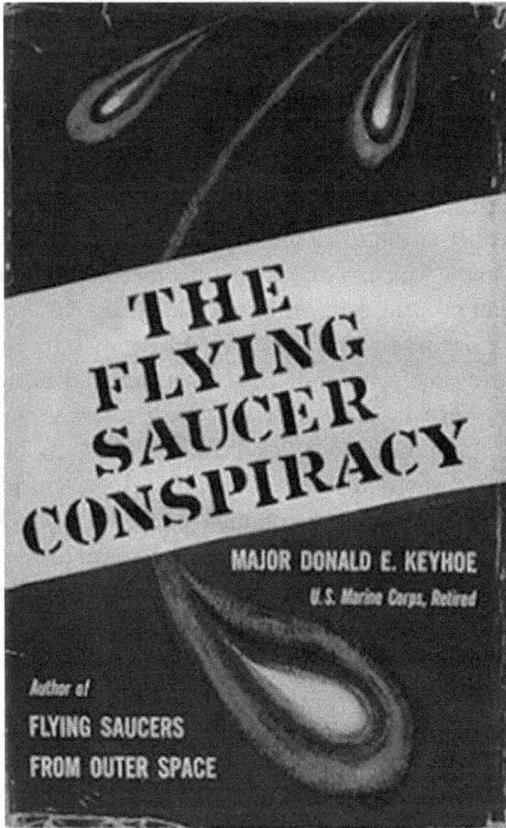

THE FLYING SAUCER CONSPIRACY

MAJOR DONALD E. KEYHOE
U.S. Marine Corps, Retired

Author of
FLYING SAUCERS
FROM OUTER SPACE

Chapter 18:
Ruppelt's Ruminations

Keyhoe's *The Flying Saucer Conspiracy*, which had been so well received by Clara John, was published in mid-December 1955, and from the very first page it hammered the Air Force for its denials about UFO reality. "The Air Force has refused to release any official reports of flying-saucer encounters," he complained in the Foreword and followed up with numerous examples of its unremitting secrecy and denials. The Moncla and Mantell sightings were, of course, brandished as prime instances of how "the silence group" kept the lid on a potentially dangerous situation. He was sure that the "entire globe" was under saucer-surveillance and that hysteria was surely imminent.

The importance of his new book may be judged by the Air Force's chicanery in reaction to it. Keyhoe was informed by one of his sources that release of the AF's *Project Blue Book Special Report No. 14* was being timed with the specific intent to damage any impact his book would have. He recalled:

> A friend of mine, pretty high up in the Pentagon, told me "they're going to let that [the report] go just in time to knock off your book that's coming out in May." I said [publisher] Henry Holt will appreciate that because the book is only about a third written and it won't be out for months and he called me up later and he said they've just found out your book's not coming out and they've slapped this secret label on this and they're gonna hold it. So they held it until October, at which time Len Stringfield who put out CRIFO, made a mistake ... and said ... [the book] was coming out in November ... and that afternoon, at 5 o'clock, Captain Robert White got orders from top side, "Let it go!" so he let it go.[304]

Consequently, in this latest rake-treading blunder, the ill-timed release of *Special Report 14* was denied any impact on Keyhoe's book, and the Air Force's hand was further weakened when, only a month later, Ed Ruppelt published his own book.

The Report on Unidentified Flying Objects was, in its way, a landmark publication. This could not be trashed as the work of a sensationalist, cultist, or money-grubbing attention-seeker. Here were the words of the Air Force's own investigator, whose work at Blue Book was key to the findings of its recently released report. He had seen the data, helped compile the statistics, read the reports, and personally investigated many famous sightings. Running to more than 300 pages, though without photographs or illustrations, his book immediately found its place in UFO history.

This unique account, of a unique time, had been in the works since at least June 1954 when Ruppelt had asked Keyhoe for advice on publishing his own book about the saucers:

> I have been dickering with a publisher for a book, but it isn't firmed up as yet. I have about seven chapters finished. I think that the book will surprise you. It will tell the <u>whole</u> UFO story, which, I can assure you, has never been told before. This is providing that I can get it by security review, but I think that I have this all figured out. As you know, the *True* piece wasn't cleared and I had a different outlook on things then.[305]

Don was keen to help:

> I'm writing HH and Co. [publisher Henry Holt] today and will let you know what they think ... My opinion ... is that HH would not be your best bet, because of my book still being on their active list. Also, unless you had some new evidence which materially changed your "middle of the road" approach, my feeling is that they would not want two books on UFO's at this time.
>
> ...There's one unfortunate angle you probably realize— all these sensational books, Bethurum, Adamski, etc. have made the factual approach seem, by contrast, a little staid. (Even mine, so I'm told.) Your approach, however, would have the advantage of your former official connection, and if you had some new material it might go over with a bang ... If our viewpoints were closer together, I could even offer to help on such a book—but since they aren't, we'd both be

at a disadvantage. I still hope that one of these days you'll discover some dramatic, convincing evidence that will make you a believer like myself ...[306]

Ruppelt wanted advice about giving lectures, so Keyhoe gave him a run-down of the pitfalls, which serve to refute the accusations often made against him that he was making big money off the saucers. This was far from the reality; he had made many errors of judgement, or had been ill-advised, and subsequently lost out. He didn't want his young friend to do the same:

[D]on't sign up unless you get a good offer, better than the one I had. My outfit took 40% of the gross and I had to pay my own expenses. I wouldn't agree to less than a 70/30 split if I talked next season ... You could arrange for evening talks, so they wouldn't interfere with your work—or Saturday and Sunday appearances, before clubs, etc.... If you didn't have to travel out of your area, you would make some money [but] my trouble was that I was scheduled for isolated talks involv-ing expensive travel—to Milwaukee, Kansas City, Buffalo, etc. Considering the lost time, plus expenses, I figure I barely broke even; however I did it at first in order to get more people talking about my book. I learned later that one good TV program, on a network, is worth twenty such lectures, probably worth a hundred of them.[307]

A couple of weeks later, he was giving Ruppelt tips on getting a good publishing contract, which he himself had failed to secure in the past:

Don't believe that deal about doing a paper cover, pocket sized book first. I did it with Gold Medal Books, in 1950, [*The Flying Saucers Are Real*] and my entire payment for one half a million copies sold was about $6,700. If it had come out in hard covers I'd probably have sold 1,000,000 copies, the way things were going then—for that was right in the middle of the big flurry of 1950, with sightings galore [so] try to get a contract clause which gives you the right to hold up the paper edition for a year. I should have done that with Henry Holt and Company; they thought my book would be dead by April, and they sold that reprint deal as of May

1 [and] the very week it came out the hard cover book was on one of the best seller lists, which shows how wrong HH was. They have lost and so have I as a result ... I think you certainly can do a book; I hear that all the phoneys and fakes are going to write new books, so it is time that a solid, honest individual like yourself should tell what he knows. I hope you will give full weight to the evidence on the interplanetary side ... I hope you will get a good deal somewhere and a good "ghost"...[308]

He added:

I'll be glad to advise you as best I can. Even though we don't agree on the final answer, I do think you have been honest with me all the way, and I'll do my best to do the same—and to reciprocate for your writing that letter, about the ATIC clearances, etc. That took courage, and also real generosity. You could have done as Al [Chop] did and wiggle off of it with the same—and reasonable answer—that you didn't want to risk your present job ...[309]

Keyhoe felt confident that whatever Ruppelt wrote, it would be honest, not least because he had written to him, stating: "I wouldn't do a book unless I told the truth exactly as it happened, and believe me this would not follow the party line."[310]

From early on in his research for the forthcoming book, Ruppelt was taking an interest in the contactees. On June 9, 1954, he paid a visit to the Greater Redondo Chamber of Commerce with his Northrop colleague, C. W. Smick, and met with a Dr. William C. Conway. Conway was one of Fry's followers and also the "leader of a small but growing Latter-day Saints restoration sect." For whatever reason, Ruppelt and Smick "both tried to be very 'mysterious'" during their visit, until Conway, "shamed them into revealing who they were ..."[311]

Despite its business-like name, the Chamber was part of the cultist saucer movement and was "primarily interested in Cosmic Energy," a supposedly free power source claimed to have been harnessed successfully by one John C. Roberts. Roberts claimed he had invented power plants that could extract energy from the air and beam it to Earth to provide power for, in particular, farm machinery and "flying saucers." Conway believed that this invention was

156

being "suppressed" by "big wigs" and "vested interests" and said that Roberts had a small model-size working flying saucer, which was similar to Adamski's "mother" ship.[312]

Conway may or may not have known that Roberts had been declared bankrupt in 1941 and sentenced to ten years in jail, not for extracting energy, but for extracting $34K from Missouri farmers who had invested in his phony "wireless power transmission" invention. Presumably his incarceration had not dampened his enthusiasm to try his luck again.

* * *

In January 1955 Ruppelt wrote to his "friend" Fred Durant to ask if he had "picked up some fairly recent information" on sightings in Europe during his 1954 attendance at the IAF in Austria, which might be of use in his planned book.[313] (Presumably, Ed was unaware that his exalted pal had been in contact with Clara John before his departure for that trip.)

For further material, Ruppelt dug deeper into contactee territory. In March 1955, he wrote to George Van Tassel:

> I am doing a book on the history of "flying saucers" for Doubleday and Company of New York. I plan to attend your meeting in the desert on March 13, to obtain material for the above mentioned book. I would like to use a tape recorder in my car consequently I would like to get a parking place fairly close to the speaker's platform if this could be arranged.
>
> I would also like to be admitted to any press conferences that might be held.[314]

Ruppelt and his wife, Liz, attended the convention and both made personal notes, which cast some light on what went on at these gatherings—lots of spouting from the contactees about wisdom handed down from the space brothers, laments about the government, the fate of mankind if it didn't mend its ways, polar tilts, "densities," and sales of books and trinkets to an adoring crowd of all ages. These revered messengers of the space brothers drove and slept in old cars, piled up inside with bedding, books, and assorted paraphernalia. Their followers roughed it similarly, or in tents, and supposedly were so familiar with the sight of saucers that they couldn't be bothered to stay up late and watch one that was scheduled to appear and dutifully arrived the previous night.

Ruppelt followed up the visit with a tape-recorded reading of his notes, describing Daniel Fry's wife as a "crummy lookin' gal" with dirty hair and clothes, and that the daughter "looked pretty ratty," but if she got herself clean she might be "pretty good lookin'." As to Fry himself (later described by Coral as "a lousy electrician, and that was all"), Ruppelt noted that he was the only one with a crowd around him, albeit small, and that he used many electrical terms and references with which he "was obviously really snowing these people."[315]

Amid his occasional yawns on the tape, it can be readily understood that, while Ruppelt found nothing particularly offensive about the personalities of the cult leaders in attendance—which included the big-hitters, Adamski, Bethurum, and Van Tassel (whom he considered to be a "very nice guy" and "very convincing")—Ruppelt personally was not taken in.[316]

His experience at this convention seemed to prompt an idea similar to Thomas Eickhoff's, that the contactees ought to be brought to heel by the law. A few days after the desert convention, he had a telephone conversation with Lt. Robert White, then in the Office of Public Information at the Department of Defense, and they talked about Adamski. Ruppelt told White that the contactees had been "signing affidavits about their stories." White already knew and had spoken to the FBI, which

> …went out there and told Adamski to stop telling people that he has the backing of the Air Force and the FBI. So he took this statement (Adamski made a statement for the FBI that he had nothing to do with the FBI and the Air Force) and altered it to show that they were backing him. He got some gold ribbons with a gold seal and was showing that. Then the FBI went out again and they told him to lay off in no uncertain terms. It's never been seen again.[317]

In reply to an earlier question from Ruppelt asking if "it was possible to prosecute people who perpetrated hoaxes," White advised him that there was no specific law that enabled this, but it may be possible for a private citizen to approach the District Attorney, who might then pursue the matter.

Nonetheless, in the summer of 1955, Ruppelt, accompanied by his brother Jim, visited Adamski at Palomar for several hours. The visit was recorded, and although only part of it survives, it tells us much about the communication styles of both men. When asked a specific question, Adamski would use his tactic of simply steering his answer away into other topics of his choosing, one following another, in a droning, self-serving, often bizarre oration.[318] Ruppelt's response was to politely listen to Adamski's ramblings and rantings, using the rare breaks in his disconnected verbiage to ask questions or make comments that gave the impression—at least to Adamski and his secretary, Lucy McGinnis, also present—that he was taking Flying George seriously. It might be expected that, on returning to their car, Ruppelt and his brother exchanged much eye-rolling and guffawing.

In the end, the contactees were given little attention in his book, which was published in mid-January 1956 by Doubleday & Co. "I'll give you the facts— all of the facts—you decide," he said in its foreword, making it clear that, despite his time at Blue Book, his discussions with Keyhoe, and the criticisms about his lack of conclusion in his *True* article, he still wasn't committing himself. His employer, Northrop, reported on the book somewhat limply in an internal memorandum:

> We are pleased with Mr. Ruppelt's achievements as an author
> and his recognition as being an authority on "flying saucers."

The memo also noted that 10,000 copies had been sold in the US, 8,000 in England, and a French translation was nearing completion. Moreover, it seemed he was now on the saucer-celebrity bandwagon:

> Mr. Ruppelt has served as guest lecturer at numerous dinners
> and luncheons (including most of the industrial manage-
> ment clubs in this area) and has served as technical consul-
> tant on the recent United Artists motion picture, "Uniden-
> tified Flying Objects." He also has been technical consultant
> for several television productions, and has appeared as guest
> on the "Paul Coates Show."[319]

The Air Force, however, said:

> As with any free-lance author, Mr. Ruppelt's theories, opin-
> ions and conclusions are his own, and not necessarily those of
> the Air Force. His book was reviewed and passed on by Hqs
> USAF from a security viewpoint <u>only</u>. While most of the
> statements in his book are factual, the inferences and implica-
> tions that he attempts to leave are definitely questionable. As
> project officer [he] was considered competent in monitoring

investigations, and collecting and correlating data for analysis. However, he was not an expert in such highly specialized fields as astrophysics, meteorological optics, psychology, radar, and photography. In sightings with these aspects or implications the Air Force has relied on many scientists and specialists, whose conclusions are considered more valid.[320]

From this chilly response, it can readily be inferred that Ruppelt's "conclusions" and "inferences and implications" were interpreted by the Air Force as supporting the interplanetary theory, thereby lending support to its main critic, Donald Keyhoe.

Reviews otherwise were generally favorable, though there was a feeling among a good number that, given Ruppelt's inside-knowledge, he should have been able to settle on, or at least lean toward, one position or the other. Noted science fiction author Arthur C. Clarke wrote:

> [O]ne is tempted to say he is the only author of a book on UFO's in a position to write about them, and it would clear the air … if all earlier volumes could be mercifully forgotten … Captain Ruppelt does a very creditable job of fence-sitting, but it is obvious that he will not be at all surprised if UFOs do turn out to be spaceships.[321]

Elsewhere, while lauded for being informative, the book was described as "bafflingly inconclusive," and "curiously indecisive," but Coral Lorenzen's opinion was scathing:[322]

> It seems conclusive that he had done what so many saucer writers are inclined to do, and that is to assume himself into the position of the foremost expert on the SUBJECT OF FLYING SAUCERS. In our opinion, the prerequisites for such a position is that that the nominee be driven by curiosity, respect for truth and tenacity. Ruppelt was literally tossed into the job, didn't particularly want it, and as an Air Force officer was beholden to conceal that which higher authority deemed judicious to conceal … [T]he book, although informative and interesting, did not particularly exhilarate old-time researchers in the saucer field. We particularly did not relish the underhanded snide remarks inserted here and

there throughout the text which seemed deliberately discrediting to Donald Keyhoe ... Ruppelt must make a choice—either he doesn't know as much about the UFO question as he claims, or he is not telling all he does know ... THE TRUTH ABOUT FLYING SAUCERS comes a long way from living up to its title ... [A]ll in all, the book was good reading, informative in parts, but certainly not on a par with any of Keyhoe's works.[323]

Despite the grammatical and factual errors in her review (Ruppelt, was not "literally tossed into the job," and his book was not called "The Truth About Flying Saucers") her visceral, negative critique showed her continuing strong support for Keyhoe.

According to UFO researchers Michael Hall and Wendy Connors, the book was undoubtedly written by Ruppelt himself, even though he had suggested to Keyhoe in 1954 that he might use a "ghost." The "snide remarks" to which Coral referred were therefore his own and were certainly a slap in the face for Keyhoe who had done so much to help him. The protégé had ungratefully slated his friend and mentor:

It is rumored among magazine publishers that Don Keyhoe's article in *True* was one of the most widely read and widely discussed magazine articles in history.

The Air Force had inadvertently helped Keyhoe—in fact, they made his story a success. He and several other writers had contacted the Air Force asking for information for their magazine articles. But, knowing that the articles were pro-saucer, the writers were unceremoniously sloughed off. Keyhoe carried his fight right to the top, to General Sory Smith, Director of the Office of Public Information, but still no dice—the Air Force wasn't divulging any more than they had already told. Keyhoe construed this to mean tight security, the tightest type of security. Keyhoe had one more approach, however. He was an ex-Annapolis graduate, and among his classmates were such people as Admiral Delmer Fahrney, then a top figure in the Navy guided missile program and Admiral Calvin Bolster, the Director of the Office of Naval Research. He went to see them but they couldn't help him. He knew that this meant the real UFO story was big and that it could be only one thing—interplanetary spaceships or earthly weapons—and his contacts denied they were earthly weapons. He played this security angle in his *True* article and in a later book, and it gave the story the needed punch.

But the Air Force wasn't trying to cover up. It was just that they didn't want Keyhoe or any other saucer fans in their hair. They couldn't be bothered. They didn't believe in flying saucers and couldn't feature anybody else believing. Believing, to the people in ATIC in 1949, meant even raising the possibility that there might be something to the reports.

The Air Force had a plan to counter the Keyhoe article, or any other story that might appear. The plan originated at ATIC. It called for a general officer to hold a short press conference, flash his stars, and speak the magic words "hoaxes, hallucinations, and the misidentification of known objects." *True*, Keyhoe and the rest would go broke trying to peddle their magazines.

Ruppelt jibed at Keyhoe's account of this 1952 press conference, at which he had questioned General Samford:

This bit of reporting makes Major Keyhoe the greatest journalist in history. This beats wire tapping. He reads minds. And not only that, he can read them right through the walls of the Pentagon. But I'm glad that Keyhoe was able to read the General's mind and that he wrote the true and accurate facts about what he was really thinking because I spent quite a bit of time talking to the General that day and he sure fooled me. I had no idea he was worried about what he should tell the public.

And he wasn't done yet:

The *True* article did come out, the general spoke, the public laughed, and Keyhoe and *True* got rich. Only the other magazines that had planned to run UFO stories, and that were scooped by *True*, lost out. Their stories were killed—they would have been an anti-climax to Keyhoe's potboiler ...

Keyhoe had based his conjecture on fact, and his facts were correct, even if the conjecture wasn't ... To say that the book is factual depends entirely upon how one uses the word. The details of the specific UFO sightings that he credits to the Air Force are factual, but in his interpretations of the incidents he blasts way out into the wild blue yonder.

Lee Munsick, in his own North Jersey *UFO Newsletter*, called the book "a must," as did Len Stringfield in his *Orbit* newsletter, though a few weeks later, he wrote to Keyhoe:

> Ruppelt's book is good, but he's highly critical in places ... Noticed his jibes at you, but this was probably a "condition" put to him by AF in order that they clear his book. At least this is my opinion and this is what I have told those who inquired about Ruppelt's rancor.
>
> Ruppelt wrote me recently and I quote one choice part: "To be very frank with you, about all I can agree with in many issues [of *Orbit*] is the date in the masthead but I must say that you have an extraordinary ability to put together a clever newsletter. Actually, I get a great deal of enjoyment out of reading it."
>
> Well, I guess that puts me in my proper spot.[324]

Stringfield may have been correct about a "condition" being imposed on Ruppelt. Keyhoe later wrote:

> In 1956 no letter was received [from Ruppelt]. Ruppelt later told me he was embarrassed because he had felt it advisable to "take a few digs" at me in his book ... He said that some AF officials suspected (mistakenly) he had tipped me off to hidden UFO cases during 1952-3.[325]

In what was to be one of his last letters to Ed, Keyhoe offered him absolution:

> I want you to know that my own silence has not been, as you may have thought, due to the little digs that you took at me in your book ... Also, I wish to heaven I had gotten rich, as you said. Actually I was making more money the two years

before I started researching UFO's than I have any year since
...[326]

Their written exchanges leave no room for doubt that, despite Ed's published sneers, Don still felt sufficient trust in, and affection for, the man he thought was his friend. If these feelings were reciprocated, they were hidden, as Ruppelt's later letters would show. Soon, he would embark on a shabby rejection of Keyhoe, his friendship, his work, and the entire UFO subject.

Chapter 19:
Strange Bedfellows

As January 15, 1956, passed through midnight, Clara John was typing a letter to Townsend Brown:

> I've been asked to give the Adamski-Leslie tapes again—two tapes you haven't heard … I know you will want to hear them …
>
> I promised the subscribers there would be "more on gravity" in the next issue of The Little Listening Post. I'm hoping to be able to go over that Dan Fry tape with you and have left the tape recorder all set up here—the way we talked about it. I somehow have a hunch about leaving Thursday of this week open—that is—Thursday evening, January 19. Hope you can find time to crowd it in. Please let me know.

It's not clear to which Fry tape Clara refers, but the Adamski/Leslie tapes were popularized in 1954, thanks to devotee Fred Dickeson, who had founded the Adamski Correspondence Group in Timaru, New Zealand.[327] Copies were distributed around the globe and were considered essential listening for Adamski-ites. Among them it seems, was Thomas Townsend Brown, a man of hard science, allegedly working on classified projects for the Navy, who was not only in frequent contact with cultist Clara John, but also willing to give up his valuable time to listen to contactees expounding their space-brother beliefs.

In February, Brown was preparing to leave for Europe and had asked Clara if there was anything he could do for her while there, to which she replied with the address of one of her subscribers, an "engineer" in Oslo, whom she said "MUST be working on saucer propulsion." She also suggested he contact the British Interplanetary Society in London because there were

> … many hundreds of top notch scientists in it and I can't believe ALL of them are necessarily hardheaded <u>rocketeers</u>. I think most of them don't quite know what to make of this

saucer thing … I've been a member for years … and have had many arguments with Arthur [C. Clarke] about saucers. I always predicted to him that we would get the satellite by rocketry but when we went beyond that it would be by some other kind of power. Told him he could call it a woman's hunch if he wanted to.

She closed cryptically:

Will be waiting to hear more about that "new organization" you mentioned.

Hope you have time to drop a line. And plenty of God-speeds go with you…You probably sense by now that I mean to HELP catch this thing—no foolin'.

PS: That line on the first page of The Little Listening Post about the TOOL OF RESEARCH—I scribbled on a bit of paper in my purse on the way down town—and two days later you came out here and told me you were a teacher of Research Methods—It struck hard![328]

This referred to an item in her February issue of the *LLP*, which said that Washington, D.C., due to massive government investment, was now "being called 'CAPITAL OF SCIENCE'—Govt. sold on Research! WITH THE TOOL OF RESEARCH MAN CAN CLEAVE THE HEAVENS!"

Evidently, this tied in with some discussion she had had with Brown—presumably two days after the publication of that month's *LLP* (February 3rd)—which suggests that their talk was relevant to his European trip.

Three weeks after his letter from Clara, on February 26th, Brown was in Leesburg, Virginia, living with his family in a grand house, which they had rented for an extended period. In his notebook, he wrote his ideas for laboratory experiments on "1. The Change of Angular Velocity to Conserve Angular Momentum, 2. the Disc-Type Inertial Differential Electrogravitic Motor, and 3. The Impulse Effect in the Force Developed by a Simple Capacitor in Vacuum," in other words, disc propulsion.[329]

Eight days later, Townsend Brown arrived at the Orly airport in Paris, but little is known of his activities there (or for that matter, anywhere else). Arriving later in London, he reconnected with his estranged son who was then in service with the USAF and stationed in England.[330] From there, he went on to Cheltenham, the beautiful Regency spa town about 100 miles west of London, which then was home to GCHQ—the Government Communications Headquarters.

He was accompanied by a former "soldier, sailor—and a spy," known as "O'Riley," who, in wartime, had been assigned to protect him during a mission in Germany.[331] On April 15, 1945, Brown had parachuted behind enemy lines and on landing had been met by O'Riley, whose instructions were:

> ... not to let this man out of my sight ... I had been told that my only real job was to "escort" Dr. Brown. That meant I was to make sure he didn't get himself killed.[332]

He had also been instructed that, in the event of his charge being captured, he was not to be taken alive (though, as it turned out, in the absence of O'Riley, Brown was said to have been shot in the shoulder and was lucky to survive). As to Brown's mission in Germany, his protector later told an interviewer:

> I must tell you with the interest in "foo-fighters" you are getting much closer to the main reason TTB intended to be in Germany. On one level it was the interest in the cipher machines but that was not the first thing on his particular laundry list. Dr. Brown often said that if you want to see how nature utilizes his "force fields," that answer could be found in the "plasma vortex" sometimes called "ball lightning." So when reports of "balls of light that seemed to be under intelligent control" reached others in the military that were familiar with Brown's work, he was put immediately into the front of the search party.[333]

Now, eleven years later, the two men were in Cheltenham, apparently at GCHQ, where Brown's scientific activities remain unknown. However, O'Riley recalled:

> I can't say much ... but I can say that Dr. Brown developed a listening device at Cheltenham that was far superior. It caused quite a stir, especially the way he sort of just "whipped it out there" full-grown. And [the British] held on to it as long as [they] could to clean up [their] own backyard. Then the Americans finally made a deal with Dr. Brown to follow his "tunnel diode" ideas with submarines out of Florida. He figured that it was an important "second step" and that he

figured was worth having that sort of wherewithal—as he put it—behind him.[334]

Brown's European visit had been brief. He departed by ship, the French SS *Liberté*, from Southampton, England, on March 29th, but his mind was still on what would appear to be saucery-matters.[335] On April 4, 1956, he was back in Leesburg, where he continued to make notes on propulsion and where the family was joined by a close friend, thirty-three-year-old Helen Brasee Towt, a former WAVE, who by 1951 was employed as a clerk at Wright-Patterson AFB. The group were seated around the kitchen table and discussion turned, as it had done before, to Brown's idea for a national organization to study UFOs, and they pondered what such a body should be called. From an assortment of words bandied between them, Towt suggested National Investigation Committee on Aerial Phenomena. "Committee," she pointed out, was "a word that always got people in Washington to sit up and take notice."[336]

Chapter 20:
The Grandiose Plan

Meanwhile the Keyhoes, despite Don's deepening commitment to UFOs, were continuing to enjoy life. He still had enough money to live well, even though he had "done very little lecturing lately" because it didn't pay; some offers were so low they wouldn't even cover expenses.[337] Still, the couple owned their magnificent home in Alexandria, were saving for their girls' college education, and in general, setting aside concerns about Helen's health, were happy and secure, living moderately high on the hog.

The happiness of their daughters, however, was less evident to their neighbors, who felt that the girls were neglected, and this feeling added to Don and Helen's unpopularity with local residents. They observed how the girls were dressed (frequently in plaid), as though they were from "an impoverished community in Alabama," and how they often bickered with each other at the bus stop on the way to school. The local maid, who worked at several of the properties on the street, commented that "them Keyhoe girls aren't treated right" and felt that Don and Helen were "so mean to those girls." Their non-identical twin-ship was reflected in both their appearance and their character. Caroline was unusually small and had a pleasant disposition, in contrast to Kathleen, who was tall, thin, and "always in a bad mood." Considered locally as being "a bit weird" and "outcasts," neither girl was part of the usual social scene typical of their generation. The neighbors felt rather sorry for them.[338]

Whatever Don and Helen thought (or didn't think) about their daughters' condition, in late July the couple embarked, *sans* twins, in New York for a 13-day luxury cruise on the *Ocean Monarch*, travelling first-class to Bermuda, for which they paid between three and six hundred dollars each (multiply by ten for the equivalent today).[339] The ship offered what then passed for high-level tourism (pool, cinema, and American food with a European slant), but the Keyhoes had no idea that this trip would be the last, relatively carefree time of their lives.

During their vacation, NICAP—which was already on Keyhoe's radar—had been taking shape, but that shape was being formed to no small extent by Clara John. She had written to Brown on July 14th, asking if he could attend the fourth meeting of her recently-formed Flying Saucer Discussion Group:

> M. K. Jessup is going to be the speaker. Perhaps you know
> him personally. He's an astronomer, you know, and one of
> our most prolific saucer authors ... He was here at the Lit-
> tle Listening Post the other night and we made a tape ...
> Another thing one keeps hearing mentioned is the idea of
> some central research organization or "Foundation," proba-
> bly located in Washington, for coordinating this whole UFO
> study. Mr. Jessup is the third man to have mentioned it to
> me recently. I think this subject may come up at this coming
> meeting.

This letter seems rather odd, given that months before, Brown had already talked to her about the Washington "Foundation." He clearly was part of her private inner-circle, which, as noted earlier, included some "very good sources," and raises the possibility that such obliqueness in her correspondence was deliberate. Clara John evidently had a clandestine life ticking away in the background that enabled her to have discreet social gatherings, outside the city, with men "in suits, others in uniform" and with Thomas Townsend Brown, a super-secret scientist working covertly on, among other things, propulsion. He so highly rated this Washington widow's knowledge of saucers that he discussed with her at least some of his work and set aside valuable time to meet with her and her fellow "New Agers." Why?

The answer may come from Brown's daughter. She said that her father believed there were other "entities" who have "always" lived on our planet and who allowed humans to retain their warlike nature because it served a purpose—it protected them against other beings from outer space who cared nothing for mankind and might take complete possession of the Earth.[340]

Such a belief was well within the range of Clara and her fellow cultists and certainly raises not only many intriguing possibilities about Brown's value to these believers, but also leaves us to wonder who else was among her like-minded contacts. Indeed, four years later, Clara would come under scrutiny from the FBI, whose partly redacted records infer that she was in receipt of secret documents supplied by a source in the Pentagon (see Chapter 31).

The tape recording of Jessup to which she referred briefly touches on the idea of a special study organization:

> Jessup: ... it's more urgent than it's ever been before that a

worldwide reporting system be set up and a centralized clear-
ing house be organized so that if the governments are going
to put pressure on, or smear the whole field into a ridiculous
state, that those who really know what's going on can get the
information ... I would honestly like to see some organization perhaps subsidized or financed —
Clara: You mean a civilian organization?
Jessup: A civilian organization of people who are serious
about the subject—we're never going to get it from our government ...
Clara: There's a lot of talk about that.[341]

This idea had been on Keyhoe's mind too, since at least 1953, by which
time it had already become apparent that "no lone-wolf investigator could
hope to crack the secrecy wall." That year, he had received a letter from
Abraham M. Sonnabend, president of the Hotel Corporation of America,
"suggesting such a group ... Leaders in other fields agreed," as Keyhoe later
recalled (though didn't specify who these leaders were). Sonnabend would
later serve on NICAP's board.[342]

While the "talk" between Clara John and Townsend Brown continued,
the Keyhoes completed their vacation, returning to the US on August 10th,
but if Don wanted to keep his attention on Brown's new venture, he had a
minor, but nonetheless aggravating, matter to deflect him, which somewhat
typified the difficulties he had to endure.

He was still enjoying the balmy shores of Bermuda, when in the movie
section of the *Tribune Star* (Terre Haute) of August 5, 1956, amid cheesecake
shots of screen beauties Yvonne de Carlo, Jane Russell, and Virginia Mayo,
his name and his work were credited as the inspiration for Columbia Pictures'
Earth vs. The Flying Saucers. The movie had been showing around the country,
paired with cheapo second-feature, *The Werewolf,* since June.[343] He was
aghast at this sort of accolade found in numerous other newspapers that year,
and insult was added to injury because the opening titles of the film were
emblazoned with, "Suggested by *Flying Saucers from Outer Space* by Major
Donald E. Keyhoe."

He wrote to Coral Lorenzen (after his usual delay in responding) and
lamented the circumstances that led to his association with this work of fiction:

First, I very much resent being misled into thinking this was
to be a documentary picture. Second, I refused to make per-

171

sonal appearances with the film. My publishers, Henry Holt
and Company, sold the film rights to "Flying Saucers From
Outer Space" to Clover Productions, which I understand is
a subsidiary of Columbia Pictures. An official of Clover Productions, and the Hollywood agent who handled the matter,
both assured me it would be a documentary film—dramatized, but fully documentary as far as the saucer items were
concerned ... I did not serve as technical director, as some
Magazines have stated. I did not go to Hollywood, never
talked with the producer, director, or anyone else out there,
after Holt signed the contract. I did agree to make personal
appearances if the film was, as I was told, documentary—a
dramatized version of the "search for the truth." Incidentally,
the relatively small amount paid for the film rights certainly
convinced me it was to be a documentary—not the science
fiction thriller I understand it turned out to be (I have not
seen the film and from what I've heard about it I don't intend
to.) ...

I apologize to the many sincere readers of mine who
went to the movie because my name was used to promote it
... I should have been smarter ... I've learned my lesson; if
another movie deal ever builds up I'll get a lawyer to handle
my part.[344]

Released at the same time, in a somewhat astonishing development, there
had indeed been a serious documentary film about the saucers: *Unidentified
Flying Objects: The True Story of Flying Saucers*, which was a dramatized,
carefully accurate recreation of the 1952 flap, as experienced by Al Chop
(played by Tom Towers), Dewey Fournet (played by Floyd Burton), Ruppelt
(played by Robert Phillips), and the radar operators who watched the event on
their screens. The film, on which Ruppelt was adviser, fully vindicated much
of Keyhoe's position—though omitted any mention of him—and revealed
that the Utah film had been analyzed, as he had earlier claimed. Both it and
the by-then famous Montana film were also shown. This short color footage
was taken in August 1950 over the Legion Ball Park in Great Falls, Montana,
by Nick Mariana, the general manager of the "Selectrics" baseball team. It
showed two luminous, fast-moving round objects traveling across the sky at
up to 400 miles per hour. The Air Force examined the film, denied Mariana's

accusation that it had returned to him an altered version, and dismissed the objects as aircraft. But now the footage was included in a film that gave serious treatment to the UFO subject.

It seemed that, at last, the USAF had performed something of a striptease, peeling away veils of denial, to reveal the near-naked interplanetary truth—or at least, a strong suggestion of it. The Air Force however, denied it had been involved with the film and had a ready-prepared statement to that effect, which pointed out that only former USAF officers were advisers to the film makers. Yet, despite the impression the movie gave and its nationwide showing, it was considered to be rather out of date and captured little attention. Some audiences drifted out during showings, which demonstrated that if the Air Force had ever been concerned about panic in the streets, this surely ought to have been sufficient evidence to prove that Americans would not lose control. Regardless of its authenticity, it was a damp squib.

Chop would later confirm that the film was "very accurate! Extremely accurate!" and added:

> Frankly, I didn't think much of the film ...because it was too honest. There was no bullshit ... I didn't get anything out of it ... the film didn't make a trickle.[345]

Fournet, Ruppelt, and Chop each had "a small percentage" in the film, though its failure meant they received nothing, but it did instigate a friendship between Chop and former silent screen star Gloria Swanson.[346] She was now in her late fifties but still fit and slender, as was evident when Al, after an, unexpected personal invitation, went to her home and found her standing on her head in a yoga position. She was keenly interested in the saucers, and after having seen Chop portrayed in the film, she "just wanted to talk about UFOs." The two of them kept in touch for some years after and he found her to be "a very lovely person." She later became a NICAP member and in November 1957 Keyhoe visited her at The Statler during her brief stay in New York. They discussed the problem of Air Force secrecy and Gloria encouraged him to keep fighting against it. She added that her main interest in UFOs was "the fascination of those other worlds" and the beings inside the saucers. Don admitted to her that "I've let that part get sidetracked" and when he left her suite, he "felt a tinge of the old excitement. Before NICAP it was the lure of the UFO mystery, the hope of finding a link with other worlds, that had kept me going. But that had been obscured in the fight against secrecy."[347]

Coral Lorenzen, still one of Keyhoe's biggest fans, wrote her thoughts on

Unidentified Flying Objects: The True Story of Flying Saucers in the September
APRO Bulletin:

> I feel that our friend Donald Keyhoe should have been given
> credit in the picture. (Editor's note: Mr. Keyhoe will prob-
> ably never receive credit for what he has done in relation
> to the saucer mystery, and certainly not in a picture which
> was executed with the aid and collaboration of the Air Force.
> There seems to be an effort underway at present to disqualify
> Mr. Keyhoe and the Director would like to go on record at
> this time as saying that as long as she directs APRO she will
> never have any derogatory opinions regarding Mr. Keyhoe's
> efforts on behalf of the UFO problem. He has done a com-
> mendable job—that's good enough for us ...)[348]

Keyhoe replied:

> Thanks for the mention [but] about my not getting credit
> in the picture ... I knew all about that film from the month
> the contract was signed; also the producer [Clarence Greene]
> certainly was quite familiar with the Chop story, from the
> way I told it in FSFOS. He didn't introduce anything new
> that I know of—except the copies of the Utah and Mon-
> tana films. But I'm not squawking about the lack of credit,
> for the film did a good job and has convinced many former
> skeptics.[349]

These unsatisfactory Hollywood offerings were insufficient to divert him
from his fervent mission, and he continued to spread his opinion that the Air
Force must end its secrecy, and that Congressional hearings should be held to
bring this about. Congress, he believed, was honest and powerful. It was only
necessary to give it the facts about sightings and it would do the right thing.
Keyhoe would be personally vindicated, the people would have "all possible
information," and there would be dancing in the streets. Now that there was
movement toward establishing a special national civilian group devoted to
the objective study of UFOs that might assist in these goals, it occupied his
intense interest.

Richard Hall (later to become NICAP's Assistant Director and general *factotum*) explained the focus of the proposed group:

> Soon after NICAP was formed in late 1956, one of the main
> goals established was to press for Congressional hearings as a
> step toward bringing scientific attention to UFOs. Hearings,
> it was felt, would clarify the problem and bring out informa-
> tion about the scope and seriousness of the phenomenon.
> Hoaxers would be exposed, and serious fact separated from
> misinformation. Then it would be possible for scientists and
> others to lend their skills to a thorough investigation, with-
> out fear of ridicule. An equally important result would be a
> more regular flow of reliable information to the public.[350]

How much Keyhoe knew of what had been going on in the background
of NICAP's formation, and for how long, isn't clear, but Townsend Brown
and Clara John had been busy. Brown had indeed attended the contactee
group's meeting, held at the YWCA on July 20th and he recalled it years later:

> The need for an organization to gather information on
> sightings became apparent. I pondered over the problem for
> quite a time. During this period Clara John was quite active
> gathering books and information on UFO's. She held many
> meetings with her friends "in her garden". I attended some of
> these gatherings and we together discussed the need and pos-
> sibilities of a group to study and report sightings. The first
> meeting of about ten persons was held (I believe) in one of
> the meeting rooms of the YWCA in Washington. I had pre-
> pared for presentation at that meeting a tentative prospectus
> of an organization which would take the form of a non-profit
> corporation, organized expressly for the nationwide surveil-
> lance of UFO sightings.[351]

At the end of this meeting, Clara made a speech:

> Today there are thousands of little research groups all over
> the world, as well as people working singly on this thing.
> The time has come to coordinate their activities into a pat-
> tern that will prepare humanity for this startling new event in
> human existence. Where better than in Washington for this
> movement to take shape and direction? That is what these

175

meetings are being called for. This, tonight, is our fourth meeting. We (have been) laying the groundwork the last couple of weeks, and you here tonight are perhaps witnessing—and we hope will be participating in—a new step, an unprecedented history-making step ...[352]

This "groundwork" was almost certainly on what to include in Brown's prospectus for NICAP, about which he had been taking advice from Clara on how to get it across to her discussion group, whose approval seemed to be essential. Her letter to him of August 13th suggests a hidden agenda between the lines:

> But MOST of these people are the type objective scientists might refer to as research "fans." I don't know if you plan to have some scientists present. The thought has come to me that one "safe" way to have the meeting would be for you to present the new Prospectus; then have a pre-picked panel to discuss it at a table up front. But at the start of the meeting—distribute little tablets of slips of paper and pencils and ask all present to write down their best contributed thinking as the meeting progresses—and hand it in at the close. This could be valuable for digesting when there was time for it later. It would also be a time-saver and would eliminate the danger of getting off into by-ways by those who perhaps did not get the full concept in so short a time ... This is just a thought. You may have some better idea.
>
> Am awaiting report of further progress since last Tuesday.

In this missive, she mentioned that she'd received a "most cordial" letter from Courtland Hastings, who hoped to attend the upcoming meeting. Hastings was vice-president of Civilian Saucer Intelligence (New York) (CSI-NY), created in 1954, and he now found himself included in Brown's plans for the new group; he'd been invited to become "a NICAP director."[353]

On August 16th, Brown again met with Clara's contactee-fan group and presented to it his "Tentative Prospectus" (dated August 11, 1956) for the "National Committee for the Investigation of Aerial Phenomena to be known as Project Skywatch," though it was changed in the final version to "Skylight." (This too was dropped in early January 1957, following contact from the

National Aviation Education council, advising that their own publication was named *Skylights*.)[354] "It was well-received and everyone both endorsed it and vowed their support for the project."[355] At some point after this, Clara wrote, apparently to Brown, that her group nonetheless had concerns about where the money for the new venture would be found, and added:

> They need to develop an <u>assurance</u> that "outsiders" with no heart interest in their beloved subject are not pulling some string. Some are afraid it leans to objective science (rocketry). Others are afraid of the reverse and that inclusion of the "Psychic" means that it will get off from the <u>factual</u> balance ... Our "liaison" angle between these two approaches is as new as it is desperately needed ... and the MYSTERY (unprecedented) with which we are dealing now demands this dual approach—an ALL-INCLUSIVE approach.[356]

This approach, which seemed so essential to Clara and her followers, would in effect be the one taken by NICAP and which Keyhoe would quickly realize was impossible to maintain, but that was yet to come. In the meantime, the Tentative Prospectus, which would be little changed when it was finalized, showed that Brown's plans were indeed "grandiose," being more suited to the founding of a major industry or academic institution than something formulated and approved by a little suburban saucer club. Moreover, he intended to study "Abstract Interpretations" of the phenomenon, including "psi concepts," which Clara John evidently thought might be a stumbling block for some of her group.[357]

He estimated that salaries alone would run to $101,500—around $1 million today—and envisaged a minimum staff of twelve, ranging from file clerk at $5,000 per year up to Director at $15,000 per year.[358] A Board of Governors would be selected and there were to be six classes of membership ranging from "Founders endowments" of $1000, $15 for Regular members, and $7.50 for Associate members. Honorary memberships were free but would only be awarded by "the unanimous action of the Board."

His ideas for funding were certainly ambitious and many were similar to those which had appeared in earlier proposed projects (see Chapter 21). NICAP would draw its income not only from donations and membership fees, but also from (a) Lecture tours (nationwide) under Committee sponsorship, (b) Motion pictures produced under Committee sponsorship, and (c) Illustrated technical lectures to aircraft, electronics, and materials industry by staff members using copyrighted material.

Further, it would derive income from "technical consulting services by staff members" given to press, TV library research, the motion picture industry, the aircraft industry, electronics, fuels, space medicine, construction materials, along with "franchises, copyrights, patent licenses on material developed by the Committee or donated to it."

No less ambitious were its aims to publish Project Skylight, "a monthly scientific journal" and "Space Flight …a popular magazine with photographs in color." Sales of this latter publication were expected to "easily support all of the operating expenses and public services of the Committee" and it also expected to be tax exempt (though the IRS did not allow this until 1970).[359] As with the aims of Brown's 1938 Foundation, it intended to grant awards "for meritorious effort or achievements in science," and now would include awards "for significant discoveries." The Committee would also support "scientific research or related investigative projects by financial assistance or otherwise" and aimed "to conduct physical and chemical analyses of materials taken as evidence."

It appears that Courtland Hastings attended this meeting and, as a result, declined Brown's offer of directorship. He later said:

> I've been familiar with [NICAP] … considerably before Donald Keyhoe became Director. I had known the previous director … the man who organized NICAP, but er, when I went to Washington to look into it and at that time the former Director had proposed that I be a Director of the organization, upon investigation of it, it didn't seem to be set up properly to do the job that it was supposed to do and er, therefore I sent regrets regarding the honor which was offered …[360]

On August 29th a meeting of the incorporators was held, at which Brown was appointed "Executive Vice Chairman *pro tempore*," with the intention that a successor would replace him, after which he would "assume a vice chairmanship for direction of the Committee's scientific affairs."[361] NICAP's certificate of incorporation was filed that day, having been signed the day before by Brown, Mary V. King, and Thomas D. O'Keefe, and witnessed by Joseph Lapiana Jr., Notary Public.

Amid these wildly ostentatious plans, Rose Hackett evidently had found high favor with Brown, for he appointed her NICAP's secretary. She had by then become engaged to a sixty-nine-year-old widower and "rich man" named Duncan Cameron "Cam" Campbell, who worked as Supervising Financial Officer at the Federal Housing Administration in Washington, D.C.[362] In May 1957, he had written an essay titled "Truth and Flying Saucers," which pondered how "truth" might be applied to the subject of saucers. The piece was dotted with Biblical references and made only restrained allusions to the "subjective" approach. Though it was faintly tinged with New Age ideas, it was a fairly rational piece, coming from the by-then husband of a devout cultist.[363]

According to NICAP's 1971 account of its own history, Campbell at some earlier time had introduced Rose Hackett to Brown, but she undoubtedly already knew of him—and he of her—thanks to Clara John. Campbell would be appointed temporary treasurer in September 1956, and his "close friend," Dr. Garrett Chamberlain Rush II, former lawyer and retired chiropractor, was appointed his Deputy.[364] Texas-born Rush, who personally knew contactee George Hunt Williamson, was in his early seventies and had been admitted to the Texas Bar in 1932, but his career had subsequently been centered on supervisory admin work with the Veterans' Association and his chiropractic work was on a part-time basis.[365] This small, eclectic group was a long way short of the minimum twelve staff envisaged in Brown's prospectus, but it was a start and Clara began "spreading the word" of NICAP's inception.[366]

She announced it on August 30th in a special *LLP* press release, informing her readers that the new organization would "act as a liaison between objective science and abstract interpretations in this field"—though the latter goal was not mentioned in the Certificate of Incorporation. Money was "already flowing in," she proclaimed—or at least $100 had been subscribed in late August by one individual. Clara nonetheless tried to create the impression that the public were tearing around the streets, frantically waving the prospectus, unable to contain their excitement:

> This announcement is bringing a surging that is palpable! ... People are alerting libraries, showing the Prospectus to bookstores, discussing it with their bankers and telling their friends. It is as though the floodgates had been opened and long-confused and pent-up forces had a last found a safe and orderly outlet through which to flow toward some great new horizon!

Meanwhile, in the real world, Keyhoe was keeping a close watch on the new group's formation and had "helped to secure Board members," among them his former Annapolis pal, Delmer Fahrney, who in addition to his work on guided missiles had become a key figure in the development of "pilotless aircraft," familiar today as drones.[367] He was by now a retired Admiral but for his own part was not yet officially involved with NICAP.

As the launch date for the new Committee drew near, Keyhoe notified a few confidantes, among them Coral Lorenzen:

> I know all about it, as they've been getting my advice for months … I've tried to steer them away from the obvious dangers, and if they get started as planned this may be a big deal, and powerful enough to force a showdown … Everyone tied in with it is trying to keep the crackpots from muscling in—it's especially important not to have them even in the dim background when the story is released. I've recommended that I be kept out of it, at least for a while, and I'm not even signing up until I see it is going to be a high-level organization and that I can do some good. Confidentially, I expect to have a hand in running their monthly publication when they get underway. I may serve as an unlisted consultant—I don't know yet.[368]

Coral followed this up with her own letter to Brown offering her co-operation, while blowing APRO's trumpet a little ("we are not small, have representatives throughout the world as well as several hundred members in this country"). She added that she was "slightly peeved" that her and Jim's recent scheduled appearance on popular TV show, *Do You Trust Your Wife*, had been scrapped "out of consideration for the Air Force." With this off her chest, she added in a P.S.:

> Watch out for the screwballs and crackpots—they creep in so easily. However—I wouldn't discount all accounts of landings and little men—we've found that many are as fully corroborated as some of the "classic" sightings.[369]

Brown never got round to sending her a personal reply, but he had been in touch with Ruppelt. On October 18th, he wrote to say that he counted him among "a few public spirited leaders whose forthrightness and intellectual honesty are established." He added, by hand, "We would especially welcome you on the Board," but his invitation evidently was declined.[370]

Though Keyhoe was keeping a low profile, his correspondence with friend and admirer Len Stringfield gives a picture of his involvement and his expectations during NICAP's gestation:

> I've had a big hand ... in getting them started ... The man who started it is T. Townsend Brown ... an inventor ... called visionary, impractical, etc., and also a level-headed scientist. He worked for Navy on a special gravitics project about a year, then they killed it (so they said) and told people (like me) that it added up to nothing. I think he is, like most of us, interested in making a living and could be called a promoter type. But I've watched this thing carefully—I've refrained from joining for several reasons—and if they follow the plans laid down (which I helped develop) it may become a well-known, high-level organization, able to force action in Congress and at the Pentagon ...
>
> They hope to get enough big names to use ... to prevent ridicule of the outfit. That's the key; I've hammered on at them for weeks not to announce anything until they get at least four or five big names to use ... I'll be behind the scenes, for a time at least, because I don't want any newspapers to try to use me to kill off NICAP. Let the big names carry the weight for a while; meantime, I'd be planning the first issue [of NICAP's magazine, Skylight], working up connections, etc. I would not be the editor—I would be either the top editorial consultant, or special advisor, but actually I'd run the magazine, at least for a while ... I'm trying to guide them right, keep the crackpots at arms' length, and leave no loopholes for wisecrack news stories.

He assured Stringfield that NICAP would work with both CRIFO and APRO, adding:

> Oh, yes, one angle I forgot ... Exactly what this means to me, personally. First, it's a chance to get rid of all the mass of un-answered mail—via letters printed by NICAP (on my stationery) apologizing ... It also means a chance to keep abreast of UFO developments without extensive work—their library

and research section would be available. Instead of writing another book (which I don't want to do) I could now and then write an article for Skylight (a name I don't like) and keep my hand in. I can develop new contacts, see what's going on behind the scenes. All this would be <u>part</u> time ... Right now it's a complete loss of time—I've donated many days, and a lot of ideas ... Added to all this is the feeling of being in on a <u>big</u> operation ....[371]

To Keyhoe, NICAP appeared to offer a real opportunity for meaningful input into an organization that could achieve his long-held ambition: to end Air Force secrecy and bring UFOs out from the disreputable shadow of contactee claims, into public and official recognition.

For the present, he expected to remain in the background and "let the big names carry the weight." As to the future, whatever his reservations, it was surely worthwhile to stick with this promising new venture and see if its exciting potential would be fulfilled.

Chapter 21: The Iceberg

Although Don was keeping out of the public eye during NICAP's gestation, he was willing to get involved in raising funds. Brown needed money and lots of it to finance his ambitious plans and was casting about for rich donors. In the first week of October 1956, he had written to 83-year-old Mrs. Anne Archbold, a noted "unconventional" wealthy socialite and daughter of John Archbold, founder and former President of Standard Oil. Brown had already met her "on several occasions ... to discuss the work of Major Keyhoe and others on the subject of aerial phenomena."[372] He asked if the three might get together to discuss NICAP's program and invited her to become "one of the ten Founding Endowment members."[373] They did meet and Keyhoe would later approach her twice more, but no donations were forthcoming.[374]

Lack of funds aside, it became very clear within weeks of NICAP's launch that Townsend Brown was not the man to lead the organization he had devised and which had been so enthusiastically supported by Clara John and her crowd. The serious UFO research community soon had misgivings about his credibility, finances, and past achievements, but these formed only the tip of a very strange iceberg. There was another story behind these doubts, apparently unknown outside of Brown's confidential circle. NICAP was not the first failed "grandiose" scheme he had instigated that had been created as a moneymaker to fund his own ambitions. Moreover, he had recently worked with "scientists" of dubious academic status, and among NICAP's forthcoming Board of Governors and their associates were men with CIA backgrounds or links. Richard Hall, later NICAP's Assistant Director, noted that, "Among the organizers were two people with past CIA connections: Nicolas de Rochefort and Bernard J.0. Carvalho."[375]

Little is known about Carvalho, though it's thought that he operated from within one or more CIA-front businesses. He was born in San Antoa, Portugal, in September 1919, the son of a watchmaker, and by age 21 worked in Boston, Massachusetts, as a printer for McKenzie Engraving.[376] When drafted in WWII, he "waived his rights as an alien" and served as radio operator/gunner on a Catalina-Navy PBY (flying boat) during action in the South Pacific, for which he was awarded the Distinguished Flying Cross Air Medal with four oak leaf clusters and the Australian Flying Cross.[377] He became a naturalized

US citizen in 1943 and by 1945 was stationed at Scott Field AAF Training Command radio school.[378] Ten years later, he was a director of "a Washington Hometown News Bureau" and had formerly headed "a group of Washington publicists."[379] His work for McKenzie Engraving may have led to his post-war position as "plate printer" and "adjutant" at the Washington Bureau of Engraving and Printing.[380] From at least 1966 to June 1970, he was Director of the USO (United Services Organization) in Fairbanks, Alaska, and then was transferred to the Tacoma, Washington, branch. In January 1971, it appears he was implicated in an "accounting discrepancy" in Fairbanks and was then no longer "employed in any capacity by the USO or any of its affiliates."[381]

The only other information available in the press and public records (aside from that pertaining to his marriages/divorces) tells us that by 1956 he and his then-wife Melba Mitchell were acolytes of Indian guru Meher Baba, who believed himself to be God in human form. How Carvalho was linked to Townsend Brown isn't known, but they both had in common their radio work and their esoteric leanings, though perhaps Carvalho's involvement with the aforementioned "Washington publicists" had brought them together.

In 1957, Brown issued NICAP's January Progress Report, which announced:

> Mr. Bernard J. O. Carvalho, Major, USAFR, Washington, DC., was named Special Adviser for the organization and implementation of the magazine, "SPACE". By resolution of the Executive Committee, Mr. Carvalho is authorized to explore the possibilities of a contract or franchise with various publishers [and] as Chairman of the Membership Subcommittee, Mr. Carvalho is now engaged in developing plans for a membership drive, together with ideas for appropriate national advertising.[382]

Russian-born De Rochefort is better documented generally, but as to his CIA activities, there is more speculation than confirmation. He had arrived in the US in 1949 and the same year was appointed to the faculty of Georgetown University, teaching summer courses in French government and politics. De Rochefort became a naturalized American citizen only in 1954, but by this time he was already a Defense Department adviser on psychological warfare and also a University teacher of political science.[383] The FBI was interested in him during 1956 with regard to whether or not he was a Commie working for the Chinese, but ultimately it determined that he was anti-Commie, in part because of his activities for the Committee For One Million Against the Admission of Communist China to the United Nations (COM).[384] How he came to be on board with NICAP isn't known, but several of those involved at the time of its incorporation had similar political/idealogical links.

Morris Jessup, who had been "very close to the horse's mouth from the beginning," was already aware that the new Committee was being formed under the aegis of "an active and competant [sic] group in Baltimore who want to help, and who have access to a small publich [sic] relations and fund raising company." The identity of this "group" is unclear, but the PR firm to which he referred was Counsel Services. Located on West Monument Street in Baltimore, it had members and clients with links that give it the flavor of itself being a CIA-front. It was launched in March 1947 by an odd trio: Mary Vaughan King, Leo H. McCormick and L. G. (Levin Gale) Shreve. Mary King— yet another Iowan—was born Mary Stoy Vaughan and studied at Yale, where she gained degrees in dramatics and theatre lighting, leading to her later becoming a lighting consultant, specializing in its domestic applications and therapeutic qualities. In 1931, newly resident in Baltimore, she authored *Importance of Lighting in Occupational Therapy*, and in 1942 she married stockbroker Francis E. King Jr. He was at that time with the OPA—the Office of Price Administration in Baltimore—a body formed to oversee wartime rationing prices, from which he resigned in November 1945. Mary had earlier joined her husband at the OPA and stayed with it after his resignation, working then as assistant to Baltimore native Leo H McCormick, state director of the organization. He was an insurance executive who also occupied high-level positions in local frozen food businesses. In May 1947, he joined the Board of the newly-formed Eastern Shore Distributors Inc., just two months after becoming co-founder of Counsel Services.

Shreve, who later wrote spy novels, served in the Army from 1941 and was promoted to Major in 1943, at which time he was "public relations and orientation officer." He served in the Pacific under Admiral William F. "Bull" Halsey (the aforementioned cousin of Adamski acolyte, Wallace Halsey) and in China on the staff of General Albert C. Wedemeyer—later a NICAP governor—becoming adviser to Chiang Kai-Shek, the leader of The Republic of China. He retired from the service in 1946 with the rank of Colonel, and that same year, due to his work for the Chinese leader on rural development programs, he was recruited by the CIA.[385] This work involved providing audio-visual aids to educate the population, under the auspices of the Economic Cooperation Administration (ECA), an agency created to administer the post-war Marshall Plan. In 1950, Counsel Services was under contract to the ECA for the provision of farm-production information in Europe and sent its "specialists," who had done the same work in China, to deliver this service. The ECA is alleged to have been a CIA-cover operation.[386]

Among Counsel Services' clients was CIA agent Colonel Ulius Louis Amoss, a man who had dedicated his life to espionage, which he described as "the second most ancient profession in the world, not as honorable as the first, nor as much fun."[387] During his wartime Army career Ulius "Pete" Amoss wore a number of hats:

> Director of the OSS [Office of Strategic Services] Near Eastern Desk, intelligence; Deputy Director, OSS, for sabotage, intelligence, psychological and guerrilla warfare; Commanding Officer, Experimental Detachment G-3 UASFIME; and Deputy Chief of Staff, U.S. Ninth Air Force'[388]

Post-war, he became founder and president of ISIF—International Services of Information Foundation, Inc.—"a non-profit, privately owned and operated intelligence service whose purpose was to collect and disseminate information from overseas countries," but which is claimed to have been a "CIA commercial cover."[389] In June of 1953, Brigadier Thomas B. Catron, who had retired from Army service in 1949, became a trustee of ISIF and by 1956 was serving on Townsend Brown's NICAP Board of Governors. (He remained on the Board for a few months after Keyhoe's Directorship began in 1957.)[390]

Among its activities, the ISIF attempted—and failed entirely—to assist disaffected Soviet Communists to escape Russia, including Stalin's son. This venture had been funded to the tune of $50,000 by noted anti-Communist millionaire Clendenin (or sometimes, Clenendin) J. Ryan Jr., whom some allege was a CIA agent.[391] According to one source, in 1955, Mary Vaughan King played an early part in bringing about this funding through a "complicated chain of contacts," though it's fair to note that this Amoss-Ryan endeavor was no secret.[392] Like other ISIF projects of this nature, it was reported in the press; indeed, Amoss himself gave his own account of the case in the *San Francisco Examiner* on Nov 8, 1953.

One of Amoss' claims to fame was the invention of a men's hair colorant, "Grecian," based on an ancient Greek formula that in 1955 was advertised in the press by Aegis Products, Inc., giving the same address as Counsel

Services.[393]

By December 1954, while Keyhoe was mopping up after the Eickhoff/
O'Mara debacle, Brown had become of interest to the cultists. Edward W.
Hermann, special agent for McGraw Hill publications, had been investigating
him, his Foundation, and one of his associates, Mason Rose, on behalf of
Meade Layne, a noted spiritualist. He'd founded the Borderline Sciences
Research Foundation (BSRF) and held many occult notions, including belief
in an alien presence on Earth.[394] Hermann was a member of this group and
felt that, as he worked "at the cross-roads of the business-industrial press," he
was well-placed to make enquiries relating to the interests of the BSRF:

> [I]t is my job to be particularly interested in any develop-
> ment in science which may have a direct or an indirect im-
> pact on our vast industrial technology. As a part of my code
> of personal responsibility to my job, I believe it to be vitally
> important to keep my ears "to the ground" for anything and
> everything that might be a clue to a news story ... That helps
> explain why I am a member of a rather unusual organiza-
> tion headquartered in San Diego: The Borderland Sciences
> Research Associates, headed by Meade Layne. At first blush,
> one might be tempted to say "A bunch of quacks?" My un-
> reserved, unqualified answer is NO ... a bunch of top-flight,
> intelligent scientists who are not afraid to explore the un-
> known.[395]

His investigation discovered that Counsel Services was secretly the
location of The Townsend Brown Foundation, which had been located at
other addresses over the years, including Connecticut Avenue in D.C., and
Adamski's old stomping ground, Laguna Beach, California.

Hermann also learned that by 1952, Mason Rose—sometimes referred
to as "Dr."—was "the principal promoter" of the Townsend Brown
Foundation when it had been located in Los Angeles, and Rose described
himself as the President of "The University of Social Research."[396] He had
written a "white paper" on the Biefeld-Brown effect, explaining how it was
relevant to Townsend Brown's research on saucer propulsion, in the hopes of
encouraging private funds for this work. He founded his alleged University
with the aim of "advancing world happiness and unity through selected
research projects," but its only project was flying saucers. His "university"—
though supposedly chartered—had no students; it considered itself to be a

"social and scientific laboratory." Rose hoped to "persuade the United Nations to set up a commission to make interplanetary contact for the furtherance of harmony in outer space." He believed that if mankind continued to make atomic explosions, "the saucer men" might get rid of the human race.

The idea that alien beings were keeping a worried eye on Earthmen and their dreadful weapons was not confined to cultists. Keyhoe himself had written about this in 1951, following "five recent atomic explosions" in Nevada. He postulated that saucers were the "observation devices" of intelligent space beings and predicted that the recent explosions might bring a "sharp increase" in sightings reports that spring. These tests, he thought, were being observed because they represented a "danger to the solar system."[397]

On April 8, 1952, the *Los Angeles Times* reported on Mason Rose and his link to Townsend Brown's research, featuring also the third man in his Foundation, Bradford Shank (a.k.a. W. Bradford Shank). The trio were photographed in front of a "twelve-foot pillar" topped by a horizontal arm, from which two flying saucer-like discs were suspended. Rose told reporters that "they have solved the flying saucer mystery" due to Brown's discovery that they function "in a field of 'electro-gravity.'" It mentioned also that for four years, Brown had been working in his basement on a "barometer" that could predict stock market behavior by registering variations in the cosmic rays that reach Earth from space, allegedly influencing human psychology.

Other newspapers carried similar reports, giving the impression that Rose and Shank were credible boffins, but none mentioned that Rose was most famous as a "Hollywood psychologist," who lectured mainly to women's groups (about 400 per year) on marital issues and war neuroses, and had at least one piece published in *Cosmopolitan* about the tribulations of former child-stars.[398]

Shank, who claimed no scientific qualifications, was a "teacher at a public school" in Chicago in 1940, but by the time he was involved with Brown was reported to be a former physicist with the Manhattan Project, under which capacity, in 1946, he wrote a series of newspaper articles for the Los Angeles *Daily News* about "problems created by the release of atomic energy."[399] By 1950 he was "vice president" working in "electrical research" and was referred to in the press as being on the faculty of George Pepperdine College, a Christian university.[400] Not mentioned in the general reporting, but frequently found in the classified ads, is that he was also a Scientologist lecturing on "Dianetic Auditing," a supposed psychological method of trauma release devised by Scientology's founder, L. Ron Hubbard, to whom, Shank claimed, he had been "formerly special assistant."[401] In 1952, the same year Shank was working with Brown, his spiritual leanings were further expressed when he published *Fragments*, a book of his philosophical poetry. One verse, from his poem "Testament," forecast events in a style Clara John would have approved:

A time is coming
When an integration of things now known
Will point clearly
And directly
To man's salvation.

Poetry and religion aside, his—apparently—serious work with Brown didn't appear to detract from his sense of humor, when in October that year, he performed in mustachioed-drag with a barbershop quartet for the delight of a PTA group in Los Angeles.[402]

As to Mason Rose's *bona fides*, Hermann's 1953 research found that his "University" didn't exist and that he had "latched on to a report" (the Biefeld-Brown report) written by Townsend Brown and "rewrote it to suit himself, cooked up a fake 'University of Social Research' merely for a letterhead and issued it …"[403] Hermann would later be told, from information relayed to him that originated from Brown himself, that the Mason Rose report was "ok" and "in essence it is correct and there is nothing secret about it, nor does he [Brown] care much who does the writing."[404]

Not mentioned by Hermann and presumably unknown to him was Rose's criminal background. In February 1942, he was accused of inflicting "serious bodily injury …with his fists and feet" on a 49-year-old man in Arizona.[405] His later success as a speaker on psychology was briefly tainted in 1960, when he and six others were arrested by the FBI for theft of a meat truck and its contents in Vernon, California.[406] Three years later, he was back in circulation, now described in the press as the "Dean of the California Institute of Applied Science," which, like his "University," may also not have existed.[407] Why and how Brown had linked with Rose and Shank, two men of highly questionable backgrounds and with new age mindsets, is perplexing.

With regard to the Townsend Brown Foundation, Hermann initially wrote, "There is considerable mystery about the Foundation. I could find no trace of it listed among the foundations at National Research Council. Nor at Nat'L Bureau of Standards. No listing in Washington telephone book …" but after further digging he learned:

> Off the record he has used up most of his funds trying to build flying saucers … Brown applied to Basic Research Corporation for funds but after the Board looked into it, the application was turned down. No flying deals, it was agreed. This is the Corporation [he] joined as chairman of its advisory board after he left the Atomic Energy Commission.[408]

He noted also that Counsel Services was

> … an outfit that goes in for fund raising for research purposes. Our Washington reporter talked with the advisor of this office, telling him that he was a science writer. He seemed suspicious and said Brown was away but that there was a big program in the offing, that he was working with the Department of Defense on it, and with the law firm of Jansky and Bailey … <u>They want no publicity</u>.[409]

By late October of 1952, Brown had submitted, through Jansky & Bailey, the "big program": a "Proposal for Joint Services Research and Development Contract" called Project Winterhaven.[410] This was a pre-echo of his later elaborate plans for NICAP, which events would show was merely another vehicle to achieve funding for conducting his own research. Winterhaven's aims were manifold and ambitious. It would participate in "philanthropic enterprise," assist charities and "religious institutions," build laboratories, fund "scientific expeditions," and even "grant awards, scholarships and endowments for meritorious effort or achievement in science, art and literature." Most curiously, it intended to promote sculpture, "dramatics," and ballet.

These objectives were no more than window-dressing and are referred to only in the list of Purposes at the start of the report, perhaps in a "catch-all" attempt to garner funds. The project really intended to undertake "pure research" into four areas: inductive effects, tidal computations, anomalous behavior of massive high-k dielectrics, and fundamental physics, each to be carried out by separate, highly-renowned institutions. The Department of Defense was proposed as the "Prime Contractor" handling "the administration of government contracts" and the funds obtained would then be distributed among "eight cooperating organizations under appropriate subcontracts."

This "pure research" would "prove the controllability of the gravitational wave, a fundamentally new system of communication" in order to "solve many of the difficulties inherent in present-day radio and, at the same time, provide countless additional channels for communication." Brown believed this would "provide a secret, almost wholly untouchable, channel for classified military communications."

The idea that any of the foregoing research might be relevant to religion and the arts seems spurious. Similarly pretentious, Winterhaven's proposal to award grants for "meritorious effort" in science had already been put forward by Brown's Foundation's when it was created in 1938 and is almost identical to one of his proposals for NICAP four years later.

Project Winterhaven did not come to fruition. In 1971, Brown recalled that "it was never approved by the Defense Department, but interest in its possibilities continued for several years."[411]

The FBI was interested in the Townsend Brown Foundation, too. In 1953, following claims that his Foundation had ripped-off two Los Angeles businessmen to the tune of $60,000, the Bureau reported that, despite being based in "luxurious, aesthetic offices," the enterprise was a lure. One potential investment broker pulled out because he felt Brown et al. "looked like a bunch of gyps" with a proposition that was too good. This proposition appears to have been in connection with a gravity-defying propulsion device, which Brown claimed was of interest to several high-profile organizations. According to the report, this device had been found to be merely "a static wind machine as is exhibited in any college physics laboratory." In short, the FBI concluded that the Foundation was a "fraudulent enterprise" and the principals were "either frauds or security risks," taking money from gullible investors.[412]

Whether or not Brown was a huckster, by 1955, with his Foundation apparently revived and now located at Counsel Services, he seemed to have set aside his scientific ambitions. Due either to fiscal distress, desire to support his in-laws, or, according to one source, possibly as part of a planned, covert action to discredit himself, he opened the Embassy Laundry in Washington, D.C., which he operated with his wife's parents, Clifford and Sara Beale.[413] Hermann wrote:

> The Townsend Brown Foundation no longer exists ... so now TB is in the laundry business establishing a chain of automatic laundries at colleges and other institutions across the country. He hopes to make enough with his business to eventually reactivate his now-defunct Foundation.[414]

How much of this Keyhoe knew isn't clear, but he would soon be privately expressing his doubts about Brown to others. It seems unlikely that Brown ever had enough money for his projects, as he never personally contributed toward NICAP's new set-up (though he would tell a correspondent that he had put in $1,000).[415] In fact, he was so strapped for cash that in August 1956, just as the new Committee was being incorporated, he had borrowed $25 from Clara John, which wasn't repaid until January 12, 1957 (with $0.68 interest). He added that he was "grateful for the lift that this timely loan has given the Committee" and boasted, either quite erroneously or with blatant falsity, that the hoped-for funds were now coming in. They were not.

Before its doors were opened, NICAP was already in trouble.

Chapter 22: NICAP

"I wince when anybody refers to 'flying saucers' ... but actually that's what we're after. We want to know whether they exist ... and we think it's high time," stated Townsend Brown on October 23, 1956, when the press first reported the birth of NICAP. He added that eventually "we'll have money in the bank—$2,000,000 or $3,000,000."[416]

Reported as *pro tempore* executive vice-chairman (but no reference was made to a "chairman"), Brown said he would return to London "as research director for Whitehall-Rand" and that he was "also a consulting physicist in Paris for a French Aircraft company."[417] These plans did not bode well for any future level of commitment to NICAP; it suggested that he was going to give birth to the baby and then put it up for adoption, while he went away to live a more fulfilling life. Nonetheless, in keeping with his ambitions, the office at 1536 Connecticut Avenue—a prestigious location—was acquired and furbished. NICAP, with a brass plate at the door bearing its name and Project Skylight, was now, supposedly, open for business.

An early visitor to the organization's spiffy new office was a friend of Keyhoe's, Robert Serling, brother of the famous Rod Serling, who is best remembered for TV's *The Twilight Zone*. Robert was aviation reporter for UPI and he called in at NICAP "about a month" after it was opened, noting that it was located in one of the "swankier" neighborhoods of the city. The office was spacious, nicely appointed, and at the time of his visit had only three occupants: Brown, Jessup, and a "rather distinguished looking woman" (Rose Hackett) who greeted him pleasantly until he told her he was a reporter, at which point, "her face froze about 40 degrees." Serling talked with Brown and Jessup, learning that the latter was connected to NICAP "in some way," but found that they were "reticent" in discussing their organization because it was new and not yet ready for publicity. Serling was told that Brown had plans for an "ambitious five-year study" to be funded in part by NICAP.[418]

Serling sent this information to Ivan T. Sanderson, the noted and frightfully posh British naturalist, whose interests included cryptozoology, unexplained phenomena, and UFOs. Soon after receiving Serling's letter, Sanderson went to lunch in Washington with Keyhoe, during which it's clear that Don's previously high hopes for NICAP had eroded because he now expressed a dim view of those involved with the new organization. He was "not impressed" with Jessup, had "warned Brown about Clara John" (she had visited the new office early on), and was "very wary about the whole thing— Brown & money angle specifically."[419]

After their lunch, Sanderson, accompanied by Don's old comrade, John Daly, went to visit the NICAP office "sans Keyhoe" and came away "puzzled." He had some of the same impressions as Serling, though with many more doubts about its founder.[420] He felt that there was "something funny" about Brown, finding him evasive and vague, especially in regard to key issues such as finances, investigative staff, and membership numbers (in regard to the latter, Brown said there were "oh, about 90"). Sanderson, in any case, was already somewhat miffed because he had earlier offered to join the organization and thought it suspicious that Brown had not responded. The notes of this meeting also record that somehow involved with the set-up was an "ex-FBI man," and that "Mrs. John has nothing to do with NICAP."

Brown's vagueness accords with Serling's earlier observation that he was reticent and seemed in no hurry to have publicity, though there were plans to publicize the outfit. Martin Heflin (brother of movie star Van Heflin), a public relations man employed by Counsel Services, was now "the group's fundraiser." He had been engaged to take care of publicity and was given the title "Chairman of Public Relations."[421]

As to Brown's future intentions, Sanderson's notes record that Colonel Emerson of Louisiana was being considered to replace him "when/if [Brown] returns to White Hall Rand."[422] (Emerson remained and would later serve under Keyhoe.)

Jessup's own reticence and his undetermined status with NICAP become clearer through his correspondence and give us an insider's view of the turmoil and uncertainty that immediately arose during what would be Townsend Brown's brief tenure. His letters to Gray Barker during 1956 and 1957 reveal both his own reasons for involvement and his grave misgivings about Brown and the new organization. He told Barker that he had "been very close to the horse's mouth" from the very beginning and that

> Brown is not a Saucer man, and knows almost nothing about
> UFO personnel over the country. Has not read the books nor
> mags. Flounders a lot at meetings. Doesnt [*sic*] fully recognize
> the difference between a local club and a national organization
> and has conducted meetings at the local level which is a mistake

and has slightly antagonized the local club ...He is appointing officials from the fringe group but trying to get Board members from the anti-UFO crowd. He has a host of UFO people wanting to help and looking to him for leadership which he is not yet able to supply because of unfamiliarity with the subject ... His purpose seems to be the creation of an income position for himself and a friend or two, which is OK, but he has not seen the necessity of getting someone of broader experience to run the show for him. He has done everything possible to get me to step in and supply the business and UFO know-how, but the one thing that would interest me: a paying job at the top level. The original moving spirit was Clara John of the Little Listening Post, and certainly if she is left to make suggestions the fringe crowd will take over. There is an active and competent group in Baltimore who want to help, and who have access to a small public relations and fund raising company, but I am beginning to doubt whether they can function with Brown's academic attitude ... on the positive side ... is [office manager] Rose Hackett, who gave up a $4500 govt job in Baltimore and moved over to DC, lock, stock and barrel. She is very religious on the UFO slant and has been working on a UFO-Bible for two years. She is REALLY dedicated to UFO, and will not let the NICAP fold if she can help it ... [NICAP's] plans are objective and very comprehensive so that no facet of UFO lore is omitted.[423]

Jessup felt however that "within a few weeks at most, Brown will be forced to give up, and turn over the management to people with business ability." He was especially agitated at the salaries proposed:

I protested to Brown that the UFO people would never associate with any outfit paying such a figure, and he countered with the statement that the UFOers should take into account that the salaries had not been paid, but were only set up in case money became available. My holy sainted Aunt—how dumb are we supposed to be?[424]

Moreover, Jessup was understandably peeved that he was not to be allowed a position at NICAP under the incumbent leadership: "I have been snubbed completely because I wrote a book on UFO and therefore might be biased.

For Christ's sake!"[425] Nonetheless, he intended to keep his powder dry and take a pragmatic approach. Mindful of openly criticizing the fringe, for the sake of his own book sales, he told Barker:

> I believe you and I have everything to gain and nothing to lose by being cooperative and sympathetic to NICAP. A little adroit politics will make it a successful UFO enterprise. I recommend that we push it for very practical reasons ... publically [*sic*] I feel I have to continue walking a tight wire in order to maintain public relations for future books ... we have to just turn the fishy eye on some of the hoaxing ... I have never accepted ANY story of space riding and take a dim view of all reports of contacts.[426]

His observation about Rose Hackett's religious slant on UFOs was, however, to some extent, in line with his own, as evidenced by his 1956 book, *UFO and The Bible* (which was an extract from his larger volume *The Expanding Case for the UFO*), but he still, privately, eschewed contactee claims.

While Jessup's doubts remained, the new organization and its Board were given a cautious welcome by the UFO research community. The Civilian Saucer Intelligence of New York (CSI-NY) commented:

> If NICAP can do what it has set out to do, it will deserve the enthusiastic cooperation of all other saucer-research organizations; a civilian UFO investigation on this scale has been sorely needed.

It nonetheless expressed deep misgivings about Brown and the unknowns of his scientific background:

> T. Townsend Brown, is something of a mystery man. Apparently competent as a physicist (though he had no degree), he is one of those who have claimed to have constructed electromagnetic devices that develop a true antigravitational effect
> ...

CSI-NY had tried to find out about Brown's work through the Gravity Research Foundation of New Boston, New Hampshire, but it "had been unable to obtain information from Brown about his experiments" and added that there had been "no breakthroughs" in electrogravitics. Also consulted was

Dr. Bryce DeWitt, head of the University of North Carolina's Institute of Field Physics, who confirmed this opinion. CSI-NY observed:

> The question as to what Brown has actually accomplished is therefore a significant one. At present, we are unable to answer it. Certain allegations concerning Brown's work, which would be disturbing if true, have come to the attention of the Research Section from persons on the West Coast and elsewhere.
>
> In addition, Dr. Leon Davidson has pointed out to us certain features of the proposed organization of NICAP which would seem to indicate a danger of excessive central control by those in a position to buy preponderant voting power ... Perhaps our reservations are mere paranoid suspicion ... but the consequences to the reputation of UFO research, if NICAP were to develop along improper lines, would be so grave that we feel it is necessary to let our colleagues know that some legitimate questions about this project have still not received a final answer. We hope that when the Board of Governors meets in January, these matters will be cleared up to the satisfaction of all concerned.[427]

In December the following year, DeWitt would visit Townsend Brown at the laboratory of his new research partner, Agnew Bahnson, Jr., son of a wealthy industrialist father, to inspect their work on electrogravitic effects in a vacuum, but he came away unimpressed.[428] (According to Brown's daughter, Bahnson was a contactee who believed that the "space brothers" had told him to seek out her father, and that later, he was disappointed when these entities ceased their visitations.)[429]

Despite the numerous peculiarities behind its creation, NICAP had been launched —but within days, it was under a cloud. On November 1st, nineteen voting members of NICAP met to select a Board of Governors. Jessup, though not a member, attended and he was unimpressed. He suspected that NICAP had been formed for a few promoters to line their own pockets, that their plans for public relations were vague and suspicious, and that the proposed salaries were too high. Moreover, it emerged that some potential donors wouldn't cough up as expected because Brown indicated that NICAP would

do "limited investigations."[430]
Nonetheless, after this meeting the Board of Governors was named:[431]

> Rev. Albert H Baller, a Congregational minister, at that time with the Robbins Memorial Congregational Church, Greenfield, Mass. He had been interested in UFOs since he sighted three in 1952, after which he presented occasional talks on the subject. He was a member of the Australian Flying Saucer Bureau, and also of APRO and CRIFO. In addition, he worked as a psychiatric counselor at a Boston clinic and was also an author of children's books.[432]
>
> Brig. Gen. Thomas B. Catron II had retired from the Army in 1949. A member of CIA agent Ulius Amoss' International Services of Information Foundation, Inc.
>
> Frank Edwards, well-known radio-TV personality and author on UFOs.
>
> Col. Robert B. Emerson, Nuclear Physicist, employed at the Kaiser Aluminum Company in Baton Rouge and also head of his own Emerson Testing Laboratories, Baton Rouge.
>
> Rear Adm. Delmer S. Fahrney, retired Navy officer, former Annapolis classmate of Keyhoe's and noted pioneer in missile development.
>
> Rev. Leon C. LeVan, Pastor (Swedenborgian) of New Christian Church, Pittsburgh. (According to astronomer Frank Halstead, later a NICAP special adviser, he had had "considerable correspondence" with Le Van "mainly trying to convince him that Adamski and other long hairs were fakers.")[433]
>
> Charles A. Maney, physics professor at Defiance College, Ohio. In 1915 he made the discovery of internal motions in Orion's Great Nebula. He had been interested in UFOs since 1950 and had given lectures on the topic.
>
> Abraham M. Sonnabend, a hotel executive with interests in a wide variety of other businesses. In 1958 he became a board member of Studebaker. He was also Chairman of the Board of Botany Woolen Mills, Inc.
>
> Talbot T. Speer, businessman, owner and publisher of several Maryland newspapers, and a former Maryland half-

back. In 1951 he founded the philanthropic Talbot T. Speer Foundation and in his honor the Talbot T. Speer Award for outstanding male athlete was created and is still awarded annually. According to Jessup, Speer had contributed the required Founder's $1000 to NICAP, at "the personal request" of Rose Hackett.[434]

With Townsend Brown's sights already set elsewhere and concerns about his background and motives mounting from within the existing research community, NICAP, before it had handled a single report, was already heading toward a crisis.

It came only twelve weeks after its incorporation, when on January 14, 1957, Keyhoe attended the first Director's meeting. It proved to be a lively event. The members were focused upon whether or not the fledgling Committee had a future under Brown's prospectus. Overall, they agreed that his aims were "too high in 'envisioning' so many projects," which would have required 50,000 or 100,000 members to achieve the necessary funding. The Board at this stage had "half of a mind" to pull the plug on NICAP, though it agreed that the focus should be on getting the "truth" out to the public. But Brown's unrealistic ambitions for NICAP were only part of the problem.

Jessup's previous suspicions about NICAP being formed for the financial benefit of a few members referred to an apparently backroom deal made between Garrett Rush and Townsend Brown. The $1000 founding members donations would give 100 votes to the donor, but this, according to rumor, was, in effect, a scam by the two men. They had not contributed in full for their memberships—Brown made no donation and Rush gave $400—but then paid themselves a large salary by cheque and donated this non-existent money to NICAP. By this means, they became the only "donors" and gained voting control. Moreover, Jessup believed, "Brown has been borrowing from loan Companies @ 3% a month against hopes of a killing in NICAP."[435]

On top of that, according to Jessup, another backroom deal had been agreed:

> Secret committments [sic] were made to certain Baltimore people to pay one private small firm $1850/month for so-called public relations work which has never materialized ... Clara John know[s] a lot about it and is very disturbed.[436]

The firm was undoubtedly Counsel Services, though the identity of these

"Baltimore people" isn't clear, but against this simmering, shady, and shaky background, Keyhoe eventually took charge of the meeting:

> [U]ntil the night of January 14 I was merely an unhappy observer [but] that night I gave Brown an ultimatum in front of a room full of members (although I tried to do it in a lowered voice, I finally got angry ...) I told him that if he and Rush didn't withdraw their names as nominees for new Board members, I'd see Admiral Fahrney that night and advise him to resign; also I'd do the same with all the Board members. So they reversed the deal ...[437]

The next day, beginning at 10 am and scheduled to run until 8 pm, another meeting was held, during which Townsend Brown resigned, confirmed on the 16th in his letter (typed by Rose Hackett), acknowledging Keyhoe's accession. He added, "I shall, of course, continue my interest in NICAP, especially in its scientific findings ...." Some years later, his version of events would differ markedly from Keyhoe's and Jessup's:

> After the [NICAP] office was established on Connecticut Avenue and continued operations seemed assured, I asked Donald Keyhoe ... to take my place and thereby allow me to go back into the laboratory and active research work in the field of electrogravitics ...[438]

According to Brown's daughter, her father was unconcerned about his removal from NICAP:

> He didn't much care anyway ... he was not planning on running the operation and he was already planning to be somewhere else ... he had made sure that it was begun because he actually needed it for his own research.[439]

Keyhoe was now asked by the Board to take over the Directorship and agreed to do so—temporarily—on the strength of promises that "big funds" would be forthcoming:

> I was told that within a very short time there would be substantial sums of money coming in to allow us to build it up—we'd have an editor, an editorial assistant and a promo-

tion man and public relations and this, that and the other, all of which were badly needed. The sum was estimated at around $50,000.[440]

A few days after Brown's departure, Jessup wrote to Barker:

Already there are rumors that a successor to Keyhoe has been contacted and has been here to look over the situation. Keyhoe, of course, is in as director on temporary basis, and he dont [sic] want it anyway ... Funny thing, but nobody who was in at the beginning except Mrs Hackett, is still in NICAP.[441]

Mary Vaughan King had by now relinquished her post "in order to assist in the Committee management liaison work," but whatever this unclear job description entailed, she appears not to have stayed at NICAP after Brown left. Rose Hackett remained, drawing praise from an admiring Jessup who believed that she was honestly devoted to the UFO cause, and that she and Keyhoe, in whom he had confidence, were now working toward making the Committee a success.

With Brown gone, debts already accumulated, $1.40 in the kitty, and no office staff other than Rose Hackett, NICAP had only faith in the future and a brass plaque at the door upon which to build a unique organization strong enough to take on the US Air Force and to garner support, enthusiasm, and cash from a public that, surely, would clamor for the truth about UFOs.[442]

Donald Keyhoe at the door of the National Investigations Committee on Aerial Phenomena. (Gordon Lore)

Chapter 23:
The "Real" NICAP

Keyhoe's decision to temporarily take the helm seemed to quickly be justified when, on January 17, 1957, Admiral Fahrney got the reborn NICAP off to a flying start by holding a news conference, at which he made a bold statement:

> Reliable reports indicate that there are objects coming into our atmosphere at very high speeds. No agency in this country or Russia is able to duplicate at this time the speeds and accelerations which radars and observers indicate these objects are able to achieve.
>
> There are signs that an intelligence guides these objects because of the way they fly. The way they change position in formations would indicate that their motion is directed. The Air Force is collecting factual data on which to base an opinion, but time is required to sift and correlate the material.
>
> As long as such unidentified objects continue to navigate through the Earth's atmosphere, there is an urgent need to know the facts. Many observers have ceased to report their findings to the Air Force because of the seeming frustration—that is, all information going in, and none coming out. It is in this area that NICAP may find its greatest mission.
>
> We are in a position to screen independently all UFO information coming in from our filter groups.
>
> General Albert C. Wedemeyer will serve the Committee as Evaluation adviser and complete analyses will be arranged through leading scientists. After careful evaluation, we shall release our findings to the public.[443]

This was just the thing to launch the "new" NICAP, and it was a smack in the face to the Air Force, whose decade-long derision of the UFO subject had held sway. Fahrney's statement, though refraining from mentioning visitors from other worlds, could hardly be interpreted in any other way. This remarkable pronouncement from no less than "the father of guided missiles," a man of serious disposition and gravitas, threw down the gauntlet.

Keyhoe was buoyed by Fahrney's forceful declaration, and in a report to the newly-elected Board of Governors in February, he gave it prominent mention, noting that it had resulted in some positive publicity and in requests for him to "appear on broadcasts or to give talks about NICAP and the UFO situation." These and other appearances already in the pipeline would result, he felt, in "thousands of members!"[444] Furthermore, he expected that his many contacts would soon "swamp NICAP with requests for memberships," resulting in 100,000 by the end of the first year. He strongly recommended the organization should publish a monthly 32-page newsletter ("the first issue MUST be good") so that important matters could be given in-depth treatment. Evidently filled with enthusiasm, he asserted that, "this organization can easily become a tremendous success."

February also saw the marriage of Rose Hackett to Duncan "Cam" Campbell. They were wed on the 22nd at the Rockville Presbyterian Church, Maryland, by which time Duncan had relinquished his position as treasurer, supposedly owing to work commitments—though he retired soon after.[445] Surprisingly, given the earlier turbulence, he was replaced by Dr. Garrett Chamberlain Rush.

The day-to-day business at NICAP was nonetheless entirely in the hands of Don and the newly-wed Mrs Campbell. Despite their differing views on the contactees, they shared a common aim to make the organization a success, each working very long days for little or, sometimes, no pay.

By the time Keyhoe's "personal statement to a very few close associates" was issued on March 7th, it was evident from its content that he had been sweeping up after Brown's parade and some of his enthusiasm was replaced by stark financial reality. Most of Brown's aims had been discarded, but the fundamental purpose of the Committee, at this stage, appeared little different to how it was originally envisaged. Nonetheless, the Major wanted feedback on the feasibility of his own ideas for moving forward. He offered reassurance that the organization was now "beginning to operate as originally planned" and laid out his suggestions. If his changes were implemented, he had "no doubt of NICAP's success" but this could only be achieved by first being realistic about salaries. Any staff would be paid below average for their work—including himself. The only money available at present was from membership fees, which had been cut from Brown's hefty $15 per year to a still not cheap

$7.50. Those who had already paid the higher amount could have a year's extension or a refund, but this unwittingly set in motion a rolling program of financial catch-up that would never be satisfactorily managed.[446]

Ambitiously, Keyhoe planned to supplement the promised monthly 32-page magazine with occasional bulletins/newsletters, but, like the extension of membership dues, this hobbled the horse before it left the stable. Indeed, throughout his entire time at the helm, the length, content, frequency, and cost of NICAP's publications became the heaviest burden of all and would weaken it more than any other challenge.

Even so, he was fired up and raring to go. Amid all the reorganization, the speaking engagements, and the need to evaluate UFO reports, March 21st saw him putting up his dukes to Dr. Hugh L. Dryden, Head of NACA (the predecessor of NASA), who in February had asserted before the House Appropriations Committee that saucers didn't exist and that he hadn't the time to refute "the science fiction people." In a letter to him, Keyhoe stated:

> If, as you imply, you can provide absolute proof that uniden-
> tified flying objects are non-existent, then NICAP will pub-
> lish this as its final conclusion and at the same time I shall
> request the board to dissolve this committee at once.

No such proof followed, but this pugnacious challenge to the illustrious doctor drew a line in the sand for all those who made sweeping dismissals they couldn't back up with evidence.

Coral Lorenzen approved of Keyhoe's appointment, not least because she had been dismayed by the poor and tardy response from Townsend Brown. Her letter to him of October 6, 1956, offering advice on avoiding the "crackpots," was answered with only circulars, which were not mailed until November 20th. Displaying the lack of knowledge and interest in UFO research groups about which Jessup had earlier complained, Brown had merely annotated her letter with "Let's send her a news release," hence Coral was justifiably unimpressed with the man and also suspicious of his financial motives.[447]

She expressed endorsement of the new order in January's *APRO Bulletin*:

> This is cause for considerable relief on our part, and we can
> feel that the group is now in competent hands ... Let's all
> wish Mr Keyhoe and the other members all the good luck
> possible in this venture ...[448]

In the March *Bulletin*, she went even further and displayed extraordinary generosity and commitment:

> We are now sure the UAO mystery and UAO enthusiasts will receive respectful treatment by NICAP… the sterling quality of the men on the Board of Governors … will be a definite asset to Major Keyhoe and the organization as a whole … we are behind NICAP 100% and recommend that APRO members support them to the best of their ability.[449]
>
> Some members, well aware of our plan to cooperate with NICAP, ask, "What if APRO members who join NICAP feel they can't afford or don't care to continue with APRO? What if this is so widespread that APRO dwindles to the point where it can't support itself?" Our answer is simply this: … If such a situation presents itself, the Director will close APRO and do everything possible to aid and abet the cause through NI[C]AP. She now feels that there is a group capable of directing the efforts of all UAO groups, and would not feel too badly about bowing out.'[450]

Given APRO's status, Don could not have wished for a more supportive and harmonious start to his Directorship, which for the next eighteen months was often followed up with assistance and information from Coral, willingly given. So manifest was her trust in and respect for Keyhoe that she soon gave him "the principle facts involved in a military sighting which we feel is too 'hot' for us to handle," though she later requested he keep it under wraps as there had been other developments. Moreover, with respect of the "hot" case, she admitted that sharing it with him was "the only confidence I've ever broken …because I felt that in your position you could verify and check better than I."[451]

Ted Bloecher, a founding member of CSI-NY, was relieved at the change of management: "Thank God T. Townsend Blemish has been taken care of. As you realize, all of us were receiving extremely poor stories about the man for the past few months."[452]

The group's newsletter also expressed approval at "The Rebirth of NICAP":

> NICAP is the most promising endeavor that has yet appeared in the field of UFO study. With excellent personnel, a sound

program, and unprecedented prestige, NICAP can dissipate the murky atmosphere of mixed ignorant skepticism and ... cultism that now surrounds us, and inaugurate a new era in saucer research ... There is no doubt that NICAP under its new management will be the closest approach to a "professional" civilian UFO-research body that the world has yet seen.[453]

On a cautionary note, it lamented the recent closure of Len Stringfield's newsletter, *Orbit*, which he had ended after three years of publication due to the high costs involved. CSI-NY's newsletter prophetically commented:

The financial burden of publishing a monthly magazine finally became more than he [Stringfield] could manage: printing costs kept going up, but subscriptions fell behind ... he believes, primarily because his editorial policy was too scrupulously factual, refusing to pander to the cultist element [and] it bodes ill for the future of UFO research if the process of economic "survival of the fittest" results in the elimination of the sensible, and the preservation of the showmen and outright cranks.

Despite this justified concern, Keyhoe was undoubtedly warmed by such gestures and accolades from those who might easily have seen NICAP as a rival, and by April 1957 he had committed himself full-time to "the cause." But that month he announced his first significant blow: Fahrney resigned.[454]

His departure, so soon after his galvanizing statement to the press, kicked off rumors around NICAP that he had been forced to quit due to pressure from the military. He answered these suspicions by letter, stating that he was not "under compulsion to resign," that he wanted to continue as a member of NICAP and expressed his confidence and trust in Keyhoe's leadership. (He would prove to be as good as his word, continuing to provide useful information for some years to come.)

The membership was informed of Fahrney's exit by special bulletin. A few days later Keyhoe, seemingly unaware that Townsend Brown had earlier tried to recruit Ruppelt, updated his young friend—who had recently suffered a heart attack—in a letter that showed his own increasing concern about finances, though he had evidently been busy and was still optimistic:

> NICAP was organized last year by T. Townsend Brown and a few others who had a good idea but failed to follow through. In January Admiral Fahrney and the rest of the Board changed the management. I found myself stuck with the toughest job I have ever had. I took it because I could see the chance for a very big build-up in publicity about the saucers, one which would help to vindicate me and also other writers who have not gone off the deep end. I am glad to say that our membership has grown steadily and it now includes many pilots, several scientists, engineers, radar operators, and other specialists besides a good cross-section of solid, substantial citizens. I am still working on a deferred-pay basis, in case you think I am getting rich. I believe NICAP will keep on building to the point where we can have an adequate though very small staff and at least make expenses.
>
> At present we are in the process of adding several new members to the Board of Governors and also to our special panel of advisers. From responses so far it appears that we shall announce several well-known names during May, and also a new Chairman of the Board to replace Fahrney, who had to resign because of his wife's serious illness and pressures of business commitments at Franklin Institute and the Naval Aircraft Factory. He is still helping us and he is a member of NICAP. However, we expect to name an even more prominent citizen in his place. I think you will be reading about some of these Board Members in the next few weeks.[455]

The "prominent citizen" turned out to be Vice Admiral Roscoe Henry Hillenkoetter, first Director of the CIA and Keyhoe's former Annapolis classmate. Recently retired from service, his inclusion on the Board of NICAP was a triumph and more than made up for the loss of Fahrney.

Hillenkoetter's tenure in the top job at the CIA gave tremendous kudos to NICAP. It demonstrated blatantly that this was no coffee klatch or cultist assembly but was an organization with serious-minded folk at the helm. On the face of it, his authority was unassailable, and it became a useful ruler for Keyhoe with which to rap the knuckles of NICAP's critics. It would also become a red flag for those who later believed that Hillenkoetter's involvement laid the foundation for CIA infiltration of the Committee, though given its pre-Keyhoe links with Counsel Services, this was almost certainly kicked off during Brown's tenure.

Moreover, it's true to say that Hillenkoetter's time at the CIA had little glory attached to it and was fraught with controversy and difficulty. His status was heavily diminished because he largely failed to overcome the administrative challenges with which he struggled during his Directorship of the fledgling Agency.

In May 1947, he had stepped—or rather been placed—into the shoes of General Hoyt S. Vandenberg, who had been Director of Central Intelligence (formerly Central Intelligence Group—CIG) from June 1946 until May 1947. The appointment of these two men in succession followed the convention of having military men in such positions: the Army had had its turn with Vandenberg, and now Hillenkoetter was, in a sense, the first cab on the Navy's rank. He had more experience in intelligence than his predecessor, but his appointment was not universally welcomed, and there were some in Washington who had never heard of him. One officer who served under him recollected that he was

> ... a thoroughly decent, unpretentious man, but a rear Admiral. In the hierarchical maze of Washington, his authority scarcely extended beyond the front door.[456]

Vandenberg, who had "no long term interest in the subject" of intelligence, had lasted for just over ten months in what was then a small going concern with an uncertain future. His short incumbency, however, did no favors for his successor. During his time as Director, he had tried aggressively and with some success to "alter drastically the balance between the Central Intelligence Group and the departmental intelligence agencies, at the expense of the latter," by engaging in a power struggle with their chiefs. This approach to securing power from other departments meant that "the uproar he provoked was still at full strength when Hillenkoetter took over" in May 1947.[457]

He initially held the same role and title as his predecessor, but in December that year President Truman established the Central Intelligence Agency, and Hillenkoetter was relabeled Director of the CIA. But the new branding did nothing to create the harmony that had been lacking, and he immediately found himself tangled in administrative barbed wire when he tried to improve relationships with those departments and individuals so adversely affected by

Vandenberg's changes.

To add to his difficulties, in January 1948, a survey of the CIA's performance and its ability to deal with future intelligence matters was begun, chaired by Allen Dulles. There is some lack of clarity as to whether or not Hillenkoetter himself felt this was necessary, but it nonetheless was undertaken, and what became known as the "Dulles Report" was published a year later.[458] In it, Hillenkoetter was heavily criticized, if not insulted, and many thought he would soon be ousted.

Matters were made worse when, after the report, his and his department's reputations were further tarnished by two significant intelligence failures. The first was a wholly inaccurate estimate of when Russia would produce the atomic bomb. Hillenkoetter predicted it would be 1953, but it was tested in August 1949 (just eleven days after President Truman had said publicly that he had no plans to replace Hillenkoetter). This gaffe was followed ten months later by North Korea's invasion of South Korea, a catastrophe the CIA had failed entirely to predict.[459]

How much of this and other shortcomings could fairly be laid at Hillenkoetter's feet is outside the scope of this work, but his term at the CIA was neither short nor sweet: he was replaced on October 7, 1950, by former Ambassador to the Soviet Union Walter Bedell Smith, having lasted much longer than many thought he would or indeed should have. He was widely reported to have requested return to active duty after the North Korean debacle, though he would counter this later by saying he made this request before the incident. After his departure, future Directors of the CIA would be civilians.

The press was, as ever, duplicitous in its appraisal of him. Some reports said he had done a good job under difficult circumstances, others were highly critical—one went so far as to label him "bumbling"—but whatever the truth, Hillenkoetter's reputation was in tatters, and until Smith's appointment was confirmed, the subject of who would replace him became open season for columnists.[460]

Despite all this, it may be inferred that Hillenkoetter held no grudge against Dulles for the scathing report that bore his name, since the two men kept a civil, if not fawning, occasional correspondence for a few years after. In 1953, when Dulles himself became Director of the CIA, he sent a brief letter to Hillenkoetter:

> As I take over this new job, which you know so well ... I

hope that when you are next in Washington I will have the opportunity to see you as there are many things I should like to talk over with you and get the benefit of your knowledge and experience in this field.[461]

In January 1957, just weeks before he cast in his lot with Keyhoe and NICAP, Hillenkoetter sent a letter to Dulles, which strongly suggests that he had long-since cut his ties with the CIA:

It was a great pleasure and a great treat for me to be at lunch today and I am most grateful and appreciative of your courtesy and kindness in having me with so many old friends and colleagues. I purposely have avoided seeing or being with too many former associates in the Agency because there is no pest worse than an "ex" who comes around and keeps kibitzing over what happens at the present as to what happened in the past.

Since, for that reason I had not seen many of these old friends, I was doubly pleased that I could have lunch with you and with them. I am most indebted to you for your thoughtfulness. Also, I should like to thank you for your kindness in sending me back to the Pentagon in your car.

Again with sincere thanks and all good wishes, please believe me. Most cordially [signature].[462]

Richard Hall (later NICAP Assistant Director), in an effort to place Hillenkoetter's former role in perspective, wrote in 1994 that:

CIA employees were simply professionals in the intelligence field, and had their own private interests and activities, including curiosity about UFOs ...[463]

Whether or not that was the case for Hillenkoetter, when he joined NICAP, the public had forgotten the turmoil of his CIA Directorship and could not fail to be impressed that he had once been head of that increasingly secretive and powerful organization. It gave him the gravitas and *bona fides* to lend unimpeachable authority to NICAP. His past failings, real or perceived, did not detract from his status; for PR purposes alone, he was worth his weight

in gold.
   Surely, things could only get better.

Chapter 24:
A Motley Crew

Although NICAP now had a large jewel in its refurbished crown, the day-to-day grunt work at head office was still mostly down to just Keyhoe and Rose. In the years ahead, it would increasingly be supported by Subcommittees and Affiliates. The former would perform field investigations within their own state and provide reports to HQ. Public relations were "a secondary function," which fell under the remit of Affiliates, whose other functions were to arrange meetings, run "membership drives," "research projects," and give general assistance to investigations.[464] These units would prove a mixed blessing—there were occasional misunderstandings, rivalries, and personal "empire-building" problems that Keyhoe had to tackle.

For the present, some relief to his and Rose's workload arrived in April, when they were joined by an able and keen Associate Editor, Lee Munsick, head of the North Jersey UFO Group.

Munsick had first been alerted to the 1956 formation of NICAP by the tentacled Clara John, though he was firmly anti-contactee.[465] He had begun corresponding with Keyhoe and consequently was well aware of the financial crisis plaguing the Committee. Don had recently admitted that he was trying "to keep from going bankrupt" and was considering doing part-time work to keep things going.[466] Against that background, Munick's decision to work at NICAP was prompted by a phone conversation with Keyhoe, as described by the latter to Ted Bloecher:

> [T]o be Director, promotions man and editor all in one has been almost impossible. I was lamenting this on the phone with Lee Munsick the other day and he offered to come down and help throw some of the stuff together. I explained that we were not even caught up with back salaries, long overdue and that it would be a gamble on his part … The upshot was that he agreed to come down for a week or so …[467]

His arrival was timely and essential because the first issue of NICAP's newsletter (optimistically called a "magazine"), the *UFO Investigator*, had yet to be completed, and pressure to release it was intensifying. The members had paid their dues, yet had nothing substantial to show for their money, and moreover it was essential to build on the momentum gained in the early weeks of NICAP's new order. The fundamental problem was, as it would always be, lack of money. Keyhoe later explained:

> On the basis of [promised funds] I announced the NICAP magazine and sent letters to all the people who'd read my books and we sent out quite a number of them and we had acceptances and then after the acceptance[s] the people who were going to donate the $50,000 in amounts of $5,000 apiece, in most cases, each one began waiting for the other. As a result, here was NICAP, committed to publishing a magazine [which we got out with] ... blood, sweat and tears ... and sheer desperation ...[468]

On June 6th, the heavy physical and emotional strain at NICAP was suddenly increased. Only fifteen weeks after his marriage to Rose Hackett, Duncan Campbell was found dead in the garage of their home. He died of "asphyxiation when he fell asleep in his car after parking it in his garrage [sic], but leaving the motor running."[469]

To one of his correspondents, Keyhoe wrote:

> This came as a tremendous shock to all of us here, and Mrs Campbell has suffered greatly, although her indominitable [sic] will and courage have been an inspiration to us all. Our work, too has suffered, both from our own shock, and from Mrs Campbell's temporary absence from the office, forcing another slight delay in the publication of the magazine ...[470]

Commendably, following this bereavement, she managed to pull her oar, and the first issue of the long-awaited 32-page *UFO Investigator* (which carried an obituary for her husband) was published in July, but its disorganized content and layout reflected the chaos under which it was put together. In his editorial, Keyhoe admitted it was "far from perfect" and gave the same reasons for the delay in publication that would be repeated in almost every issue thereafter—staff shortages and lack of money. Moreover, it set the tone and content of future issues: criticizing Air Force secrecy, laying bare its contradictions, lambasting uncooperative officers, and taking it to task for disparaging Keyhoe and NICAP.

Don's choice of lead item was hardly spectacular, though was in keeping with his aims; it was merely an account, albeit detailed, of "four saucers over California" to which was devoted the greater part of five pages, spread inconveniently throughout the magazine. The item boasted up-front that the radar report, which had been signed by the operators who tracked the objects, had been "certified by NICAP board members" who had "seen the signed reports." How much ice this cut with members isn't known, but it gave a clear message to the Air Force that Keyhoe considered his Board to be so important that simply having seen a document ought to be sufficient evidence. He managed also to take another swipe at General Joe Kelly, with whom he had locked horns back in 1954. The California sightings were broadly under Kelly's remit and Keyhoe sent him two letters and a telegram requesting relevant AF reports, but he pointedly informed readers that no reply had been received. (He would mention the Kelly issue many more times in the years to come.)

Having given so much attention to these sightings and the Air Force's shortcomings in respect of them, he whipped out the equivalent of a dead rabbit from his hat:

> [A] complete analysis by NICAP's Special Advisers is not possible without the report of the 4602 Intelligence Squadron, now at Air Force Headquarters.

In other words, if the Air Force wouldn't co-operate, NICAP was stymied.

To further guarantee he would make no friends among the Men in Blue, he reproduced a piece by journalist Gene Wortsman from May 1957 in which the Air Force disparaged Keyhoe and his "upstart" NICAP, accusing both of playing up its alleged secrecy in order to keep the "organization alive." The unnamed spokesman mocked: "Those birds keep yelling and that makes the subject enticing … That's their bread and butter."

As to the impending release of NICAP's first publication, the spokesman had said, "We couldn't care less."[471]

The Air Force, however, did care about NICAP. In March its collective nerves had been set jangling thanks to Keyhoe. He had written asking for its report on a visual and radar sighting on the 23rd in the skies over Oxnard, California, which had been reported in the press. ATIC sent a "Joint Messageform dispatch" to the 4602nd Air Intelligence Service Squadron in

Colorado Springs, that demonstrated no concern about what the object was, but demonstrated plenty of concern about the AF's public image. The sighting was

> ... recognized as potentially dangerous in that it could give Air Force unfavorable publicity, if exploited by fanatic or die-hard "flying saucer" proponents. This now definite possibility, with receipt of letter from NICAP ... Officially, this incident does not warrant action required, but [Keyhoe]'s ability to slant material and create unwarranted trouble for Air Force, his stock in trade for almost ten years.[472]

To aggravate the Air Force even further, it was now beaten with its own stick—Ruppelt. His support for Keyhoe was given prominent mention in NICAP's first issue, which detailed his clearances of ATIC material, the revelations made in his own 1956 book, *The Report on Unidentified Flying Objects*, and the Air Force's blunders in verifying whether or not it was given clearance before publication.

But perhaps most infuriating was the second lead item, announcing an "8 Point Plan Offered Air Force," which amounted to a condescending proposal for a deal in which NICAP would "agree" to cooperation with the Air Force if it played ball. Keyhoe had written to Air Force Secretary James H. Douglas with an offer that

> ... would mean [the AF] providing the Committee with all UFO sightings reports now labeled as "solved" for evaluation by the Board and the Special Advisers, with NICAP's conclusions given to the Air Force and the public.[473]

In a final blast from NICAP's trumpet, the Board of Directors were each given their own mini-biographies, including a lauding of Hillenkoetter and a statement by Joseph B. Hartranft Jr., "President of the influential Aircraft Owners and Pilots Association," which supported NICAP's stance against censorship and hoaxers. Adding to the military luminaries on the Board was Lieutenant General P. A. del Valle, noted for leading the WWII invasion of Okinawa and for his far-right views. Also included was a careful statement by Dewey Fournet:

> Although I do have my personal opinions about the UFO, I have steadfastly refrained from making them public because

no matter how much I might emphasize that they are only private opinions, they would undoubtedly be construed by the general public to reflect official US Air Force conclusions ...[474]

The official Air Force conclusion was, of course, that UFOs amounted to nothing, a view with which Fournet, as a civilian, was free to agree, so along with his prominent status at the new Committee, it was easy to draw the inference that his personal opinion disagreed with that of his former employer.

As to the contactees, NICAP's policy was given at length, which amounted to stating it would give a fair hearing to, and make impartial examination of, any evidence presented.

Overall, the greater part of the "magazine" was taken up with the biographies of Board members, but of the twenty other pieces, ten were critical and accusatory toward the Air Force, including the lengthy item about Ruppelt's book. Taken together with Keyhoe's condescending offer of the "8 Point Plan," it's hard not to infer that the need for containment of the AF's most vocal critic was felt more keenly than ever. The issue also reported that General Wedemeyer had withdrawn from his role in evaluating UFO reports due to "the unexpected publicity and flood of mail" he had received since his name had, it seems, erroneously been made public.[475] These reports would now be assessed by an "adviser panel." As to Wedemeyer, press reports of the time note that he had now been elected as head of the advisory board and Director of Townsend Investment Company (no connection to Thomas Townsend Brown).[476]

Rose Hackett had been crucial to the completion of this issue. She had brought with her to NICAP her own IBM proportional spacing machine, an expensive piece of office equipment for which special training was needed to operate and which the Committee could not afford to buy. It gave a professional look to the publication and though the finished copy was disjointed and wordy, it represented an important step for the shaky new organization. At least members now had something to show for their dues, and without her commitment, it undoubtedly would not have been achieved. But her devotion came at a cost.

Keyhoe did not know that soon after her husband's death, Rose began secretly copying "stacks" of UFO documents and sending them to Thomas Townsend Brown, an act which, aside from its disloyalty and its inescapable inference that she filled some covert purpose, placed a significant financial burden on NICAP, which was eternally strapped for cash. Brown's daughter remembered sorting through these "stacks." Her father told her the saucers that wobbled "are ours," but she was unsure what this meant, nor did she know why he continued to be interested in NICAP's doings.[477]

Rose at this time was receiving barely a pittance from NICAP, yet in August 1957 she anonymously sent a cheque for $1,000 to cover its crippling outstanding printing bill. However, given her need to keep NICAP going to facilitate her own contactee ambitions and to continue providing Brown with reports, this was unlikely to have been the selfless act Keyhoe believed it to be when he later discovered she had been the donor.[478] Neither did he know that, when Brown held meetings with some of his large "groups," his faithful secretary would attend.

Even without knowing the wider picture of his secretary's perfidy, Keyhoe knew he was in a fix. Though she kept the organization going, she was at the same time putting it in jeopardy; her devotion to the contactee cause constantly threatened to undermine NICAP's sober aims, and in his heart Don knew that, widowed or not, eventually she would have to go.

* * *

The persistent difficulties that had marked Keyhoe's first months at NICAP were given a welcome respite in early July. He was elated by a call from NICAP's lawyer, Sam Borzilleri (originally appointed by Townsend Brown), who told him to get material together for a possible Senate Sub-committee hearing that had asked for NICAP's help. This would be part of the Government Operations Committee, chaired by Senator McClelland, and its chief investigator, Jack Healey, would phone within the week.[479]

Keyhoe and Lee Munsick moved like lightning and had "an impressive pile" of case documents ready that afternoon, but Lee urged caution, pointing out that they might be giving away too much at this stage, thereby allowing the Air Force to "have the drop on us." Keyhoe ran this suspicion past NICAP's board and Hillenkoetter agreed. "I knew it was getting hot," he said, and advised: "don't use your best cases." Frank Edwards and J. B. Hartranft concurred, so the most compelling examples were held back for presentation at the hoped-for hearings.[480]

Meanwhile, with this encouraging development in the background, there was still a mountain to climb and allies old and new to be cultivated. High on Keyhoe's list was Ruppelt, whose value to NICAP, if the Congressional hearings went ahead, was foremost in his mind. In anticipation, he had written-up Ruppelt's comments taken from his *Report on Unidentified Flying Saucers* and inserted them as answers to hypothetical questions he might face in the potential hearings.[481] It was this anticipatory mind-set and behavior that would prove to be both a strength and a weakness for Don in the years to come.

On July 17th in New York, Keyhoe and Munsick met with Ruppelt, who was appearing on the panel game show, *I've Got A Secret*, hosted by Garry Moore. This was similar to the highly-popular *What's My Line*, and came from the same Goodson and Todman stable. A celebrity panel would question a small group of contestants to figure out what was their shared "secret," i.e., a common experience or occupation.

In this episode, the contestants were witnesses to some of the most persuasive UFO sightings of the time: Captains Chiles and Whitted, who saw a "double-decked rocket ship over Alabama"; Nick Mariana, who had taken the famous Montana film; former Marine, now photographer, Ralph Mayher, who had snapped a UFO over Miami; and Carl Hart, who had a still image of the "Lubbock Lights." After these men revealed their link, Ruppelt was interviewed by Moore and confirmed that he believed UFO witnesses had "seen something" and that 20% of sightings were unsolved.

Following the show, Keyhoe and Munsick went backstage to see Ruppelt, who told them that "some AF officers were angry about his book, especially his disclosure of the censorship and the secret Intelligence conclusion that the UFOs were interplanetary. But he insisted he was not being pressured ..."[482]

Keyhoe asked Ruppelt to join NICAP's board. "All right," he replied, "I'll do it. I consider it an honor," but two weeks later, his weathervane had swung in the opposite direction, and he sent a telegram withdrawing his agreement.[483] Don replied, expressing his disappointment at this reversal, and attempted a bit of not-so-subtle pressure:

> The two men you met at the Taft Hotel, Ted Bloecher and Lex Mebane, both overheard our remarks about your joining the Board, and sending a statement. There is nothing to prevent their making this public and then I would have to explain why you had changed your mind. I can ask them not to do this, but cannot guarantee it.
>
> Also, my associate editor, Lee Munsick ... publishes a UFO magazine and it is possible the incident might be de-

scribed there. I shall do my best to keep this story out of print since I understand what happened: I am assuming that Northrop suggested that you reconsider your acceptance.[484]

Ruppelt sent him an inconclusive and contradictory reply, saying that his decision was unconnected with his work—but that because of his work, he couldn't give his grounds for not getting involved:

> If the situation were such that I could conveniently do it, it would be interesting to work with NICAP but as things stand right now I just can't. Northrup [*sic*] didn't have anything to do with my decision, it was strictly my own, incidentally. It's difficult to give you a good, solid reason why I've decided to stay as far out of the UFO controversy as possible because I can't get specific about my work. You'll just have to take my word that I have a good reason.[485]

He added that the first issue of NICAP's newsletter was "good," that Keyhoe had "an impressive list of people on the board," and perhaps as a warning shot for what was to follow, remarked, "I thought Dewey's statement was good and I admire him for pointing out that his conclusions were his own." He enclosed a slide he had earlier mentioned to Keyhoe, showing a split cloud photographed over Newfoundland in the late 1940s, and hoped they could meet up sometime "in the next few months" in Washington.

Keyhoe didn't know it then, but this would be the last helpful communication he would ever receive from Ed Ruppelt.

Chapter 25:
Strong-Armed by Armstrong

Television ownership in America had soared from a few thousand in the mid-1940s to six million in 1950, and by the end of the decade it had increased ten-fold. Now fully established as the dominant medium, it was Keyhoe's preferred outlet to showcase NICAP, and he welcomed the opportunity to appear on the recently-revamped *Armstrong Circle Theatre*.

Beginning on NBC in 1950, it was a low-budget though successful anthology series, which in its earlier years offered fairly standard dramas. In 1957, when the program moved to CBS, more of its content became fact-based, and thanks to this shift the topic of UFOs would be given an airing. Keyhoe was contacted in December that year by scriptwriter Irve (Irving) Tunick, a 45-year-old New Yorker who had been writing for the program since 1954 and would later go on to write for primetime shows including *The Virginian*, *Ironside*, and *The High Chapparal*. He asked Don to participate in Armstrong's live, televised discussion, "The Enigma of The Skies," to which he agreed. Slated to appear with him were Kenneth Arnold, Captain Chiles, and Ed Ruppelt, the inference being that these three would be for the "positive" on saucers. "For the negative," Tunick hoped to bring in Donald Menzel, but the Air Force had declined to participate.

"Thinking that it was going to be a panel discussion," Keyhoe later recalled, "I said [to Tunick] be sure to get the Air Force in there [and] tell them that if they don't put somebody on you'll simply announce on the air that the Air Force was given full chance to explain its side and they refused to have anyone on." Soon after, Tunick "called back and said the AF has now reversed itself and everything's fine and they're giving us full co-operation."[486]

The broadcast date was fixed for Wednesday, January 22, 1958, and Keyhoe was keen to make his case against the Air Force in this arena. He was always well-prepared for lectures and debates; indeed, it had become an almost effortless procedure, beginning with a mantra-like statement of NICAP's aims, followed by naming the most illustrious board members and advisers, before getting down to specific cases drawn from his comprehensive knowledge and an ever-ready sheaf of documents. But what should have been a straightforward opportunity to espouse NICAP's position on TV became yet another burden on his time and energy. From the very start, he was tangled in barbed wire laid down by the Air Force.

He was dismayed to realize what lay behind its willingness to face him on live TV. The "discussion" would be entirely scripted by Tunick, "no ad-lib," and the Air Force would "put on their part separately." They wanted to see Keyhoe's script in advance, and he would be allowed to see theirs. Sensing trouble, he was tempted to decline but on balance felt it was best to comply and make the most of the opportunity. As he would have the backing of Arnold, Chiles, and Ruppelt, it still seemed a strong enough line-up for the "positive."

"Air Force stooge" Menzel had now confirmed he would take part, and with him for the Air Force "negative" angle was its spokesmen from Wright-Patterson AFB, Lt. Col. Spencer Whedon, and Richard E. Horner, Assistant Secretary of AF Research and Development.[487] Despite being scripted, it appeared that both sides were about equally matched—but any notion of égalité evaporated when Keyhoe was told that, of the thirty-two minutes available, the Air Force and Menzel would speak for twenty-five, leaving him and the others only seven. His heart sank:

> [A] script came down showing the Air Force had all of part two and I had five minutes of part three, Ruppelt had three minutes and Menzel and the Air Force had the rest of it ... I kicked about it and they said "well, you should have asked for equal time at the start," which was true, but I had thought it was a discussion show.[488]

He complained to Tunick about the paltry time allotted to him, but Irve, though uncomfortable, told him it was too late now and suggested, ridiculously, that Keyhoe could "cram a lot into seven minutes." He said the show's balance was already weighted in favor of the "positive" because the host, Douglas Edwards, would present the issue "more from NICAP's viewpoint," therefore requiring a counterbalance.

More strictures were applied. The Utah film would not be shown because, according to Tunick, the Air Force "will call them [the formation of UFOs] seagulls." Keyhoe cried censorship, which Tunick denied, but he remained absolutely firm about the Utah film: "we can't buck them on those pictures."

Despite the bludgeoning unfairness of the set-up, Don grappled with his script, which he now squeezed and pared down to the essentials, reckoning that if he talked fast, he could get across the most important information. He worked overnight preparing the first draft for approval by NICAP's Board of Governors on the Sunday before the broadcast. They felt it was "too weak," however, and should include certain crucial documents: the 1948 "Estimate of the Situation," which concluded that UFOs were interplanetary; the 1952 Air Force (Fournet) analysis of UFO maneuvers that reached the same conclusion; and the findings of the 1953 CIA secret panel report (Robertson), which recommended expanding UFO research as required to solve the problem of instant positive identification of unidentified flying objects.[489]

Along with several juicy cases, he also included NICAP's response to Blue Book's *Special Report 14*, flagging up points about which the Air Force's own claims were contradictory. Among the examples he gave was its assertion that there had been insufficient numbers of detailed descriptions of UFOs to make "even a rough model" of a saucer, although Project Grudge had given specifics of dimensions and stated that accurate models had been made. He went on to quote Senator Barry Goldwater, physicist Dr. Hermann Oberth, and William (Bill) Lear, inventor of the famous jet which bears his name, among others whose opinions supported his own. He made his "high point" the hidden Air Force conclusion that "UFOs were interplanetary spaceships." The finished script barely scratched the surface, but despite the limitations imposed, he had done a good, concise job, carefully timed to be delivered in seven minutes.

Though he'd met all the constrictions laid down, Tunick told him by phone, "We had to cut it, it was too long."[490]

An incredulous Keyhoe now threatened to pull out, and after an argument Irve caved and matters were back on course. But when rehearsals began on Monday, there was bad news. The script handed to him, prepared by *Armstrong*, omitted most of the changes he had agreed over the phone with Tunick. Worse still, Chiles' employer, Eastern Airlines, had forbidden him to appear—and Ruppelt had backed out.

In yet another weathervane swing, Ruppelt had at first agreed to participate, then declined, and Keyhoe was never able to confirm the real reason for his withdrawal, though he had his suspicions. Tunick thought that Ruppelt couldn't get a leave of absence to attend, while late-night radio host Long John Nebel (not a wholly reliable source) said later he had heard Ruppelt didn't want to appear and had sent a wire to say so, though Tunick, when asked, wasn't aware of it. Don had wondered if Ed's recent heart attack had caused him to pull out, then thought his withdrawal was because he hadn't known rehearsals were required. A month after the show, he wrote to Lee

Munsick:

> When invited to appear on the Armstrong program he
> snapped at it very eagerly and said he would not be able to
> come because of pressure of business. He could have come in
> as late as Tuesday afternoon for the rehearsals and been on
> his way back to the Coast Wednesday night or early Thurs-
> day. Also, Armstrong would have covered all his expenses
> and paid him a little bit besides. I am positive that he was
> pressured into withdrawing.[491]

At some later point, Ruppelt in a "strained" manner, phoned Keyhoe and
said he had cancelled because of "business, not pressure," though Don was
unconvinced.[492]

With his main man out of the picture, Keyhoe was already hampered and
now "kicked" about the missing changes to his rehearsal script but was assured
they'd be forthcoming. He was told to read the version at hand for "timing,"
but when Armstrong's mimeographed pages arrived, only the references to
the three documents confirmed by Ruppelt were included. Equally irritating,
Whedon now began to rehearse his own script, which consisted of six minutes
detailing the outlandish claims of contactees, which made it evident to Keyhoe
that "It was a systematic debunking job."

Then it was his turn, but when he read the section about the three
documents, Whedon hurried over to Bob Costello, the show's producer.
When the rehearsal finished, Tunick told Keyhoe he had to cut this portion,
too. The two men debated back and forth about censorship, and even though
Keyhoe pointed out that the documents were "official statements, already on
record," Tunick wouldn't budge—the Air Force had said it would deny them,
along with their source (Ruppelt) and that the Armstrong people "couldn't
have any fight of that kind." Moreover, there could be no mention of any cases
where the source was not named; the Air Force would claim Keyhoe had made
them up. Also forbidden was any reference to "gagging orders," which meant
he could not mention JANAP 146 or AFR-200-2. In short, almost everything
that Don knew was essential to include in the script was vetoed.

Frustrated and angry though he was, it was no picnic for the unfortunate
and harassed Tunick, who was trying to keep matters on course but was caught
in the crossfire between the participants. He would initially, if reluctantly,
accept Keyhoe's arguments demanding this and that should be included, but
he always caved to the Air Force's insistence that more cuts had to be made

and found himself subject to Don's occasional explosions, protesting about censorship.

Keyhoe was now forced to decide between swallowing all this or pulling out but felt the latter action would give the impression that "we were afraid to talk back to the Air Force." Moreover, he wanted to protect Ruppelt from being branded a liar. Then, as he debated with Tunick, he noticed Kenneth Arnold in the background, watching the mess unfold. There was something in his expression that led Don to wonder if all this was part of an Air Force plan to ensure that NICAP would quit and leave the field clear for them.

"It's a raw deal," Arnold told him when he got the chance, because he'd been having similar problems from the beginning. Talent Associates Ltd, the agency handling guest appearances on the show, had failed to send him the first draft of the script in advance of his departure for New York, but gave him verbal assurances that "the true story as far as we know [it] was [to be] portrayed for public interest." On that basis, he made the long journey from Idaho, but after two frustrating days of rehearsal, believed that the constant script changes meant the final outcome was wholly uncertain. Moreover, he had "sent to the studio photographs and photostats of things that I know and could substantially prove to be true," but their use had been forbidden by the Air Force. It was evident there was to be no even-handed presentation of both sides.

At this point, the strong quartet for the "positive" originally scheduled was already halved, but by 1 pm on the day of the broadcast, it was down to just Keyhoe. In the hotel lobby, he saw Arnold checking out and learned that he was throwing in the towel; he felt the whole thing was obviously rigged and would not be party to it. At 2:44 that afternoon, he sent a telegram to Costello and Tunick, explaining his reasons:

> The persons or agencies who protect information of national interest have a serious responsibility. A correctly informed public is one of the greatest assets this nation can have. This is to inform you that I will not be a participant on any program that obviously misrepresents and distorts facts available on any subject broadcast for the public interest nor could I allow any photographs or material properly copyrighted to be used on any program without written permission of the owners. PS: I am not making an appearance on any television program on January 22nd 1958.[493]

Keyhoe was tempted to follow Arnold out the door but knew that would leave the entire program to be a platform for Air Force flimflam. He tried another tack, suggesting to Tunick that he could get Hillenkoetter to stand in, but Tunick rejected this and said he would read Arnold's material in his absence. Desperate now to retrieve something from this fiasco, Keyhoe pondered holding up to the camera the censored page about the Air Force's conclusion that the saucers were interplanetary, but he didn't want to make trouble for Costello and Tunick. Then he thought of something else:

> I was getting more burned up at the fact that the AF had too much time and that [so much] had been cut out of the script and that the public was getting an unfair picture so I mentioned to one of the Armstrong representatives, that we had been working with a Senate subcommittee on UFO secrecy for about 6 months and they had a lot of evidence and they were considering the possibility of public hearings and I said, if I put that in there, how would that be and he said he thought it would be terrific ...[494]

This, at least, would be something, although he would have to ad-lib because he had nothing prepared, but it might be worth a shot. He didn't realize, however, that the representative "had no authority to okay such a thing and that what I should've done was go to Bob Costello, the producer."

At 10 pm, Eastern Time, the program aired and if it had been a radio presentation, listeners tuning in part-way might have been forgiven for thinking they were hearing a *Bob and Ray* comedy sketch. The first sixteen minutes were taken up by Doug Edwards' overview of the topic, which at least was rational, if not gently slanted in favor of UFOs. Then the Air Force got under way, rolling out its usual, tired, party line, while Keyhoe nursed his increasing frustration beneath a polite silence.

Whedon went into some detail about the Mantell incident, admitting that the Air Force no longer thought the pilot had been chasing Venus but had seen a Skyhook balloon, and then made a lengthy, pointless spiel about crackpots and their hoaxes, complete with photographs, sounding very satisfied at his own erudition when making these well-worn pronouncements. Moreover, he stated confidently that the cost of investigating each UFO case was $10,000, but this was later refuted by the Air Force when it somewhat threw him under the bus: "Whedon was a reserve officer on a two-week active duty tour at the time he made his statement ... Whedon now says 'This sounded like a good

226

round number.' He had no basis of fact for making this statement."[495]

After the commercial break, it was Keyhoe's turn. He still hadn't decided whether or not to go ahead with the ad-lib and began to read his denuded script from the teleprompter. Then suddenly, unable to contain himself, he decided to wing it:

> And now, Mr. Edwards, I would like to make a disclosure ... something which has never been revealed to the public. For the last six months our Committee has been working with a Senate Committee which is investigating official secrecy on UFOs. If the hearings are held, open hearings, I believe it will prove that the flying saucers are real ..."

Silent pandemonium ensued. The teleprompter began wildly racking up and down in a desperate attempt to signal him stop, while in the control room Bob Costello "grabbed the sound control knob and turned it way down."[496] Keyhoe, unaware that he had been faded out, kept talking. The sound was briefly turned up and then down again, checking to see if he'd reverted to the teleprompter, then turned up fully a few seconds later when he had finished his ad-lib.

Next up was the asinine academic, Menzel. In his usual huffy, self-important style, he put on a display that outdid even his previous balderdash:

> It's gone far enough. In my opinion it's not the reports of the flying saucers which should be analyzed, it's the non-qual-ified interpreters themselves who argue that these saucers come from outer space.

He declared that Project Blue book hadn't "paid enough attention" to weather phenomena, then bit the hand that fed him with a dismissal of the Air Force's Skyhook balloon statement, pronouncing instead that Mantell had been chasing a "mock sun, perhaps." Finally, he attributed many sightings to "owls that glow in the dark." It was surely a mark of how desperate the Air Force was to defend its position that Menzel and his risible nonsense was the best they could find to bolster their case, live on national television.

The Air Force's Horner gave the last word, quoting selectively from the Robertson Panel summary—which Keyhoe had been forbidden to even mention—that no evidence of any kind had been found, and he concluded with

227

his assurance that the Air Force would continue its "detailed investigation."

* * *

The CBS switchboard was jammed for 45 minutes after the end of the broadcast with calls complaining about Keyhoe's cut-off. Even more written complaints were sent to the network, the Air Force, and NICAP about what was perceived by the public as blatant censorship, more in keeping with Communism than American free speech. Though Don's ad-lib was not a world-shattering announcement, and some viewers managed to hear or lip-read most of it, it was the principle of the thing, and many were outraged. He responded to members' concerns with a circular:

> The statement I began when cut off the air was as follows:
> "In the last six months, we (NICAP) have been work-ing with a Senate committee investigating official secrecy on Unidentified Flying Objects. If open hearings are held, I feel it will prove beyond doubt that the flying saucers are real machines under intelligent control."[497]

He also was obliged to issue a statement absolving CBS and the program of blame:

> Due to a misunderstanding on my part ... the producer and director had no alternative but to order audio-cut-off since they had no idea of what I was about to say. I regret the mis-understanding and wish to make it plain that this was not an attempt at censorship by CBS or *Armstrong Circle Theatre*.

He admitted to Ted Bloecher of CSI-NY that studio staff said they'd have let his ad-lib go if he hadn't begun it with "I am about to disclose something," but he remained positive overall that interest in NICAP and UFOs had increased as a result of the show, and that "the Senate committee is now stepping up its work and is actively considering open hearings. All of this is to the good ..."[498]

Keyhoe was nonetheless much concerned about any detrimental impact his impromptu action might have on his chances of future CBS appearances and also on Costello and Tunick, both of whom he considered to be the "nicest" people he had ever encountered in TV, but he needn't have worried.

Costello wrote him a letter of thanks, adding:

> The response to the show has been very good … You may
> be interested to know that you have thousands of fans as ev-
> idenced by the CBS switchboard which had calls backed up
> for forty-five minutes following the show.[499]

Others were on his side, too. Staunch ally, Pan-Am pilot Captain Bill
Nash (of the famous Nash-Fortenberry UFO sighting), although still grieving
from the recent death of his wife, wrote to Keyhoe about the cut-off:

> Frankly, I think that this is the best thing that has happened
> since Russia fired off Sputnik.[500]

Equally supportive was Len Stringfield. The day after the broadcast, he
sent a short note to say he had been "swamped with calls—everybody quite
upset… Count me in on any showdown. I have much to say."[501]

Even Barry Goldwater got in on the act. He wrote on behalf of NICAP
Board member Reverend Baller to Richard Horner "concerning the Air Force's
position regarding unidentified flying objects as expressed on the Armstrong
Circle Theatre." Horner replied with a fair account of the reasons for Keyhoe's
cut-off, but the rest of the letter was the standard explanation given to any
citizen who made enquiries about UFOs, accompanied by the Air Force fact
sheet.

Keyhoe's initial optimism about the effect of the *Armstrong* debacle was
short lived. In early March, he issued a bulletin to members, advising that,
"Many Americans, uninformed on UFOs, took the Air Force statements
without question … As a result, there has been a sharp drop in membership
applications …[502] He pleaded for members to recruit at least one other person,
to make donations if they could "until we are on our feet," and to publicize
NICAP wherever possible.

He also flagged that on March 8th he was due to be interviewed by Mike
Wallace on the ABC network, followed immediately by an appearance on
Long John Nebel's midnight to 5:30 am radio talk show. In this then-rare
format, guests went free-range, pecking at morsels and scratching up ideas on
non-mainstream topics, including UFOs and contactees, reaching an audience
in thirty-eight states and some parts of Canada. Though the program lacked
polish and suffered from long periods of stultifying boredom when Nebel
would spend minutes slowly explaining or repeating irrelevant or obvious

points, it had nonetheless acquired a hallowed status among night-owl listeners and was a good platform for Keyhoe to try and "offset" the damaging effect of his appearance on the *Armstrong Circle Theatre*.

He hoped for a similar effect on *The Mike Wallace Interview*, whose intense, stern style was challenging for his guests. Though he often elicited from them a frankness and depth that standard celebrity interviews neither sought nor achieved, it made for uncomfortable viewing. "I knew they could be rough," said Keyhoe in dread anticipation of his ordeal, but at least he had received assurance from the host that there would be no restrictions on their discussion.

The studio set evoked an interrogation chamber with Wallace perched on a low-backed stool, wreathed in cigarette smoke, focused and inquisitorial. The victim, starkly lit against a black background, sat opposite his tormentor who mercilessly probed and goaded, sometimes asking deeply personal questions, like a doctor interested only in the diagnosis of, but indifferent to, the suffering of the patient. The camera was equally merciless, zooming in close enough to see the beads of sweat and the twitching of the captive's face, laying bare the fear in his eyes.

Keyhoe's eyes, however, showed no fear. His demeanor was calm, attentive, and confident, and the interview overall covered much of the ground upon which the Air Force had feared to tread in the *Armstrong* broadcast. In fact, Keyhoe rather breezed through it and more than once made Wallace flounder, notably when he picked up on the host's careless accusations of pilots being counted among hoaxers and again when he sycophantically lauded Menzel's scientific prowess. Don sidestepped this gushing accolade and Wallace, seeming to sense that he was on the wrong track, nervously moved on to another topic.

In the meager 30-minute format, of which several were taken up by adverts for Parliament cigarettes, Keyhoe gave no Earth-shaking information; essentially he banged the same drum with which he had been making noise since 1949, and both he and Wallace missed the opportunity for a revelatory examination of NICAP's evidence. Many of the questions were prosaic and exposed a basic flaw in both media and public understanding of what was really important. When asked by Wallace the usual, "Where do they come from?," "What do they look like?," "Why are they here?," and "Why don't they communicate with us?," Keyhoe could only answer that he didn't know. (The contactees, in full contrast when asked these questions, were able to answer all of them in detail, rendering any negative admissions dull in comparison.)

However, one significant point was touched upon. Wallace told Keyhoe that according to the Air Force, a member of the Senate subcommittee had now said there was no interest in having hearings on UFOs. In reply, Don pointed out that within the last two weeks he had been giving information to its Chief Investigator, but Wallace's information proved to be correct. The prospect of hearings appeared to have been dashed.

In April, Keyhoe wrote to Coral Lorenzen that "the McClelland Committee now seems to be backing down—under Air Force pressure ... It was only after the *Armstrong Circle Theatre* and *Mike Wallace* shows that they began to deny they had any plans for public hearings."[503]

The Air Force, despite its shaky assertions and the risible posturing of Menzel, seemed to have scored another victory, sending Keyhoe back to square one. Yet, for a few strange days in August, it looked as though he might overturn their advantage.

The Under Secretary of the Air Force must have been startled to receive a memo (date unclear but likely August 5th or 6th) from USAF Major W. P. Fisher, Director, Legislative Liaison, telling him that "informal notification" had been received from the House Select Committee on Astronautics and Space Exploration, to advise that "hearings ... on the subject of unidentified flying objects" would commence at 1400 hours on August 7th and were expected to last four days. The Air Force was asked to testify on August 8th. "The Subcommittee has specifically requested that no publicity be given to the hearings."[504]

John W. McCormack, chairman of this House Select Committee, presided, and the surviving documents from the "closed secret session" were written by the Air Force, hence the word "hearing" was crossed out and replaced with "study." In short, A. Francis Arcier of ATIC scientific intelligence and Captain George T. Gregory, now Blue Book chief, presented the usual party-line, which was apparently well-received by the committee members, and the Air Force came away feeling that the outcome would be a "vote of confidence in the Air Force, ensuring the public that the Air Force is not hiding any information on UFO's."

It was noted also that "additional witnesses from public life" were to be called, apparently to be heard without the presence of the Air Force, who "may be required to return to answer questions posed by public witnesses." Keyhoe was listed among them—though the others were all in the "negative" camp, notably Menzel. Nonetheless, Don's inclusion surely held out the possibility that he would present his own compelling counter-evidence to the

AF's version.

For reasons unknown, apparently before Keyhoe had been approached, the hearing was shut down and no public witnesses were heard.[505]

Chapter 26:
Annus Horribilis

Keyhoe's first year as Director of NICAP had been the most difficult since his *True* article hit the stands in December 1949. He was no longer an independent writer and investigator, free to deal with saucer-matters in whatever way he thought best. Now he had to manage a national organization devoted to a subject that was widely ridiculed, navigate the turbulent waters of finances, staff, public relations, and editorial demands, while facing off against the Air Force, the press, and the contactees, along with trying to tempt Congress to participate in UFO hearings.

The latter possibility had now diminished, but if NICAP hadn't gained any members due to the *Armstrong Circle Theatre* debacle, Keyhoe had at least bolstered his reputation, though the resultant strain upon him was evident a few days later. In a letter to *Boston Globe* editor Otto Zausmer, who wanted biographical information on him, Keyhoe admitted that he had "been ill—an after effect of a week with little sleep."[506]

With *Armstrong* and the Mike Wallace interview now behind him, if he hoped that 1958 would be more settled and productive, he would be disappointed.

Even before these two strenuous appearances, his burden had been increased when Lee Munsick left in October 1957; he needed a reliable and higher income, but his amicable departure created an enormous editorial void that Keyhoe was unable to fill. He was therefore thankful when 28-year-old Richard "Dick" Hall, a philosophy graduate of Tulane University, came aboard in June 1958.

Hall's own interest in UFOs went back to at least his time as a student when he'd edited and published *The Satellite*, a newsletter that took a "strictly factual" approach to the saucers. In the early fifties, while an enlisted man at Keesler AFB in Mississippi, he had read UFO press items pinned on the service club noticeboard and had later read Keyhoe's books. The 1952 flap convinced him that UFOs needed serious attention, and when he heard about NICAP's formation under Keyhoe's directorship, he began a correspondence with him, culminating in being offered a position as Assistant Editor. Hall would immediately prove to be a crucial asset to NICAP. Highly literate, with a remarkable clarity of expression and capable of rational, in-depth analysis, he had deep respect and admiration for Keyhoe, who came to regard his young protégé as a "godsend."[507]

Dick's arrival might well have seemed tinged with an aura of divine intervention, for it coincided with one of the most stressful and tempestuous periods of NICAP's existence, and without his help, the organization—and Keyhoe—would certainly have collapsed before the end of the year.

Shortly before Hall joined, NICAP had moved out of its large office on the second floor of 1536 Connecticut Avenue to smaller rooms on the fourth floor in an effort to cut costs.[508] The change of location, however, made no difference to a fundamental problem that had hampered the organization since its creation. Hall soon became aware that NICAP's stalwart, Rose, had a thorn. Years later, he recalled:

> Mrs. Campbell was a great believer in "contactee" stories, and she was trying to steer NICAP in the direction of being a credulous fan club ... In a private meeting with Major Keyhoe, I expressed my concerns ... He was already aware of the problem but lacked the resources to hire other staff members. Mrs. Campbell was a highly organized person and a skilled office manager, and she was all he had.[509]

Keyhoe knew plenty, though not all, about his secretary's cultist interests and had long tried to set aside his disquiet, even though the situation was further aggravated by her assistant, Bessie Clark, who was brought in to the fold by Rose herself and who shared her commitment to contactees. Dick Hall's arrival redressed the balance somewhat, bringing the total permanent staff percentage to 50/50 for and against the lunatic fringe, but the simmering tensions between the two camps remained a dangerous undercurrent, around which Keyhoe and Hall were obliged to navigate, and it was taking its toll.

By the summer, a rumor was circulating that Keyhoe had suffered a heart attack (the previous year he had confided to Ruppelt that he had "had some funny feelings in my left side"), which according to Dick Hall was "partly true."[510]

> Major Keyhoe has not been too well in the recent past, and he did have electro-cardiograms taken showing, I believe, some sort of minor heart damage. However, he has not been

hospitalized or even put out of circulation. Since I have been here, he has been to the office frequently, has appeared on a local radio show, and has done all the usual routine office work.[511]

Word of this had also reached Adamski, who wrote to Keyhoe expressing his concern and hoped he was

> ... fully recovered by now. As you know, I had a similar experience several years ago and realize that it was caused from too much tension. May I suggest that your life is more important to you than all the work you are doing ...[512]

Keyhoe replied with appreciation for his kind wishes and agreed "that tension of course does add to such condition." These gentle sentiments aside, the meat of their letters was in connection with yet another of Adamski's claims that, thanks in no small part to Clara John, had been doing the rounds. This further added to the strain on Keyhoe, NICAP, and the relationship of both to Rose Hackett Campbell and the contactees.

It had begun in December 1957, when Adamski received the notorious "Straith Letter." Typed on official-looking notepaper, impressed in the top-left corner with a seal and postmarked December 6th, the supposed author was "R. E. Straith" of the "Cultural Exchange Committee" in Washington, D.C., who gave Adamski his personal opinion that was critical of official secrecy on UFOs. He wrote: "It will no doubt please you to know that the Department has on file a great deal of confirmatory evidence bearing out your own claims ..." Similar letters were sent to CSI-NY and APRO. Both organizations smelled a rat and set them aside without public comment, but for Adamski the letter was unquestionable proof that everything he had spouted was true. This "proof" had been provided by his old ally, Clara John. Adamski had written asking her to find out about Straith, and as a consequence of her own enquiries, the trouble began.

According to James D. Villard, publisher of *The Ufologer*, an infrequent periodical that gave space to advocates of subjective beliefs, Clara had phoned him on February 12, 1958, and asked, without giving a reason for her enquiry, if he knew of an R. E. Straith working in the State Department. Villard's contacts there suggested that, though Straith was not known to them, it was possible he might be someone who was on "special work," but not with the Department. Villard, according to his own account, told this to Clara, explaining that if this man was doing such work, he would not be listed in the usual directories.

She then wrote to Adamski:

> I have just gotten a small amount of information about R. E. Straith. I am told he is in the State Department and is on se- cret work. Probably this is why he was hard to track down.[513]

Unsurprisingly, this was good enough for Flying George, and he began to proclaim the contents of the letter, being fully convinced it was authentic.[514] When Villard became aware of this development, he gave Clara the benefit of the doubt and thought she had misunderstood his information, so he phoned her and made it clear there was no Straith in the State Department or anywhere else, and that he believed the letter to be a hoax.[515] On receiving this news, Adamski entirely rejected it and merely escalated his claims that Straith existed; he was not about to relinquish a supposed official acknowledgement of his beliefs, no matter how flimsy the evidence and how unlikely it was that an official would send out a personal opinion on a high-security matter using Departmental stationery. Moreover, he refuted the information that the Cultural Exchange Committee didn't exist and insisted he had "spared no effort" in his investigation—but his "effort" amounted only to what Clara John had told him.

In reality, the letter was a piece of mischief born of a drunken prank by Jim Moseley and Gray Barker, aided and abetted by James Villard himself, who had earlier supplied them with some pilfered, albeit no longer used stationery, bearing the impressed insignia. Villard denied this already-circulating rumor in his own account of the Straith debacle, published in UFO researcher Max Miller's winter issue of *Saucers*.[516]

Later independent analysis of the letter showed unequivocally that it had been typed on Barker's typewriter.[517] After this was revealed, he and Moseley— who also was suspected of involvement—took accusatory pot-shots at each other in their respective newsletters, but old hands in the saucer business knew this was how they operated and weren't fooled by their faux antagonism. It would be many years before the hoax was admitted (by Moseley), but a seed had been planted in Adamski's fertile mind and it grew rapidly into a giant beanstalk.[518]

Among those to whom he wrote extolling this apparent vindication from on high was Gray Barker himself, whose amusement upon reading Adamski's letter can readily be imagined. He told Barker he had investigated "in every way possible" the identity of Straith, had acquired information from "unimpeachable sources," and that "Mr. Straith experienced quite a battle within himself before writing that letter."[519]

Adamski now went on a jag, sending out photostats to all and sundry, and writing in his own booklet publication, *Cosmic Science*, that he could "prove" the letter was genuine:

> The original letter … carries the impression of the official
> Seal of State just above the salutation. This Seal is NEVER
> found on blank paper. It is impressed only AFTER a letter
> has been written and signed. Our Seal of State is rigorously
> guarded … for documents bearing this official badge carry
> weight throughout the world.[520]

He clung especially to the significance of this seal, which he was certain could mean only that it was genuine, despite Keyhoe's written insistence that:

> The letterhead on which the so-called Straith letter was writ-
> ten was imprinted with this seal, but by machinery. That is,
> this letterhead was turned out by tens of thousands with the
> seal impressed on blank paper with the usual Department of
> State heading.[521]

In his June issue of *Cosmic Science*, Adamski again declared that he had "made a thorough investigation of the authenticity of the letter" and that "a correspondent in Washington, DC"—evidently Keyhoe—had told him that the paper on which the letter was typed was produced in "tens of thousands." "This, I do not believe!" he exclaimed, adding, "If anyone is deliberately misusing our Seal of State, he should be located and exposed."[522] Even after Adamski was visited by an official from the State Department, who told him the paper was nowadays used only as "scratch paper" at "the New York office in the UN," he—and his similarly deluded secretary, Lucy McGinnis—interpreted the conversation to mean that Straith existed and would be found at that location.[523]

Matters were made more difficult thanks to Los Angeles KTTV's *Bill Welsh Show* of July 17th, on which the host (who described Adamski as "one of the outstanding leaders in the field of Unidentified Flying Objects") interviewed Carol Honey, then an Adamski-devotee.[524] Honey claimed that the "Cultural Exchange Committee" did indeed exist because according to press reports it had been instrumental in arranging Bob Hope's visa for his recent visit to Russia. But he was in error on this; press reports made no mention of a "committee," as confirmed at the time by Max Miller, who contacted several official sources that admitted there was a cultural exchange program, but it had no "committee."[525]

This latest absurdity dragged on for over a year, creating a significant headache for Keyhoe. His enormous backlog of correspondence was now swelled by letters from within and without NICAP, demanding to know what was his real position about the Straith letter. Having set himself up as the foremost civilian authority on the saucers, he was inevitably the go-to guy for the public when they wanted answers. Their enquiries couldn't be set aside, given the increasing interest arising from the case and the potential for damage to the Committee, so more time and expense was unavoidably and pointlessly incurred. Flying George refused to believe Keyhoe's repeated, patient, written explanations, nor any of his assurances by phone that he had been the victim of a hoax.

All sensible efforts, however, were merely logic off a contactee's back. Adamski dismissed official denials received "orally and by letter" from the State Department and was unswayed by its firm request that he "inform all who inquired about the letter that it was spurious and to cease distributing copies of it." These refutations simply made him more entrenched; he didn't want to be bothered with the facts and would never depart from his conviction that the letter was real. Even Wilbert Smith kicked against Don's insistence that it was a "phony." In a telephone conversation between the two in March, Smith had become "a little irritated" at this idea, claiming that he "knew 'somebody' who knew Straith … was working in a super-secret agency partly under State Dept. control."[526]

For Keyhoe, however, 1958 was to bring further trouble. Another Adamski incident was about to erupt, which would eclipse the Straith debacle, create more turbulence for NICAP, and bring about the inevitable, bitter showdown with Rose Hackett Campbell.

Chapter 27:
Cleaning House

The break had been a long time coming and it would later be realized that Rose's cultist meddling in NICAP's affairs had begun even before Keyhoe's takeover from Townsend Brown.

It was thanks to her that another of her adored contactees, "Dr." Daniel Fry, would for many years be under a—somewhat justified—apparent misconception that he was a "Founder Member" of NICAP. This belief was based on her letter to him of late September 1956 in which she acknowledged receipt of his cheque for $15 (the cost of membership under Townsend Brown) and his application as a "regular voting member." However, the receipt attached to the letter was clearly marked "Founder Membership," which she further confirmed in February 1957 when she wrote to inform him that his recent book, *Steps to the Stars*, would be placed in NICAP's library:

> Since you became one of our Founder Members, NICAP has continued to struggle for general recognition … more "big names" are to be added to the Board of Governors. The "big money" continues to hold off—except for tentative nibbles, but sooner or later the Big Truth will out! (These remarks are my own, please, so do not quote me! Ever since hearing your most impressive recordings at the home of Mrs Walton Colcord John, I have felt as if I know you quite well—and favorably indeed!)[527]

His membership fee of $15 was, of course, $985 short of the amount to be a Founder Member, as per Brown's original requirement for donors, who, in return, would receive voting rights. Moreover, it was submitted after the closing date for such applications, so it can be inferred that, either this concession was approved by Brown, which seems unlikely given that he had to borrow $25 from Clara. Keyhoe later suspected that this mess resulted from a decision taken independently and without authority by Rose herself, but whatever the reason, even though the matter would not be exposed and resolved until 1967, it gave apparent status to a major contactee and was among the earliest written examples of her determination to turn NICAP into "a credulous fan club" for contactee cultists.

She caused other difficulties between NICAP and Fry during what would be the last few weeks of her tenure, when she accepted from him a small disc,

> … about 2.5 inches in diameter, one-fourth of an inch thick, with a hole in the center about one-fourth inch in diameter. It is a dull black in color, with a few specks of what appear to be tiny bits of metal. It is moderately flexible, like some kind of rubber composition.[528]

In June 1957, Fry had appeared on Long John Nebel's program and had shown the disc to him and his other guests, with the strong implication that it was of "extraterrestrial origin." This resulted in a "touch of unintended slapstick," unseen by the radio audience, of course. One of the guests was Lex Mebane of CSI-NY, and he immediately recognized the disc as "a toroidal ferrite magnet of the type used in high-speed computers and children's toys. It was a good choice for astounding the ignorant." Mebane decided he would "expose the deceit" and quickly pocketed the disc, at which point "Fry dived from his chair to recover his exhibit," but it fell out of a hole in Mebane's pocket and rolled across the floor, from where "Fry quickly retrieved it."[529]

It otherwise caused no great interest, but through a series of "Chinese Whispers" over the next year, the disc became reputed to have strange magnetic properties and to hover in the air. In letters to NICAP in August and September 1958, Fry denied these attributes, but in an effort to refute claims that it was merely an "ordinary piece of ferritic material," explained that he had left the object with Mrs. Campbell during the first week of August and made an agreement with her that half of it would be subjected to a "complete analysis" by NICAP.

When Dick Hall contacted Fry for further information about the disc, he refused to say where he had obtained it because "it might cause the specimen to be impounded, and the analysis to be classified." He would say only that "it was upon the surface of the earth when I obtained it" and that all its elements were "common to this earth." As to his reason for leaving the disc with Rose, he later contradicted himself, saying that, "I have never requested Nicap [*sic*] to examine or to analyze this object. I handed it to Mrs Campbell at her request because she expressed interest in it."[530]

NICAP ultimately concluded, via analysis by Colonel Emerson, that the disk had no unusual properties, but the fundamental problem was that Rose's independent collaboration with a contactee had incurred time and expense that the Committee could ill afford, adding further to the mounting tension.[531] The issue was still rumbling in early September, but by then, another matter had erupted, in which Adamski was the unwitting catalyst that caused the simmering antagonism between Keyhoe and his secretary to boil over.

David Jesus, a NICAP member based in Hollywood, informed the Major by letter that, on July 25th, Adamski—only a week after his previous appearance on the *Bill Welsh Show*—had again been his guest on the show, and this time he triumphantly brandished a NICAP membership card:

> Adamski: NICAP was battling me a little bit ... yet I get a Membership Card that costs seven and a half dollars from them altogether free of charge just last week.
> Welsh: They've made you an honorary member and still they argue with you about your claims.
> Adamski: Yeah, that's right. Here it is ... By golly, I got it last week. I was so surprised.
> Welsh: ...He's a member in good standing.
> Adamski: Good standing![532]

Dated July 30th, the letter was received on August 4th. By then, Rose Campbell had received a letter from Howard Menger, another notorious contactee whom she revered. Menger said he came from Jupiter, had married a woman he claimed was from Venus, and the planetary pair held Rose in high esteem. They had invited her and "the staff of NICAP and especially Major Keyhoe" to attend a "UFO space convention" at their farm in mid-September, along with Adamski, Van Tassel, Fry, and their enablers, Gray Barker and Long John Nebel.[533] He claimed in his letter that he possessed a film showing "four discs," which had hovered over his property the previous week.

Rose had the gall to show the letter to Keyhoe, who politely declined the invitation in writing and enclosed a form asking Menger to detail his claims about the four discs. It's worth noting that Menger didn't specifically ask for NICAP to get involved in the case—he had merely said "You may wish to check into this, and we will be glad to give you any assistance you need." By asking Menger for more information, Keyhoe was creating work for himself, expense for NICAP, and unwittingly gave a contactee credence by offering unasked-for consideration of his claim.

Moreover, the fact that Rose would push such an invitation under Keyhoe's nose demonstrates how determined she was to bend him to her cultist agenda and suggests either a profound obtuseness on Menger's part for making such an offer to Keyhoe, or that she had given him cause to believe it would be accepted. She was evidently playing both ends against the middle, since only two months earlier she had given an excellent interview to George Todt, press reporter and NICAP special adviser, which had been entirely supportive of the Committee and wholly without any hint of her cultist leanings.[534] Behind the scenes, however, she was becoming restless in her devotion to the contactee cause and unhappy about Don's position thereon.[535]

During May 1958 she'd been exchanging letters with Adamski's secretary, Lucy McGinnis, in which her increasing frustration and disloyalty was apparent:

> Let me say (and this is entirely between you and George and me, please) Donald Keyhoe is vastly ignorant of the contact angles of truth in the saucer story and I personally think that is shocking and shortsighted …

She did admit that out of "thousands and thousands" of letters received by the Major, only about six were in favor of giving prominence to contact "angles," and lamented that things would go nowhere "with the practical promotion of the pround [sic] messages of truth that our space brothers are bringing us …even their use of men like DEK are all in the picture of enlightenment to mankind …"[536]

Even before the Menger letter, Rose's nerve was increasing. She had shown Keyhoe a letter she'd written to NICAP member John Weigle (former president of the short-lived Ventura County UFO club), inferring he should disregard NICAP's policy of not endorsing any book and that she considered the Major to be an *ipse dixit*, i.e., a person whose assertion of authority is based not on proof, but solely on their own opinion. This was surely rather rich coming from a contactee-follower, and when Keyhoe read it, he was furious ("My first reaction was to blow up").[537]

At this point, he evidently hadn't yet read the letter from David Jesus about Adamski, but when he did, he became incensed.[538] He'd been entirely unaware that Adamski had received a membership card and on checking the office files, found that six other notorious contactees—Orfeo Angellucci, Truman Bethurum, Howard Menger, Buck Nelson, Reinhold O. Schmidt, and George Van Tassel had also received cards for which they had not paid, nor had acknowledged receipt of them.

Adamski's TV appearance on July 25th soon brought a flood of enquiries, causing Don to complain that:

> I have received phone calls, telegrams, and air-special letters at home, demanding to know whether I gave Adamski, secretly, an honorary membership, unpaid ... this story has spread like wildfire and has angered a number of NICAP paid-up members. To quote: they feel they've been tricked; they paid, even sent donations in some cases—and here Adamski gets an unpaid membership, when he is very well able to pay. Also, NICAP apparently did this secretly ...[539]

In Keyhoe's view, Adamski's bragging had been done specifically to annoy NICAP members and to gain publicity at the organization's expense, but further investigations discovered that the contactees—except for Adamski—had been sent membership cards due to "addressograph list error." Don fired off telegrams to each, informing them of the mistake and that

> You have never been a NICAP member. You were meant to receive only publications dealing with your claims ... Please return unauthorized membership card. Any use now will constitute false pretenses. [sic]

To Adamski's telegram he added:

> You have been warned by telephone and by my previous telegrams. Any further claim to honorary NICAP membership will be false pretenses [sic] and will be dealt with as such.[540]

At some point during all this turmoil, matters got even worse when Keyhoe discovered that Adamski's card was indeed valid; someone had paid for his membership and it was suggested to him that Rose was responsible. At first he "was sure this was not correct" but suspected she at least knew who was the culprit and took her to task. He wrote to her:

> [T]his was my first knowledge of it, and I think I should have been notified of this development ... I am not disputing the right of anyone to purchase a gift membership for Adamski

or anyone else. But under the circumstances ... for anyone in NICAP to give him such a paid membership would inevitably lead to trouble. In any case I should have been consulted and notified ... But you do have influence with Adamski ... Regardless of your having known about his membership, you could still show him the bad results.[541]

Meanwhile, the happy recipient—evidently not in on the decision to gift him a membership and unaware of who had paid for it—stirred the waters even harder in his letter to Keyhoe of August 15th, (received on the 18th) thanking him for the card, "since I had neither asked for such a gift, nor had sent payment for membership" and did himself no favors when he added:

> This afternoon I am leaving for a two or three week lecture tour up the Pacific Coast. I shall take both the membership card and your telegram with me and let the people decide what they can make out of the two.

On the 13th, before Adamski's threat arrived, the heated showdown between Keyhoe and Rose had finally come. Two days later, when he'd cooled down, he wrote to her a nine-page letter, in which he calmly addressed the festering mutual resentments that their confrontation had exposed. She had accused him of attacking the contactee groups, complained that NICAP's policy excluded consideration of their claims and that he had "struck" at her behind her back in regard to her contactee associations. Moreover, he was not in the office enough, didn't do any "NICAP work" at home, and had no idea how much work got done, while she and Bess Clark put in regular hours. He had "used" her merely for her assistance.

In response, he fully acknowledged her vital work but reiterated at length NICAP's policy on contactees, "which you yourself helped shape and have often endorsed as the only logical one," rebutting her accusation that this was "Keyhoe policy." He felt "very much resentful" about the John Weigle letter and demanded to know who had paid for Adamski's membership. He didn't deny the right of contactees to become members but made it clear that in future they would not be accepted without his approval.

In an apparent attempt to garner her understanding, he listed his many problems that tell us how, less than two years at the helm, his life was falling apart:

> My personal problems ... are a nightmare ... I went through
> my savings, borrowed, and at present am heavily in debt. My
> taxes (Virginia) have been unpaid since early 1957; I have
> had to buy items on long-time contracts. We had no vaca-
> tion last year, only a few days (from my wife's small savings)
> this year. I am in a desperate financial situation, entirely be-
> cause of NICAP ... I have written and sold only one article
> since I became director—payment, $300 ... This situation
> has caused serious problems at home; I live in constant wor-
> ry about the future, knowing I have risked the welfare of
> my family, and may well lose my home and whatever else I
> possess.

He insisted that he was still determined to keep NICAP going. If it closed, then "the Air Force will jump in and play it up as proving we found no proof of UFO reality," the press would do the same, and Congress would "not initiate a drive for hearings ... but I am determined not to let it fail without a last-ditch fight."

He admitted that the Adamski membership issue had made him feel "violently bitter," but though he had since calmed down, he made it clear to Rose there would be no change toward contactees. She must accept it if she wished to continue at NICAP.

She did not accept it. By the time Keyhoe was preparing notes for a NICAP members' meeting in Washington, D.C., on August 27th, she had resigned, but so desperate was his need for office help, he was giving her time to reconsider whether or not her decision was "irrevocable." When the *UFO Investigator* was issued in September, he had his answer:

> We regret to announce the resignation of Mrs. Rose H
> Campbell ... In recent weeks, Mrs. Campbell has frankly
> rejected the NICAP policy on contactee claims, urging that
> our publications give favorable consideration and approxi-
> mately 50% space to contactee stories...
>
> In resigning, Mrs. Campbell has frankly warned that she
> plans to fight NICAP ... [I]t is unfortunate that a former
> NICAP official should believe it necessary to launch such an
> attack.[542]

Her "sidekick," Bessie Clark, also quit, so it seemed that the last of the contactee acolytes had gone, and presumably another office assistant, Margaret Kruckman, also departed. She was an early funder of NICAP under Townsend Brown and was the wife of Arnold Kruckman, noted aviation pioneer, press reporter, and Adamski-ite. He'd been pressing his friend, Republican representative Wint Smith, to lend support to creating the aforementioned HR 7843, particularly so it could be used to "make mandatory the registration of any persons who are in our country from space." According to Kruckman, Smith had "more than just a casual interest" in the saucers and had "read about everything on the subject."[543]

The Kruckmans were among Clara John's fervent group, so evidently the contactee infestation in NICAP's tiny staff had been significant. The surviving records don't show if Margaret Kruckman left at the same time as Rose (though Keyhoe's later correspondence indicates she did), nor if she was responsible for the reference initial "k" on the letter sent to Adamski enclosing the membership card. The other "k" in the organization was Elizabeth Ann Kendall, a fresh hire at that time, who used the reference initials "eak." But the initial "k" was still used a year after Rose's departure, so it remains unclear who sent the troublesome card. NICAP employed many volunteer or part-time staff during Keyhoe's time and there are no detailed records of their names.

Meanwhile, word of all this reached loyal member and supporter Idabel Epperson, later head of NICAP's Los Angeles subcommittee. She wrote hastily and at length to equally loyal Isabel Davis of CSI-NY with her suspicions that the Major, as some now complained, was secretly a contactee, but Davis' reply was straightforward and rational. "[M]y confidence in Keyhoe and NICAP is about 200%" and she wrote six pages in his defense, pointing out the enormous burdens his directorship placed upon him and her views about the problem of handling the contactees:

> CSI finally learned to make short shrift of the crackpots; we get written applications and refuse to take money from members of the lunatic fringe, and take the resultant criticism of our "intolerance" with mighty few sleepless nights. We can afford this because we're a very small organization and because Lex Mebane pays half our costs of operation. Can Keyhoe do this? … not while support from serious people is inadequate for NICAP's operation. Promises of lump sums were made to Keyhoe, you know, when he took over the Di-

rectorship from Townsend Brown, who appears to have been nothing but a promoter .... I'm not even sure that NICAP could or should reject the crackpots entirely .... I think [the policy] of sending questionnaires to the contactees, offering to have a NICAP panel hear their claims in person, etc., is the only possible course.[544]

Idabel would follow up with an apology for her original knee-jerk letter and reiterated that she was firmly on Keyhoe's side. Nonetheless, it's clear from the exchange between these two women that the ripples of the membership card incident had spread right through the UFO research community and were immensely detrimental to Keyhoe and NICAP. Amid the flurry of letters, calls, and telegrams that Don fired off in August and September, there seemed scarcely time to draw breath and many crossed in the post, requiring him to withdraw some of his comments and demands, while grappling with what was now a damage-limitation exercise.

He chose not to publicly air specifics about which staff member was responsible for the Adamski debacle, but after the whirlwind upset and his knee-jerk responses, he had to perform something of a climb-down to the other contactees who had received cards. He didn't deny their right to be members but insisted their memberships had never been valid, and if they wished, could reapply. Menger chose to do so, following what amounted to an apology from Keyhoe.

As it now stood, the "lunatic fringe" element had been ousted from inside NICAP, and there was a feeling of relief within and beyond. Keyhoe acknowledged it would be "tough going" until they could get more help—it was now just himself, Dick Hall, and Elizabeth Kendall "holding the fort"—but "at least we do not have to worry about little tricks being pulled behind our backs."[545] Rose, it later emerged, had carried out a last petty stunt before her departure: she pilfered NICAP's "form book"—presumably the forms that were sent out to contactees to ask for proof of their claims. "God, what a woman!" wrote Lee Munsick to Keyhoe, feeling very happy to hear she had gone, particularly as she, for reasons he could not fathom, blamed him for the whole mess.[546]

Both Coral Lorenzen and Idabel Epperson were among many who wrote to express their pleasure at Rose's departure, and in late September Don received a letter from Morris Jessup who, despite his involvement in the early NICAP and his attendances at Clara John's meetings, took a dim view of Rose and the contactees:

> Rose Hackett wrote me a letter this week, and then phoned
> me. She told me of resigning. She didn't give any reason but
> I know enough to know that she is disgruntled because the
> crackpot element is barred from NICAP. I am on your side of
> the fence as you know ... Rose is driving out to Indiana to see
> me AND Pelley. That's no compliment to me as I would[n't]
> believe anything Pelly [*sic*] said on a stack of Korans ... I
> know that she has always wanted to get me to be active in
> the inner working of NICAP because she has thought that I
> would embrace the so-called "subjective" simply because I do
> not take an open stand against it. I suspect that she is going
> to try to get me to start another organization, or to go into
> NICAP with a view toward changing the policy. Nothing
> doing on either count. I've had a belly full of the "Subjec-
> tive." It worse than stinks.[547]

"Pelley" was William Dudley Pelley, a controversial figure at the time. He'd had a short career as a writer in Hollywood where he unsuccessfully "labored among the Flesh Pots," though later twice won the O. Henry Award (in 1920 and 1930). By his own admission, he prided himself on "being a good hater," but in April 1928 he claimed to have undergone what today we would call an out-of-body experience.[548] This, he felt, changed him for the better, and he afterwards looked with a kindly eye on his fellow man. His epiphany, however, was short-lived because by 1932 he had founded the anti-Semitic Silver Shirt Legion, based on Hitler's emerging Nazi movement, and was known to his followers as "beloved Chief."

None of this deterred Rose from being prepared to drive nearly 600 miles to enjoy Pelley's company, and according to Jessup, she was still hopeful of changing NICAP into her idea of what a UFO investigating organization ought to be—to serve the contactees.

In the end, she took no action against Keyhoe but maintained her interest in "new age" notions. In September 1960, she was a scheduled speaker at a convention given by Reinhold O. Schmidt's International Space Craft Project, held on a field specially reserved for saucer-landings near Bakersfield, California, and attended by Fry, Wayne Aho, and several other notorious contactees. (In April the following year, Schmidt was imprisoned for defrauding $5,000 from one of his elderly followers.) She was listed as Rose Hackett Campbell, but this was no longer her name, for she had remarried in D.C. on November 6, 1959, to Kentucky-born Otho Lee Hiett, fourteen years her senior, becoming his fifth wife. Hiett was referred to variously as poet, author, travelling salesman, and doctor, seeming to claim a new career in each of the several states where he married and then divorced, or was divorced by, most of his wives.

His fourth wife, Reverend Dorothy Hiett, claimed to be a psychic medium, though she presumably failed to prognosticate that, during preparations for a spiritualist convention in Indiana on June 18, 1959, she would drop dead. Five months later, Otho married Rose, and in 1963 they purchased the Central Hotel on Main Street in Jerome, Arizona, as part of a local effort to revive the area. The building still stands and is a remarkable example of Old West wooden-balconied architecture.

Rose became involved in local women's GOP politics and for many years kept in touch with Townsend Brown, receiving letters from him in which he would send his good wishes to "Lee." Eventually the couple moved to Chesterfield, Indiana, where Otho, now said to be a registered pharmacist, died aged 92, in 1981.

After his death, Rose settled near her children in Puyallup, Washington, and she died there, aged 94, in May 1996. She was buried with her first husband, Dutton Pioneer Hackett, in Seattle.

Chapter 28:
Ruppelt's Reversal

At the same time Keyhoe was negotiating his way through the Straith letter debacle and handling the increasing tensions with Rose, another long-simmering issue was demanding his attention.

His relationship with Ruppelt had been showing cracks since August 1957, when Ed had given his contradictory reasons for not getting involved in any official position with NICAP. The two had never shared full accord on the interplanetary theory, but Keyhoe, even during and after the rift that was to come, would maintain that his young ally was constrained by Air Force/Northrop pressure. He may well have been correct and, if so, both men were to blame.

Ruppelt's writings and interviews over the years had exposed much that would otherwise have been under wraps—which of course lent fuel to Keyhoe's arguments about Air Force secrecy. Ruppelt himself admitted that, during his stint at Blue Book,

> I was being quoted quite freely in the press and was repeat-edly being snarled at by someone in the Pentagon. It was almost a daily occurrence to have people from the "puzzle palace" call and indignantly ask, "Why did you tell them that?" They usually referred to some bit of information that somebody didn't think should have been released.[549]

It was bad enough for the Air Force that Keyhoe had been publishing books, articles, and giving interviews that exposed its shortcomings, but Ruppelt had in effect been doing the same, thereby handing a great deal of ammunition to Don, which he fired off at every opportunity. Now, eight years after his first book, Keyhoe was head of his own investigating body, backed up by many big hitters in the military. Moreover, in the first issue of NICAP's magazine, Ruppelt and the information he had provided were given prominence. It seems no coincidence that after this went out, Ruppelt began to try and distance himself from Keyhoe and his saucers, as first indicated by his July 1957 acceptance, and then, two-weeks later, rejection of a place on NICAP's board. Evidently something had occurred during this period.

Keyhoe, though, was not giving up on his young friend. He liked him and knew that his former status at Blue Book was of high value to his and NICAP's aims. His letters to Ruppelt had always emphasized his feelings of gratitude, trust, and admiration, but privately he had some doubts. As early as 1954, in a letter to Coral Lorenzen, he confided:

> I'm not 100% sure about Ed. We are now very good friends; I've tried to figure him carefully, and I'd almost swear he is on the level, nor any stooge for the AF. If so, then it means he was not given all the dope when he was in Blue Book. He swears he was … My honest opinion is that Ed has told what he knows, that he wasn't told ALL, that he's beginning to wonder.[550]

To Lee Munsick in February 1958, he wrote:

> What Ed Ruppelt told you about the F-89 and Lieutenant Moncla as far as I am concerned is all bunk. Ed was not on duty at that time, and anything he got was picked up later, at ATIC …
>
> This is completely off the record, but don't believe everything Ed Ruppelt tells you. I have two or three cases in mind in which details he gave me at one time vary considerably with another telling of the story. This, of course, could be accidental, but Ed blows hot and cold on this subject as his recent action [pulling out of the Armstrong broadcast] has shown.[551]

Nonetheless, Keyhoe was still trying to cultivate him. Only 72 hours before his letter to Munsick, he had written to Ruppelt with some friendly and informative chat about the *Armstrong Circle Theatre*, though he inserted a gentle dig about the effect of his last-minute decision not to participate. "The program might have taken a different course," he wrote, but he still offered Ed the get-out clause of blaming his absence on Northrop. He further stroked his ego by asking him for assistance on the forthcoming Mike Wallace interview: "I am wondering if you can think of anything I might use on the program other than what you know I now have." He asked him to change his mind about becoming a NICAP Board member, while dangling the option to otherwise become a Special Adviser, suggesting that "there would be less chance of criticism" directed toward him.

Ruppelt sent no reply, so on March 13th Keyhoe wrote again, with more detail about the Armstrong program and the now recently-broadcast Mike Wallace interview. This was a chatty, four-page letter, but it was evidently an attempt to capture Ruppelt's attention and prompt a response. He even tried to lure him with suggestions about how he might become a celebrity authority on UFOs:

> Once this thing really breaks ... there will be a scramble by syndicates, networks, and magazines for "top authorities" on the subjects ... you would be one of those called upon immediately ... you would be quickly established as a network commentator with a program originating in Los Angeles ...

As to the still hoped-for Congressional hearings, Keyhoe wrote that "off the record" Fournet had confirmed the existence of the 1948 Estimate of the Situation document, and if he was called to testify at a Congressional hearing, Don felt sure he would make a statement to that effect. He asked Ruppelt to help by "giving me the names of any others" who know about the four documents he had revealed in his own book, so that he could "give this material to ... the Senate subcommittee."

Jack Healey (or, Healy) of the subcommittee had earlier contacted Ruppelt, asking him to appear at the potential hearings, but he had refused, and Keyhoe now tried, somewhat desperately, to persuade him to change his mind by suggesting difficulties that might arise if he didn't appear:

> I can understand that you might think it wise not to become embroiled in such an investigation. However, if there is an open hearing, they can insist on your appearance and it would be better if you had a number of others who are sympathetic to what you have revealed and would already be on record as to that effect ... I know the spot you're in, Ed, but I do think that sooner or later you will be called for detailed reports on all of these points and many others, including a re-statement of your opinion on Special Report 14.[552]

On the same day he sent the foregoing to Ruppelt, Keyhoe also wrote to no less than the CIA's dark and soulless Director, Allen Dulles, and in a four-page missive, performed a foolish and ultimately destructive display of multiple rake-treading. He informed Dulles of the Air Force's *Armstrong Circle Theatre* censorship and devoted 25% of the letter to the published revelations made by Ruppelt regarding the four vetoed documents. Moreover, he took pokes at Lt. Col. Whedon and Major Lawrence Tacker, then PIO for the Air Force (and soon to become a noted adversary to Keyhoe), for their denials about the documents and especially about the "1953 panel report." He requested that NICAP be "given a copy of the full panel report for comparison with the items listed by Captain Ruppelt in his book."

He also raised the complaint made by photographer Ralph Mayher that his 1952 UFO picture had prompted a visit from CIA agents who warned him not to discuss the matter. Naively, Keyhoe asked Dulles if the Agency had been interrogating and intimidating UFO witnesses:

> If it is true—and the witness has said he can name the two CIA agents involved—then we should like to know on what authority he was ordered to keep quiet. Since the Air Force states there is no security involved and I have personally been assured by Air Force officers and by high-ranking Naval Academy classmates of my own that I was in no way doing a disservice to the country by my own revelations, I am seriously concerned—as is our Board—with the apparent censorship. If it does exist, we should like to know under what laws, and by what authority, it has been established, and also the reasons for requesting witnesses to keep silent.
>
> It is not NICAP's purpose to create dissention [*sic*], but rather to get the facts into the open and answer this question once and for all.
>
> A Senate subcommittee is conducting a preliminary inquiry considering ... the possibility of holding public hearings. NICAP is cooperating with this subcommittee.[553]

In these four pages, Keyhoe had brought to the attention of the CIA's Director the public errors made by the Air Force, the contradictions in its denials, the shortcomings of specific officers, and the revelatory writings of Ruppelt. He also accused the CIA of intimidating witnesses (and expected Dulles to own up if it had done so), flagged up the Senate subcommittee's interest, and in effect demanded that documents be provided to NICAP for consideration by its illustrious board—which included, of course, Hillenkoetter. If he had specifically tried to make trouble for himself and Ruppelt, he could not have done better.

The effect of this might be inferred when, eighteen days later, Ruppelt sent Keyhoe a short, dismissive reply offering no comment on his recent letters:

> As I told you, I'm completely out of the UFO business. I still believe you think that someone is forcing me out but this is not true. As long as the UFO subject stayed on a conversational plane I was willing to go along with it. But when it is pushed so far that a Senate sub-committee is conned into devoting their valuable time and effort, I bow out. I think the chances of UFO's being real are a billion to one and there are other problems in this world that are far more important for a Senate sub-committee to look into.[554]

If Ruppelt truly thought his earlier writings and discussions about UFOs had been on a "conversational plane," he was either deluding himself or trying to delude Keyhoe—it was a ludicrous new posture. He had talked about the saucers and Blue Book many times in the media, had been adviser on the pro-UFO 1956 film *Unidentified Flying Objects: The True Story of Flying Saucers*, and at his own volition had published several hundred pages on the subject. At no time in these arenas had he flatly refuted the idea of "UFO's being real"— indeed many felt that he and some of his fellow officers rather leaned toward the interplanetary theory and that his writings exposed Air Force chicanery. And of course, he had been the source of information about the "secret" Air Force documents and the Robertson panel, upon which Keyhoe had placed so much importance and that had ultimately resulted in his letter to Dulles. (Dulles did not reply himself but delegated it to others who evaded Don's questions.)

The combined effect of all this appeared to be that Ruppelt, six years after leaving Blue Book, had now come down off the fence and kicked UFOs into the trash. His remark that a sub-committee had been "conned" was a dirty slap at Keyhoe, but it smacked of desperation on his part. It was an effort to distance himself from being dragged into an arena in which he would have to do battle with the Air Force. He had been one of Don's most vaunted helpers, thereby helping the Major and NICAP to become the biggest public relations challenge the Air Force had ever faced. It was now time to pay the piper, and he clearly had decided to ditch UFOs and show fealty to the party line. Though he would always insist he had been under no Air Force pressure, his wife would later say that was not the case and that its displeasure about his 1956 book was made clear to him.[555]

Despite Ruppelt's obvious cooling, Keyhoe still held out hope that it didn't mean a complete *volte face*, but in May 1958, he began to realize how far his young friend's position had changed. A NICAP member in Florida copied to him a letter received from Ed in which he'd stated that UFOs were "nothing more than reports of balloons, aircraft, astronomical phenomena, etc. I don't believe they are anything from outer space."[556]

Ruppelt reiterated this new stance of total denial in a reply sent the following day to chemical engineer Dr. Leon Davidson, the almost lone and much-maligned proponent of the theory that UFO sightings, radar blips, and contactee experiences since 1951 were the result of CIA activity.[557] Davidson was pressing the CIA for release of the full 1953 secret CIA Panel report and wrote to Ruppelt asking for clarification on his participation in the proceedings. When he received Ed's letter denying the saucers, he sent—with Ruppelt's permission—a copy to Keyhoe.

It's evident that by now Ruppelt's wings were being clipped. Davidson's badgering of the Air Force and the CIA in late April had prompted a four-page reply from Tacker on May 20th, in which he denied Ruppelt's account of the Robertson Panel's recommendations to expand the project and to keep the public fully informed in order to "dispel any of the mystery that Security breeds." These, Tacker said, were only the "comments and suggestions of individual members of the panel" taken from "an unofficial classified supplement ... inappropriate for inclusion in the Formal Panel Report." He pointed out also that the idea to expand Blue Book had been proposed by Ruppelt himself.

In a further thinly-veiled criticism of Ruppelt's former co-operation with Don, Tacker wrote:

> The Air Force was compelled to generally adopt the press release approach because in the past when we furnished factual information to certain writers of UFO books and articles upon their individual requests our section was interpreted as granting approval and clearance to the books and articles in which the information was used.[558]

In mid-July, pro-saucer Washington newspaperman Bulkley Griffin was working up some articles on the subject and wrote to Ruppelt asking him to confirm the comments attributed to him in NICAP's January *UFO Investigator* (which were included in a piece condemning Air Force secrecy). He told him that the Pentagon now "assert you did not head Project Blue Book" and that Major Tacker first described Ruppelt as "chief analyst" for the Project, "then later seemed to back down on giving you even that measure of responsibility."[559]

In his disdainful reply, Ruppelt implied that the *UFO Investigator*, which he said he hadn't read, might have "badly misquoted" him and that "I never have believed that the reported UFOs were anything but a heterogenous collection of reports of misidentified, common everyday objects." He haughtily ascribed reports to "a certain degree of excitement associated with a sighting which tends to bias the observer's power of reasoning." All sightings were merely "balloons, aircraft, astronomical boddies [*sic*], etc." and added, "I can assure you that all of the people who worked for me at ATIC had the same opinion."

He couldn't resist a swipe at Keyhoe:

> As far as the Air Force's statements that an added effort on the UFO project would be a waste of time, I concur. As far as I'm concerned the project has been a wast [*sic*] of time for the past years. Everything should be declassified and put in the National Archives so organizations like NICAP can play around with it.[560]

Griffin replied, "I admit I was surprised you never have believed in the UFOs."

Keyhoe had also got wind of these curious Air Force denials about Ruppelt's role at Blue Book, and when he received Davidson's letter with the enclosed copy, he wrote to Ed and attempted to stir his indignation toward the Air Force. He told him that both it and Major Tacker were now denying the "key points" in his 1956 book and saying that he was removed from Blue Book for "inefficiency, incompetence, and a wrong approach to the investigation." As to Ruppelt's *volte face* on the saucers, he wrote, "I am puzzled, because this is so completely at variance with your book," and listed numerous examples that he felt demonstrated he had been "completely convinced that UFOs were real." Keyhoe by now had further concluded that Tacker, supported by Richard E. Horner, was waging a "campaign against NICAP and of course me."[561]

On July 30th Ed sent a two-page reply to Don's letter about Tacker's trashing of his reputation. He continued to dismiss the saucers, insisted that his own UFO writing had deliberately excluded his personal opinions, and reiterated that the saucers were balloons, etc. He insisted, again, that he was not being intimidated and closed the letter with "I haven't been in Washington for some time and doubt if I'll be there soon. If I do come east I'll give you a call."[562]

As late as September 1958, Keyhoe was still trying to bring Ed back into the fold by offering him sworn affidavits from those who had been told about the Air Force's trashing of his reputation, but it was to no avail. Ruppelt's position became more firmly aloof and entrenched. He was now making it clear that his loyalties lay with the Air Force, and if he felt any pangs of guilt about throwing Keyhoe under the bus, it would never become apparent.

Meanwhile, only six days after Keyhoe had written his showdown-letter to Rose Hackett Campbell—the outcome of which he was still awaiting—he wrote to Al Chop:

> Probably you know that Ed Ruppelt has been backtracking rapidly for several months. He now says he never did believe that flying saucers were real—that they are mirages, hallucinations, mistakes, etc. I simply cannot accept this—I think he is under heavy pressure at Northrop because of their Air Force contracts.
>
> Ed has made too many contradictory statements to fall back on this answer now.[563]

Of course, Ruppelt was wasting his time denying that he had been told to renounce the saucers because Keyhoe believed that security would prevent him from making such an admission, so he was damned if he did and damned if he didn't. Still, his recent distancing from Don and his sneering attitude toward the saucers and their proponents were markedly different from his behavior since 1952 and the pro-UFO inferences given in his writings. The latitude allowed him by the Air Force, which had permitted—or at least, hadn't prevented—his revelatory writings, seems to have been curtailed by August 1957 and applied strongly thereafter.

We can now only speculate on what warnings he might have received; he was, after all, a sick man with a young family who depended on his job at Northrop and who would have to rely on his Air Force pension if he should die. The implied threat created by Tacker's assault on Ruppelt's reputation and status can only have contributed to his insecurity and emphasized that he had no real power to defend himself. Perhaps he had been encouraged to consider these factors.

The cold rebuff in Ruppelt's latest letter set the tone for his future dealings with Keyhoe and the UFO subject for the rest of what would be his short life. Two and half years later, aged 37, he would die from a second heart attack; but before that he would make his foulest public assault against his friend and mentor.

Chapter 29: The Feud

Keyhoe's relationship with Coral Lorenzen had always been strong and cordial, so he had no idea that their correspondence between April and July 1958 would precede the end of her endorsement and admiration for him. The incident that brought this about had not yet occurred, but these last letters are additionally noteworthy, for they were more than just the usual updates on sightings, accompanied by pleasantries and shared grievances. Some of their content was markedly odd.

In relation to the now well-known experiences of Albert K. Bender and Edgar Jarrold, who both claimed in 1953 to have been visited by some mysterious "men in black," Coral and Don had been recently exchanging thoughts on these alleged encounters. She wrote:

> We, I feel, have made the mistake that the AF is the group holding back the information, and I know now that we were very wrong. One of my members has been "visited"—but he had the nerve to put down everything that was said and sent it to me. What he said, if it were given nationwide publication, could actually cause a panic—and I'll frankly admit that I do not feel I have the moral right to do so. I do not believe the Orson Wells [*sic*] panic could even compare with what would happen ...[564]

A few weeks later, she wrote:

> This thing is much bigger than any of us thought ... I still have a feeling that the "people" have a right to know. You're right—there are a lot of things I don't care to put into a letter. We have things in our files that we don't dare print because of the trouble it would cause for us and the individuals involved. About those off-the-record deals; we get our information through devious means: when a PIO or high-ranking officer tells us something we discount it entirely ... The time will be here shortly, however, when CIA will realize that we have quietly entlisted [*sic*] the aid of their (the

US's) best research men, who by then will be ready to talk. I can hardly wait.[565]

Keyhoe was more cautious, but shared with her his own additional, confidential concerns:

> I still am not sold on the Bender story, although of course it could be true. Am getting suspicious of a great many information items given to me "off the record" [and] here in Washington I often get tips that I now realize are at least 50-50 distorted or maybe some without any foundation.[566]

Two months later, he had given more thought to her earlier letter and wrote a follow-up:

> There are some other things that I don't care to put on paper right now, but they add up to reasons for the fear I suggested.
>
> I notice that you, too, feel you have knowledge of such reasons—that is, the answer to present secrecy—and it has been suggested to me that if I were to make public one of the suggested causes for secrecy I would immediately be in hot water. I do not accept this without proof, but it does lead to a need for reconsideration ...
>
> I wonder if we can work out a method of exchanging the information—on a confidential basis—unless mutually agreed that it shall be released later—to see if there is any similarity in supposed reasons for secrecy. I am willing to put down these reasons in an unsigned letter—or even a signed one if you wish—with my opinion as to how likely they are. I shall do this if you feel you can do the same in regard to reasons you have ...
>
> One reason given me by two persons well recognized in missile and space development programs would certainly cause alarm if broadcast officially as fact. Even so, I still believe that hiding the answer—no matter how ominous—is wrong and inherently dangerous ... Certainly the peril indicated, if it is true, could not be any worse than that from the H-bomb. I'll admit that there is a certain element of horror because of the "unknown," which the H-bomb does not have.

He gave his thoughts on who was really behind the UFO cover-up, which is at odds with criticisms leveled at him then and later that he placed the blame solely with the Air Force:

> Regarding your idea that a higher agency is back of the secrecy: I fully agree and have for some time said that I was sure the CIA is deeply involved and also NSC [National Security Council]. I know now that on certain angles the FBI has been called in, and also a section of the Atomic Energy Commission. In fact, there is hardly any high level secret agency which is not connected at least slightly with the UFO problem.[567]

Whatever information Don and Coral had on the "peril" and "horror" to which they had been alerted would never be shared, because three weeks after these letters, her attitude toward Keyhoe, which had started with such effusive, almost embarrassing cordiality, began an irreversible decline and became regarded in saucer-circles as a "feud" between APRO and NICAP. In later years, UFO authors and investigators Ann Druffel and Stanton Friedman believed, as others did, that the tension between the two research organizations was due to their differing views on humanoid/alien beings. Druffel said:

> [T]he fact that the Lorenzens accepted some of these humanoid cases was against NICAP's principles. They felt that they had to concentrate fully on the unidentified aircraft ... so this was the disagreement between NICAP and APRO. I wouldn't call it a real disagreement because I know that there was no disagreement on Keyhoe's part with APRO, but it seems that the two organizations were going after different aspects of the same problem.
> Keyhoe felt that he must be as scientifically oriented as possible because he worked with congressmen and scientists ...[568]

Friedman's opinion was the same:

> [The Lorenzens] were more ready to listen to talk about alien beings, abductions and so forth ... [O]ne of the big feuds was about the whole question of alien beings ... Keyhoe liked to control things ... Coral called me [in regard to the

Hill case/Marjorie Fish map] [and that] wouldn't have happened with NICAP, they were still kinda holding back on all this business with aliens ... they would take potshots at each other in their newsletters from time to time. It's kind of shame because if they'd worked together it would have all moved forward much better ...[569]

NICAP's own take on the feud was similarly expressed:

When APRO began to consider seriously contact cases we knew to be of dubious value, questions from members and the public forced us to take a stand.[570]

Their divergent views on the "little men," however, was not the root of their falling-out. Both were intelligent enough and more than sufficiently committed to objective research to allow this one point to interfere with their accord. They had long accepted each other's positions on this issue because fundamentally they shared the ultimate goal of bringing UFOs into serious consideration. What had happened?

The feud took root in the summer of 1958, due to an omission and an erroneous assumption on Coral Lorenzen's part that resulted in a mini-maelstrom, which was played out in the press and proved to be a humiliation for her and for APRO.

It was well known that eminent psychoanalyst Carl Jung for some time had expressed interest in, and curiosity about, the UFO phenomenon. Given his status in the culture of the era, it was natural that any exposition he made on the subject would be of interest to both pro and anti-UFO reality camps.

Coral had corresponded with him occasionally and understood the PR value of Jung's analytical thoughts on the subject. Consequently, she offered and believed he had accepted both an honorary membership and a consultant position with APRO. To mark this, the *APRO Bulletin* of July 1958 now listed him as APRO's Consultant in Psychology and reproduced a 1954 article, written by Jung, that gave credence to the reality of UFOs. Unfortunately, Coral had omitted to give the original publication date of the piece, and the Associated Press, assuming the item to be current, seized upon it and sent it round the wires, resulting in nationwide reporting. Jung, it seemed, had just stepped firmly into the UFO-reality camp and this was big news.

As soon as the story hit the press, NICAP was swift to offer congratulations. In the absence of Keyhoe, who was out of town, Rose Campbell, during what turned out to be her last few weeks with the Committee, sent a short letter to Coral congratulating her on "the REAL SPLASH" the story had received. Five days later Keyhoe sent a personal letter, offering his own congratulations, generously expressing his view that "if we had released it here it would not have received one-half the attention." He mentioned that Jung had recently become a member of NICAP, and added, "By now you must have established very good relations with the wire services there, which, of course, will help with future releases."[571]

Only four days later, those relations had soured, and APRO's apparent coup turned into an embarrassing fiasco. Had the only error been failure to give the original date of Jung's piece, a simple correction would have sufficed, but the problem proved to be more fundamental and damaging. Coral was unaware that the article was neither an accurate nor a complete version of Jung's German original, which had been first printed in the Swiss newspaper *Die Weltwoche* and later translated into French for a Swiss saucer magazine, *Association Mondial Interplanetaire*. The version Coral used was yet a third translation, into English, for Britain's *Flying Saucer Review (FSR)*, which she believed to be a correct transcription from the French. However, the *FSR* had selectively abridged the item to rather lean Jung's view in favor of saucer reality and downplay his somewhat nebulous thoughts on the subject.

By August 8th all was revealed and the fallout commenced. Jung was in Switzerland when he was apprised of the story and then gave an interview in which he rejected APRO's article, prompting a joyously sarcastic piece in *Time*, written by its notoriously inaccurate and foolish science editor, Jonathan H Leonard, in which he took unsubstantiated pot-shots at Coral Lorenzen and APRO. She now found herself hit by "an avalanche of mail" and sent to Keyhoe a brief, glum letter, regretting that she had caused "erroneous publicity for Dr Jung and APRO."[572]

By the end of the month, she had evidently spent much time evaluating her position and was "preparing a full statement for the next bulletin," which would do "the ethical thing—apologizing to a great scientist for being instrumental in misrepresenting his views." She would not "weasel out of it" and wanted to make amends "not out of fear of Dr. Jung, or need of him, but rather because he has been wronged."[573] True to her word, the September bulletin contained a lengthy, self-flagellating apology:

> We were in no way aware that this article was misrepresenta-
> tive but in over one year of occasional correspondence with

Dr. Jung we had never checked the accuracy of this material with him—a very serious oversight on our part. Now it appears that the *FSR* article was somewhat wishfully translated (from his 1954 interview for *Der Weltwoche*) and shortened.

She further admitted that, among its failings in the matter, APRO had "mistook" Jung's acceptance of an honorary membership to mean his name could be listed among its officers, which she had now removed. Her contrition was unalloyed, displaying a professionalism that did her credit, though the press seemed rather delighted at this opportunity to gloat at her error, using the *Time* article as the basis for its shadenfreude. Its view that people who saw or "believed" in saucers were crazy was both stabilized and reinforced, leaving Coral to remark in her *Bulletin*, "What [the] final result all of this unfortunate publicity will be in the long run cannot be prognosticated at present."

She ended the piece with brief thanks to Keyhoe for his own article in NICAP's August *UFO Investigator* that clarified the misunderstanding but in which—yet again—he trod on a few rakes. He published in full a praiseful letter he had received from Jung, but in doing so, unintentionally seemed to gloat at Coral's mortification:

> Thank you very much for your kind letter! I have read all you have written concerning UFOs and I am a subscriber to the NICAP-Bulletin. I am grateful for all the courageous things you have done in elucidating the thorny problem of UFO-reality. The article in APRO-Bulletin July 1958, which caused all that stir in the press, is unfortunately inaccurate … I follow with my greatest sympathy your exploits and your endeavours to establish the truth about UFOs.
>
> It is a curious fact, that whenever I make a statement, it is at once twisted and falsified. The press seems to enjoy lies more than truth.[574]

Thus, for the delectation of NICAP members, Keyhoe showed how he was lauded by the illustrious Jung as "courageous," while Coral Lorenzen and APRO were held responsible for "all that stir" and the "lies" in the press.

By October, it seems that Jung was still unhappy about events. He wrote to Keyhoe:

> My recent experience with APRO shows me that I must be

careful in getting mixed up with UFO-organisations. Although I am vividly interested in these questions, I prefer to detach my name from organizations of this kind ... If I am able at all [to] help in psychological matters, I am glad to do so, but I prefer it in an in-official [*sic*] way.[575]

For Coral, her triumph had turned into an embarrassing failure from which NICAP had benefited, and she wanted now to put the whole ghastly affair behind her. She would succeed in so doing; the Jung misunderstanding proved to be only a seven-day wonder and APRO's briefly-dented reputation and her relationship with Jung recovered. Indeed, by the following June she wrote that he was "still our consultant on psychology" and soon after boasted that he[576]

... is giving us helpful advice. We are still on excellent terms with him, by the way ... Whether or not we agree with Carl on fundamentals is unimportant—I admire the man for even taking the time and trouble to investigate the UFO mystery ... He is still quite upset at the way the press cut our throats (his and APRO's) last year. A press release calculated by him to take the blame off our backs and put it where it belonged was issued, but never carried ... His initial statement after the mixup started was cut and twisted so that it had little resemblance to the real facts.[577]

Yet, despite mending fences with Jung, her attitude toward Keyhoe rapidly deteriorated, and if he ever figured out the source of Coral's change of heart, it's not evident from his subsequent letters. Hers, however, reflect a distinct coolness toward the man she once so strongly advocated and admired, which was first indicated in her response to his letter of August 13, 1958. Following the recent fuss surrounding George Adamski's claim of honorary NICAP membership, Keyhoe asked her to give "as wide publicity as possible to counteract the false impression made." Her response was entirely lacking in the effusive co-operation and support she had previously demonstrated. The *APRO Bulletin* of August tersely noted:

Donald E. Keyhoe of NICAP, Washington, D.C. has asked us to inform the membership that George A Adamski is not an honorary member of NICAP—that the membership card which Adamski carries was an error in addressing.

By December, her feelings were apparent to others. Following a recent meeting, Idabel Epperson wrote to Isabel Davis:

> Did you know that Coral is <u>very anti</u>-NICAP? (I'm sure you must have guessed it). I think Don Keyhoe has been darn nice to Coral. I can't understand her "beef"—nothing of any substance or importance. I'm sorry she feels as she does. She stands to lose—not Keyhoe—by lack of cooperation. I can't help but feel that she would have felt out of place at the meeting anyway—most all were loyal NICAP members.[578]

Matters had still not improved when, years later, Idabel would write to Dr. James E. McDonald with her comments on Dr. Phillip Seff, professor of geology at the University of Redlands, California, who was APRO's geology advisor/consultant. She observed:

> [I]t seems that Dr. Seff is very disillusioned with the Lorenzens and recently made a comment about Jim [Lorenzen] before a group where he was giving a talk—and he noticed someone taping his talk and asked them to erase what he had said (about Jim) [so] if he feels the way he does, I wonder why he continues to associate with them. (I gave it up a long time ago!).[579]

Coral's last letter of 1958 to Keyhoe was a short note updating him on APRO's analysis of a "great cloud cigar" recently sighted, which turned out to be "an unusual combination of contrail, angle of vision and lighting conditions." True to his usual delay, he wrote her a brief reply on January 13, 1959, thanking her for the "frank report" on this sighting and promising to soon send her "a very long letter." Clearly, there was no resentment from his side, nor any awareness that her attitude toward him had changed irrevocably.

* * *

An interesting codicil to the Jung affair is found in *Lindbergh* by A. Scott Berg. He wrote that Lindbergh visited the psychoanalyst, then aged 75, at his home in Bolligen, Switzerland. During a conversation on another matter, Jung suddenly turned the topic to UFOs and admitted to an astonished Lindbergh that he believed the reports he had read and that he was uninterested in the psychological aspect of the phenomenon. He added that he had read Keyhoe's book (*The Flying Saucers Are Real*) and ended their discussion by telling Lindbergh that there were "many things going on around this earth that you …don't know about."[580]

Neither Coral Lorenzen nor Keyhoe appear to ever have been aware of this opinion, and if Jung believed in saucer-reality in 1958, he had certainly not played fair when he denied that such was his position. The resulting cessation of good will between APRO and NICAP meant that the future benefit to serious UFO study by the two foremost research organizations of the era was lost.

As to Lindbergh's own views on UFOs, in 1979 Keyhoe recalled hearing from Pentagon sources that when "Slim" had been brought back to active duty (in 1954), he was told not to discuss UFOs. Don wrote to him about this story, though received no reply, but some years later met him at a function and "kidded him" that he must have a "blank spot" about UFOs. Slim said nothing and merely grinned, leaving Keyhoe to speculate that his hero hadn't dismissed accounts by "the hundreds of good witnesses that he knew were on record."[581]

After the Jung incident had quieted down, Coral Lorenzen's letters to Keyhoe became infrequent and mostly brief, though gave no indication of her resentment. However, those written to noted Swedish UFO researcher and one-time NICAP translator K. Gosta "Gus" Rehn show her real thoughts about NICAP, Keyhoe, and some of his associates, which were distinctly unpleasant, ignoble, and duplicitous.

Coral began corresponding with Rehn in January 1959 with a polite and business-like exchange of information about recent Swedish UFO sightings, but over the next several months their missives became of a deeply personal and at times, creepy, nature.

In her earliest letters, she kept her powder dry, offering only mild criticisms of Keyhoe, as if testing the Swedish waters:

> Mr. Keyhoe has never been particularly disposed to believing in "little men", etc., so whether or not it will be played up in their next *Bulletin* or not, I don't really know—I certainly don't expect it.

This was an innocuous and not inaccurate comment, but in her next letter she was leaking a little more negativity, thanks to a question in Rehn's letter of January 19th asking if NICAP or any similar organization had any money. She replied:

> No saucer organization has money to speak of. NICAP had big plans ... and are still having a hard time. APRO, (second largest in this country) on the other hand, does not maintain offices on a grand scale as does NICAP ... We cooperate in any way possible with any SERIOUS group, but have not noticed any reciprocation ... Keyhoe tends to over-dramatize and sensationalize. We have sent detailed reports on good sightings in this area several times, but have received no reciprocal cooperation.[582]

From this initial grumbling, she progressed to suspicions of a conspiracy against APRO by "a US agency" and took more thinly-veiled swipes at NICAP:

> The cover of one of my letters to an out-of-country representative was ripped and part of the contents removed recently ...APRO was visited by a Security Agent ... I am becoming especially leery of any group which presents few facts but harps continually on the Air Force angle ... it goes a lot farther than a mere military group—the conspiracy involved ... the CIA and National Security Board ... the Air Force is ... "the whipping boy" or "front" for the real culprits ...
>
> We have followed a policy of not allowing military members to dominate our headquarters setup—because they are too easily planted. Apparently our adversaries have realised this and are taking other steps to get us out of the field. We feel that we have smelled out their tactics ... they realize that we are one group which is concentrating on building a mountain of facts and real evidence instead of mere accusations ...[583]

By September, her digs now extended to others in the UFO field whom she disliked, and her thoughts became more tinged with paranoia:

> [Leon] Davidson is a member of CSI New York, and has a PhD in something, which has never been made clear to me. He is convinced that saucers are US secret weapons—he is either crazy or a tool of the military. It must be one or the

other.[584]

Rehn concurred: "I agree he is nuts about the US secret weapons. Or that he is in collusion with the AF like Moseley."[585]

Coral escalated the point and now included Keyhoe as a suspect in the perceived collusion:

> I see that I do not need to warn you about the Davidson-Mo-seley-NICAP collusion … I do not believe that Keyhoe is a willing collaborater, [sic] but I think he has surrounded himself with the military with which he is so familiar and cannot conceive that they are working at odds with his goals … [Davidson] is a plant …
>
> We have received no less than 8 requests for membership lists of APRO in various states and areas recently, and visits from members of another group who were obviously sent to pump us for as much information as they could get out of us … I see that I do not need to warn you about any cooperation with Davidson. The "opposition" is attempting to infiltrate and swallow or literally smother the few clear-headed researchers left.[586]

While being sour about Keyhoe behind his back, she still offered him an occasional sweetener. In what may have been a genuine effort to help him avoid embarrassment—or conversely might have been a way of salting his wounds—she tipped him off that a card had been in circulation that implied he "would attend the spacecraft convention at Tulsa."[587] He wrote a friendly reply in early October, with thanks for her kindness, and enclosed "a copy of a letter to Moseley in answer to his attack on me in his latest publication … I am convinced now that he is motivated by pure malice." In his *Saucer News*, Moseley had published a trashy and inaccurate piece by Adamski-acolyte Michael G. Mann, which mocked and criticized Keyhoe, prompting from him a letter to Moseley, threatening legal action.[588]

Coral wrote back to Keyhoe with a chatty letter, entirely free of any malice toward him, but which displayed her duplicity in regard to the Moseley factor:

> Thanks for the mimeographed letter to Moseley—he's been harping on the "government secret weapon" theme for so long that I think this is his last-ditch attempt to qualify any-

one who has established anything for the interplanetary theory.

She even went so far as to offer "any help in the future," and in November's
Bulletin made a very brief comment that Moseley's attack on Keyhoe was
without basis.[589]

By the end of October, Coral and Rehn had gone on first-name terms—
she would in future call him "Gus"—and this marked a big shift in the
intimacy of their communications. She told him, "Now that we are on a first-
name basis, I feel more relaxed about confiding certain information."[590] This
"information" took the form of her increasingly paranoid predictions about a
forthcoming alien invasion of Earth:

> We expect an attack of some kind in the not too distant fu-
> ture. We think we know how they will do it, and control
> the panicked population at the same time. We are convinced
> they are building bases in preparation, at the present time ...
> I think we would be fools to try to defend ourselves ... This
> whole "silence" attempt is not just the Air Force as so many
> have been fooled into believing—it is fostered by American
> Intelligence, but is a worldwide conspiracy made up primari-
> ly of top intelligence groups as well as the military.[591]
>
> ... I must be careful in divulging these facts. I have been
> constantly pressured for the past 6 months to "cooperate"
> with NICAP—they know what we have and they want it. I
> do not think Keyhoe is a willing cohort—I think he is mili-
> tary and egotistical enough to be very efficiently used by the
> wrong people—the military members of NICAP, including
> the former chief of the CIA who was in on the big deal when
> UAO investigation changed hands in 1952 from the Air
> Force to CIA ...[592]

She credited her alien-doom theory to a young man who had replaced
Keyhoe as her most revered and respected UFO researcher, thirty-four-
year-old Dr. Olavo Fontes, Chief of the Gastroenterological Section of the
National School of Medicine in Rio de Janeiro, who became APRO's Special
Representative in his home country of Brazil. He had become interested in
UFOs thanks to Keyhoe's *The Flying Saucers Are Real*, which eventually led to
him contacting Coral Lorenzen in March 1957. She was immediately taken

with his ideas: her ten-page July *APRO Bulletin* that year was almost wholly given over to his article titled "We Have Visitors from Outer Space." After the 1958 Jung debacle, her adoration for Fontes increased in inverse proportion to her scorn for Keyhoe and anyone whom she considered to be his ally. Even CSI-NY was not exempt; she praised its *CSI Newsletter* but snarked that it was published only "when they are not working for Keyhoe."

Now that she had come to despise her former hero, she bestowed her patronage and her confidences elsewhere. Her two new collaborators, however, were different from Keyhoe and each other and she treated them accordingly.

Fontes was a married man with two young children, and though Coral didn't meet him personally until 1961, she felt he was

> ... a curious individual. I am very fond of him; he is one of the most unusual personalities I have ever encountered. He can be cold and ruthless, sneaky, conniving, and just plain ornery when he needs to be in order to gain his ends, but actually he is a very warm, humble, fine man—and one of the most naive, trusting romanticists I have ever known.[593]

She also found him to be somewhat shy and prudish, with an embedded cultural disdain for female intellect, so even though she chafed at the sexist limitations imposed on women by American society, she refrained from discussing with him anything that might offend his misogynist sensibilities, or which might bring a blush to his cheek.

Her relationship with Rehn was rather different. He was unmarried, certainly not prudish, and though her early letters to him were similar to her letters to Keyhoe—a respectful exchange of UFO thoughts and some personal chat—they soon degenerated into a rather earthy discourse of a type she never shared with the Major. This was expressed particularly in relation to the infamous case of a young Brazilian farmer, Antonio Villas-Boas. In October 1957, he claimed he had been abducted by aliens and forced to have sexual intercourse with one of their females. Dr. Fontes had personally interviewed Villas-Boas and in confidence told Coral of the man's claims. She in turn told Rehn, initially giving him a censored version of what had supposedly occurred, but added "There are many more details which I will go into if you care to discuss them."[594] He certainly wanted more:

> Dear Coral, I did not get offended at all by your relating the intercourse between the boy and the space woman. More,

more details—if Fontes have them—concerning the way she got his seminal fluid in her ... Gasping for breath.[595]

She obliged him, though pointed out that "Despite Olavo's reticence about speaking of sex ... he didn't hold anything back because he knows I wouldn't be satisfied with anything less than <u>all</u> the details."

Now keen to arrange a get-together in the US with Fontes and Rehn, she suggested how it might be achieved, adding:

> I wouldn't want anyone to go back and tattle to Keyhoe and his crowd about just how much we know so far.[596]

He replied, "Jeez, I got so excited when I got your letter...that I wanted to run upstairs and rob my own trunk [i.e., masturbate]."[597] She wrote back with her thoughts on what they would discuss during the proposed meeting:

> Don't worry about the clean fun—the subject of "Lover Boy" [i.e., Villas Boas] and his interplanetary wench will come up and the going will get dirty, you can bet your life on that... And the first one who makes a remark about keeping the conversation on a "lofty" level will get put in his place.[598]

The seduction of "lover boy" was, she speculated in some detail to Rehn, to see if "interbreeding was possible" as a prelude to an alien colonization of Earth. The progeny of this un-asked for mating would be used to test "if cohabitation and fraternization would weaken the hold of their troops on earth."[599] She entreated Rehn to keep quiet about her theories: "I do not want anyone in the 'silence' conspiracy to know exactly what we have deducted about the UAO mystery and their plot."

As to Keyhoe and NICAP, she continued to express her feelings about both to Rehn. In November 1959, he had complained to her that Keyhoe had "refused to take in landing reports from his Swedish representative, a competent engineer whom I know." She responded:

> I am suspicious of that whole outfit ... NICAP still plays up the "hate the AF" theme, playing down the CIA part, and reports play a very small part of the whole. I think that also Keyhoe is afraid to feature the cases or efforts of "foreign" investigators such as your engineer friend ... because they might attain some status in the field and therefore unthrone

him from his position as titular head of UAO research the world over. I think it is regrettable that such a man became the main figure, myself.[600]

This was a far cry from her feelings in her *APRO Bulletin* of 1955, when she stated:

The collective hand of the Aerial Phenomena Research Organization is again extended in a clasp of congratulation to Major Donald E. Keyhoe for the fact of bringing to heel ... the USAF ... their fear of him and his facts ...aimed at shooting down Keyhoe's theories and contentions.

Evidently, the Jung fiasco had caused Coral's tide to turn. Her pride had been irrevocably wounded, and the immense admiration she had previously held for Keyhoe had changed to scorn, suspicion, and resentment.

The honeymoon was over.

Chapter 30:
Et Tu, Ruppelt?

On April 20, 1959, Morris Jessup took his own life. He was found dead in his station wagon in the parking lot at Matheson County Park, Dade County, Florida, after inhaling exhaust fumes from a pipe connected through the rear window.[601] The June issue of the *UFO Investigator* noted that "Although he did not accept the claims of the contactees, he urged tolerance by the other groups or at least neutrality. NICAP joins his many friends in regretting his untimely death."

Jessup had been suffering from depression for some time. He and his wife, Kathryn Ruth (*née*, Jones), had divorced in 1956, and presumably she had custody of their daughter, Mary Alice, but his woes were thought to be exacerbated by criticisms of his work, particularly in respect of his 1955 book, *The Case for the UFO*.[602] It had made no waves on its own merit, but a year later was thrust into ridicule and infamy thanks to the bizarre actions of a 30-year-old Pennsylvanian, Carl Meredith Allen, a.k.a., Carlos Miguel Allende, who may have suffered from a multiple-personality disorder. He began corresponding with Jessup around the start of 1956, claiming he had witnessed a Navy experiment in teleportation in which, by "utilizing principles of Einstein's Unified Field Theory, a destroyer and all its crew became invisible during October, 1943."[603] In the summer of 1956, he annotated a copy of Jessup's book with comments supposedly written by a trio of aliens, sent it to an officer at the Office of Naval Research, and the story of the Philadelphia Experiment was born.

The details of this well-known and perpetually popular story are beyond the scope of this work, but Clara John's tentacles reached even into Jessup's unfortunate tangle with Allende: it was she who, according to Townsend Brown's daughter, had ensured that the annotated version, after it curiously had been printed privately by a Navy contractor, Varo Manufacturing of Garland, Texas, reached some of the military and civilian men who had attended her elegant soirées. The "Varo" version overwhelmed Jessup's carefully written and deeply researched book. When later shown a copy, he was unimpressed. According to ufologist John Keel, Jessup considered it a "joke" and Allende to be mentally ill.[604] Despite this, Jessup's name became linked with the Philadelphia Experiment story, detracting from the serious objectives of his own book and adding to his depression.

Meanwhile, NICAP's publications were still floundering. Their ambitious 32-page monthly magazine was a dead-duck, and for the most part, the best that could be managed were either eight-page newsletters or four-page bulletins, almost all of which contained pleas for money and occasional membership "drives," some descending to the level of offering a reduced renewal fee—which had by now been cut from $7.50 to $5—in return for bringing in a new member. A good many issues contained questionnaires, asking facile questions such as, "Do you wish to end the blackout to learn the truth?" and asking to what extent members believed contactee claims. This, of course, added to the administrative burden on Keyhoe and his small staff; when members responded, someone had to handle the extra mail, sort through these replies, and compile the statistics, which then culminated in the results taking up valuable space in the next issue. To make matters still more burdensome, when members expressed dissatisfactions or preferences about the newsletters' content, Keyhoe would try to take these into account and make what seemed to be the required changes, but this kept him and NICAP's publications in a constant state of checking and changing, trying to please all of the members, all of the time.

Though the newsletters and bulletins offered detailed information about sightings (written by Keyhoe in the dramatized style of his books) and his gripes about the Air Force, from the very start they were equally a vehicle for him to air his grievances against his civilian detractors and rebut their "attacks." For example, in September 1958, while the Rose Campbell/Adamski membership issue was still rumbling, Keyhoe ran a column in the newsletter taking issue with arch-detractor Jim Moseley, who had recently slated him for failing to live up to NICAP's original promises. A year later, Don was again rebutting another attack by Moseley, who had just published in his own newsletter, the aforementioned, poorly-researched piece by Michael G. Mann, which trashed Keyhoe and his UFO work. Moseley had now added to the insult by sending copies of Mann's piece "to all NICAP members whose addresses had appeared in" its publications, leading Keyhoe to threaten "legal action against both you and Mr. Mann."[605] Though this was certainly a foolish and arrogant move by Moseley, Keyhoe laid out the saga in the newsletter, thereby drawing members into his angst, a response he used many times throughout his directorship. Several NICAP supporters were indeed outraged by this latest

Moseley mischief, notably Lee Munsick, who wrote: "I am just furious and ready to punch the two M's if I see them. Bastards."[606]

The June 1959 issue of the *UFO Investigator* was of particular note for, along with the Jessup obituary, two other long-standing matters gave Keyhoe an opportunity to air his problems.

Although Rose Campbell's welcome departure held the promise that NICAP could now move further away from contactee disruption, Adamski was still in the saucer business and, like the Hydra, always grew a new head when one was cut off. Page one of the newsletter proclaimed that one of his tales from late 1958 had now been "blasted," and it devoted almost six columns detailing how it had been exposed as being "completely contrary to factual evidence."

Adamski said he had been traveling by train from Kansas City, Missouri, to Davenport, Iowa, to give one of his "lectures," but he was happily diverted from this Earthly mode of transport by the offer of a lift in a flying saucer. He claimed that, following an announcement, the train had stopped on the tracks and while he was taking the air at an open door, a car pulled up and offered to take him and his luggage to a waiting UFO from which he alighted eight hours later somewhere outside Davenport.

NICAP became involved in trying to expose this latest hooey, thanks to Arthur Campbell (no relation to Rose), Director of NICAP's Kansas City Affiliate. After his own his investigation, he provided Keyhoe with sworn affidavits from train staff stating that the journey was unbroken aside from a brief pause of two seconds at a crossing, and that there were no doors that could be opened where Adamski claimed to have hopped off. Campbell pointed out also that to drive from Kansas to Davenport just happened to be a journey of eight hours.

This was the second stunt Adamski had pulled that year. In March 1959, he lectured in Melbourne, Australia, where his antics were observed by a member of the VUFORS (Victorian UFO Research Society):

> He left a meeting … claiming that he was going out to com-
> municate with the Space People. One of the members fol-
> lowed him and reported later that he went out of the build-
> ing, looked in a few store windows casually, and then came
> back in and gave his report on the Space People.[607]

Richard Hall, now increasingly taking charge of matters at the office, was embroiled in the affair and, surprisingly given his usual pragmatism, seemed no less determined than Keyhoe to expose Adamski. Among many letters NICAP sent and received on the subject, Hall wrote to Arthur Campbell that, "we intend to follow up on your investigation, and would appreciate your continued cooperation until we are ready to report the conclusions."[608]

However, the larger and far more troubling feature in the June 1959 issue was "in the form of an open letter to Ruppelt" from the Major, which began with an introduction:

> In the past month, rumors that Capt. Edward J. Ruppelt has been pressured into debunking his own UFO book have been circulating in Washington. This is a personal report on the facts as far as I know them.[609]

Occupying two pages, Keyhoe reminded Ruppelt of all his apparent support for UFO reality over the years and expressed astonishment that he was now said to be revising his book, which would not only deny the saucers, but also was being written in collaboration with the Air Force:

> To me, this new AF cooperation is extraordinary. From the start, your book has been a real danger to the secrecy group … So I can't understand why they would help you now, reviving your book—giving further publicity to the very revelations they so bitterly deny. It doesn't make sense, unless they expect drastic changes—changes practically nullifying your earlier disclosures.'

If Ruppelt read this letter, it can scarcely have encouraged him to return to the fold. It detailed the public and private written and verbal disclosures he had made in apparent support of Keyhoe and the interplanetary theory, along with his exposure of crucial documents that would otherwise have remained unknown. This open iteration, of which "a copy will go to Air Force HQ," was a desperate and ill-considered harangue that served only to lay bare to the public and the Air Force how far from the official path Ruppelt had strayed. Though the Major tried to temper his entreaty with generous acknowledgements of his friend's valuable assistance over the years, it was still a blundering and chastising reminder of Ruppelt's betrayal and his foolish audacity in kicking against the Air Force's "nothing to see here" policy. Don asked:

> [H]ow can you justify this with your earlier frank disclosures? … Don't let them [the Air Force] trick you. If you try to re-

tract, you will be bitterly attacked by many readers, including influential book reviewers, who hailed you for speaking the truth, for daring to put the record straight … You could even be accused of writing your book solely for profit …

He ended the letter with a comparison between what Ruppelt had said in 1954—"I wouldn't do a book if I didn't tell the truth exactly as it happened, and believe me this would not follow the Air Force party line"—against his recent denials—"I have always been convinced that reports of UFO's were nothing more than reports of airlines, balloons, astronomical phenomena, etc."

Don added, "Ed, that IS the Air Force party line."

As a final, unintended humiliation, he closed the piece with a note to members asking for their opinions and promising to publish any reply received from Ruppelt.

It was all too late. As Keyhoe suspected, Ruppelt had indeed been revising his book and with the Air Force's blessing. By May 1959, it was "providing information" to him for his update and "was to review the material written … prior to its release to the publisher."[610] Ruppelt had approached Major Robert J. Friend, now in charge of Blue Book, and requested some statistics. He wanted those on UFO reports that had been classed as "unidentified" through 1955 to 1958, information on the current functioning of "UFO reporting, investigating and analysis" systems, and a summary of "four reports which occurred since September 1958."

Ruppelt's contact at the USAF's Public Information Office during the writing of his revision was Major James F. Sunderman, who liaised with Colonel Gordon C. Hoffman in the Office of the Air Force Chief of Intelligence at the Pentagon, and with Major Lawrence J. Tacker, all of whom were monitoring Ruppelt's new draft. In May, Hoffman wrote to Tacker that Air Force information would be provided to Ruppelt

> … with the understanding that close control will be exercised on the Ruppelt manuscript, and that the ATIC will be allowed an active part in [illegible] that the inclosed [sic] information is forwarded to your office for release to Mr. Ruppelt.[611]

Finally, it suggested that Ruppelt "be advised that he make his associations of the Unidentified Flying Objects Program with the AF and not the Air

Technical Intelligence Center." This sentence was underlined by Sunderman and annotated,"Ed: note this please!"

In July, Sunderman wrote again to Ruppelt informing him that his three new chapters had been reviewed by the Air Force and "cleared for publication just as you wrote them, with no amendments," but the letter enclosed a two-page list of points with which it took issue. Almost a page was devoted to batting down Ruppelt's (somewhat surprising) praise of Len Stringfield, yet it told him he was "in no way required to make any changes in your manuscript as a result" of any comments, even though exception was taken to his account of pilots being scrambled just for fun, about which Ruppelt had written:

> The official answer you'll get, if you ask the Air Force, is that they scramble against any unknown target as a matter of defense. But over coffee you get a different answer. They write the UFO scrambles off as training cost. Each pilot has to get so much flying time and simulating intercepts against an unidentified light is more interesting than merely "burning holes in the air." If appropriations are ever cut to the point where training must be curtailed, and Heaven forbid, there will be no more scrambles after flying saucers. And the colonel who told me this was emphatic.

The Air Force commented, "This is absolutely not true, no matter who told Ruppelt." It further listed several cases to which he had referred that were not recorded in ATIC files and noted he had given an incorrect figure for the number of UFO reports in 1952 (he gave 918, the AF said 1,501). However, it approved of his "good treatment to the 'contact' group such as Adamski, Bethurum, Fry, et al.," likewise his defense of the Air Force. As to Don, "Ruppelt gives adequate treatment to Keyhoe and his organization."[612]

The result, published in January 1960, was three new chapters tagged on to the end of the original book, which were a total refutation the seventeen that preceded them:

> Before anyone gets the idea I've turned hypocrite since the first seventeen chapters of this book were written four years ago let me explain. In the first seventeen chapters I made a concentrated effort to keep my opinions out of the book and present the facts as they exist. Since then, I've learned that many people were interested in my opinions.[613]

This statement, from Ruppelt's handwritten draft, didn't make it into the revised book—in which he offered no explanation whatsoever—but tell us the unconvincing rationale he considered using to justify his sell-out of the saucers, done under the watchful eyes of the Air Force.

In an attempt to find at least one ally for his new anti-saucer view, he had written to his former Blue Book assistant, Andy (Anderson) Flues, who by now had left the service and was settled in Chicago, running a general store. Asked by Ruppelt for a statement to be included in his new chapters, Flues replied that, although up until he left the Project in 1952 he thought there was a possibility the sightings were of space vehicles, that was no longer the case:

> I agree with you that in our investigations we did not find anything solid enough to warrant the conclusion that we were dealing with interstellar space vehicles ... [T]here was not one single case which, upon the closest analysis, could not be logically explained in terms of some natural phenomenan. [*sic*][614]

Ruppelt's surviving papers available to this author give no indication that he contacted his pro-UFO former boss, Dewey Fournet, whom he had praised in his original seventeen chapters and who would have been the most authoritative source for his revision. This omission suggests that he wanted no clouding of his new view: Fournet knew that Ruppelt had quit Blue Book due to the "negativism" toward the saucers that arose after the 1953 CIA secret panel meeting and this surely would lend no support to his new anti-saucer stance.

This "negativism" had now—apparently—become his own mindset. Whether or not Keyhoe ever knew what Ruppelt had told Fournet about his reason for quitting Blue Book, he was surely correct that pressure had indeed been applied to him to make his ludicrous reversal.

The "adequate treatment" of Keyhoe in the revision, of which the Air Force approved, was Ruppelt's blatant kowtowing to his former employer and a rancid betrayal of his friend and supporter, which vaunted deliberate and provable distortions of facts that clearly were written to inflict ridicule on Don and NICAP.

In particular Ruppelt gave special mention to the demands of the "Eight Point Plan," published in the first *UFO Investigator* that "went over like a worm in a punch bowl" (which was probably true) and that the Air Force "decided to ignore NICAP" (which was not true). As a result:

> Then NICAP headquarters called in the troops and members
> from all corners of the nation cut loose. The barrage of mail
> broke the log jam and just enough information to constitute
> an answer dribbled out of the Office of the Secretary of the
> Air Force. But this didn't satisfy Keyhoe or his UFO hun-
> gry NICAPions. They wanted blood and that blood had to
> taste like spaceships or they wouldn't be happy. The cudgel
> they picked up next was powerful. The Air Force had said
> that there was nothing classified about Project Blue Book yet
> NICAP hadn't seen every blessed scrap of paper in the Air
> Force UFO files. This was unwarranted censorship! While
> Congress was right in the middle of such important and cru-
> cial problems as foreign policy, atomic disarmament, rack-
> eteering, integration and a dozen and one other problems,
> NICAP began to bedevil every senator and representative
> who was polite enough to listen.
>
> It's the squeaky wheel that gets the grease and in No-
> vember 1957, the United States Senate Committee on Gov-
> ernment Operations began an inquiry concerning UFO's. I
> gave my testimony and so did others who had been associ-
> ated with Project Blue Book. A few weeks later the inquiry
> was dropped. But NICAP had made its name. Of all of the
> thorns that have been pounded into the UFO side of the Air
> Force, NICAP drove theirs the deepest.

Thanks, he added, to the "mess" created by NICAP, Admiral Fahrney, General Wedermeyer, and Lieutenant General del Valle "politely and quietly, resigned," though Ruppelt did offer a crumb to the Major:

> Keyhoe has taken a beating, being accused of profiteering,
> trying to make headlines, and other minor social crimes.
> But personally I doubt this. Keyhoe is simply convinced that
> UFOs are from outer space and he's a dedicated man.

In the almost 15,000 words of his revision, that was the best he could say of the man he once called his friend.

Moreover, his scorn was not reserved just for Keyhoe; he poured it upon anyone and everyone who had ever reported something in the sky they couldn't identify, *a la* Menzel:

> [W]e heard the words "experienced observer" so many times these words soon began to make us ill. Everyone, except housewives with myopia, were experienced observers. Pilots, "scientists" (a term used equally as loosely), engineers, radar operators, everyone who reported a UFO was some kind of an "experienced observer." This man had taught aircraft recognition during World War II. He was an experienced observer. That man spent four years in the Air Force. He was an experienced observer. We soon learned that everyone is an experienced observer as long as what he sees is familiar to him. As soon as he sees something unfamiliar it's a UFO.
>
> Pilots probably come as close to falling into this category as anyone since they do spend a lot of time looking around the sky. But even those who can rattle off the names and locations of stars, planets and constellations don't know about a few relatively rare astronomical phenomena. The bolide, or super meteor, is a good example. Few pilots have ever, or will ever, see a deluxe model bolide but when they do they'll never forget it. It's like someone shooting a flare in front of your face. There are a number of reports of bolides in the Blue Book files and each pilot who made each report called each bolide a UFO. The descriptions are almost identical to the classic descriptions of bolides found in astronomy books.

The entire *volte face* was reprehensible and at total odds with his clear statement in the original book—still, bizarrely, included in the new edition:

> [T]his report is written exactly the way I would have written it had I been officially asked to do ... the Air Force has officially said that there is no proof that such a thing as an interplanetary spaceship exists. But what is not well known is that this conclusion is far from being unanimous among the military and their scientific advisers ...

It is certainly very odd that the Air Force would take strong issue with parts of his three new chapters, yet not demand they be amended, or why they were allowed to be published preceded by the revelatory and contentious originals. Perhaps this was intentional: by agreeing to tag on the additional material in this way—which Ruppelt must have known would trash his reputation and credibility—was a sort of plea deal. To prevent destructive action against him, he had to totally abase himself before his former employer, humiliate himself before the public and, by his insulting reversal, ensure he would cut himself off irretrievably from Donald Keyhoe.

The Major's response to the "revision" came in the March 1960 *UFO Investigator*, which informed members that Ruppelt had recanted. He made some valid observations:

> [T]he added chapters contradict the first part of the book, without any explanation [and] with no additional information, Ruppelt has reversed himself completely and now says he considers all of the reports explainable as natural phenomena ... . It seems odd that while active as the Project Blue Book chief, Ruppelt could find no explanations for ... good cases; but now that he no longer has access to all of the sources of information necessary to check a UFO sighting he has been able to find answers. Guesswork of this sort hardly provides the "realistic and knowledgable explanation" which the Air Force says its personnel must give the public. The strained reversal would not appear to be of Ruppelt's own choosing.

Keyhoe could no longer hope for any support from his former ally, who in any case died on September 19th that year. Few were aware of his death, and it received bare coverage in a handful of newspapers, in which he was identified as a "saucer prober," while his bazoo, the *Ames Daily Tribune*, simply referred to him as a former resident.

NICAP published his obit in the December 1960/January 1961 issue of the *UFO Investigator*.

> We sincerely regret his passing. Ruppelt was instrumental in opening up the secretive UFO policy and revealing the existence of the secret AF conclusions, that UFOs are real and interplanetary. Although the second edition of this book "The Report on Unidentified Flying Objects" last year was revised to debunk UFOs in three added chapters, this was

believed done under pressure from the Air Force. His original findings as project chief still stand as an indictment of the official secrecy policy.[615]

Chapter 31:
Tacker's Tack

If Menzel was Keyhoe's most ridiculous and obtuse critic in the scientific community, Lieutenant Colonel Lawrence James Tacker was his equal in the Air Force. Along with Menzel, Ruppelt, and a great many others, he would be unknown to the wider public today had it not been for his involvement with Donald Keyhoe.

None of Don's critics had made an iota of difference to his belief that the Air Force was involved in a cover-up about the saucers. He reinforced his claims in May 1960, when he published what would be the only book he wrote during his tenure as head of NICAP and which was perhaps his best—*Flying Saucers: Top Secret*. Like all his writings before and after, it whipped the Air Force for its hapless obfuscations and bludgeoning attempts to keep a lid on credible sightings. Among many cases cited in the book, that of United Airlines DC-6 Captain Peter W. Killian was given detailed attention. On February 24, 1959, he and the pilots of two American Airlines planes in the area had a clear sighting of three powerful "brilliant lights" in the skies over Pennsylvania; they were undoubtedly not aircraft nor natural phenomena. One of the lights, bigger than his own plane, approached and then returned to the other two. Killian dutifully made his report but was soon ridiculed in the press, discredited by the Air Force, and told to keep his mouth shut.

The release of this book—which included a chapter suggesting the Air Force had tried to weaken NICAP by faking UFO reports—was certain to inflame former PIO Major Tacker. He had recently been promoted and now occupied the wholly unglamorous position of "Chief of the Magazine and Book Branch, Secretary of the Air Force, Office of Information (SAFOI 3-D)"—in other words a uniformed librarian. Despite this dull posting, he inadvertently achieved lasting fame entirely due to his childish criticism of Keyhoe, which is forever enshrined in his vituperative debate, live on air, on NBC's *Dave Garroway Show*.

Broadcast on December 5, 1960, Tacker made himself and the Air Force look utterly foolish while trying to defend the well-worn party-line. Such was his arrogance and aggression that Keyhoe began to quickly lose his usually unflappable demeanor, and the debate slid into a noxious debacle, heading toward what today would surely climax in expletives and a vigorous exchange of studio chairs.

Tacker had recently published his own short book, *Flying Saucers and the US Air Force*. Of its 162 pages, plus index, only 87 were text and the remaining 72 were appendices, which included, no less, AFR 200-2 and JANAP 146—the very documents that Don had been forbidden to mention on the *Armstrong Circle Theatre*. A great deal of the book was given over to refuting what Keyhoe had said in that program and elsewhere. It made no specific mention of him or NICAP but devoted a chapter largely to a verbatim account of what the "experts" had said on the *Armstrong* broadcast, including Menzel's assertion of glowing owls. Some of its refutations were clearly aimed at Keyhoe; the flyleaf referred to "the sensational claim of certain UFO clubs or groups and certain individuals that flying saucers are spaceships under intelligent control." Elsewhere, Tacker huffed about these "clubs" whose "planned campaigns" had engendered interest from members of Congress and had demanded public hearings.

Overall, the book was a defense specifically against Keyhoe's accusations and was a clear illustration that, despite Ruppelt's desperate assertion that the Air Force had long since decided to ignore NICAP, it was not and never had been the case. Tacker's book, predictably, merely trotted out the usual, tired, unsupported, and often risible explanations for UFOs that had done so much damage to the Air Force's image since 1947—though presumably the author didn't realize that his own somewhat pulpish writing style rather resembled Keyhoe's. As to its content, even before publication, Dick Hall was anticipating NICAP's reaction: "we are going to pick it to pieces and hang up the bones to dry."[616]

The book, emblazoned on the cover with "The Official Air Force Story," had a brief foreword by General Thomas D. White, Air Force Chief of Staff, which stated: "So far, not a single bit of material evidence of the existence of spaceships has been found." It was later said to have sold around 10,000 copies, and during the infamous NBC interview, Tacker was not going to be deflected from the claims he made in it.

Host Dave Garroway was a keen and highly-knowledgeable amateur astronomer. He politely challenged Tacker's erroneous claims about how the distance and angular size of an object can be determined, but the floundering Colonel, clearly unprepared for such a test, simply became more foolishly defiant as he struggled and failed to explain himself.

He took an early, pompous swipe at Don when he referred to "the science fiction type of thing that Major Keyhoe writes," but became inflamed when Keyhoe began to reference several Congressmen who had told him they were unsatisfied with the Air Force's denial of secrecy. He mentioned in particular Representative Joseph E. Karth, who had raised his concerns in executive session, complaining that "the Air Force took refuge in security and said this was involved with the nation's safety." Tacker vehemently denied this, to which Keyhoe asked, incredulously, "Are you calling Representative Karth a liar?"

Tacker shot back with, "Are you calling General White a liar? Did you read [his] Foreword to the book?" and the two then began brandishing high-ranking names at each other. Most egregiously, Tacker sneered at NICAP as a "hobby group," shrugged-off contemptuously the illustrious names of its Board of Governors ("You're impressing me immensely, Major"), and snarled, "Why don't you get off that kick—you don't believe it yourself!"

Of course, after the program, Don had his own outlet for venting his feelings, and the next issue of the *UFO Investigator* devoted a large, space-wasting verbatim segment on the debate. Some six-hundred letters were received at NICAP, expressing disgust at Tacker's performance, and allegedly thousands of similar complaints were received by the Air Force. Lee Munsick pulled no punches when he wrote to the editor of the *Air Force Space Digest* in D.C., pointing out that its recent praiseful review of Tacker's book ignored its numerous flaws, and with respect to the Keyhoe debate added:

> Garroway and many of his viewers were shocked with the pigheaded, snotty, stubborn attitude of the Air Force, epit-omized by Col. Tacker. I am most sorry to see your journal suckered into being a party to this travesty of official com-petency.[617]

Ted Bloecher wrote personally to Tacker in a letter that is a model of polite pungency:

> Having had the misfortune of missing your televised appear-ance with Donald Keyhoe ... I was pleased to read excerpts of your contretemps with the flying saucer dragon in the NICAP *UFO Investigator* ... Those of us who are seriously concerned about the lack of official responsibility toward this

subject are indeed indebted to you for confirming our suspicions of bureaucratic flim-flam in dealing with this subject.

You succinctly display your own ignorance [regarding
angular size of unknown objects and temperature inversions]
... Your personal vendetta toward Major Keyhoe is childish
at best and certainly not befitting an officer of the US Air
Force ... Your rudeness was intolerable, and certainly disas-
trous to your side of the argument. I would like to thank
you for this enlightening display of inexcusable official han-
ky-panky.[618]

Largely unknown, however, is that the anger Tacker displayed on
Garroway's show was not simply attributable to his personal shortcomings;
it had been building for long time, thanks to Keyhoe's unrelenting attacks
on the Air Force and on him personally, which had continued despite the
setbacks resulting from the *Armstrong Circle Theatre* and the Mike Wallace
interview. Undaunted, Don had continued to pursue Congressional hearings
and support from politicians, notably in 1960, when he had gained interest
from then-Senator Lyndon B. Johnson (LBJ), who in July had been named
as John F. Kennedy's running mate in the upcoming presidential election.
Johnson sent an encouraging letter to NICAP:

At my direction, the staff of the Preparedness Investigating
Subcommittee is keeping a close watch over new developments in this field, with standing instructions to report to me
any recent significant sightings of unidentified flying objects
along with an analysis of the conduct and conclusions of the
Air Force Investigations of each such sighting.[619]

This was in response to receiving from Keyhoe, "the NICAP digest of
evidence—key cases and documented proof of censorship," which had been
copied to "other members of Congress who have shown serious interest
in the UFO problem." The digest was précised in the July-August *UFO
Investigator*—which devoted three of its four pages to unremitting criticism of
the Air Force—and asserted that "the complete document proves beyond any
reasonable doubt" that:

1. The UFOS are intelligently controlled machines superior
to any known earth-made devices.

2. The USAF knows these facts and has kept the truth from Congress, the press and the public.

It went on to list examples where "AF denials of secrecy are untrue," where "cases [have been] explained away," and "documented, verified UFO cases concealed, denied or falsely explained by the AF." The rest of the issue reported at length on the Air Force's "attack" on the Brazilian government, because it had labelled "as a hoax a UFO photograph released by the President of Brazil" (this was the famous Trindade Island sighting). And for good measure, Keyhoe laid the blame largely with Tacker for what he considered to be the Air Force's "attack" against "Brazil's official circles," then packaged up this material and sent it to sympathetic Congressmen and LBJ, a potential vice-president.

If this wasn't sufficient to create the outrage within Tacker that spilled out on Garroway's show, there was already plenty originating back until at least soon after the *Armstrong Circle Theatre* fiasco.

In early April 1958, W. E. (Wilton Enlund) Lexow, the CIA's Chief of Applied Science, sent a memo to the Assistant Director, SI (Scientific Intelligence), with respect to Keyhoe's and Davidson's written requests for a copy of the 1953 secret (Robertson) panel report:

> In response to our query as to whether the Air Force has any objection to our answering these letters enclosing a copy of the panel report, Major Tacker indicated that he had rather the CIA forward the letters to him … and he will answer the letters. He stated that the Air Force is endeavoring to impress upon Major Keyhoe and others in a similar position, that his office is the proper place to come for such information.
>
> In view of my conversation with Major Tacker, I called Frank Chapin in the DDCI's office and advised him that the Air Force not only preferred to answer the letters, but was most insistent that they be permitted to answer them … I think we can use this procedure as a precedent henceforth in all inquiries regarding UFO's.[620]

Thus, the CIA happily off-loaded UFO enquiries onto the Air Force and, in Keyhoe's case, specifically into the lap of Tacker at his own request. Evidently he was keen for a fight long before the NBC contretemps. But unknown to Garroway and Keyhoe, his long-festering anger had undoubtedly been fueled by a very strange security matter that had arisen six months before the debate aired, which allegedly involved Don and can only have served to deepen the Colonel's feeling that Keyhoe and his turbulent NICAP ought to be neutralized.

On June 7, 1960, Tacker had received a phone call alleging "that Top Secret and Secret documents relating to unidentified flying objects (UFO) were being surreptitiously removed from the Pentagon long enough to be reproduced" and then returned to the Pentagon. The informant was a British Army colonel who was now an American citizen. He had "served with the Australian government as an Assistant Liaison Officer for North America" and had once "served with the British Internal Security" (presumably MI5).

Tacker met the next day with the informant, whose credentials were checked and found to be reliable. The source told him that he worked in premises "adjacent to" Mercury, Inc., a.k.a. Mercury Enterprises, which was located at 1025 Connecticut Avenue NW, a few minutes walk from NICAP headquarters at 1536 Connecticut Avenue, NW.

The man said he had been shown "photostats of documents marked Secret and Top Secret" by two individuals (names redacted), both of whom were known to Tacker. It appears that these individuals were the same men who, in May 1960, had visited "Major Ben Fern, Chief of the Magazine and Book Branch, Office of the Secretary of Defense, Public Affairs." They had written an article on UFOs for the June issue of *Argosy* magazine, which was based on the "NICAP viewpoint" and now wanted to follow up with a piece from the Air Force's angle. It's inferred that these men were connected with Mercury Enterprises, which the informant described as

> a promotional organization set up to exploit information on
> space exploration and technology with the intention of sell-
> ing stories, scripts and articles based on it.

There had indeed been an article on UFOs in *Argosy* as described. It was "Flying Saucers: Menace or Myth?" by Keyhoe "as told to Harold Salkin," a writer, publicist and UFO researcher who happened to be one of Clara John's "associates," as she herself described him.[621] It's not clear from the document if any of the redacted names might refer to Salkin, but a Memorandum of Record dated June 14, 1960, from Major Robert J. Friend (at that time, Blue Book chief) confirms he was one of them. Friend reported that during the week of May 30th, Tacker had been visited by Salkin and another man who claimed to represent *Argosy* magazine. They were researching for a UFO article to be published in *McCalls* (a needlework and craft magazine). It was apparently these two men for whom, according to the FBI document, Tacker had subsequently arranged a visit to "Wright-Patterson AFB where they would be given background on the Air Force viewpoint on UFOs because hitherto they had only been exposed to the NICAP outlook."

This interview and subsequent visit is confirmed in the *UFO Investigator* of July-August 1960, which gives the name of Salkin's accomplice at the interview with Tacker:

> Most of the ATIC statements were tape-recorded by maga-zine writer Harold Salkin, at Dayton [and] Washington ra-dio producer, Richard Vaughn, of WTTG, who was seeking material for a documentary UFO program. The dual inter-view began on May 31, had been arranged by AF HQ, and the AF had flown the two men to Dayton.[622]

Indeed, Salkin had provided NICAP with a signed certification regarding his visit to ATIC, accompanied by Vaughn [a.k.a. Vaughan] on that date, with handwritten notes of the meeting with Friend and a Colonel Hiaett.[623] The salient points of the tape recording were listed Q&A style in the July-August issue of *UFO Investigator*, which devoted almost half its content to lambasting the Air Force for its denials and contradictions with respect to various sightings reports during this interview.

Tacker's informant claimed that the Pentagon documents shown to him by the redacted individuals (presumably Salkin and Vaughn) were being taken to a place referred to as the "listening post," where they were copied, "delivered to Mercury Inc" and returned to the Pentagon by unknown means or persons.

The most damaging claim made, however, was that Keyhoe had a desk at Mercury Enterprises, and "on several of these occasions" was present during examination of the documents, which were "gloated over."

Tacker had also received, apparently from his informant, a copy of the Apr-Jun 1960 issue of Clara's *The Little Listening Post* in which Mercury Enterprises is mentioned. A note containing the illegible initials of several persons was attached to the issue, and it claimed that the editor of the *LLP*

> ... has the contact within the P. and from whom [name re-dacted] (Rtd) obtains certain documents. Name of contact unknown as present ...

The Apr-Jun issue of the *LLP* does indeed refer to Mercury Enterprises and the address is given as 1025 Connecticut Avenue, NW, though the "files of the Directorate of Special Investigations were checked" and no record of the company was found. Research by this author, of public and press records of the period, also found no trace of it, nor of any "Industrial Relations" business "adjacent" to the address. The premises at 1025, like many on the street, then and now, comprised several office suites serving a number of separate businesses. In 1960, it also happened to be the address of NICAP's lawyer, Sam Borzilleri, who had been hired by Townsend Brown.[624] This was later confirmed by Brown himself in 1971:

> The [Townsend Brown] Foundation also retained an attorney (whose name I do not remember) in the same building where our offices were located, to file the incorporation papers for NICAP.[625]

From available records, the only Industrial Relations business listed on Connecticut Ave NW that year was directly on the opposite side of the street, at 1028. The occupant was one Ella G. Roller, an "Industrial Relations Counsellor," who was a noted figure in Democrat political circles, and in 1945 she had been "information specialist" at the OPA—the same organization in which Mary Vaughan King and her associates were involved. This of course might be entirely irrelevant but is nonetheless another odd coincidence that commands heightened interest when viewed in the context of the NICAP story. No less interesting is information directly from Townsend Brown, in which he said:

> For several years prior to NICAP's incorporation, the Townsend Brown Foundation maintained an office on Connecticut Ave, near Farragut Square ...[626]

This, according to his own later correspondence, was 1025 Connecticut Avenue, NW.[627] He gives this as the location of the Foundation while he was "preparing and submitting" his proposal to the Defense Department for Project Winterhaven—though the address given on that proposal, 416 Bowen Building, Washington, D.C., is some streets away from Farragut Square (which is a small park). Number 1025 must therefore have been in addition to his location at Counsel Services office, which Edward Hermann confirmed to be the Foundation's office in 1954, when Brown was submitting (or perhaps, re-submitting) his Project Winterhaven proposal. The FBI's failure to link the address on Connecticut Avenue with the Townsend Brown Foundation inevitably implies that Mercury Enterprises was a front, though it may simply be that it was either unconnected to Brown, or that the FBI conducted an inadequate investigation. The Bureau was not infallible, as is evident from many errors in the files of the period in question. However, given Clara John's connection to Mercury Enterprises and the informant's allegations of a link between the two, it seems more than coincidental.

Moreover, in March 1960, the *LLP* reported on an Adamski lecture given at D.C.'s Hotel Willard, sponsored by Mercury Enterprises, marked by a 65-strong "red-coated" band in his honor, which was led by Courtland Hastings, who had earlier declined Townsend Brown's offer to become a Director of NICAP. The same issue further mentioned Mercury Enterprises as the distributor of "a 30 minute documentary re Anti-Cancer Agent KREBIOZEN which has been suppressed for last decade," available free for non-commercial use.[628]

Adding further oddness to this episode, it appears that one of the men who had met with Major Fern and Tacker had, in December 1957, represented himself as a USAF Reserve Officer. He had given Fern as a reference for a check that subsequently bounced and then had obtained permission from another individual—presumably an Air Force officer—to give that person's name as reference for a successfully cashed check for $100. The man cashing these checks appears to be the same individual who had impersonated the aforementioned USAF Reserve Officer. The case was at that time referred to the FBI, which interviewed him, but the result of that investigation is redacted in the memo.

The allegation of the pilfered secret Pentagon documents was investigated by the Air Force. On June 13th, personnel interviews were conducted at AFCIN, which ascertained that none of those interviewed "could recall ever having seen a Top Secret document relating to this subject, but several had seen Secret documents."

On June 23rd the matter was turned over to the FBI, but in spite of the apparent credibility of Tacker's informant and the documents he provided, the Bureau decided to take "no action in this matter in the absence of information indicating a violation of a Federal statute within our jurisdiction."[629]

Today, more than sixty years on from this strange episode and without complete documentation, we can only speculate on what the full story might have been. The simplest explanation may be that the informant had mistaken Keyhoe for Townsend Brown, who may well have still kept a desk at 1025

Connecticut Avenue. It seems highly unlikely that Keyhoe would attend such meetings as the informant described; he tolerated, yet distrusted Clara John, and she would be among the very last people with whom he would share clandestine allegiance. That said, Keyhoe would have known that Salkin and Clara John were linked, yet he co-operated with Salkin on the *Argosy* piece and mentioned him uncritically in the *UFO Investigator* during 1960. But it should be remembered that Keyhoe would deal with contactees if they served some productive purpose. Wilbert Smith's 1955 conversion to cultism didn't cause him to be ostracized by Keyhoe.

As to Tacker's snarl at Keyhoe "why don't you get off that kick—you don't believe it yourself" on Garroway's program, perhaps this was rooted in the recent information that the Major and cultist Clara John were in cahoots. Such an association would inevitably imply to Tacker that Keyhoe was a closet-cultist.

Of course, seen today through the prism of NICAP, any mention of "secret" Pentagon documents coming under Keyhoe's or Clara John's scrutiny inevitably suggests they had seen the "smoking gun"—written evidence that there was indeed a high-level cover-up of interplanetary visitors. But this may not have been the case. There is one final observation to be made on this strange episode. In Clara John's *LLP* of May 1963—which happened to be the largest she ever published—she remarks, with a hint of gleeful sarcasm:

> Pentagon documents are sometimes tagged "SECRET" merely to cover up <u>mistakes</u> or to avoid <u>criticism</u>. Pentagon classifies enough documents every week to form a pile higher than the Empire State Bldg ...!!

It's unclear whom she quotes, or from where this information comes, but *if* she and Townsend Brown (or, far less likely, Keyhoe) had indeed "gloated" over the alleged documents, were they merely examples of Pentagon folly, which for a time, were being passed to the *LLP* to demonstrate the fallibility of anti-saucer officialdom? It stretches logic somewhat to draw this conclusion, but given the bizarreness of the episode and the strangeness of NICAP's journey to this point, perhaps it has a tinge of merit.

With this in the background, and now that the FBI had dismissed the case, Tacker—who must have been salivating at the prospect of bringing down Keyhoe and NICAP—was surely frustrated at being thwarted, so he tried another approach. On August 29th he wrote to FBI Director J. Edgar Hoover, enclosing a press clipping that reported the first arrest made under a new law "designed to prevent trading on the name of the Federal Government for non-governmental purposes." A woman from Silver Springs had been arrested for naming her debt-collection agency the National Deposit System so that it would appear to be a government department, with the intent to mislead the public. The number of such cases had been increasing, hence the law was enacted. Tacker wrote:

> As you well know, the National Investigation Committee on Aerial Phenomena has done this for many years and has been a thorn in the side of many governmental agencies during this period including the FBI, the Air Force, Department of Defense, various Congressional Committees and individual Congressmen and Senators.
>
> Could not we possibly invoke this law to curtail the activities of this organization in a manner similar to that described in the inclosed article?[630]

Two days later, Hoover sent Tacker a personal reply:

> The public law to which you refer, Section 712, Title 18, U.S. Code, applies only to skip-tracing or collection agencies for bad debts, and private detective agencies. In view of this fact, no investigation can be conducted concerning the National Investigation Committee on Aerial Phenomena under the afore-mentioned statute.[631]

Clearly, Tacker could elicit no action against NICAP by the FBI, nor by the Pentagon, despite the serious allegations that had been made in June.

This double-thwarting surely stoked the fires of his indignation, which resulted in the scorching he inflicted on Keyhoe when they did battle on Garroway's show barely three months later. He had entered this debate with information no doubt fresh in his mind that his adversary was not only party to theft of secret Pentagon documents but also was in secret collusion with the lunatic fringe.

In the immediate aftermath of the show, Tacker came off the worse. In February 1961, he was transferred to USAF HQ in Germany (Wiesbaden) to an obscure posting as Director of Information.[632] The April-May 1961 issue of the *UFO Investigator* announced triumphantly, in its lead story, "Tacker Replaced As Spokesman" and laid the cause to the "flood of protests against his public UFO misstatements and his arrogance toward anyone who questioned the AF claims."

If the Air Force had expected their spokesman to undermine NICAP on TV, it had not only failed but had also rattled Keyhoe's cage all the harder, causing him to ramp up his unwelcome demands. Getting rid of Tacker was not enough; "the situation requires far more," he complained. He now "requested that the AF Secretary ... correct all official mis-statements" and "end the unwarranted UFO censorship." For good measure, he gave Tacker a petulant kick over a "misleading photo" in his book, *Flying Saucers and the US Air Force*, accusing him of cropping and tilting an image of Comet 1957-d, taken from an astronomy magazine and labelling it as a "moderately frequent" fireball meteor. "Presumably, this rare picture was used because it is more spectacular than most meteor photos," Keyhoe added, snarkily.

Tacker was to some extent neutralized, and the Air Force tried to distance itself from his book. The October 1961 *UFO Investigator* gleefully headlined, "AF Disavows Tacker Book As Official," quoting a letter to NICAP from Major William T. Coleman, current "UFO Project spokesman," in which he wrote that the book

> ... was undertaken as a private project in Colonel Tacker's off-duty hours ... The book was published as a commercial enterprise ... Since this is not an Air Force document, a discussion of the relative merits of the book is not within our official purview ... If you are distressed with the contents of the book, you should correspond with Col Tacker personally.[633]

Despite this, Coleman admitted a few months later that the book had been reviewed by the Air Force under order AFM 190-4, which "covers books, articles and scripts for talks and broadcasts" in a review process that had the power to delete "classified matter." Keyhoe, in a rather reaching attempt, interpreted this admission to mean that even if Tacker's book had contained "positive UFO evidence, this would have been prohibited."

In 1966, Tacker would surface again to bang his anti-UFO drum on a CBS program entitled *UFOs: Friend, Foe or Fantasy*, hosted by America's "most trusted" man, Walter Cronkite. The program trotted out the old Air Force denials, supported by interviews with Menzel and the current Blue Book chief, anti-UFO Major Hector Quintanilla, though they did interview Keyhoe, who brandished his usual defense. Interestingly, Thornton Page, who made a brief appearance in the program, had his own fingers in the pie. In a letter to Fred

Durant, dated September 16, 1966, he wrote that he had "helped organize the CBS TV show around the Robertson Panel conclusions."[634] Evidently, it was slanted against Keyhoe's view from the start.

The following year, Tacker's career appeared to be rather lackluster in comparison to his role as UFO debunker. He was now "academy information officer" at the Colorado Springs Air Force Academy, where he was reporting on a rash of forced resignations among cadets due to a "cheating scandal." Four years later, he was living a well-paid civilian life, serving as either president or vice-president of public relations for various firms, before ultimately entering a comfortable retirement. He died in 1996, aged 89.

His Air Force replacement was Major William T. Coleman, whose debunking would later appear to be even more profound than his predecessor's. In July 1955, when piloting a B-25 over Southern Alabama, he and his co-pilot had a lengthy close-up sighting of a "titanium-type finish" disc of about 60 feet diameter and about 10 feet thick "through the center."[635] In 1976 Coleman took his turn at debating Keyhoe on air and described his experience, but the sighting hadn't changed his debunking mindset, even though he admitted that "it could have been a test vehicle, but I doubt it."[636]

But that was yet to come. For the present, Donald Keyhoe could savor this small victory.

Chapter 32:
Forwards and Backwards

Though Colonel Tacker had been temporarily quelled, NICAP still had the unending distractions emanating from the contactees. In April 1961, the Committee had been dragged into the sort of story the press liked to print because it shone a poor light on serious research.

A Wisconsin plumber, Joe Simonton, claimed that a flying saucer had landed in his backyard, and its three "Italian looking" occupants gave him "some pancakes in exchange for a jug of water." County Judge Frank W. Carter, without consultation, informed the press that he'd sent one of the cakes to NICAP for analysis. Instead of justifiably rejecting this unsolicited item, the Committee sent it for analysis by Board member Charles Maney, who expended time and money to determine it was merely a "common type of hydrogenated-oil shortening." Further tests would have cost around $300, which NICAP could not afford. When told that no further analysis could be done, Judge Carter then launched "attacks" on the Committee in the press, and Keyhoe, yet again, felt he had to expend time and energy rebutting these accusations.

Later, in Coral and Jim Lorenzen's 1967 book, *Flying Saucer Occupants*, the Simonton case was detailed in a guardedly favorable way, but APRO's loathing of NICAP was now such that its name in relation to its investigation of the "cookie" was not even mentioned, though criticism was nonetheless given. They huffed that "the UFO group" that had obtained one "planned no further action and had more important things to do."[637]

While the cookie crumbled, NICAP cancelled the membership of evangelist "Dr." Frank E. Stranges, who claimed to be in personal contact with "Valiant Thor," a Venusian who looked perfectly human (apart from having no fingerprints) and worked in the Pentagon. Stranges headed the National Investigations Committee on UFOs and liked to pass himself off as both "a personal friend" of Keyhoe's and as a spokesman for NICAP. He was warned to cease giving "this impression."[638]

On a positive note, the Committee now had an "International Panel of Advisers" located in France, Sweden, Brazil, Venezuela, England, New Zealand,

and Canada. The latter nation was represented by contactee-convert Wilbert Smith, whose defection to the other side had not sufficiently impacted his usefulness to Keyhoe and his organization. However, according to Dick Hall, advisers and also Board members were not as useful as their status implied:

> Some of our Board of Governors and Panel of Advisers (vary-
> ing from individual to individual) have little time to devote
> to UFOs, and do little more than allow use of their names for
> prestige purposes. The Panel ... does not actually convene as
> a panel since the members are scattered all over the country
> and no funds are available to pay their transportation costs,
> even for a yearly meeting.[639]

Meanwhile, Keyhoe's raison d'étre was still to bring about Congressional hearings on UFO secrecy and the more he was thwarted in this ambition, the more resolute he became. He was of course, up against *Project Blue Book Special Report 14*, which had been successfully used by the Air Force to assure most "congressmen that the Air Force's UFO program was adequate to the task," but Keyhoe had doggedly stirred doubt in enough minds in Washington to keep alive the possibility of hearings.[640]

As frustrated as he was with the Air Force, it was no less exasperated with him. Since 1949 he had picked apart every statement, jumped on every error, named names, made pompous demands, and sent letters and reports to the highest levels in government and the Air Force, though he was only a civilian and had no more power than any other. Neither was he a politician, a prominent scientist, nor an industry leader—though many such figures were NICAP members—and along with some of the higher-profile members of his Board, he was merely a retired officer. Moreover, he was head of an impoverished organization that was constantly teetering on the brink of collapse, but somehow he and NICAP were still standing. These deficits, though, were still not sufficient to render him without enough influence to maintain his relentless criticism of the Air Force and to thrust it under the noses of people who mattered.

A possible solution to the Air Force's troublesome stewardship of the UFO subject had presented itself in October 1958 when Blue Book had acquired yet another chief, Major Robert J. Friend, who tried to systematize the neglected project. Like Ruppelt, he was hampered by lack of staff and finances, but his efforts enabled a reassessment of Blue Book's "role in studying the UFO phenomenon."[641] He realized that the project's interest went no further than determining whether UFOs were a national security threat or had intelligence value. Therefore, if they

> ... did not fall into one of these two categories, they were then a scientific problem and, as such, did not come within the purview of what the Air Force called the intelligence community.[642]

Additionally, the study found that the project "was 80 percent public relations" due to the "unfavorable publicity" generated by private UFO organizations that exploited the subject for "financial gain, religious or other more devious reasons." These groups were blamed for witnesses complaining to their congressmen and "causing congressional hearings," which of course, meant NICAP.

As a result of these findings, which appeared to confirm that the Air Force had limited interest in the project (and that Donald Keyhoe took up 80% of Blue Book's time), it felt the best way to deal with the problem was to make it somebody else's by getting rid of UFOs from ATIC's remit altogether. Rather than trying to keep tighter control of the saucers, it was anxious to relinquish them to whoever was willing to take them on, hence other Air Force divisions were approached but none wanted the poisoned chalice. To what extent these rejections were caused by the sure and certain knowledge that with the saucers would come Keyhoe can only be speculated upon, but the upshot was that ATIC—even though in 1961 it quietly "became part of the Foreign Technology Division [FTD] of the Air Force Systems Command"—remained stuck with both.[643]

In March 1961, Jim Lorenzen attempted to garner interest in UFOs from America's new president, John Kennedy, in a somewhat terse if not pompous letter/memo, displaying the self-congratulatory tactlessness that Keyhoe often displayed in his communications with authority. Headed "Unconventional Aerial Objects," the five-page missive lacked even a polite introduction or closure, but pointed out the Government's shortcomings in investigating UFOs and informed JFK of, among other things, specific sightings and Aimé Michel's "Orthoteny." Lorenzen described this theory as "the fact that UFO sightings for discrete periods of time formed straight line ... patterns." Emphasis was made of Jung's interest in UFOs, and a bibliography of fifteen publications was enclosed, which included some of APRO's own bulletins and even Tacker's book.[644] None of Keyhoe's works were mentioned. At this time, however, Kennedy was rather more concerned with Earthly matters regarding the impending Bay of Pigs operation.

While the Air Force was hoping to get rid of UFOs, Keyhoe was even more vigorously thrusting them at sympathetic Congressmen. He had long expressed concern that the saucers might trigger an "accidental war" and in August 1961, it seemed to him that this possibility was increasing. Kennedy and Khrushchev were eyeball-to-eyeball over the occupation of Berlin, and tensions were rising by the hour. Don felt that this escalating crisis might provide tragic validation of his fears, and he was now even more anxious to draw attention to NICAP's quest for an end to secrecy.

Whether or not Kennedy took interest in APRO's or NICAP's missives isn't known, but Keyhoe's own broader efforts to alert higher authority to the need to investigate seemed to be paying off. The October 1961 *UFO Investigator* encouragingly announced that "Majority Leader Support Indicates Early Congressional Hearings," but this had been achieved only after an awkward and almost catastrophic misunderstanding in August and September between Minnesota Congressman Joseph E. Karth and NICAP.

House Select Committee Chairman John W. McCormack had apparently retained his earlier interest in the saucers, and due to his influence a "UFO Subcommittee" had been created. He had discussed this with Keyhoe in early August, advising him to contact its newly-appointed chairman, Karth. (It appears that Coral Lorenzen knew of this before Don; she wrote to Karth on July 13th offering APRO's assistance.)[645] Since Karth was unavailable at that time, Keyhoe wrote instead to Congressman Overton Brooks, chairman of the Science and Astronautics Committee, whom he knew was not in favor of hearings, but had reluctantly responded to McCormack's urging and appointed Karth.

Keyhoe's letter of August 11th detailed NICAP's "plan" for ending "UFO secrecy" in order to prevent accidental war and outlined its idea for a "new UFO Information Agency." This "Agency" would release "all reports of unknown or so-called unidentified flying objects from December 8, 1941 to date, these not to be summaries, but complete reports ..." Much of the content was, of course, heavily critical of the Air Force and employed Don's usual tactless language with which he unwittingly made condescending, imperious demands and proposals.[646] Among them were:

> A. NICAP Board members, officials and advisers will submit the evidence and proof ... in executive sessions of the UFO Subcommittee, with the Air Force assigned representa-

tives present and authorized to explain the Air Force policies and answer specific questions. The Air Force representatives will be directed by the Subcommittee to answer all of NICAP officials' questions in regard to specific UFO sighting reports and to all phases of the Air Force investigation.

B.   The Air Force representatives will similarly be permitted to question NICAP officials, and the NICAP representatives will answer fully, except for revealing names and certain details of a few reports given to NICAP confidentially.

...

E.   If the Subcommittee decides, after hearing Air Force and NICAP evidence and answers, that the Air Force has withheld, denied or wrongly explained specific UFO reports, and that it has withheld UFO information from or given untrue answers to Members of Congress, the press and public, then it will set to reduce the secrecy dangers by ending the censorship.

F.   If this Subcommittee decision is made, insuring the prompt release of all UFO information in the hands of the Air Force, NICAP will immediately end its criticism of the Air Force past policies; it will make available all its own UFO information; and it will cooperate fully ... in carrying out the new policy and educating the public.

If, however, the Air Force could "disprove all of NICAP's documented evidence," Keyhoe would resign, allow NICAP to fold, and forever after hold his peace.

What Brooks thought of this isn't known—he had never read any of NICAP's documented evidence—but in early August he suddenly became interested. He had only just learned that Hillenkoetter, whom he held in high regard, was on NICAP's board, so he arranged to meet with him and Keyhoe on August 24th. But on August 16th, fate intervened when Brooks died of a heart attack, and he was replaced by Congressman George P. Miller, who would not permit UFO hearings.

Setting aside this latest blow, Keyhoe copied the letter and plan—eight pages in total—to Karth a week later and on August 28th received a three-page excoriating reply:

> [I]t was my belief that you ... actually had proof that UFO's did exist and that you would be prepared to prove this during the course of a hearing ... I cannot help but feel ... that your primary if not sole objective, is to "be-little," "defame," "ridicule" ... and therefore cause the U.S. Air Force embarrassment.[647]

With respect to Keyhoe's plan, Karth felt it was almost entirely concerned with his "evident dislike and malicious intent toward a great branch of the military. In fact it sounded to me like nothing more than cheap service rivalry" and accused him of "grandstand acts of a rabble rousing nature." As to hearings, Karth was "not interested in listening to headline making accusations (prompted it seems by past gripes) in open debate between you and the Air Force."[648]

Finally, he made clear his feelings about Keyhoe's peremptory terminology and how it had altered his former "vital interest" in UFOs:

> You dispelled any hopes I had relative thereto in the language heretofore cited ... If I have anything to say about it, your terms, conditions and suggestions will not be accepted.[649]

On September 1st, in Keyhoe's absence, Dick Hall sent an interim reply to this scorching rebuke, employing his usual calm and succinct manner. He gave clarification on some of Karth's concerns and offered NICAP's "regret that you have misunderstood our reasons for keeping after the AF about UFO's."

Keyhoe's own nine-page reply to Karth on September 12th was far more contrite, admitting that he had given "unwittingly, a totally erroneous impression of NICAP and its aims." He had been "shocked" and "hurt" by Karth's letter but now abased himself, acknowledging that his "poor choice of words" was the result of being under pressure to present the facts before "the inquiry sessions probably would be closed."

Karth evidently possessed a truly open mind, for a week later he sent a brief letter to Keyhoe, reversing his former hostile position: "Now that we have a better understanding of each other, I would hope we could properly proceed with a hearing early next year—providing the new chairman authorizes hearings."

Promising though this was, Keyhoe still had to grapple with NICAP's usual problems, which were as troublesome as any of the brickbats hurled at him by the Air Force and other critics. The 1962 January-February *UFO Investigator* devoted a page and a half to his report on its ongoing internal difficulties. "I am sure most of you do not fully realize our constant financial ordeal," he began and went on to lament at length how the lack of money and the resulting lack of staff were hampering its aims, highlighting in particular the consequent delays in meeting with Congressmen. He was additionally chafed that contactee Major Wayne Aho—a NICAP member—who was often mistaken for himself, "spent months on Capitol Hill," but the ongoing financial crisis meant Keyhoe could not "visit every Congressional office, to correct such errors." (Aho's membership was revoked later that year due to having "urged" a Baltimore radio station to broadcast a tape "denouncing" certain military and scientific personnel.)[650]

The lead item, however, which was sure to rile the Air Force, announced that NICAP had offered to "AF Secretary Zuckert …private AF-NICAP conferences, [to present] its specific evidence and majority conclusions that UFOs are real and under intelligent control." (By April, Zuckert had rejected this offer, which was repeated in May and was again rejected.) Page three provided the latest report on the "Congressional Situation," in which Keyhoe refuted what he believed were circulating denials that a Congressional UFO Subcommittee ever existed, by reproducing supportive letters from John McCormack and Congressman Perkins Bass.

Behind the scenes, however, there was unexpected and exciting movement toward hearings. In February, one of Karth's supporters, whom Keyhoe identified only as "a congressman," met with him and requested he select one of NICAP's "hottest cases," with the intention of using it to create big publicity and force Congressional Hearings. Keyhoe gave him one of the best in his files: the February 1951 case in which Navy pilot Lt. Graham Bethune, his crew, and military personnel passengers had a near-collision with a metallic, glowing disk, around 300 feet in diameter, during their flight from Iceland to Newfoundland. To protect Bethune's identity, Keyhoe had changed his name in the report (and in his 1960 book, *Flying Saucers: Top Secret*) to "George Benton" (though in his 1973 account of the incident in *Aliens From Space*, called him "George Brent").[651]

The congressman was also apprised of how the crew were interviewed by Naval Intelligence and ATIC, during which Bethune had been shown photographs of similar craft by a "government scientist" thought to be with the CIA. None of these interrogators would answer any of the pilot's questions.

The case appeared ideal, particularly as Bethune and the other witnesses, who were still in service, would be guaranteed immunity if they testified at any hearings. The congressman laid out to Keyhoe his plan for holding a press conference featuring, among others, Barry Goldwater and Hillenkoetter. The latter, he felt, was key to getting the issue exposed, and he was "counting on him" to "spearhead the show."[652] Keyhoe agreed to sound-out his old pal, whom he felt sure would want to participate.

Before he approached Hillenkoetter, Don needed to speak to Bethune but didn't know where he was now stationed and felt it unwise to phone Naval Personnel and ask for his location. Instead, he used a reliable go-between, "Jack Morton," a "personnel specialist" who had dealings with government departments and who had helped him twice in the past. They agreed on how "Morton" could get the required information without rousing attention—he knew there had been a "flag" on Bethune's file at one time but thought it was likely removed by now, so he would make the call and give Keyhoe "the dope" the next day.

Two days passed without a word, so Don phoned Morton's secretary, who said he was "taking time off." After several calls to his home number went unanswered, Keyhoe drove to his house that evening, but no-one came to the door. Soon after he returned home, a panicked Morton, who had secretly observed Don arrive and depart from his residence, phoned him, and a somewhat cinematic conversation followed.

Morton had made the call to Naval Personnel and, within an hour, realized that the flag on Bethune's file was still active. Two CIA agents arrived at his office, told him to get rid of his secretary, then gave him "the third degree" about why he wanted to contact Bethune, who was behind it, and to what purpose. He was "grilled" until he spilled about Keyhoe, the intended hearings, and Hillenkoetter's participation. The "Congress meeting deal" worried them, it seemed to Morton, and now his wife was "scared to death." The agents, he said, "ordered me not to see you or tell you anything ... [so] for heaven's sake don't try to call or see me again."[653]

After this startling and unsettling development, Keyhoe knew it was now imperative that he meet face-to-face with Hillenkoetter in New York and bring him up to speed. The next morning, while waiting at Washington National for his flight, he phoned his secretary, Mrs. Lelia Day, to tell her his plans, but when he spoke to her, he knew instantly there was trouble. She told him an important letter was waiting for him, which he ought to read for himself. By the time he got back to the office, he had guessed it would be from Hillenkoetter:

> Dear Don
>
> In my opinion, NICAP's investigation has gone as far as possible. I know the UFOs are not U.S. or Soviet devices. All we can do now is wait for some action by the UFOs.
>
> The Air Force cannot do any more under the circumstances. It has been a difficult assignment for them, and I believe we should not continue to criticize their investigations.
>
> I am resigning as a member of the NICAP Board of Governors.

Keyhoe reread several times this "astonishing" and "incredible" letter, reflecting on the numerous anti-secrecy/pro-Congressional hearings statements his old friend had made during his NICAP tenure. "How could he have been pressured into this complete reversal?" he asked himself.[654]

He would never get an answer. Indeed, the matter would become less clear over the next three years, when Dr. "Owl Glow" Menzel would vaunt on radio in 1964 a letter he had received from Hillenkoetter the previous year, written in response to receiving a copy of his recently published book, *The World of Flying Saucers*. Hillenkoetter praised the book effusively and said it had "effectively put to rest all surmises about flying saucers being from 'outer space.'" He referred also to a conversation the two had had at a dinner the previous December, in which he told Menzel he had quit NICAP because:

> ... it had degenerated from an organization honestly trying to find out something definite about possible unknowns into a body bickering about personalities. The Air Force, too, could have helped by not being so secretive.[655]

When Keyhoe heard about this in December 1964, he wrote to Hillenkoetter asking about Menzel's boast, to which he received only a short reply a month later, stating that the two had indeed met at the dinner but had merely exchanged "Good Evening—Merry Christmas." They'd had no discussion about NICAP or UFOs, but he confirmed he had received a copy of the book, on which he "took no position."[656]

Who was lying? It was almost certainly Hillenkoetter. Even Menzel's bloated ego was unlikely to result in faking a letter from the former CIA chief. The writing style is certainly that of Hillenkoetter, and it closed with the unusual phrase "please believe me," which he regularly used in his personal correspondence. Moreover, Menzel continued referring to its laudatory content for some time after, to which Hillenkoetter made no denial.

Hillenkoetter's brief reply to Keyhoe in January 1965 offered no explanation and made no apology for the enormous setback that he surely knew his resignation from NICAP had inflicted upon his old friend and how far it had damaged the cause that had for years united them.

Like Ruppelt, Hillenkoetter had become Menzelian, and similarly, if he felt any doubt or shame about his betrayal and abandonment of Don, he would forever keep it to himself. If he had truly accepted Menzel's meteorological theory of the saucers, then we must ask what "action by the UFOs," to which he referred in his letter to Keyhoe, could be expected from mere weather phenomena and what pressure had been applied to the former head of the CIA to bring about his astounding reversal.

Chapter 33:
Staggering On

Now bereft of Hillenkoetter, NICAP's prestige was severely dented, and the ongoing financial crisis was worsening. In April 1962, Dick Hall wrote to Max Miller:

> Our situation has deteriorated so badly that we are having to discuss the possibility of disbanding NICAP. Taxes have almost put us out of business, and the response to our last appeal left something to be desired ... There is very little reason for optimism. Our Five-Year Report is in the advanced talking stage, but no money to print it ... Don is worn out, and it's an awful strain on all of us to plod along unable to make ends meet [and he] has done as much as humanly possible if not more. I agree we should give up unless we get a real break within the next month or so.[657]

NICAP's desperate plight was embarrassingly evident in its March-July *UFO Investigator*, its cheap mimeograph printing more befitting a suburban "hobby" club than the foremost civilian investigative body of its kind on the planet. Funds were so tight that the issue had been printed and mailed due only to the Washington State Subcommittee's good graces.

Keyhoe admitted that, despite receiving many letters from members pleading for NICAP to keep going, only 6% of the membership had put their hands in their pockets to save it. (This attitude, however, was unfair. Members paid the dues demanded, yet were harangued frequently to send additional money because Don would not set a higher membership fee.) Nonetheless, he remained optimistic and pugilistic, insisting that "We are just one step from Congressional action" and "Congressional interest in UFOs" was increasing. To bolster these claims, he devoted a good part of the newsletter to the importance of NICAP's impending "Five-Year Report" (later published as *The UFO Evidence*), which he felt sure would be the ultimate blow to Air Force secrecy: "THIS IS A SHOWDOWN ... Do we sneak away like scared dogs with our tails between our legs? OR DO WE STAND UP AND FIGHT?"

He would of course fight, even though Dick Hall was continuing to despair about NICAP's situation:

> I sometimes get the impression no one gives a damn about us and what we are fighting for. Don and I both have about reached the point where we consider the Five-Year Report a do-or-die proposition. If it doesn't stir things up, we might as well quit.[658]

Still, by the end of 1962, two new Board Members had been appointed, though both lacked the luster of Hillenkoetter: Dr. Charles P. Olivier, President of the American Meteor Society, and Col. Joseph Bryan, III, a retired USAF officer who, unknown to Keyhoe, was a CIA psychological warfare expert. He was also the author of a 1947 authorized biography on the aforementioned Admiral William F. "Bull" Halsey, under whom the CIA's L. G. Shreve had served in the Pacific (see Chapter 21). Bryan's reason for joining NICAP remains a matter of speculation, but after some initial doubts about his motives, Keyhoe welcomed him to the Board.

The sense of deflation expressed by Hall was perhaps reflected in the first *UFO Investigator* of 1963, which seemed to lack the combative vigor of earlier issues. It was partly given-over to speculation about life on other worlds in what seemed a rather desperate attempt to fill its pages, but it remained Keyhoe's personal soap box from which to rail at the Air Force; he couldn't resist swinging a punch in return for its latest denunciation of him. He devoted a space-wasting full page to his rebuttal of just one letter sent to just one NICAP member from USAF's spectacularly-named Lt. Col. Lookadoo, in which he had trashed Keyhoe's reputation and integrity. This prompted Don to respond with a numbered listing of each "charge," followed by "the facts." His justification for this fulminating riposte was that "the untrue charges reflect on all NICAP members [so] they must be fully refuted. If not, they might endanger the success of our Five Year Report, on which Congressional action depends. It is not impossible that this is the purpose behind the attacks."

Despite the typical overkill of his response, he may well have been correct. If there was one thing guaranteed to inflame NICAP's director, while increasing the already substantial pressure on him, it was Air Force criticism, and he fell for it every time. He was to the Air Force what the contactees were to him—an unremitting nuisance that could not be reasoned with, nor ignored, so perhaps the best that could be done was to repeatedly undermine him and his turbulent Committee at every opportunity, just as he had always done with the contactees. It was a costly and time-wasting strategy that didn't work for either side, but it was nonetheless maintained.

At the start of 1963, NICAP's administrative tangles and managerial ineptitude continued, evidenced by its attempt to improve and clarify its wieldy membership procedures. In response to "past confusion," it had discarded the incomprehensible annual renewal system, which had somehow been tied to whether or not a member had received a "full quota" of publications and now had a "simplified renewal policy":

> Under the new system, if the first issue you received was V. I. No 11, you would not have been due to renew until you had received V. II No 4, your sixth issue, which was mailed in June 1962.
>
> (If you joined in September 1961 at $5, the first issue you received was V. II No 1. The membership covers six bi-monthly issues, therefore it expired with V. II No 6 which was mailed in December 1962. If the first issue you received was V. II No 2 (October 1961), your membership expires with this issue, V.II No 7, etc.)[659]

Whether or not this encouraged members to renew, or simply instilled in them the loss of will to live, can only be speculated upon.

The issue also reported on the recent death of Wilbert Smith (December 27, 1962), giving diplomatic, but dignified acknowledgement of his work: "Although Mr. Smith and NICAP differed about certain contact claims, his technical advice and leads to valuable information were greatly appreciated."[660]

The March-April newsletter was little better than the previous and had more than a tinge of desperation in its content. NICAP now was in such a parlous condition that it lacked even basic office equipment, so thanks were extended to members who had donated such, or had given their services. In a further testament to the Committee's desperation, members were asked to join in a "Stamp Project," instigated by none other than Jan Aldrich, nowadays a senior figure in UFO research but who was then a member of the recently-formed Connecticut Affiliate. Those with "access to cancelled postage stamps" were asked to send them to him for sale to stamp dealers and the proceeds would go to NICAP.

It also had a personal, slightly hectoring message from Don:

> I am now past 65, an age when some men stop work and relax. I'm not stopping and this isn't any self-pitying bid for sympathy. I can take the pressure ... If you're tired of hearing about NICAP's financial problems, we don't blame you. We're tired of them too. But we shouldn't have to plead for help to do the job. We shouldn't have to beg, as if for charity, when overdue members forget their back dues.[661]

The Five-Year Report was still in the works, but its completion was now reliant on members who had offered free art-work or editing services. Funds for printing were still lacking, which was unsurprising given the size of the intended run—a copy would be sent to "each Member of Congress and about 500 copies" to the media and "influential citizens." This was in addition to copies available to members at a reduced cost, bringing the total run to potentially in excess of six thousand.

Perhaps Keyhoe had briefly taken to heart Hillenkoetter's recommendation that NICAP should "not continue to criticize" the Air Force, for his only real dig in this issue was to complain that the Air Force knew of the funds crisis with respect to the report "and is informing Congress and citizens that NICAP has no such documented evidence." He warned members, "MAKE NO MISTAKE: Ending UFO secrecy depends on this Report. Congressional hearings depend on it ... If we get the Report to Congress well before the session ends, NICAP's biggest job is done."[662]

Its fumbling administrative procedures remained evident with respect to the ongoing membership card fiasco, which was now bordering on the Kafkaesque. The cards were ready but could not be sent due to some problem about envelopes, so an interim card was printed in the current issue. The real cards would carry an expiration code so that "non-coded members can easily figure when their memberships expire":

> For example, V II, No 12 means the membership expires after receipt of Vol. II, No 12 (four numbers after this double issue.) ... The figure "1963" on interim cards is merely to show the year when they are issued; a current membership may expire before the end of 1963 (after the sixth issue.) The coded cards will eliminate any confusion; meantime, any

non-coded member wishing to know his or her expiration
code can secure it by sending us a self-addressed postal card
...

By summer, Keyhoe was getting back into his combative stride. In the
June-September newsletter, he delivered blasts to the Air Force and to Menzel,
who was spared a full rebuttal of his latest anti-NICAP rantings due to space
needed for other stories, especially the progress of the now titled "Six Year
Report." Despite the crisis in 1962, it was "near the final stages," but "hold
out witnesses" were begged to come forward with their sightings reports to be
included "before it is too late."[663]

Argosy magazine was once more in Keyhoe's focus regarding a July
1963 article, "The Spaceniks of Giant Rock," written by NICAP Adviser
for Photography, Max Miller, which heralded yet more aggravation and
distraction from important matters. Hall and Keyhoe interpreted the piece
to be in support of contactees (though it seems to have been rather a tongue-
in-cheek dig at them) and "several members" had "denounced" it, leading the
UFO Investigator to state that Miller had "done a grave disservice to serious
investigators" and urged members to "help nullify this article by stating the
true evidence."

This was strong condemnation coming from the Committee to one of
its own advisers, but it had been building since at least 1959, when Idabel
Epperson wrote to Ivan Sanderson and Keyhoe about Miller's admiration for
Gabriel Green and other contactees.[664] Green at this time, amid the tension
surrounding Ruppelt's defection, had received from Don a severe reprimand
for claiming that NICAP was part of his Amalgamated Flying Saucer Clubs of
America outfit. Keyhoe made his feelings clear in a blunt telegram:

> This is to warn you against repeating any claim that the
> National Investigations Committee on Aerial Phenomena
> is part of your flying saucer club organization. NICAP is
> emphatically opposed to your Los Angeles program which
> focuses attention on unproved and often absurd claims of
> contact with space men. Many of these claims are known
> to be false. Practically all are regarded with suspicion by the
> press and general public. Your carnival approach to the sub-
> ject of unidentified flying objects is sure to cause public rid-
> icule, offsetting serious work by NICAP and other reputable
> fact-finding UFO groups.

Any claim or insinuation that NICAP agrees with your views will be publicly denied. The Los Angeles press and broadcasters are being informed of this warning.[665]

Undaunted, in 1960 Green announced that, having been selected by his spacemen friends for the task, he was a write-in candidate running against Richard Nixon and John F. Kennedy for the Presidency of the United States, and promised "Utopia," "Paradise," and "abundance" for all Americans. The press reported that his saucer club's co-chairmen were Daniel Fry and Reinhold O. Schmidt, leaving no doubt as to the basis of Green's platform and the electorate to which he appealed.

In May 1962, Miller's position on the contactees was made clear when he insouciantly remarked in a letter to Dick Hall that he was now working for Green, who was "running for the Senate." He believed himself to be a positive controlling force on Green and boasted to Hall in his letter that he was "fully responsible for [Green's] total omission of the [UFO] subject from all literature, speeches, etc.," though he admitted that he was "fully aware of what a thorn in the side he has been to UFO research." Nonetheless, Miller happily admitted he was "in effect, his public relations coordinator and advisor."

Hall's response was to the point:

> I was shocked to the core … Don's reaction was similar. What on earth do you have in mind? … I am appalled to see an extremist and phoney like Green espousing some liberal causes … I have always respected you and your contributions to UFOlogy, and hate to see you tied up with such a clown.[666]

On August 29, 1963, Miller was kicked out of his role at NICAP. Hall wrote: "It is with regret that that I must inform you that Don and I have decided to remove your name from the list of our Panel of Special Advisers." He explained that his association with Green was a "source of embarrassment," that the *Argosy* article gave the impression that only contactees were interested in UFOs, and that Miller had failed to make timely analyses of photographic material. This latter point was justified—Hall had sent several letters requesting the return of, or reports on, items in response to complaints from members. Miller denied he supported Green but admitted he had been "extremely lax and frankly, irresponsible, in my obligations to NICAP."[667]

The same month that Miller was ejected saw a change of staff at ATIC.

Lt. Robert J. Friend was replaced by Major Hector Quintanilla, Jr., an officer who considered Blue Book to be a "$20,000,000 Fiasco" and who thought the project was a waste of his own time. His tenure is considered by some to have been similarly worthless. The manuscript of his book, dated 1974 but written some years earlier, was a nose-to-tail rebuttal of all views that did not accord with the Air Force party line on UFOs.[668] Much of it, either directly or implied, was targeted at Keyhoe and NICAP, though he poured scorn on many others who dared to counter the Air Force's facile explanations.

His appointment, however, was certainly convenient and timely for the Air Force. Though Keyhoe had yet to achieve Congressional Hearings, he continued to press for them, which meant that Blue Book, unable to find a home outside the Air Force, now surely needed a chief who would not turn out to be another Ruppelt. Quintanilla was the perfect man for the job; the party line sat well with him, and he supported the Air Force's debunking without question. His book manuscript leaves no room for doubt that he loathed the saucers and their proponents, and he felt that neither of them deserved an iota of attention. From this point on, whatever usefulness Blue Book may have had to serious and open UFO investigation—little though it had ever really offered—was now ended. Its own description of the project and of Quintanilla shows the neglected and apathetic condition into which it had descended:

> There is only a minimal, permanent, full time staff [that is] only necessary to provide direction and administration to the program. All other personnel are used only on an "as needed" basis … . Major Hector Quintanilla, Jr, a physicist by train-ing, is primarily the <u>administrator</u> that screens the incoming reports of sightings and decides the specific investigative and analytical requirements of each. He then directs the action to be taken, monitors the results and determines what, if any, further action need be taken. On rare occasions, time per-mitting, he personally conducts some phase of an investiga-tion.[669]

This structure, Blue Book claimed, "eliminates the possibility of a permanent staff member becoming narrow or un-scientific in his approach to the problem." Hence, both the project and the remit of the man in charge were watered down to homeopathic-remedy proportions.

Blue Book's usefulness to Keyhoe had in any case died with Ruppelt's apostasy, but it seems the Air Force had learned a lesson from its former chief's co-operation with NICAP; no "permanent staff member" would be allowed to go his own way, regardless of where Blue Book's cases might lead. Without resources or an inquisitive mind at the helm, the project was guaranteed to become satisfactorily moribund.

Additional perspective on NICAP and Blue Book comes from J. Allen Hynek, who in the 1970s reflected on his thoughts about both in *The Edge of Reality* (1975), a book written in collaboration with Jaques Vallee, which was a transcription of tape-recorded discussions on their thoughts about the UFO phenomena. In it, Hynek admitted:

> Oh, well, my impression of NICAP was completely soured and prejudiced, perhaps because I never had any direct contact with them: all I knew about NICAP was through Blue Book and they were painted to me as a bunch of crackpots; Keyhoe was presented as a scoundrel and a mountebank, and all I remember was that, time after time, when Keyhoe seemed to be getting a little ascendency and calling for congressional investigations, suddenly there was a big flurry at Blue Book, key congressmen were called and told not to pay any attention to him, so there was a real counter-offensive mounted ... I wasn't sharp enough to see that this was a highly political move. I really thought then that NICAP was a bunch of nuts.[670]

In 1978, Hynek wrote more on Blue Book:

> [It] was always regarded officially as "unclassified," but this amounted to a standing joke among those who knew better. Not only were many of the reports labeled "Confidential" or "Secret," but the citizen who tried to examine Blue Book files was given a polite runaround or an outright refusal on various grounds. Those who sought to find out about the Air Force's investigation of UFOs were usually brushed off on the basis that the UFO files contained information that might reveal secrets about experimental military aircraft and hardware, new and advanced radar equipment and its secret locations, missiles, and military bases and installations.

In short, what was true in theory was not true in practice. Blue Book files *were not* open to the public, even though the Air Force claimed publicly that Blue Book was an open book.[671]

By autumn 1963, Keyhoe had begun to question Hynek's own position and gave what later proved to be a correct interpretation of the latter's quandary about the saucers. In that year's June-September *UFO Investigator*, he quoted from a recent article in *Yale Scientific Magazine*, in which Hynek had acknowledged the "decidedly above average" level of intelligence among UFO witnesses that was "in some cases embarrassingly above average."

Keyhoe's use of this quote from the Air Force's own consultant was an evident attempt to bolster his own cause—he was always keen to offer statements from credible sources, even if their conclusions about the saucers did not accord with NICAP's. But he noted, accurately as it turned out, that Hynek was "struggling between a private conviction of UFO reality and his duty as the AF UFO chief consultant to support the denial policy." Don concluded with the remark that "It would be interesting to learn exactly what he believes—and what he knows."[672]

Chapter 34:
A Gas Explosion

"We are confident of making significant progress in the New Year," Keyhoe told readers of 1964's first *UFO Investigator*, despite acknowledged setbacks with respect to the still not-quite-ready Six-Year Report, now named *The UFO Evidence*, and the "log-jam in Congress caused by the assassination of President Kennedy." His murder also brought about the end of Lyndon Johnson's active interest in UFOs. America had become a bubbling cauldron, and LBJ's attention would be elsewhere for the rest of his Presidency.

Clara John, alert as ever to what was ticking away in saucerdom, was plugging the forthcoming *The UFO Evidence* in her *Little Listening Post*:

> NICAP members & advisers are being primed to get on the air over local and regional radio/TV, & will keep up a barrage until the full truth re Saucers is made known ... The battle will soon get hot![673]

Taxes continued to be a burden on NICAP; yet again it had been denied tax-exempt status, due in part to the IRS's orally-expressed displeasure that the Committee "spent too much time" criticizing the Air Force. Faced with such bias—the legality of which was surely questionable—and the IRS's additional accusation that NICAP's "broadcasts were mainly self-promotional," Keyhoe appealed the decision but was unsuccessful. He admitted that "until UFOs are more openly recognized, it is doubtful that the ruling could be reversed by the tax courts."[674]

The saucers, however, were unconcerned with taxation. Late April saw the start of the biggest wave of sightings "since November 1957," which "continued steadily [and] included an unprecedented number of landing, near-landing and close-approach cases."[675] Still famous today is the Socorro incident of April 24, 1964, involving patrolman Lonnie Zamora. It received wide press coverage and the *UFO Investigator* of July-August devoted a detailed account to the sighting, even though it involved "little men."

Officer Zamora had abandoned his chase of a speeding car along the highway just outside Socorro, New Mexico, because he was diverted by the sound of an explosion nearby. He hurried to investigate, fearing that a "dynamite shack" that he knew to be in the area had exploded. When he turned off the highway onto a dirt road, he was astonished to see, from about 150 yards away, a white egg-shaped craft on metal legs. Two small figures "about 4 ½ feet tall" in white suits stood next to it and seemed startled by Zamora's arrival. They made a swift departure in their craft, which roared and spewed "flame and smoke from its underside" before it took off.

NICAP's own member, Ray Stanford, had quickly investigated and obtained "metal scrapings" from the site, where scorched ground was also noted and what may have been imprints from the craft's legs were photographed. Hynek also attended and came away mighty puzzled, unable to find any explanation for what had happened.

When analyzed, the "metal scrapings" were found to be silicates, which "under a weathering environment display a submetallic luster." Though the case had characteristics of both a potential alien craft and something of a terrestrial nature (the flames and smoke), it at least served the purpose of reigniting public interest in the saucers.

It therefore happened to be a good time for publication of the long-awaited *The UFO Evidence* and NICAP's summer newsletter headlined that "World-Wide Impact" had resulted from its July 1st submission of the "184-page six-year study of UFOs," which had, at last, been sent to every member of Congress. The editorial described it as "an achievement of gigantic proportions," which was no idle boast. It remains an outstanding piece of work and is a testament to NICAP's knowledge, to its analyses of cases, and to Dick Hall's talent for writing clearly, concisely, and under pressure. During the preparation of this report, Keyhoe had withdrawn from active participation in writing it because his wife had suffered "her first heart attack." This had necessitated a house move in 1964 to Luray, Virginia, where she could avoid climbing stairs and live "in some place with less pressures and tensions."[676] As a consequence, the burden for *The UFO Evidence* had fallen on Dick Hall, who had compiled and written it almost single-handedly. The Abstract read:

> A synthesis is presented of data concerning Unidentified Flying Objects (UFOs) reported during the past 20 years through governmental, press and private channels. The serious evidence is clarified and analyzed. The data are reported by categories of specially trained observers and studied by

patterns of appearance, performance and periodic recurrence.

During the process of selecting the most reliable and significant reports, emphasis was placed on the qualifications of the observer and on cases involving two or more observers. This resulted in 746 reports being selected, after consideration of over 5000 signed reports and many hundreds of reports from newspapers and other publications.

An overall look is taken at the UFO problem: The historical development of the mystery, Congressional attitudes and activity, consideration of the problems and dangers involved, and discussion of what is needed in the way of organized scientific research.

Evidence is presented in support of the hypothesis that UFOs are under intelligent control, making plausible the notion that some of them might be of extraterrestrial origin.

In the Introduction, Hall stated that the fundamental focus of the report was "to remove the fog of mysticism and crackpotism which has helped to obscure the real issues. These issues are (1) the factual evidence for UFOs and its interpretation; (2) official secrecy and its effect on efforts to arrive at [the] truth."

He made two further points that succinctly distilled the entire UFO mystery into a few words:

There are basically two explanations for the consistent, world wide reporting of UFOs every year: (1) widespread and presently unaccountable delusion on a scale so vast that it should be, in itself, a matter of urgent scientific study; (2) people are seeing maneuvering, apparently controlled objects in the atmosphere.

The report garnered positive if cautious responses from many Congressmen, and Keyhoe's optimism was high. He told NICAP members that "the UFO problem has currently reached a new phase in which hearings are a definite possibility if enough people request them."[677]

Clara John praised *The UFO Evidence* in her September-October newsletter:

[C]opies ordered by high Pentagon offices, the Library of

Congress, "Time" magazine, the UN Library, scientists at
NASA, etc. Special radio shows in US discuss it; in Canada,
an afternoon program of the CBC Network carried it coast-
to-coast! Big city newspapers are backing it editorially. One
aviation editor wrote, "NICAP has proved its point. The Air
Force should lift its veil of secrecy, make public its investigations & stop trying to <u>kid</u> the people." In Congress, support
grows for an <u>open hearing on UFOs</u> ... about 50 Congressmen now favor a real probe ... Air Force is worried about
the Report [and said] PUBLICITY ON IT SHOULD BE
STOPPED ... since the public is "getting suspicious of the
Military."[678]

Dynamic language aside, she had the nub: the public were beginning to
question the credibility of official pronouncements, and the press was less
amenable to the usual Air Force explanations. This no doubt encouraged
Keyhoe to publish a six-page piece in *True*'s January 1965 issue, "US Air Force
Censorship of The UFO Sightings," which, as always, delivered a kick in the
pants to the Men In Blue. He detailed numerous cases that the Air Force had
covered up over the years and accused it of now shifting from a strategy of
debunking sightings to one of "total suppression."

Keen as always to make his case on TV, Keyhoe also took the opportunity
to plug NICAP's *The UFO Evidence* with an appearance on ABC's *The Les
Crane Show*. "As far as possible, be on good terms with all persons. Speak your
truth quietly and clearly and listen to others." So said Les Crane in his 1971
prose-poem recording hit, *Desiderata*, but in January 1965 he was far removed
from this philosophy.

Crane had been an early radio "shock jock" and carried his rude and
combative method onto TV. But whatever freshness the show perhaps hoped
to bring to the late-night slot—already enlivened and given a new path by,
in particular, Steve Allen (a NICAP donor) and Johnny Carson—it quickly
became a vehicle for Crane to showcase his meanness and to score points off
his guests.[679]

Keyhoe should have taken warning from the fact that the program—
barely eight weeks since its first broadcast—had been sliding down the ratings.
Scheduling was partly to blame because it aired opposite Carson's show, but
also because Crane's flippant, disrespectful style did not sit well with viewers
who were accustomed to polite and cheerful light-entertainment. Don's doubts

had been dispelled, however, because in prior discussions with the Bad-Boy of the Box, Crane had "agreed to be neutral, asking about important cases in *The UFO Evidence*," so on that basis Keyhoe, accompanied by Colonel Bryan, went ahead. Aired at 11:30 pm, on January 27, 1965, its importance to the cause may be inferred from the fact it was advertised in the press at NICAP's own expense, but it turned out to be a waste of time for all concerned.[680]

From start to finish, Crane unremittingly demonstrated his determination to be childish and demeaning. Keyhoe, fully prepared as always to engage in a serious discussion, supported by documents and his encyclopedic knowledge, was a lamb to the slaughter. The host quickly marked his territory in his opening questions by sneeringly calling NICAP, "Kneecap," which drew a good-natured laugh from the Major, because he naively perceived it to be a genuine mistake; but it was followed by an unceasing barrage of ridicule and puerile interruptions from Crane, turning the opportunity for an informative session into an obvious, cruel joke at Don's expense.

In the next *UFO Investigator*, Keyhoe, with unusual restraint, described it briefly to NICAP members as "The Crane Show Fiasco":

> When he began his ridicule we could have refused to contin-
> ue and walked off the set. But the show was taped; he could
> have deleted our words and substituted some gag as we were
> shown leaving. It seemed wiser to go ahead, try to offset low
> comedy with a few facts, and get it over with ... This farce
> taught me a lesson which I'll pass along. Any of you invited
> to discuss UFOs on the air should get a guarantee ...that it
> will be a fair discussion, without ridicule or personal attacks
> ... I hope you will be fully prepared for any kind of attack—
> which I was not—or turn down the invitation.[681]

The ever-supportive Lee Munsick remarked, "I have spoken to so many people about Crane since and all agreed he was a pricque [*sic*] if you'll pardon my French."[682]

Some NICAP members had written to ABC to protest Crane's behavior, and this no doubt influenced its decision to cancel the already-failing show. On February 23rd Crane was dumped, though he would be nonetheless resurrected by the same network the next month to again host the show, now renamed *Nightlife*, on which he was slightly better behaved. But with less than a million viewers, he was again dropped in April and in the hope of gaining audience numbers, he was replaced by comparative good-boy Dave

Garroway.[683]

Crane continued to be resurrected and dropped until 1968, when he hosted his last television program, *The Les Crane Show*, on WNEW-TV for a few months. On March 22nd that year, he at last made amends for his former insult to Keyhoe, when he interviewed NICAP Board member Dr. Leslie Kaeburn and a subcommittee member, pilot Donald Hazelman. Keyhoe was satisfied to note that Crane "strongly modified his previously negative stand," conducted a serious interview, and now had "praise for NICAP."[684]

Though it would be three years before Crane redeemed himself, ridicule was not among NICAP's biggest problems in 1965. Still running a close second to the Air Force's chicanery and intransigence were the contactees and their supporters. In early April, the *Press and Sun-Bulletin* of Binghamton, New York, published a letter to the editor from Dick Hall, in which he complained about the favorable publicity it recently gave to Adamski, a man who made "wild claims" and had a "dubious background and history," while the paper ignored documented sightings by credible witnesses, but Hall could not know that such endorsement was about to cease.[685]

Twelve days later, George Adamski, beloved of the space brethren, was dead.On April 23rd, he suffered a heart attack at the home of one of his acolytes in Washington, D.C. He was rushed to the Sanitarium but died without regaining consciousness, though his death went unmentioned in the press until early May. He had erroneously been admitted to the facility under the name of "Adams," hence the potential for timely public lamenting and rending of garments by his followers was lost as few newspapers reported his passing.

Perhaps his departure created a sigh of relief within NICAP, or even the desire to throw a few hats in the air, but it wisely marked the death of its most persistent and damaging contactee with only a simple notification in the April-May *UFO Investigator*:

> George Adamski, 74, of Vista, Calif., died April 23, 1965, in the Washington Sanitarium, Takoma Park, Md., of an apparent heart attack.

* * *

By summer, Dick Hall's position at NICAP was clarified for the benefit of members. His former appellation, "Acting Director," had given the impression he was temporary, but he was now rebranded "Assistant Director," befitting his actual status. At the same time, a new appointee had stepped on board: 28-year-old Gordon Lore.

Lore and Hall had happened to meet one evening at the Unicorn Coffee House in Washington, D.C., where Gordon, an editor at "a US News and World subsidary" but "a folksong enthusiast and singer" in his leisure time, was performing. By the end of the evening the two men had become "fast friends," resulting in Lore quitting his day job to become NICAP's Assistant Editor. He had long ago read Keyhoe's saucer books and was excited to join his outfit.[686] Years later, he would remember his work at NICAP as "one of the most rewarding and, at times, most frustrating experiences of my life."[687]

Keyhoe's books by now had become significant to other UFO groups, too. Jacques Vallee, then a 26-year-old scientist, astronomer, and close associate of Hynek, was at this time researching material for his forthcoming book, *Challenge To Science*. Between January and August of 1965, he had issued a questionnaire to the "more than 200" UFO groups in America that had been formed since 1947. In reply to the question "what are the books on UFOs your organization recommends," Keyhoe's came in first, *The UFO Evidence* fourth, while Coral Lorenzen's was fifth. The results, Vallee admitted, represented only "a sampling" of the groups, but he felt they nonetheless showed "a good indication" of how things stood among civilian research organizations.[688] He added: "These answers show that the ideas expressed by Keyhoe still had, in 1965, the strongest influence on the leaders of UFO organizations in the US." It was perhaps this analysis that later led Coral Lorenzen to agree with Gus Rehn's complaint that "Vallee should not get away with his constipated, stilted circumventions" in this book and in his earlier book, *Anatomy of a Phenomenon*.[689]

Keyhoe, meanwhile, via his own questionnaires, was still trying to please all of the NICAP members, all of the time. Yet another poll of their preferences about the content of the *UFO Investigator* suggested that not only the Air Force was tired of NICAP's unrelenting criticism, but also that "a great majority" of members felt the same and had voted for more information on sightings and fewer "censorship stories, unless of unusual importance." Consequently, the summer and autumn issues focused much less on the Air Force, though an exception was made with respect to a newspaper report from July, which was reproduced in full. In a reflection of the changing mood in the press, the *Charleston Evening Post* of July 15th, took a swipe at the Air Force's repeated, complacent denials:

> Confronted by a UFO report, the service immediately begins
> to crank out of the wild blue yonder the same pre-record-
> ed announcement it has been playing for 20 years: "scratch,
> scratch, the Air Force has no evidence, scratch, scratch, the
> Air Force has no evidence ..." It all depends, of course,
> on what is meant by evidence. If our courts shared the Air
> Force's professed suspicion of creditable witnesses our jails
> would be empty.[690]

This was worthy of inclusion in the newsletter, for by now, the saucers
were once more abundant and the Air Force's explanations continued to be
unsatisfactory:

> Although ATIC recorded sighting reports at an average rate
> of 30 to 50 per month for the first six months of 1965, it
> received 135 reports in July and 262 in August. The increase
> in reports prompted widespread press and public criticism of
> the Air Force UFO program and an outpouring of popular
> articles and books on UFOs ...
>
> Because no significant wave of sightings had occurred
> since 1957, newspaper editors thought the UFO fascina-
> tion had ended. But in August 1965, following a series of
> spectacular UFO sightings in Texas, press interest revived.
> The new attitude seemed to be a product of frustration over
> the Air Force's inability to explain UFOs. Since Air Force
> pronouncements had not affected the number of sighting
> reports, more newspaper editors and reporters became suspi-
> cious of the Air Force's role. Some newspapers even seemed
> to agree with NICAP's conspiracy theories ... By the end of
> 1965 ATIC had received 887 reports ...[691]

For Keyhoe, this new "flap" was a welcome downpour after a desperate
drought. Since 1949 he had been banging his faintly-heard, often ignored
drum, complaining about the Air Force's tactic of hapless obfuscation, and
now it seemed, thanks to the glut of saucers, there was growing support for
his claims. To strike while the skies were hot, he and his staff embarked on a
blitzkrieg of public talks, TV interviews, and radio spots. Since the start of his

directorship, Keyhoe and his staff had made some 1,500 such appearances and the latest flap had increased demand.

Judging by the surviving recordings of Keyhoe in action, even from his pre-NICAP years, during these talks he would receive largely the same questions from each audience. Where are they from? Why don't they make contact with us? Are they from Mars? Aren't you biased in favor of your theory? What proof would you accept from the Air Force that they're telling the truth? He had long since become adept at responding patiently and fully to these questions with undimmed enthusiasm, though he did reply with a hint of weariness when asked, yet again, about the physical appearance of the saucer's occupants: "I don't know why it always deteriorates into little green men."[692]

In these arenas the Air Force was taken to task every time by Keyhoe's lengthy, detailed accounts of their denials and contradictions, but often he would lighten the mood with tales of the contactees, recounting with seasoned wit their claims of journeys, lunches, romances, and even marriages with space beings. These always drew laughter, but he emphasized that the point of telling these stories was to "show you that it goes on constantly so that you'll be prepared to differentiate between the kooks and the deluded people and the serious observers."[693]

On September 3, 1965, one of the most high-profile cases of the decade occurred near Exeter, New Hampshire, and it proved to be the first crack in the Air Force's dam. The "Exeter Incident" was witnessed in the early morning hours by 18-year-old college student Norman Muscarello and three local police officers, who saw a red-glowing UFO over the treetops about 100 feet away and at one point had to throw themselves to the ground to avoid it. John Fuller, columnist for the *Saturday Review*, though a skeptic, was sufficiently intrigued by the story to investigate, after which he was far less skeptical. Consequently, on October 2nd, he published a piece about the case in his regular feature, "Trade Winds," highlighting the involvement of NICAP's own investigation.[694] *Look* magazine then published excerpts from it in February 1966, *Reader's Digest* planned to soon give it their own treatment, and publisher G. P. Putnam commissioned Fuller to write a book about the case titled *Incident at Exeter*. Amid all this, he made important TV appearances of his own. The current *UFO Investigator* was upbeat at these developments:

> In the last two months, over 20 million Americans have
> learned of NICAP and its impressive UFO evidence ...
> The tidal wave of UFO publicity was set off by an article in

LOOK magazine on the now famous Exeter, NH., case. [In it] Fuller credited NICAP's massive documented evidence, also citing NICAP on the TODAY show ... On the Carson show Fuller revealed he had seen a UFO during his investigations [and] said the hypothesis that some may be from another planet is the one that has the least holes in it.[695]

Though all this was grist to Keyhoe's mill, there were still the usual nuisances to take the gilt off the gingerbread. Jim Moseley, always inflammatory and antagonistic toward NICAP—despite being a member—had crossed a line and Keyhoe had had enough. Moseley had been making wild accusations, claiming that Keyhoe held a reign of terror over members who were "forbidden" to appear on radio or TV, or even talk on the phone with "unbelievers." He had ranted that NICAP staff were "helping the AF hide UFO facts," that its Director was "overpaid," and that, essentially, the whole outfit was corrupt and inept.

Don responded:

As of this date, your membership is canceled. Your current membership is returned herewith, by registered mail. You cannot legally rejoin under an assumed name, as you have threatened if ejected.[696]

Puerile provocations aside, there was still much to be enthusiastic about. The increase in sightings brought increased interest in NICAP, which was now receiving around a thousand letters a week, swelled by the Rex Heflin case of August 3, 1965, which had erupted in the press in September. Still among the most famous of UFO sightings, Heflin, a highway maintenance engineer in Orange County, California, had taken daylight photographs of a disk maneuvering over the road in Santa Ana. The subsequently much-beleaguered Heflin had been interviewed in depth and somewhat aggressively by Dr. James E. McDonald in January 1966, who then met with Idabel Epperson, vice-chairman of the Los Angeles Subcommittee (LANS). In that capacity she had coordinated NICAP's own thorough investigation. McDonald's eventual conclusion was that the photographs were "among the very few which could be considered 'genuine,'" but they were quickly dismissed by the Air Force as a hoax done with a "small model." NICAP believed that they genuinely showed "significant evidence of a real, structured, craftlike UFO."[697]

During this period, Dick Hall began keeping a log of events, which serves now to indicate NICAP's response to the flap. Beginning on October 26, 1965, and ending on December 8, 1966, he made sparse notes on the blitz of phone calls, meetings, interviews, and other actions involving himself and key personnel during this hectic period. Aside from noting the effects of John Fuller's piece on the Exeter incident, Hall was evidently as keen as the Major to provoke interest among Congressmen with regard to both *The UFO Evidence* and the Heflin case, as extracts from the log attest:

> Oct 29: Prepared press release [and sent] copies w/photos to Calif Congressmen.
> Nov 1: Completed mailing of letters and photos to Congressmen ... Extra copies of press release sent to House space committee.
> Nov 2: 10.45 am. Call from ...Cong. Utt's office requesting more info on Heflin case ...
> Nov 10: Call from secretary at Rep. St. Onge (Conn.) office asking copy of UFO Evidence. Check revealed he received 2 in July '64.
> Dec 8: Jim McDonough of Speaker McCormack's office phoned, requested 2nd copy of UFO Evidence ... need copy for office reference.

The Betty and Barney Hill abduction case had also broken around this time—NICAP's Walter Webb had investigated—and the log notes that Barney had phoned Hall in November, urging NICAP "not to comment on news stories, hinting psych[ologist] may release conclusions next year. Admiral Knowles called, urged same. Confidence should be kept."

Increasingly, Hall, Keyhoe, Lore, and NICAP staff writer Don Berliner were in high demand for interviews, and their efforts had gained the attention of U-Thant, Secretary-General of the UN, who had "been appraised of" *The UFO Evidence*, so a copy was dispatched to him in mid-February. By early March, Hall noted that U-Thant was "considering forming investigating committee. Had *UFO Evidence* on desk."[698]

As 1966 kicked off, Blue Book was of course, still vaunted by the Air Force as the only true authority on UFOs, but thanks to its own man, J. Allen Hynek, a one-day review of its procedures—to which NICAP nor any other civilian body was invited—was held. This had resulted from a letter he had written in early 1965 to General E. B. LeBailly, USAF Director of Information, suggesting "that a scientific panel from outside the Air Force be set up" for that purpose. As a consequence, LeBailly issued a memo on September 28, 1965, to the "Military Director, Scientific Advisory Board," which noted that, though

> ... the Air Force has found no evidence that any of the UFO reports reflect a threat to our national security ... many of the reports that cannot be explained have come from intelligent and technically well qualified individuals whose integrity cannot be doubted. In addition, the reports received officially by the Air Force include only a fraction of the spectacular reports which are publicized by many private UFO organizations.[699]

LeBailly recommended that "a working scientific panel ...be organized to review Project Blue Book ... to advise the Air Force as to any improvements that should be made in the program.

The outcome was the February 3, 1966, "O'Brien Committee," formally known as the Ad Hoc Committee to Review Project Blue Book. Chaired by Dr. Brian O'Brien of the National Academy of Sciences, it comprised five members, of which only one, astronomer Carl Sagan, was not a member of the Air Force's scientific advisory board. It mainly reviewed the 1953 Robertson Panel report and heard from Quintanilla, so from the outset there was no hope of anything other than the Air Force's view up for consideration. It did, however, wittingly or not, come up with a suggestion that helped the Air Force in its desire to rid UFOs from its remit; it suggested that they should be studied under contract by "one university or non-profit organization" working with "AF investigating officers ... to coordinate this research with Project Blue Book." In other words, it would not be scientifically or objectively independent — it would still be informed by the Air Force. The Committee also recommended that the "UFO program should be strengthened" because some reports might "have scientific value," if better data had been available. To that end, it proposed that the AF negotiate contracts "with a few selected universities to provide selected teams to investigate promptly and in depth certain selected sightings of UFOs." Further, it suggested that a single university should be contracted to coordinate these teams to "provide a far better basis than we have today for our decisions on a long-term UFO program."

Even with these proposals, and allowing for the interest raised by NICAP's *The UFO Evidence* along with the handy flap that followed, no further action might have been taken. But soon, thanks to J. Allen Hynek's infamous "Marsh

Gas" pronouncement, the saucers began to slip from the Air Force's buttery fingers when its biggest-ever public relations debacle hit the headlines.

* * *

"In all due respect to Professor Hynek, he's all wet," commented Sheriff Douglas Harvey of Ann Arbor, Michigan, who, along with many officers and residents, had reported seeing strange glowing objects maneuvering at speed around the skies of the city in the early hours of March 20, 1966.

In response to the excitement caused by this latest flap, Hynek—suffering at the time from a broken jaw, which had been wired—was dispatched to interview witnesses. He also checked with "specialists" who told him that such phenomena were caused by rotting vegetation in marshy areas, i.e., marsh gas. Consequently, when interviewed by the press, Hynek suggested—not concluded—that "marsh gas" might be an explanation in those instances where lights had been seen in the area's marshy terrain. "Only two [witnesses] reported any object connected with it," he emphasized, defensively, when cornered by reporters. "All the others when I questioned them closely confined themselves to lights and particularly a glow of light, red, yellow and green lights."

Though Hynek was still the Air Force's instrument and had played their tune for years, his analysis of the Michigan sightings turned out to be a bum note. Hurried, harried, and without having spoken to *every* witness at the scene, he was, according to Sheriff Harvey, under pressure to come up with a quick answer:

> Last night he was in my office ... and at 11:00 he had no statement whatsoever to make, he told me he had no idea what it was but he said the Pentagon said he had to make a statement tomorrow. He said I don't know what I'm gonna say. So overnight he comes up with this theory.[700]

Hynek firmly denied this, insisting that Harvey had misunderstood him and that the Pentagon told him he could "say whatever he wanted," but as other witnesses continued to give compelling accounts that in no way matched a "marsh gas" explanation, the theory rapidly fell into ridicule, dragging him with it. Gerald Ford, then the House Minority Leader from Michigan and already interested in the UFO problem, issued a press statement calling Hynek's interpretation "flippant." He then wrote to the "chairmen and the ranking Republican members of the House Committee on Armed Services and Science and Astronautics," delivering another slap to Hynek:

> [H]e dismissed all of them [the reports] as the product of college student pranks or swamp gas or an impression created by the rising crescent moon and the planet Venus. I do not agree that all of these reports can be or should be so easily explained away.[701]

Ford, according to Hynek, "resented the ridicule the State of Michigan was getting, being called the 'Swamp Gas State.' The cartoons, the editorials ... I was lampooned ..."[702]

The public and the press were now even less impressed with the Air Force's facile explanations, and Hynek, as its spokesman, seemed to fully represent its determination to either ignore or conceal what was really going on. It was at this point he threw in the debunking towel: "I've had it! This is the last time I'm going to try to pull a chestnut out of the fire for the Air Force."[703]

Consequently, what had been an excruciating embarrassment for Hynek, became a watershed in his own approach to the problem and in the public perception of official pronouncements about the saucers. The events that resulted from his blunder both opened, and later slammed shut, the door on full-scale congressional hearings, but in between those two actions, there was much excitement at the prospect of a true, unbiased, and meaningful examination of the UFO subject.

Gerald Ford issued a two-page press release on April 21st:

> The Air Force has informed me it is arranging for a study by high-caliber scientists of some of the UFO sightings which have never been explained. This study will be placed under contract soon after July 1, start of the new fiscal year. It will be carried out by a university which has no close ties with the Air Force so that the findings will be completely objective, Air Force officials tell me ... It was as a result of my call for a congressional investigation that the Air Force now is arranging for a study of UFO's by topflight scientists not connected in any way with the Air Force.[704]

This announcement seemed to promise that, at last, Keyhoe's almost decade-long push for a serious, open-minded investigation of the saucers would be realized.

Soon, NICAP would be hungrily following a carrot, which unfortunately turned out to be a stick, called Dr. Edward Uhler Condon.

Chapter 35:
Keel and Jacks

The Air Force was slow to act on the O'Brien Committee recommendations, but the Swamp Gas brouhaha brought urgency to the situation, and it was now quietly, but unsuccessfully, casting about to find universities that would agree to take part in the UFO study.

During this hiatus, on April 11, 1966, Keyhoe was banging NICAP's drum on a popular TV panel-game show, *To Tell the Truth*, where three contestants each claimed to be a person of some unusual occupation or activity, and the panel of four celebrities tried to work out who was telling the truth. The panelists in this case were quick to pick out "the real Donald Keyhoe," but the few minutes allotted to him didn't provide a suitable platform for attacking the Air Force. It did, however, help to keep him and NICAP in the public eye.

A few days later he received yet more confirmation of the Air Force's hapless approach to UFOs, thanks to journalist John Alva Keel, a man of many parts, some of which were leaning heavily toward an interest in the saucers. He was compiling a lengthy article on the subject for *Playboy* (potentially 30,000 words), but between receiving the assignment and meeting with Keyhoe, the Swamp Gas fiasco had erupted, lending impetus to his investigations for the piece.

On April 18th, Keel visited NICAP and met Keyhoe for the first time. The organization was "in the process of expanding their offices and [it had] taken over the whole third floor." The two men sat facing each other in a freshly painted room, empty apart from their chairs. After Keyhoe's initial doubts about whether or not he intended to write a serious article, they talked for two hours and Keel came away impressed. NICAP, he felt, was indispensable "to any writer or newsman engaged in an investigation of UFO's," and with only six staff, was doing "a remarkable job." He intended to give NICAP "a generous plug" in his article.[705]

Keel's research had by now revealed how the Air Force dealt with—or rather, failed to deal with—UFO reports, and he had already been in touch with 50-year-old USAF Lt. Col. Maston Mayfield Jacks, Chief of Operations, Public Information Division in Washington, D.C., about paying a visit to

Blue Book for research material. Jacks had sent a cheerful reply, confirming that interviews with relevant officers would be arranged. In a P.S. he punned, "If there are any little green girls in those saucers, PLAYBOY will probably have to elbow aside little green men."[706]

Jacks' sense of humor, however, was entirely absent when on April 19th Keel arrived unannounced at Blue Book's office in room 4C922 at the Pentagon. It was immediately apparent to him that Jacks, "a harassed man with graying hair," expected to be rid of his visitor within a couple of minutes, but their tense, sometimes heated, though ultimately pointless meeting, lasted for two hours.

Keel made it very clear he didn't buy the Air Force party line and berated Jacks not only for his evident lack of knowledge about the history UFOs (aside from those mentioned in the Bible), but also for his steadfast position that "after twenty years of investigations the Air Force did not have any files" containing photographs and films of these objects, despite hundreds of complaints in Keel's possession that images submitted had never been returned.

Jacks seemed worried about who else would be interviewed for the *Playboy* article and offered to arrange a meeting with Hynek, to which the response was a verbal boot in the rear:

> I told him bluntly that Dr. Hynek made a public fool of himself in Michigan and that the general public would no longer accept him as an "expert". Disturbed, he told me that Hynek was not a skeptic. I agreed but repeated that he no longer [was] publicly acceptable.[707]

Keel was then offered a meeting with Major Quintanilla at Wright-Patterson, to which he responded:

> I told him I was not interested in traveling that distance to listen to another man parrot the Air Force line [and] I again expressed my incredulity that after twenty years of investigations the Air Force had no files or other material on the UFO subject ... I went on to say that it seemed to me as if the Air Force were not interested in investigating the UFO's, but only in debunking them. I again asked to see some kind of tangible proof that the Air Force had investigated <u>anything</u>. Again he told me there were no files.[708]

Jacks made the mistake of bragging that the Air Force received "about 4000 letters a year"—mostly from children—asking for UFO information, to which Keel "added the crowning insult by telling him that NICAP is currently receiving 4,000 to 8,000 letters a *week*," then delivered another kick to Jacks by telling him that "NICAP was the accepted authority in UFO matters."[709] These were not idle boasts or guesstimates. Membership was "surging close to 7500," and in the first week of March alone 925 letters were received, though Keel didn't mention to Jacks, or probably didn't know, that the increase in members exacerbated NICAP's ongoing bare-bones situation. It was now faced with an even larger backlog in correspondence and was "flooded with demands for speakers, assistance with articles and programs, etc." for which it lacked "a large enough staff to cope with this situation."[710]

Keel added that Air Force ridicule had driven "every reporter and every UFO investigator into the arms of NICAP." Jacks, he proposed, was either hiding something, or Blue Book "was really as incompetent and as disinterested as it seemed."

As their meeting, which had been punctuated by heated exchanges, drew to an unsatisfactory close, Jacks—evidently a man without a sense of irony—suggested Keel obtain a copy of *The UFO Evidence*. (In 1964 the Lt. Col. had acknowledged receipt of one from NICAP and "indicated he would read it carefully.") Then, "something very curious happened." While Keel waited for a photocopy to be made of his *Playboy* letter for Blue Book's supposedly non-existent files, he tried "one last gambit" to get a response from Jacks. He told the officer that he didn't believe the UFOs were extraterrestrial, to which he "reacted as if I had kicked him in the groin."

A few days after the meeting, Keel submitted his report on it in confidence to NICAP, APRO, Ivan Sanderson (with whom he was intending to write a book, later abandoned) and to *Playboy*. He concluded that the Air Force didn't want to be bothered with the "sticky problem" of the saucers, that few citizens reported their sightings to it nowadays, and that newsmen were wasting their time in approaching Blue Book. He felt, however, that

> There is, without a doubt, another project being conducted
> in secrecy to examine photos and other evidence ... Proj-
> ect Bluebook is just a shabby cover up effort and it has now
> reached the end of its effectiveness.[711]

Ten days after Keel's report, the still-desperate Air Force went public about its search for universities to become involved in the study, but "the prospects looked dim."[712]

Things also looked dim for Keel's UFO investigation. The *Playboy* article was not published; by August, he admitted he'd "been battling with them for weeks about length," and it was dropped, but he had managed to make several pungent points to the Air Force's latest PIO. He made it clear that NICAP was doing a better job and had more credibility across the board, while the Air Force had lost what remained of its own, due to the Swamp Gas fiasco. These blows can only have strengthened and added exigency to the Air Force's need to restore its reputation, to wash the saucers right out of its hair and to negate NICAP.

Soon after Keel had visited Jacks, Quintanilla was visited by Dr. James E. McDonald, who was conducting his own UFO research, and from June 6th-8th was permitted access to Blue Book's files (even though Keel had been told they didn't exist). He also came away unimpressed with the set-up, leading him to conclude that the extraterrestrial hypothesis was "the least unsatisfactory" and further concluded that the CIA had ordered the Air Force to debunk the saucers. This view was based on an extraordinary blunder by Quintanilla—he had shown McDonald an uncensored copy of the secret 1953 Robertson Panel report convened by the CIA in January 1953. Thirteen years earlier, Keyhoe had been tipped off to this document, of which only a summary was eventually released. A few days later, McDonald wrote to Paul Cerny, chairman of the Bay Area NICAP subcommittee:

> All evidence suggests foulup, not coverup. Quintanilla much worse than I had suspected ... Decided I'd better get out and see our hometown UFO group, so spent an interesting evening at the Lorenzen's [*sic*]. They are not as extreme as I feared.[713]

In September, Keyhoe delivered his own kick to the Air Force's groin in an article for *Saga: The Magazine for Men* titled "The Air Force Is *Lying* About UFOs!"[714] The content lived up to his blunt accusation; it was a nose-to-tail recital of the Air Force's duplicity and stupidity in its handling of UFO reports and mistreatment of witnesses. When asked about the recently-announced (May 9th) forthcoming investigation by a panel of "independent scientists," Keyhoe was not hopeful: "If the Air Force is controlling the evidence ... I'm afraid this is just more window dressing."

It was soon after heralded that the University of Colorado had been chosen to undertake the study, and despite Keyhoe's misgivings expressed to *Saga*, by

October he was cautiously hopeful that, after so many years of ridicule and obfuscation of the subject, this announcement would represent "far and away the most significant development in the history of UFO investigation."

He would be proven right, but for all the wrong reasons.

Chapter 36:
Condon's Low Trick

"For over a year, as NICAP director, I saw the inside workings of the Colorado Project. [It] was a strange and sometimes shocking operation."[715] This was Keyhoe's recollection in 1973, when he looked back on the calamity of the *Scientific Study of Unidentified Flying Objects*, a.k.a., the Condon Report.

In 1966, Edward U. Condon, PhD, was a 64-year-old physicist at the University of Colorado, Boulder, with a long and somewhat colorful career behind him. Noted in particular for his brief tenure on the Manhattan Project, his work on quantum mechanics, his tussles with Richard Nixon and the House Committee on Un-American Activities (which accused him of being a Commie), and for his sense of humor, it was perhaps the latter attribute that led him to treat the saucers as a joke.

The Air Force had tried to implement the recommendations of the O'Brien Committee, but as the subject of UFOs was already tainted by crackpotism and was admitted to be "99%" a public relations problem, it was a poisoned chalice and no-one would touch it. Ultimately, the plan that teams from different universities would be coordinated by another was abandoned, and the decision was made to offer the entire project to only one. Still there was no interest, until Dr. J. Thomas Ratchford of the Office of Scientific Intelligence (which wanted a psychological input to the study) buttered up the psychology department at the University of Colorado with the fiction that it had been the Air Force's first choice. This was also swallowed by Walter Orr Roberts, head of the National Center for Atmospheric Research (NCAR), an Air Force contractor and sister institution of the University of Colorado. He was certain that "others have not been approached and turned it down."[716] Moreover, his view was that if the project were done "objectively and critically ... having the project here [at University of Colorado] would not put us in the category of scientific kooks."[717]

However, thanks to Ratchford, the project was already worthless. Besides lying to the University, he had already made up his mind about UFOs and the people who were interested in them. In July 1966, he told Dr. James E. McDonald that only "kooks and cultists ... who'd never shut up" criticized the Air Force's handling of the UFO subject.[718] Moreover, it must be implied that he was under the misapprehension that Keyhoe was himself a cultist. In 1968 Ratchford had visited Lynn Catoe, archivist at the Library of Congress, with "someone from SAFOI," unnamed, who said that "eight to ten years ago, Keyhoe told him he was in daily and constant contact with the 'brothers' who were dictating his activities."[719] This, of course, cannot have been the case. Either it was a blatant untruth, or it opens up the faint possibility of memory conflation: Townsend Brown—who was NICAP's head ten years earlier— might have made such a risky admission to this "someone" who later told Lynn Catoe.

Ratchford's fib to the University of Colorado was bolstered with cash, initially in the form of a $300,000 federal grant, which was then turned into a contract, adding another $13,000 to further sweeten the pot, but the project needed to be led by "a prestigious scientist and to have the proper political outlook. [Dr.] Condon fit the job description in every way."[720]

Assisted by Dr. William T. Price, Air Force Office of Scientific Research, Ratchford sprinkled sugar on the illustrious Condon to persuade him to take on the job of project director. He initially wasn't interested, until

> Ratchford told him that the job was "a dirty chore" but somebody had to do it. If Condon did, people would believe him more than "just some ordinary guy." Condon later said: "I fell for this. Flattery got him somewhere."[721]

Hence, the "dirty chore"—the scientific study of UFOs—and a pile of cash had been placed in his lap on October 7, 1966, and from that moment the project and the future of serious UFO research were doomed. Then unknown outside of a few within the University of Colorado team, the ship had been launched with the seacocks open.

Robert Low, Assistant Dean of the University's graduate school, was on board with the Project by August 1st. He had already "become friends" with Condon, "even to the point of considering writing a biography of him," and his mission now was to sell the project to the University of Colorado and assuage its fears that taking it on would lead to ridicule.[722] In his soon-to-be infamous "Trick" memo of August 9, 1966, Low revealed the worries about credibility that had been expressed to him at the time. Lewis McAdory Branscomb, then a research physicist at the National Bureau of Standards (to which he had been appointed by Condon in 1951) said:

> ... one would have to go so far as to consider the possibility that saucers, if some of the observations are verified, behave according to a set of physical laws unknown to us. The simple act of admitting these possibilities just as possibilities puts us beyond the pale, and we would lose more prestige in the scientific community than we could possibly gain by undertaking the investigation. [He compared] it to Rhine and the [discredited] ESP study at Duke.[723]

In a response that would live in infamy, Low made his pitch to allay these concerns:

> Our study would be conducted almost exclusively by nonbelievers who, although they couldn't possibly *prove* a negative result, could and probably would add an impressive body of evidence that there is no reality to the observations. The trick would be, I think, to describe the project so that, to the public, it would appear a totally objective study but, to the scientific community, would present the image of a group of nonbelievers trying their best to be objective but having an almost zero expectation of finding a saucer. One way to do this would be to stress investigation, not of the physical phenomena, but rather of the people who do the observing—the psychology and sociology of persons and groups who report seeing UFOs. If the emphasis were put here, rather than on examination of the old question of the physical reality of the saucer, I think the scientific community would quickly get the message ... I can't imagine a paper coming out of the study that would be publishable in a prestigious physical science journal. I can quite easily imagine, however, that psychologists, sociologists, and psychiatrists might well generate scholarly publications as a result of their investigation of the saucer observers ... if we set up the thing right and take pains to get the proper people involved and have success in presenting the image we want to present to the scientific community, we could carry the job off to our benefit.[724]

Whether or not this was merely salesmanship on Low's part (for a detailed defense of his motivation and purpose for writing the memo, see Chapter 14 of *UFOs and Government*) is outside the scope of this work, but the effect it had on Keyhoe and NICAP, after it was revealed in early 1968, was devastating.

Condon, however, being "draped with dignity," had a reputation that stood him in good stead as an objective investigator, and this in effect gave legitimacy and credibility to the project.[725] His battle against accusations of communism, from which he had been fully exonerated, had, in the minds of many, established him as "a fighter against the establishment." But it would soon be apparent that as far as UFOs were concerned, he was not interested in setting foot in the ring.

NICAP and APRO, as the foremost civilian UFO research organizations, had already been approached for their input, and Keyhoe was monitoring the project's development closely and cautiously. He noted that the University of Colorado's contract with the Air Force stipulated that "The work will be conducted under conditions of the strictest objectivity by investigators ... who have no predilections or preconceived positions on the UFO question."[726] On October 8th, only twenty-four hours after the contract was announced, Condon tossed that idea into the gutter:

> It is highly improbable they exist. The view that UFOs are hallucinatory will be a subject of our investigation, to discover what it is that makes people imagine they see things.[727]

The following day, Low, now designated "UFO Project Coordinator," backed up his boss:

> The project came close to being unacceptable [but] you don't say no to the Air Force. [The project] will probably yield more information about witnesses who report UFOs than physical information.[728]

Don was disturbed at these comments from the project's two key men, but when he phoned them and said it appeared they had already drawn their conclusions, both insisted they had been "badly misquoted" by the press ("three days in a row," Keyhoe noted, dryly). Low added that they didn't want to "risk alienating NICAP," on which they were relying to "urgently" train their own investigators, and were "counting heavily on its assistance. Frankly," he admitted, "we don't know how to start."[729]

Condon's choice of other senior staff—all PhDs—were Stuart W. Cook, a psychologist and chairman of the psychology department at the University of Colorado; Franklin Roach, astrophysicist, a "specialist in astronomical spectroscopy and upper atmospheric physics"; and William A. Scott and David R. Saunders, both professors of psychology at the University of Colorado. (Saunders joined NICAP when the contract was awarded to Colorado, in order to "keep up with current sightings.")[730]

This selection, with its majority of psychologists and minority of other relevant disciplines, confirmed what Condon and Low had effectively said— that mental interpretations rather than quantifiable data were considered more important. It was seeking to reinforce the view that UFOs were all in the mind, and its supposed objectiveness would prove to be, as Keyhoe had feared, merely window-dressing. In response to the selection of staff, "there was an uproar regarding the preponderance of psychologists; people suspected that a study of 'abnormal persons' rather than abnormal aerial phenomena was about to take place."[731] Perhaps to try and allay accusations of bias, Cook and Scott stayed only briefly and were replaced by Dr. Norman Levine, an electrical engineer at the University of Arizona, and Dr. Roy Craig, a physical chemist.

It was soon evident, though, that another problem had arisen that would further help to fatally undermine the project. As described later by Hynek:

> Almost from the start, the Condon Committee ran into troubles. The foremost of these stemmed from the personalities of the director, Dr. Condon, and his chief administrator, the late Robert Low ... The committee never worked as a coherent body and was torn by much internal strife.[732]

This was not apparent to Keyhoe at the project's launch, and he was therefore prepared to be cautiously encouraged:

> If this project is carried out as an independent probe, as the AF has stated it will be, this could emerge as the most important development since the first official UFO reports in World War II.
>
> According to the official agreement with the University of Colorado, Dr. Condon will be free to make the project's findings public—even if they conclude that the UFOs are real, contrary to AF views.[733]

Keyhoe noted Condon's earlier negative remark but added that he had "qualified" it by admitting he'd not seen sufficient evidence to form an opinion, and that NICAP was unconcerned about the abundance of psychologists. He said that the University of Colorado project was "in general approaching the unique problem of UFOs with admirable objectivity and thoroughness" and there was "no reason to go along with the skeptics who interpret the project merely as the latest gambit in an Air Force propaganda campaign."

Two days before the project was announced, Dr. James E. McDonald had given a speech at the American Meteorological Society in D.C. and spoke of his own "intensive study" of the UFO subject. Not a man to mince words, ("intense and bluntly articulate") he told the audience that Blue Book's published figures on UFO sightings were "completely worthless," that its explanations were often "absurdly erroneous," and that its investigations had been performed using "a very low level of scientific competence."[734] NICAP's work, he said, was "much more thorough and open-minded" and should form part of any future study of the phenomenon.

The report in the *UFO Investigator* on this speech appears to have drawn APRO's ire and reveals that the contempt in which the Lorenzens held Keyhoe paled against that which they felt toward McDonald. Without naming him, the September-October *APRO Bulletin*, in a piece which extolled Hynek's approach to the UFOs, ranted that

> We have heard of one scientist who decries this "scientific scandal" (the lack of scientific scrutiny of the UFO problem) while all the time admitting his own interest for several years. DURING WHICH TIME HE HAD NOT THE FORTI-TUDE TO SPEAK UP. He, like others, waited until the sub-ject was SOCIALLY ACCEPTABLE.[735]

* * *

The launch of the University of Colorado project ought to have brought together the nation's two foremost civilian research groups in their common cause. Both had agreed to be involved in the "study," but it served only to increase the animosity between NICAP and APRO, and each continued to take sharp pokes at the other in their newsletters.

Perhaps in retaliation for the snippy criticisms of NICAP and the veiled attack on McDonald, the January 1967 *UFO Investigator* delivered its first kick to APRO's rear when it reviewed Coral Lorenzen's recent book, *Flying Saucers: The Startling Evidence of the Invasion From Outer Space*, to which it gave the thumbs down. It was judged to include "a heavy dose of sensationalism," while presenting "extravagant" and "outlandish" stories that were "not substantiated by convincing evidence." In addition, the book was accused of giving "exaggerated emphasis" to the "alleged threat to human society from UFOs, a claim for which NICAP has found no convincing evidence in 10 years of investigation." This, of course, was somewhat counter to the strange content of the 1958 letters between Keyhoe and Coral Lorenzen in which they had confessed to each other some knowledge of impending "peril" and "horror" for humankind, too terrible to put in writing. Nonetheless, the review dismissed the book as "below par."[736]

While the relationship between NICAP and APRO continued to fester, the University of Colorado project was already floundering, and Low and Condon admitted publicly that they were somewhat at a loss. Only "2½ months" in, Condon said:

> The total situation's much more complicated than we appreciated at first so that while we have some notions of what we're going to do I don't have any feeling at all of a very orderly or well organized thing at this stage.

Low confessed:

> It's hard to know how to go about studying this thing. How would you do it if somebody suddenly handed you the job— you investigate unidentified flying objects—how d'you go about doing that? That's the problem that we've had, we've been wrestling with it.[737]

From behind the scenes, one of the project support staff, James Wadsworth, described how things functioned from the start:

> It's as though the first concern of the group is to protect themselves from getting tainted by the quasi-scientific animal known as a UFO. [Consequently] their value as open-minded scientists has suffered greatly. They are too busy maintaining a role to let loose what little creativity they have.[738]

As Keyhoe and others would learn over the next two years, there never would be an "orderly or well organized" set-up. Condon's ignorance of, and indifference to, the subject—funded by the taxpayer ultimately to the tune of $530,000—was so profound that he didn't even know how to pronounce the acronym of the objects under study: he called them, "OOfo" (specified as the proper pronunciation in the eventual report).

Condon himself was disparaging the project in public. On January 25, 1967, he infamously told an audience from the "research fraternity" of Sigma Xi at a New York high school, that there was nothing to the saucers, and added with a smile, "but I'm not supposed to reach a conclusion for another year."

Keyhoe admitted to project member David Saunders, who felt that the saucers deserved a proper, scientific examination, that he was "shocked" by Condon's remarks but publicly said only that he "retained some reservations" about the effect of such comments. He said he still felt there was "no reason to go along with the skeptics who interpret the project merely as the latest gambit in an Air Force propaganda campaign."[739] He acknowledged, however, that the recent "outpouring of UFO literature, good and bad" had increased membership to "over 12,000."

With this in mind, it was surely not a good time to air his real concerns, so despite the backroom posturing and the negative noises emanating from Colorado, the spring issue of the *UFO Investigator* remained optimistic and complimentary about the Colorado Project, saying it had shown "remarkable objectivity ... flexibility and open-mindedness." As to what the outcome would be, it was admitted that insufficient funding and time would likely mean that no "final answers" would result, but "as a pilot study, the program is invaluable." Even so, a warning shot was fired across Condon's bows:

> The only event which might force NICAP to withdraw its support would be evidence that outside pressures were causing the project to retreat from objective, scientific investigation.[740]

APRO's response to the project's supposed intent was, like NICAP's, both optimistic and cautious. Coral Lorenzen considered Condon to be "open-minded" and "more than amply qualified on the subject of UFOs," but noted that the stated aims of the project—to find a scientific explanation for, and to allay public fear about, UFOs—"sounds strangely like the directive [in the]

Robertson report."[741]

* * *

In the May 1967 issue of the *APRO Bulletin*, perhaps in retaliation for NICAP's negative review of her book, Coral Lorenzen fired her own salvo, quoting her husband from a speech he gave at a recent "conclave" on UFOs in Tucson, Arizona, at which McDonald had also spoken. The *Bulletin*'s report showed evident contempt toward McDonald and NICAP. It complained that "the negative contributions of the C.I.A., Dr. Donald Menzel, and the Bluebook-NICAP controversy are only now being overcome." As to McDonald, he was referred to as merely "James MacDonald," or just "MacDonald," omitting his status as a PhD and incorrectly spelling his name, while huffing that his "Keyhoe-NICAP" focus on Blue Book meant that "his whole approach smacked of over-simplification." He was accused of questioning "APRO's objectivity (largely because of our heavy reliance on foreign representatives such as Fontes)," and the report snarked that his "personal study of UFOs is only about a year old."[742] In this, the Lorenzens were entirely erroneous.

McDonald's own curiosity about UFOs went back to at least 1954, when he and three other scientists sighted an aluminum-looking object hovering in the skies over Tucson.[743] These men could scarcely have been more ideal to investigate and understand what was in the atmosphere at the time, but they had found no explanation. McDonald sent to the Air Force a detailed account of the sighting, for which he received thanks, but no follow-up.

By 1958 McDonald's interest became more active, and he had begun correspondence and phone calls with Dick Hall and Keyhoe. He held both men in high regard and thought NICAP a "thoroughly trustworthy and effective research organization." When he then began re-investigating some of its recorded sightings and interviewing witnesses, he realized that "all suspicion of 'hallucination' as a causal factor" could be discounted.[744] Following his examination of the uncensored Robertson Panel report during his June 1966 visit to Blue Book, he now confidently "placed the blame for the Air Force's secrecy policies on the CIA" and had embarked on making his views public. He was, therefore, in no respect a newcomer to the field of UFO research.

As 1967 progressed, Coral Lorenzen's feelings about McDonald were bundled together with her over-arching paranoia. Her letters to Gus Rehn are, once again, revealing. In September, she wrote:

> Concerning McDonald—we have found out that he is a se-
> cret member of NICAP. For months he ran around making a
> lot of noise and constantly claimed that he was not affiliated
> with any group. He seldom mentions APRO, and when he
> does, it is not very complimentary; but he is constantly push-
> ing NICAP. I am still convinced that NICAP is a government
> sponsored organization, whether they know it or not.[745]

A month later, she continued her criticism:

> McDonald is a headline hunter and if something which will
> get him more attention comes along I imagine he'll dump
> the saucer subject like a hot potato.[746]

As to his "secret" association with NICAP, McDonald had requested
confidentiality, which Keyhoe, like Coral in many of her own dealings, was
honor-bound to keep. Indeed, according to her, APRO had secretly "been
working with Hynek since 1964, and [we] have known that he stayed with the
Air Force and kept his mouth shut about his own ideas in order to have access
to the files." She also later boasted that Hynek

> … has quite a set of files of his own that he copied from Air
> Force files. From now on, when he gets tips about reports
> he will turn them over to us for investigation … Dr. Hynek
> contributed $100 to APRO to help out; we were very sur-
> prised that he wanted to participate to that extent, but he
> sure saved the day.[747]

It would appear that she was prepared to keep quiet about APRO's work
with, and support from, a leading scientist but found it unacceptable that
NICAP should do the same. What had McDonald done to so inflame Coral?

The origin of her loathing for him, which increased over the period of
the University of Colorado Project, was perhaps rooted in a remark he made
to Hynek prior to his June 1966 visit to the Lorenzens and is reminiscent of
the Jung episode, which brought about Coral's dislike of Keyhoe. According
to Ann Druffel:

> He [Hynek] asked McDonald if he knew Coral and Jim Lo-

renzen [whom he] felt "were the most scientific of any 'club members' he'd ever met." McDonald also had met with the Lorenzens and was impressed by certain aspects of their research. He told Hynek that he felt NICAP's overall approach was better than APRO's.[748]

Hynek's opinion of Keyhoe and NICAP at this time was, of course, based on his entrenched belief that they were a bunch of crackpot swindlers unworthy of his attention, and the Lorenzens were unlikely to give him any encouragement to change his view. If his closet alliance with APRO was factual and not an exaggeration by Coral, he would certainly have informed the Lorenzens of McDonald's comment, and there was, in any case, already discord between the two scientists. Early on, Hynek had been severely taken to task by McDonald (who had "pounded" on his desk) for his persistent debunking of the saucers and for shirking his scientific duty to properly investigate them— accusations which, only a few years later, Hynek would accept.[749] Moreover, the positive effect now enjoyed by NICAP, as a direct result of McDonald's preferred association with it, can only have aggravated Coral yet further. Dick Hall later recalled that, due to McDonald's involvement,

> At a certain phase in NICAP, during the years the Condon Committee was active, we had so many requests for information from scientists, even clinicians—people who were household words—showing an intense interest.[750]

In March 1967, the *APRO Bulletin* reported that the Lorenzens had been visited earlier that month by Robert "Lowe," which resulted in the couple's agreement to "help the project in any way possible." Members were now urged to "redouble efforts" to provide the University of Colorado project with photos and negatives. However, Coral's letter to Rehn (whose most recent letter to her disclosed that he was "still full of indecent dreams" of meeting her in person) told a different story. She complained that Colorado was approaching individual APRO representatives in order to by-pass her outfit because "Jim doesn't have a degree (Hall and Keyhoe do) and they don't want to moneky [*sic*] around with 'uneducated' slobs like us." Alternatively, she speculated it was part of a plot to "render ineffectual all American groups. They already have NICAP effectively cancelled ... Do you now understand our hesitancy in going overboard with the U. of C. as NICAP has done? We frankly prefer to stand on our own feet."[751]

Meanwhile, matters at Colorado were deteriorating and internal doubts and disagreements were already tearing it apart. Condon and Low increasingly disturbed project staff with their blatant indifference, poor methodology, and bizarre non-scientific focus. Among other egregious actions, in June 1967 Condon (whom Dr. James McDonald later described as having an "over-interest in the nuts") attended a contactee event in New York at which he stood and took a bow.[752] Two months later, Low went on a junket to Europe where he declined meetings with "leading UFO researchers" in favor of a trip to Loch Ness. He said that "neither UFOs nor the monster existed, [but] it was important to compare the two phenomena."[753] Keyhoe meanwhile, at least in public, was still keeping faith with the project and defended Condon's attendance at the contactee-fest because it was essential he should do so to achieve a "comprehensive view" and observe these people "at first hand."[754]

As to his desire for NICAP's assistance, Condon's true interest in its documentation is perhaps indicated in a CIA memo, detailing a "UFO Briefing for Dr. Edward Condon." It was attended by photoanalysts from the CIA's National Photographic Interpretation Center—NPIC—which was playing an "unofficial role" in developing photogrammetric techniques to analyze UFO photos. On May 5, 1967, Condon and Low, along with Ratchford and some other project staff, discussed photo analysis techniques for UFO photographs used by the NPIC, with respect to a 1952 picture taken in Zanesville, Ohio. Condon was "most enthusiastic," stating that "he had for the first time a scientific analysis of a UFO that would stand up to investigation."

It was then decided that

> ... contractual arrangements could be made to carry on anal-
> ysis by [redacted] but under financing from US Air Force/
> University of Colorado ... . This would transfer most of the
> future analysis to the University of Colorado control, but Dr.
> Condon indicated he wished to keep a channel open into our
> organization.

Toward the end of the meeting

> ... it was suggested that it might be advisable to review all
> the photography NICAP holds, and conduct photogram-
> metric analyses on any that have the appropriate and neces-
> sary information available. This would put Dr. Condon in

a position to say that he had reviewed and analyzed all the photography in NICAP files.[755]

There should, of course, have been no "might" about the need to review NICAP's photo evidence; the project had specifically requested its input and was anxious to keep it on board. The inference in the memo is, as Keyhoe suspected, that the whole affair was merely "window dressing," a suspicion that would later be confirmed to him by Low.

From the start of NICAP's involvement with the project, some members had been pressuring Keyhoe to disassociate from it, though his unfortunate inclination to maintain faith in anything that might further the committee's (therefore, his) aims, kept him on board. He never suffered fools gladly, being reluctant to throw out any babies with their bathwater, or risk accusations of bias. As a consequence, he tolerated far more than he should have in his dealings with contactees, officialdom, and others who drained his money and energy. And the Colorado project was, after all, the only time such a (supposedly) independent, high-profile academic focus had been publicly bestowed on UFOs. In reality, he had little choice but to stick it out as long as possible, not least because he had been "privately informed by friends on Capitol Hill" that no Congressional hearings would be held until after Condon's report had been published. This meant that NICAP could either take part and hope its evidence for the ETH would convince Condon, or do nothing and hope for the best.

By June however, Keyhoe felt he had to act before things deteriorated further. He and broadcaster Frank Edwards decided to expose Condon's laxity on air, fueled to an extent by the recent announcement that the University of Colorado had asked for more money—$210,000 "partly so they can examine more of NICAP's information." Even so, Keyhoe displayed either duplicity or extreme politeness when he praised this development in the *UFO Investigator* that month, quoting columnist Roscoe Drummond, who had written, "I am convinced that the Condon team is going to do a thorough and scientific job."[756]

According to Keyhoe's own account in 1973, Edwards was now fired up at the "gall" displayed by the University of Colorado project and intended to approach McCormack and Goldwater for interviews on his program.[757] It would, he felt sure, be "a blockbuster," but once again fate intervened. On June 23, 1967, Frank Edwards died suddenly from a heart attack, and another NICAP ally was gone at a crucial moment. Keyhoe's reaction, aside from an obit for Edwards, was to do nothing. In what had become a too-frequent response over the years, he simply withdrew from following-up on the momentum of recent developments. His excuse was that only Edwards had sufficient clout to expose the University of Colorado story and despite all the evidence prepared for the exposé, he simply dropped the idea.

APRO, though frequently griping about NICAP and its involvement with the Colorado project, continued making its own (mostly South American based) contributions to it, but privately was still convinced of CIA interference. Coral Lorenzen wrote to Rehn in June 1967:

> We have been studying data which indicates that the Air Force Project Blue Book in this country is nothing but a front and has no meaning at all. Inasmuch as intelligence reports on *anything*, which would automatically include UFOs, are routed to Central Intelligence Agency, we are reasonably certain that they have a gold mine of beautiful reports which no one is going to see, including the Condon Committee.[758]

This was in line with McDonald's own views that she had earlier disparaged. But even as she was expressing her doubts to Rehn about the Colorado project, the following month saw the publication of her and Jim's book *Flying Saucer Occupants*, which extolled the Boulder study:

> It is not conceivable to us at APRO that this new project could be part of any cover-up program. The only way it could possibly be manipulated is through control of its input but we are assured that Dr. Condon will be free to develop his own sources of reports.
>
> [T]here is good cause for optimism. It seems likely that the University of Colorado study will be the means through which the public will be accurately informed concerning the true nature of UFOs.[759]

Meanwhile, NICAP's financial problems continued. It had insufficient funds for a July-August newsletter and in September sent out an emergency appeal to members for money. Rehn and Coral gloated over this latest crisis. He wrote to her:

> Boy, is NICAP down! A cry for help came to me: "We are in serious trouble. We shall have to suspend operations, at the

most crucial point of our ten-years struggle—unless we get help immediately" ... "Unexpected dwindling of new memberships and renewals" ... No help from me.[760]

She replied:

Yes, NICAP is in trouble. They have never been realistic about their expenses, in my opinion. They try to be too impressive with their offices, etc. No help from us, either, although some of their members had the cheek to write and beg us to help them.[761]

APRO's schadenfreude, however, paled against NICAP's other crisis that month: Dick Hall resigned. *The UFO Investigator* was complimentary and dignified in announcing his departure, "effective September 11, 1967," and extolled his great value to NICAP, noting that he "wants to change his activities and concentrate on other interests," but would "probably be available" as a special adviser.

This somewhat anodyne explanation concealed a storm that had been brewing behind the scenes for years. The Colorado project, though increasingly a source of concern and a drain on all at NICAP, had little effect on Hall's decision to quit. The fundamental reason was Keyhoe himself. Hall, still bitter two years later when he wrote about his resignation, had become increasingly furious and exasperated with Don since about 1963 and compared him somewhat to the commander in *The Caine Mutiny*:

Not that Major Keyhoe is demented. The parallel is otherwise very close ... I have, on the one hand, been very reluctant to hurt or thwart Major Keyhoe in any way, or, on the other hand to see NICAP reach the state that it presently has.[762]

The fundamental issue was his management—or lack thereof. Hall later recalled:

Keyhoe had not really run NICAP ... as far as day-to-day operations were concerned. I was the real Director, with all of the headaches and responsibilities, and none of the real authority. Don was simply not there, physically, in the office, to the point where it became a hard-to-suppress scandal.

Furthermore, he became progressively remote from meaningful contact with day-to-day operations and became—not intentionally, I am sure—an obstructionist who would not take action, who procrastinated, bottled things up, and would not delegate the authority to get anything done. On top of that, he began to have people channel things privately to him at his home address (primarily for use in his private writings) which were withheld from NICAP files and awareness. Often he would not be heard from for days or weeks, and then it would be to lay down some policy or plan which he had thought up without consultation with us, and without consideration of practical difficulties ... I remember meetings, frustrated discussions, which would typically end with, say, Ted [Bloecher] proclaiming "Keyhoe has to go," and we would all more or less agree guiltily.

Moreover, Hall found that the Major's temperament made him

> ... an *extremely* difficult man to work with and I almost gave up several times. Hartranft at one point alludes to Keyhoe's alienating everyone he worked with; that also holds true for every editor and publisher he ever wrote for, sad to say ... he became his own, and NICAP's own, worst enemy.[763]

While the internal tensions at NICAP were bubbling and the staff was losing faith in Keyhoe, he was increasingly losing faith and patience with the Colorado project. Each time he met with or spoke to Low and demanded to know what, if anything, was being done with NICAP's submitted cases, the short answer was "nothing." He had even gone so far as to surreptitiously include more than a hundred Air Force "explained" cases that had "absolutely false answers," in order to test Condon's promise to perform "spot checks." When challenged, Low admitted none had been checked because his boss "hadn't found any AF explanations he considers untrue."[764]

In mid-September, Keyhoe was made aware from staff at Boulder that the "project heads had ordered a search for negative evidence," and he responded by giving notice to the University of Colorado that NICAP would now withdraw its co-operation. Condon and Low were dismayed, and the latter was dispatched to Washington to meet with Keyhoe and Lore, where their discussion was "at times so strange it was almost incredible."[765]

Low admitted that Condon had not interviewed a single witness, nor did he intend to, and that he was "fascinated" by the contactees. Indeed, the only field trip he had made was to an Air Force base after a contactee had told him a UFO was due to land there. "I might as well tell you," said Low, "if he had to make a conclusion now it would be negative." Keyhoe wanted to know why then did the project want NICAP's reports? The answer confirmed what had been strongly intimated in Condon's meeting with the CIA in May 1967: "Because we can be accused of reaching a conclusion without examining all of your evidence."

The discussion now became heated, and when Keyhoe pointed out that some in NICAP didn't believe the project was "on the level," Low became snotty, telling him that it wasn't his job to find out if that was the case. His "job" was to keep submitting his "best evidence and try to change Dr. Condon's present disbelief." Keyhoe refused, unless Condon agreed in writing that he would do investigations and checks, to which Low reluctantly said he would try to persuade his boss.

Then, as Low turned to leave, a rather odd exchange occurred. Keyhoe asked him how, before the University of Colorado signed the contract to undertake the project, the Air Force had described the problem at hand. Low "blurted out" that "they didn't know how to prepare the public," and he would say no more.[766]

Setting aside his astonishment, Don, as usual, procrastinated and waited three weeks before writing to Condon and Low asking for their written assurances to investigate. Meanwhile, NICAP had stopped submitting reports. Members were not told about this change, though Subcommittees and Affiliates were instructed "do not send reports directly to the University of Colorado."[767] Keyhoe did, however, continue to allow members to participate in the study's Early Warning Net (EWN). This had been set up to facilitate rapid reporting to the project of UFO incidents (APRO was also a participant), and the eventual University of Colorado Report claimed it was a worthwhile arrangement.

> [T]o supplement Air Force reporting, we set up our own Early Warning Network, a group of about 60 active volunteer field reporters, most of whom were connected with APRO or NICAP. They telephoned or telegraphed to us intelligence of UFO sightings in their own territory and conducted some

preliminary investigation for us while our team was en route. Some of this cooperation was quite valuable.

The system, at least in one case the year before, had been praised for its rapid response. George Earley, the very active and respected president of NICAP's Connecticut Affiliate, wrote, "Well, those UColo people don't mess around ... if it sounds like a hot one or a good one, whizzzz! And they come fast ... Certainly it is encouraging to see the quick response on the part of the UColo team ... So it does appear that the UFO EWN is working well."[768]

APRO, meanwhile, was still submitting data to the Colorado project and was boasting of its connection. The Lorenzens had toured South America in August 1967, carrying with them "a letter from Robert Low ... endorsing the efforts of APRO and asking cooperation of UFO study facilities on that continent." On their return they went to Boulder "to brief the Condon Committee," concluding that "The Colorado University UFO study is in good hands."[769]

Only a week later, on October 17th, Coral Lorenzen reported to Rehn a different version:

> We were up to Boulder, Colorado last week to brief the Committee on our South American trip. Condon is a strange duck—he had been spending a lot of time running around talking to the nuts—which is strange—as he is a physicist, not a psychiatrist. I have a notion that either he or Lowe [*sic*] or both are CIA contacts inserted into that committee to keep them in line. If we get a negative report out of them—i.e., to the effect that the UFO mystery does not need further investigation—then we'll know that it is those two. The rest of the committee—or at least most of them, are very concerned about Condon and Low's attitudes and I can't say that I blame them.[770]

By this time, the Lorenzens' *Occupants* book, which a few brief press reviews considered worth a read, had now been reviewed by NICAP, and in tit-for-tat style it gave the authors a taste of their own sour grapes. *The UFO Investigator*'s appraisal, titled "Another Wild Book," made no comment on the couple's faith in the Colorado project, but criticized them for creating a "disjointed book," which gave "a tired recounting of the Villas-Boas ... and Hill cases" and took them to task for a work that was "sloppy" and "replete with incorrect information." This latter criticism was justified to some extent. James McDonald was mentioned five times, out of which four spelled his name "MacDonald," and the Zamora sighting in Socorro case was said to have occurred in 1966, not 1964. These were indeed "sloppy" errors, not worthy of experienced researchers and writers who considered their organization superior to all others of the same kind. With unusual bluntness, the NICAP critique concluded, in a style worthy of Coral Lorenzen herself:

> If the Lorenzens intended to add to sensationalism and confusion by issuing such a book, they have admirably succeeded. If, by any chance they feel they have served the cause of science and reason, then they have been hopelessly deluded.[771]

Coral would address the Zamora/Socorro error in the September-October *Bulletin*, offering no apology, but blaming the error on the initial investigators of the case. In the same issue, she tried to take credit for informing UN Secretary General U Thant's position on UFOs. APRO had contacted him "in early 1966," offering to send him their regular bulletin, which he had accepted, and it therefore boasted that "his opinions may well be, at least partly, based on what he has received from APRO."[772]

Meanwhile, Keyhoe's doubts about the Colorado project can only have been reinforced by a letter from Idabel Epperson. In late November, she wrote that Dr. Robert Nathan, a computer-enhancement scientist at the Jet Propulsion Laboratory, with whom her subcommittee had been working on the Heflin photos, had concluded that the pictures were genuine and had reported this to Brian O'Brien (Chairman of the 1966 Ad Hoc Committee to Review Project Blue Book). O'Brien refused to listen to Nathan and "sarcastically snorted, 'You must be kidding,'" adding emphatically that he thought "the Condon committee should be disbanded and stop wasting all that money—the whole thing is ridiculous."[773]

On December 1st, Condon and Low had both replied—without answering—Keyhoe's letters in which he had asked them to conduct proper research. Neither made any mention of his requests, but lavished praise on the importance of NICAP's documents to the project, which in the light of admissions already made, would appear to confirm that its case reports served a purpose other than for research.

Moreover, Low had made it clear from early on that no "old" cases would be considered because they had no value (this was even extended to reports from 1966), but he was quietly following up on at least one. In January 1968, he wrote to Ratchford updating him on his enquiries regarding the 1952 case of Commander Alvin Moore's "experience and subsequent findings of stones, which he thinks are in some way related to the UFO problem." Moore said a report had been sent to Dayton (i.e., ATIC) at the time, but on checking, Low found they had no document, which led him to remark to Ratchford:

> This, of course, may be another grain of evidence—I don't know—that Ruppelt made off with some of the files of sightings. You know that I visited Ruppelt's widow and was not able to find out anything, although one might possibly judge her assertion that she didn't have anything, that, "Ed would never have taken any Air Force files," was a little too ready and a little too vigorously asserted to carry total conviction.[774]

Chapter 37:
Fiasco Fallout

About a month after the meeting with Low at NICAP, David Saunders arrived unexpectedly at Keyhoe's office and showed him Low's "Trick" memo. "Incredible, isn't it?" he said.

The memo had been ticking away since August 1966, when it was seen by the Colorado project's Dr. Roy Craig. He showed it to Levine, who was disturbed by its content—both men experienced a "funny feeling" in their stomachs when they read it.[775] In January 1967, project assistant James Wadsworth had showed it to no less than Dick Hall when he was attending a Colorado meeting in Denver. Hall later admitted that he failed to understand the significance of it and didn't even mention it to Keyhoe. Hall's wife, Marty, was also present and recalled that Wadsworth said it revealed that the purpose of the Colorado project was to "show that there was nothing there."

When Keyhoe read it almost a year later, he was shocked. Despite its astonishing content, it was not restricted—it had been kept in open files—and he was keen to expose it to the press. Before taking any action, he told Dr. McDonald about it in confidence and on December 12th gave him a copy.

"This is dynamite," McDonald responded and wanted to write to Condon and Low, believing it would "scare them" into changing direction and start conducting a proper scientific investigation. Such action, however, would have implications for Saunders, so with his permission, something of a ruse was created to try and keep his name out of the affair. McDonald visited Boulder, where staff did not show him the memo, but pointed him in the direction of the open file named "AF Contract and Background" where it was kept.[776]

After some discussion, Saunders, Levine, and Mary Lou Armstrong, Low's administrative assistant who had long been troubled about the negative and bizarre approach of the project heads, permitted McDonald—on the agreement that he did not implicate any staff—to inform Condon, Low, and the National Academy of Sciences in writing that he had seen the memo.

Low received his letter on February 5, 1968, and according to Mary Lou, who was present at the time, he "exploded" and wanted "whoever had given the memo to McDonald" to be sacked. A similar volcanic response erupted from his boss—who apparently did not know of its existence—when Low showed him the letter.[777] "Condon had every member of the staff in for a grilling" and as a result learned who had been involved in the memo's exposure.[778] Saunders and Levine were verbally attacked by an angry and abusive Condon: Saunders, he barked, ought to be "professionally ruined," and Levine was accused of treachery. Both were fired, and Mary Lou, who could not be bullied into submission, resigned over the staff's "lack of confidence" in Low.[779]

McDonald, in his naive expectation that scientific integrity would be the result of his action, had scored a catastrophic own-goal:

> The fat's in the fire. My letter to Low ... led not to deep scientific concern and response to the scientific implications and criticism, but to raging concern for the image of CU and the principal investigator.[780]

Mary Lou Armstrong personally phoned APRO and told the Lorenzens about McDonald's exposure of the memo and the resultant firings. Consequently, the January *Bulletin* commented that this action was "only the culmination of an internal dissent which goes back more or less to the beginning of the study," which now would suffer from "the loss of two key people at this stage of the game."

Privately, yet again, Coral had more to say to Rehn in Sweden about "this clown McDonald" and his actions regarding the memo:

> From Jim's and my observations we felt [Saunders and Levine] were the most competent of the whole lot ... Mac-Donadl [*sic*] succeeded in getting the two most competent and effectual members of that committee fired. Adn [*sic*] we don't think it was just an "error" either. MacDonald still has done nothing to further UFO research. He gets a lot of publicity for himself, grabs off a lot of reports which he won't show to anyone or share with anyone. And he is a SECRET MEMBER OF THE NICPA [*sic*] BOARD OF DIRECTORS.
>
> Now, inasmuch as NICAP does not like secrecy, what is all this secrecy bit? Why can't MacDonald [*sic*] admit his affiliation with NICAP? We think he is part of the whole NICAP coverup. They have kept UFO research in a pit through their domination of publicity (keeping other groups

from growing, for instance), refusal to study landing or occupant cases, etc.[781]

Rehn was in agreement and added his own take on matters when he replied in March:

> Yes, I'll give McDonald "the cold shoulder" if he should contact me. Imagine, those tales of his! And criticizing APRO. As to NICAP, I recall Dr. Leon Davidsons [sic] stuff about Keyhoe. Keyhoe was useful to CIA, providing an outlet for the UFO cranks, helping to make a mess of the UFO question. CIA probably helped Keyhoe to get money. Air Force never bothered to answer Keyhoe's grave accusations. CIA wanted Ufo as a mess, financed Adamski etc. Davidson is not so dumb …[782]

In her reply, she ramped up her vitriol. A "forum" on saucers would be held in Phoenix on March 16th at which McDonald would speak. Coral wrote:

> McDonald thinks that he is going to swoop in and take over the press conference—but he's going to have to fight tooth and nail [with other speakers, one] of whom doesn't like his efforts and publicity hogging.
> We're pretty sure that McDonald is tied in with the CIA just as NICAP is. And he gets no more from us. He is a "secret" member of NICAP's Board—and they are the people who are constantly yakking about secrecy.[783]

While the fall-out from the memo was dropping all around, journalist John Fuller was already writing an article about both it and the failings of the Condon project. He had been at the January 1968 meeting (attended by Thornton Page) and McDonald had shown him memo. Fuller was galvanized and immediately began planning his article. Soon after, he approached Keyhoe for his collaboration and "NICAP agreed to delay its [own] *UFO Investigator* story" until after the piece came out, "provided our part in the struggle was fully covered and a NICAP box statement was included."[784]

Meanwhile, Condon was railing to McDonald and others that the memo had been "stolen," despite being told that Low himself had earlier stated that all project files should be open and unclassified. Even so, when one of

McDonald's former colleagues, Dr. Joach Kuettner, later visited Condon, he found him still "complaining about the 'trick' memo [and] claimed the memo was taken from Low's personal files." Kuettner was apparently convinced that Condon's accusation was true because "Low was standing right there when Ed said that."[785]

Colorado aside, Gordon Lore, now burdened with the role of Assistant Director at NICAP, had attended the aforementioned Phoenix event in March, which was not a "forum" as much as a press conference held at the Phoenix Executive Club. Afterwards he sent to Keyhoe a four-page letter reporting on it and other matters. A comparison of this letter with Coral Lorenzen's to Rehn and the subsequent APRO report about Phoenix, tells us much about the childish level to which the "feud" had descended. Coral had earlier confided to Rehn about APRO's involvement in the planning of this event:

> NICAP doesn't know the extent of our effort—we are furnishing the art and photo display for the lobby, and ... a big TV producer is going to visit us from Hollywood. He produces such epics as "Lost in Space, (!!!), The Red Skelton Show and the Jonothan [*sic*] Winters show ... He will be filming the press conference and the forum [and] he wants us to advise him. NICAP knows nothing about this because we called him ourselves.[786]

Dr. Menzel was among the participants and Lore related to Keyhoe how he "made a fool of himself" by storming out red-faced when a fellow speaker, Dr. Frank Salisbury, said it was "regrettable that more scientists did not have an open mind about UFOs." Two hours later, when Menzel had been persuaded to return to the debate, he hogged the stage and refused to leave it when requested to do so by the moderator. This was referred to in APRO's next bulletin merely as "an exchange between Menzel and Kaeburn [not Salisbury] on a remote point."[787]

On the positive side, Lore felt the scientists in attendance had perhaps "gained a new, favorable impression of NICAP ...rather than just relying upon negative hearsay from others." He added that he'd had friendly conversations with "even the Lorenzens" but told Keyhoe about a contretemps over the display set up by APRO (about which Coral earlier had told Rehn) and NICAP's own display, for which it had been given permission by the organizers:

> I heard they were saying things behind my back. Jim Loren-

zen even tried to remove our application blanks (about 1,000 were gathered [by him] from the table at the dinner); ... but Dr. K. [Leslie Kaeburn, NICAP Board of Governors] caught him at it and angrily set the display up again.

The Lorenzens own report in the *APRO Bulletin* made no mention of this but gushed that they had "had the privilege' of meeting with Menzel and wife, whom they found to be "attractive charming people" and described their "brief' encounter as "most amicable." This of course, was counter to her griping about Menzel's "negative contributions" in the May 1967 *APRO Bulletin*.

Lore's displeasure and distrust during this trip was not limited to APRO's antics. His report to Keyhoe tells us something of the mounting internal tensions within NICAP, in this instance from the Los Angeles Subcommittee (LANS) headed by Idabel Epperson. After leaving Phoenix, Lore visited LANS and came away with doubts about her attitude and motivation:

> She appears to have inaugurated a sort of "battle of the sexes" situation in which the 4 women on the Subc have taken over and are excluding the 4 men. (Dr. K[aeburn] thinks this is psychologically due to the fact that Idabel's alcoholic husband deserted her, thus turning her against men). Both Ann Druffel and Marilyn Epperson [Idabel's daughter] appear to be (to use a harsh word) stooges of Idabel's ... She also gave me the impression of being dogmatic ... she does not appear to be objective in her evaluation of a person's true professional worth ... if she likes a person, he can do no wrong; if she doesn't, he can do no right.[788]

Lore nonetheless acknowledged that Idabel had been a good friend to NICAP, which was certainly true, but his appraisal of the tensions within LANS, apparently arising from one of its most loyal foot-soldiers, indicates the fracturing, misgivings, and back-biting that increasingly undermined the effectiveness of the Committee.

Less than two months later in the May 14, 1968, issue of *Look*, Fuller laid bare the whole discouraging Colorado story and exposed the troublesome memo. "Flying Saucer Fiasco," which was summarized as "The extraordinary story of the half-million-dollar 'trick' to make Americans believe the Condon committee was conducting an objective investigation," pulled no punches.

NICAP was mentioned prominently throughout, and on April 30th, Keyhoe gave a press conference at which he handed copies of the memo to reporters. When Ratchford heard about this, his initial, somewhat curious unconcern about the *Look* piece changed to anger. The explanation for this appears to be found in James McDonald's journal. On June 19th, he wrote:

> Before Keyhoe's press conference (re LOOK) Ratchford in-
> clined to let Condon fight it out. But Keyhoe's having the
> memo [which Ratchford considered to be "a private paper"]
> turned them negative.

"From that point on, the Air Force defended the Condon study with no holds barred."[789] Condon, meanwhile, had phoned *Look* with his complaints about the article and intimated that Fuller should be fired.

The May-June *UFO Investigator*, having previously withheld its account of events, now revealed the story to members. Headlined "NICAP breaks with Colorado project," it detailed the numerous doubts and difficulties experienced from the very beginning right through to the decision to withdraw assistance, yet astonishingly, in the light of all that had happened, Keyhoe absolved Condon and Low of blame. "Strange as it might seem," he wrote "both appeared to believe their approach was correct and fully justified," even though he admitted that their beliefs were bolstered by not having examined any evidence.

Now that NICAP had split with Condon, Keyhoe began pushing from a different angle. On April 30th, he had written to President Johnson with details of the Colorado project's failings and offered suggestions for how LBJ might create an independent commission to "replace the wrecked project" with "a commission of capable scientists, selected by you and completely independent of any military or civilian Government agencies."[790] In reply, he received only a dismissive letter from the Air Force (a "curt brush-off") to which the matter had been passed.[791]

As to what would be the conclusions of the coming Colorado report, there was little expectation of anything other than a negative verdict, and now that one door had almost certainly closed, Don tried to force open a window. He urged members to become involved in a "vitally important program" to expand NICAP's operations with the goals of creating "the largest UFO reporting and investigating network in the world." He wanted to redesign its "evaluations system" to have "20 times" more scientists and engineers than the Colorado project had utilized. "WE HAVE TO DO THIS JOB!" he insisted.[792]

In addition to the grand plan for this vast expansion of NICAP's "network," Keyhoe increased the pressure further with an excessive response to the reaction of "[T]hirty-odd members" who had taken exception to NICAP's October 1967 critique of the Lorenzens' book, *Flying Saucer Occupants*. Among them was its own Board Member, Rev. Albert Baller, who had "courteously disapproved" of the negative review. Keyhoe felt that this "long-time Board Member" ought to have known better and did "not realize all the complex factors" involved. As a result, he made a typically over-the-top decision to "give all members, and the press, a full-scale coverage of the problem." Work had already begun on a

> ... complete discussion, which will include specific reports and claims and developments, and a precise, detailed statement of NICAP's position and operating policy in regard to both contactee and "encounter" claims.[793]

Too much was never enough for Donald Keyhoe.

* * *

The loss of Adamski in 1965 had deprived the contactees of their highest-profile advocate, and three years later one of his most enduring supporters had also departed the Earthly dimension: Clara John. A few months after Adamski's death, she had suffered a stroke, which rendered her right-side paralyzed and brought to an end her *Little Listening Post*.[794] On January 29, 1968, she had died of arteriosclerosis and heart disease.[795] The woman who had been fundamental to the creation of NICAP passed unmentioned in its newsletter, but her death was a silent marker on the road to NICAP's collapse, which, thanks to Condon, had now become inevitable.

Following NICAP's withdrawal from the Colorado project and Fuller's *Look* article, the blame for everything that had gone wrong with the Condon investigation, according to APRO, should be laid at NICAP's door. The May 1968 *APRO Bulletin* featured three columns written by Jim Lorenzen, who, in the guise of playing "The Devil's Advocate," gave a high-handed critique of Fuller's article, complaining that it was "obviously slanted to support a particular viewpoint." The "other side" to the story, he said, emanated from NICAP, Dick Hall, and James McDonald, aided and abetted by Levine and Saunders, "the chief offenders," who had the temerity to try and undermine their boss. The latter three, it was noted, "are also members of NICAP and were part of a sustained effort to undermine Condon." In Jim Lorenzen's opinion, Saunders and Levine had evidently now fallen from being "the most competent of the whole lot," to upstart troublemakers who got what they deserved.

Lorenzen then trashed NICAP's dealings with the Colorado project, huffing that its "offer to help was really an attempt to control the study. Keyhoe wanted the committee to endorse his own conclusions, adopted twenty years ago without the benefit of research." Though he conceded that APRO and NICAP were "in general agreement" about what might be shown by a "truly objective study," he was

> ... in specific disagreement with NICAP's attempt to "take over" the Condon Study. To me it is inconsistent to advocate an unbiased scientific study while attempting to impose one's own bias on such a study.

This oddly pre-echoed what the Condon Report itself wrote about NICAP when it was published the following January:

> NICAP made several efforts to influence the course of our study. When it became clear that these would fail, NICAP attacked the Colorado project as "biased" and therefore without merit.

Jim Lorenzen wasn't done yet. In the *Bulletin* he went on to defend Low's memo, insisting that it:

> ... was written chiefly for the purpose of convincing certain University staff members that the UFO study could be undertaken without the University's public image suffering as a consequence. Since most of these members were convinced that there was absolutely nothing substantial to the UFO mystery, Low felt it was necessary to approach them in that frame of reference. Nothing in the memo was binding on the study. It was merely the sort of "puffing" that goes along with any selling job.[796]

If this was merely "puffing," Condon's reaction to the memo had been somewhat extreme, a point which Lorenzen didn't address. In what might be interpreted as a ploy to cozy up to Condon, while not getting too close in case NICAP's doubts proved correct, Lorenzen wrote, "without attempting to insinuate anything more than cooperation," APRO's own contribution to the study amounted to the October 1967 briefing it had delivered in Boulder, the provision of members' names to assist with the project's Early Warning Network, and copies of the best 300 South American cases in its files. He concluded, "we still continue to cooperate with the committee in any way possible without attempting to influence the resulting report."

Yet in spite of the Colorado project's simultaneous implosion and explosion, "almost a miracle" occurred. Long-time NICAP supporter Congressman J. Edward Roush (D-Ind) went public about his dissatisfaction with the "floundering" Condon Committee's actions, citing on the floor of the House Fuller's article as grounds for doubt about the project's objectivity. On April 30th he called for a Congressional hearing—which happened to be the same day Condon announced that the project was "effectively" completed.

As a result of Roush's call, a "Symposium on Unidentified Flying Objects" was hastily organized and heard before the Committee on Science and Astronautics on July 29, 1968, but as with every other potential break, the Air Force had the upper hand. It was made clear in advance by letter, and frequently during the hearing, that no discussion or criticism of the Air Force's involvement in UFO investigations would be permitted, nor would any criticism of the Colorado Project be allowed.[797] When speakers gave the merest hint of reference to either, they were reminded of the taboos and were shut down. Moreover, NICAP could attend only in the capacity of silent observer, so it had to rely on McDonald to present his case, which was to a large extent also NICAP's. His fellow speakers, as listed in the report were:

> Dr. J. Allen Hynek, Head of the Department of Astronomy, Northwestern University, Evanston
>
> Dr. Carl Sagan, Associate Professor of Astronomy, Center for Radiophysics and Space Research, Cornell University
>
> Dr. Robert L. Hall, Head of the Department of Sociology, University of Illinois, Chicago, Ill. [Hall was the brother of Dick Hall]
>
> Dr. James A. Harder, Associate Professor of Civil Engineering, University of California
>
> Dr. Robert M. L. Baker, Jr., Senior Scientist, System

Sciences Corp., of El Segundo, Calif.

Each of them made a statement, but McDonald's was the longest, running to sixty-eight pages. It supported what he termed "the seventh hypothesis," i.e., "that UFOs may be some form of extraterrestrial devices." He gave considerable credit to Keyhoe for his "reportorial accuracy [which] was almost uniformly high" and stated that, despite the use of "extensive direct quotes and suspenseful dramatizations" in his books, "his reliability must be recognized as impressive." He rated NICAP's publication, *The UFO Evidence*, as having a "generally very high reliability" and in an oblique swipe at the Air Force, said that the UFO problem had been "swept under the rug."

Menzel, of course, spouted his usual nonsense in a submitted paper and managed to give a slap to NICAP, though not by name. He criticized "the heads of a few amateur UFO organizations" for stirring up their members to ask Congress to investigate. The renewed requests made by this "vociferous group," due to the expectation of a negative conclusion from the Colorado study, made "just about as much sense as reopening the subject of Witchcraft," he said. He even insulted Congressman Roush by enclosing with his statement the telegram he'd sent, accepting Roush's invitation to submit his statement. He wrote:

> Am amazed, however, that you could plan so unbalanced a symposium, weighted by persons known to favor Government support of a continuing, expensive, and pointless investigation of UFOs without inviting me, the leading exponent of opposing views and author of two major books on the subject.[798]

Though Keyhoe was naturally jubilant about the Symposium, there was little interest elsewhere. During the meagre six-hour session, only a dozen congressmen attended, of which nine "were in and out," and only a dozen press reporters turned up.[799] (Don later admitted that the Symposium had attracted "very little publicity.")[800]

After the hearing closed, some of the group, including Keyhoe and Roush, went to the DuPont Plaza for celebratory cocktails, but as events would later show, there was no cause for celebration. Though the Symposium "was more encompassing and ambitious than the one in 1966," it ultimately achieved no more than its predecessor, despite the sober and meticulous statements given by the participants. Yet, even allowing for the veto on discussing the Colorado project, their testimonies collectively laid bare its staggering neglect and avoidance of the subject it had failed to study at enormous public expense.[801]

The underwhelming after-effect of the session was reflected in Keyhoe's last book, *Aliens From Space*, published in 1973. He devoted barely five pages to the Symposium, while Gordon Lore in his 2018 memoir, *Flying Saucers From Beyond the Earth*, wrote only four.[802] It's fair to say, however, that at the time many factions were, not unreasonably, withholding judgement until the Colorado report was released.

Of course, timing is everything and retrospective consideration tells us that Fuller's *Look* article and the Symposium were delivered too soon and were both, in effect, ill-timed rebuttals of the Condon Report, which had yet to be published. The publication of Fuller's piece may well have been simply due to bad judgement, but it seems somewhat strange that, given the repeated thwarting of Keyhoe's unrelenting attempts to instigate Congressional hearings since 1957, Roush's plea was not squashed; within only a few weeks, the hearing was done and dusted. Some time later, Jacques Vallee may well have been correct when he suggested to author Ann Druffel that the Symposium was really "a classic tactic" used to allow "potential opponents to the Condon Report to 'let off steam' to give them a harmless day in Court."[803]

The Symposium had indeed been "harmless," unlike the Condon Report that, when published seven months later, drew a line in the sand that neither Keyhoe nor anyone else could erase.

Chapter 38:
The Bitter End

As 1968 drew to a close and the release of the Condon Report was anticipated, a storm was brewing inside NICAP. Dick Hall, despite having left the previous September, was still involved with its activities; he was now a "part-time consultant" working in an advisory capacity and as a consequence remained tangled in its administrative and management woes. His relative distance from NICAP, however, had only increased his exasperation with Keyhoe, and now, with Gordon Lore's help, he was trying to "wake him up and get him to take action."[804]

The Major's rare appearances in the office, his remote decision-making without consultation, the ongoing struggle to meet the target for publishing the *UFO Investigator*, and the increasing workload from yet another editorial burden, a follow-on to *The UFO Evidence* entitled *UFOs—A New Look*, were taking their toll. This forthcoming publication, though only a large format booklet, gave consideration to, among other UFO subjects, the Colorado project and, surprisingly, occupant cases. As ever, the cost of printing had delayed publication, but by autumn sufficient advance orders had been received and it had gone to the printers.[805]

In October, Hall had unsuccessfully tried "to convey to Keyhoe the degree of disorganization and the need for action." By December "things had deteriorated badly," so Don agreed to meet with staff for a "gripes" session. He asked for "written complaints" to be submitted to him in advance, and on the 5th, a special meeting was held at the office. It was attended by, among others, Hall, Lore, Bloecher, and a 1967 appointee, Editorial Assistant Stuart Nixon, who brought along Kathy Price, his fiancée and administrative assistant. Nixon, from the first moment he joined NICAP, had been a problem for the staff, in part due to what were perceived to be his antagonistic, underhand working methods that, combined with his actions and peculiar connections, soon gave rise to suspicions that he was a CIA plant.

The purpose of the meeting was for staff "to clear the air" with the director, but though the detail of the meeting is not recorded, it was evidently hostile and heated. Ted Bloecher, who had always been fond of Keyhoe and whose letters imply a calm and good-humored fellow, "blew up, called Don 'a liar' to his face and stormed out." Hall's own criticisms caused Keyhoe to react "strongly, personally" to him, but after reflecting on the meeting, Dick felt that the experience had been somewhat cathartic. The "mass confrontation" with Keyhoe had made it clear that the discontent was "largely caused by his handling of editorial matters."[806]

While the dust was still billowing at NICAP, January 1969 saw the public release of the dreaded Condon Report. Its negative conclusion, which went so far as to recommend "against the mounting of a major effort for continuing UFO study for scientific reasons," surprised nobody, but appalled many. Moreover, it demonstrated that the 1968 Symposium, about which Keyhoe had been so hopeful, was merely a device to be used by Condon to support his dismissal of the phenomenon. He wrote:

> We have studied this symposium record with great care and find nothing in it which requires that we alter the conclusions and recommendations that we have presented in Section I, nor that we modify any presentation of the specific data contained in other sections of this report.

Like the infamous Warren Report into the assassination of President Kennedy, the Condon Report successfully used the same tactic of publishing a reassuring summary and relying on public gullibility and apathy to deflect any interest in its details. And also like the Warren Report, the full version contained much that went entirely against its conclusion, yet it immediately became the last word on the subject: there was no cover-up, witnesses were mistaken, photographs were of no value, and everyone should just move along. The press largely reported on it with a "we told you so" yawn. There were, after all, far more urgent matters erupting in America.

Whatever Keyhoe felt about the social and political upheavals throughout the nation, his focus was now wholly on discrediting the Condon Report, which, among its staggering flaws and biased ineptitude, was clear on how it felt about NICAP. It complained:

> NICAP devotes a considerable amount of its attention to attacking the Air Force and to trying to influence members of Congress to hold hearings and in other ways to join in these attacks. It maintained a friendly relation to the Colorado project during about the first year, while warning its

members to be on guard lest the project turn out to have been "hired to whitewash the Air Force."[807]

The Report was generally much kinder to APRO, but nonetheless criticized it and NICAP with regard to the mindset of its members:

> When field studies are made by amateur organizations like APRO or NICAP, there are often several members present on a team, but usually they are persons without technical training, and often with a strong bias toward the sensational aspects of the subject.

In his summing-up, Condon evidently couldn't resist a thinly-disguised swipe at Keyhoe and also, it seems, McDonald:

> This conclusion is controversial. It will not be accepted without much dispute by the UFO amateurs, by the authors of popular UFO books and magazine articles, or even by a small number of academic scientists whose public statements indicate that they feel that this is a subject of great scientific promise.

Keyhoe now went all-out to expose Condon's con in the press, on air, at lectures, and especially in the *UFO Investigator*. The January and February issues were devoted almost entirely to shredding the Report, detailing how it had failed in its supposed purpose and had possibly fleeced the taxpayer. He tried to rally the troops with an exhortation that NICAP must now devote all efforts and yet more money to mount an irresistible rebuttal:

> We need your help. It is crucial that we continue a full-scale campaign to bring the UFO subject out in the open in order to offset the Condon report. But the cost of doing so will be great. There will be costly printing and postage bills in preparing and sending vast amounts of material to scientists for evaluation ... we must hire a lawyer and an accountant [to attain] tax exempt status.[808]
>
> The next few months will be most crucial ... We have overwhelming evidence to neutralize the report. But it will be useless unless we can make this proof known nationwide—to Congress, the press and the public. We expect the first big

impact not later than June, probably sooner.[809]

This vigorous call to arms was accompanied—inevitably—by an emergency plea for funds, and in response, "the overwhelming suggestion" from members was to raise US rates to $10 a year, but in an over-cautious and foolish move, dues were now pegged at $8.[810] Though NICAP desperately needed money and members were prepared to pay more, this lifebelt was tossed back.

As to Condon's actions, Keyhoe was not alone in his doubts. He had support from many stalwarts, including New York Congressman William F. Ryan, who on the floor of the House asked for an "immediate probe" of the Colorado project, and those few press reports that didn't simply jump on the "Keyhoe is a fool/Condon is a genius" bandwagon, expressed misgivings.

Of course, some reporters were gleeful in their ridicule. "America is laughing at Don Keyhoe again," wrote Tom Tiede of the News Enterprise Association, even though he had interviewed him and gotten his side of the Condon coin, while journalist William Hines lauded the report and accused Don of calling a subsequent press conference merely to plug his own book:

> Keyhoe is the nearest thing to a tycoon in the UFO industry, which derives its income largely from the sale of sensational paperback, hoo-hah magazine articles and the donations of excitable ladies in tennis shoes ... Leave the Keyhoes to the boob-tube, the paperback shelves and the barbershop reading racks.[811]

The remarks of these two journalists were particularly hurtful and Don drew attention to them in late February during a desperate attempt to bring under control a burgeoning mutiny within NICAP's walls, where matters were rapidly descending into acrimony and chaos.

Gordon Lore's own frustrations as Assistant Director, inherited from Dick Hall, had already come to a head, and he now "was so emotionally upset" that he had written a letter of resignation on January 24th, but changed his mind about submitting it. Three days later, after explaining matters to Keyhoe, he vented his feelings in a confidential, eleven-page memo to staff. He acknowledged that the negative effect of the Condon Report would be "difficult to successfully refute," but it's clear from the content of his epistle that NICAP's internal problems were long-standing and getting worse.

Meltdown had begun.

The solution, in the minds of management, was to increase office efficiency, and Lore's memo tells us a great deal about the day-to-day problems that by now were rampant in the office. He made plain his annoyance at staff intransigence and rapped its collective knuckles for inefficiency generally and insubordination toward him personally. He appealed for harmony, effectiveness, and putting the Committee's needs above their own. His anger was manifesting itself with a strong flavor of autocracy:

> I have noticed frequent, stubborn resistance to my instruc-
> tions ... I have bent over backwards to consider other peo-
> ple's feelings and, frequently, all I have received in return is
> resentment, resistance and even a certain amount of scape-
> goat treatment ... Feelings of jealousy, possessiveness and se-
> crecy among some staff members has got to stop. They can-
> not be tolerated any longer ... When I make a decision or lay
> down a particular guideline, it should and must be followed,
> if we are to operate at our best level. There is no reason, in
> most cases, to stubbornly argue and resist orders.

Moreover, there had been "occasional emotional explosions," staff were keeping irregular hours, were not signing in and out as they should, were not telling Lore personally when they had to take sick leave, nor were they informing him when "important" persons visited or phoned. Filing was not being done on time, and staff were taking long lunches. Some, due to "individual personality quirks," resented being challenged and often would refuse to break off from their regular tasks when requested to do other work in between. "This situation must cease, beginning now," Lore declared.[812]

These absolutist demands were rather out of character for him, but Dick Hall understood his friend's situation. He would later write:

> Gordon found himself in the unfortunate position of me-
> diating between an unhappy staff and an adamant Major
> Keyhoe who had lost his grip on things and who remained
> removed from the office. For the man in the middle, this can
> be an extremely frustrating position.[813]

While NICAP was struggling to quell insurrection and Keyhoe was making grand, desperate plans to "neutralize" the Condon Report, APRO's response to it was comparatively limp and confined mostly to the January 1969 *Bulletin.* Jim Lorenzen himself had written this issue because Coral was enduring a painful recovery from surgery, but she undoubtedly agreed with his criticisms.[814] Among them, he questioned Condon's bizarre rant in the Report about how school children were being encouraged to read UFO material and how it ought to be stopped. He had offered no supporting evidence for this claim and it had not formed part of the project's remit, nor of its so-called investigation. Jim also remarked that the Report was

> ... journalistic rather than scientific [and its] approach is what one would expect of a news feature writer who starts out with a particular theme in mind and emphasizes those aspects that will support his theme while generally discrediting all that which does not.

Such a criticism, it might be argued, was a bit thick given that this tactic had been employed by APRO many times with respect to NICAP. Similarly avoided was any reference to APRO's earlier proclaimed support for and faith in Condon, but instead the *Bulletin* hid behind the skirts of an anonymous "prominent biologist" to give what "appears to be the most representative" view about the report, held by APRO members:

> I never shared the hopes of the directors of APRO that anything would emerge from it ... Dr. Condon did not enter his investigation with an open mind ... He was no more able to divest himself of the assumptions and principles upon which present day science is based than a bird is able to divest itself of its wings and grow forelegs to walk on.[815]

Jim now washed his hands of Condon's "study," stating "We find that the Report as a whole fails ...and should therefore be dismissed and discredited."[816]

Over in Sweden, Gus Rehn had known how things would turn out. He wrote to the Lorenzens that "Colorado will make us all appear to be liars. That's what it amounts to. I mean, the press, the mass media will distort the report to that effect."[817] He was quite correct, and his subsequent letters—and Coral's replies—make little mention of the Colorado debacle, but reflect a sense of resignation to the inevitable.

While the Lorenzens were trying to brush off the Condon Report and distance themselves from it, Keyhoe was doing the opposite. In the Feb-Mar

UFO Investigator, he vehemently insisted it was "imperative to circulate strong rebuttal material to Members of Congress, press-media and scientists":

> A complete factual rebuttal by NICAP, with the aid of scientists, is being prepared … this rebuttal is certain to have a powerful—and we believe devastating—impact. In addition, NICAP is furnishing important evidence to certain influential groups and individuals preparing scientific critiques that also will deal a blow to Dr. Condon and the report …
>
> NICAP's most important activity now is the preparation of its full documented rebuttals, being prepared with the aid of advisers and outside scientists … the harmful effects of the Condon Report, unless fully offset, will be greatest in the scientific community … Our final rebuttal is being prepared as proof of factual errors and serious omissions, for comparison with each aspect of the Condon Report. Although Condon's unwarranted attacks on NICAP should be answered … we believe it will be the most powerful and convincing document NICAP has ever published …[818]

He admitted this would "add heavily to NICAP's expenses" and that matters were made more difficult because the Condon Report had "forced a delay in mailing the Investigator." The cost of the rebuttal, including regular operational costs until June, would total $39,530—yet he had already done NICAP no favors by rejecting members' offer to pay $10 per year. Moreover, the usefulness of the smaller increase to $8 was further detracted from by yet more printing and postage costs because "Affiliates, Subcommittees and Associate Members" were instructed to destroy their supplies of "old literature," to be replaced by new copies that reflected the new rate. It was a never-ending cycle of bad planning and ineptitude, fed by Keyhoe's personal determination to "get the truth" out at any cost.

As to Gordon Lore's situation, Keyhoe set about handling it in his typical, overkill, procrastinating fashion. He issued a "Confidential Letter to NICAP Staff," an *apologia* running to twelve pages, with more expected to follow.[819] It had been written on February 20th though was not copied to staff until March 19th, and its content was yet another account of his pre-NICAP achievements and the tribulations and deprivations he had endured since becoming its director. Little of what he had to say was new, but it reveals that, fundamentally, nothing had improved for him or NICAP since 1957.

Keyhoe admitted he hadn't realized "how much the frictions and resistance" had affected Gordon's authority, and though he fully endorsed his January memo, he once again aired his own problems to his disillusioned and beleaguered staff. Like the brick-bats he had long experienced from outside, criticisms from within were taken personally and had to be fully rebutted:

> I freely admit I have made errors in my 12 years as head of NICAP, errors I have always tried to correct. But some complaints about me are without any foundation at all. Here are a few recent examples:
>
> I was blamed for bypassing Isabel Davis, who was acting as coordinator for [*UFO Investigator*] Vol. IV, No. 9 copy, causing her to be indignant and upset. The facts: I was not the one who forgot to coordinate with Isabel. Because of illness with the Hong Kong flu, I had to dictate my page 1 material and message to members by phone ... I have been criticized for not pushing the tax-exempt drive. The facts: The lawyer will not proceed further without a guarantee of a minimum $500 fee, and at least $100 down, and a $100 a month ... I am blamed for not knowing staff members' problems. This is completely untrue ...

He in turn, accused staff of "an almost complete failure to know what I am doing, and what I have done as head of NICAP. Some indicate practically no real understanding of me as a person," and he complained that

> I have been pictured ... as indifferent to staff members' personal problems, unappreciative of their hard and loyal work. It has been implied, if not said, that I don't trust [their abilities], that I do very little work, except occasionally on publications—which usually results in long and unnecessary delays. If all this were true it would be an appalling picture.[820]

He went on to refute the accusation that he was "quick to criticize, slow to praise" and told how he had "skipped pay month after month," though was not asking for any thanks. He pointed out that he was "legally responsible for any NICAP taxes," which were currently overdue to the tune of $4,000 for the last quarter of 1968. As to his own finances, he lamented that "twice in the early years of NICAP I had to mortgage our home and borrow money separately," and that he had turned down better offers that would have given him financial security, when his NICAP pay was averaging less than $150 per week:

> Several times I had tempting offers: To be a chief program writer for CBS-TV (non-UFO subjects); to be a magazine associate writer and roving reporter; to do a syndicate column; and once, to write a UFO cartoon for syndicate cartoonists … The CBS job would have paid, to start, $750 a week

With regard to the post-Condon Report press comments of Tiede and Hines, he told staff that, though they surely had experienced "ribbing, or sneers" over the years,

> … this is far different from seeing yourself attacked in nationwide syndicate press stories. Though I don't like it, I can take it. But it has had a bad effect on Mrs. Keyhoe and our two daughters. Until you see yourself publicly ridiculed, misquoted, lied about, you won't know what it can do to you.[821]

He went so far as to admit, unwittingly, of being unable to overcome his dog-with-a-bone nature and then bared his feelings of guilt about the impact of his involvement with NICAP on his family:

> I have always hated to give up something important and admit defeat—so I stayed with NICAP. I know now I had no right to do this and put a heavy burden on my wife, leading to her heart condition, also forcing us to curtail our daughters' college education. I constantly feel this load of guilt and even if I suddenly had the money to afford real vacations for Mrs. Keyhoe and buy her things she has had to do without, it would be too late to make up for all the bad years.

It's perhaps worth noting here that although Keyhoe adored his wife— indeed he was uxorious—his neighbors in Luray, Virginia, disliked her. They felt that Helen was a rather "high-maintenance" woman and a "snob" who was trying to "sandpaper" her husband to "turn him into something he was not."[822] If this was the case, it would underpin the anguish expressed in his *mea culpa* to staff. He was caught between his addictive never-give-up personality and

Against the Odds

the resultant failure to provide his wife with material things he, and perhaps she, felt she deserved.

After ten pages of self-defense and reiteration of his life before and during NICAP, he addressed "some specific criticisms" that concerned his tardy handling of tax matters, pointing out that staff had ignored his instructions to record their own earnings and deductions. Gordon Lore, however, recalled that on one occasion around this time, he had visited Keyhoe's home and "found checks behind the piano," which in the context of his *mea culpa* supports the idea of his drastically poor financial management.[823] Moreover, due to his fiscal ineptitude, he was now considered by some to be "a second Townsend Brown."[824] Dick Hall would later write:

> Don was the world's worst businessman, keeping only the sketchiest of business records, and keeping us on the brink of being locked up on more than one occasion.[825]

Two days before Keyhoe's lengthy lament went out to staff, Ted Bloecher wrote to Ray Fowler regarding the June 1955 sighting of a disk east of Utica, New York, which was observed by civilian pilots and tracked by radar. Like Dick Hall, he was aware that Keyhoe withheld documents from NICAP:

> It's truly embarrassing to have to ask you—for the second time in as many weeks—for copies of sighting material we *should* have in the files, but cannot locate. It's very possible that Major Keyhoe might have seen it some time while he was in the office and taken it up to Luray with him; this has happened on a number of other occasions, and while I've repeatedly ask[ed] him about the Utica case, nothing has been forthcoming.[826]

On top of simmering tensions behind NICAP's doors, Keyhoe also had to address current dissatisfaction among members. In the latest NICAP box-ticking survey, the majority had agreed "they have had too much about Condon and the AF" and Don decided it was once more necessary to change tack to avoid losing members. In the future, there would be more attention on NICAP's "New Program," which would give much greater coverage to "the whence and why of UFOs" and would come out of "the wide blue yonder, instead of concentrating on reporting UFOs and their effects."[827] Keyhoe gave his assurance that, from now on, the *UFO Investigator* wouldn't "blast the

CR," though he had not abandoned the rebuttal and would continue to work on it.

The December falling-out between Bloecher and Keyhoe seemed to have been set aside, and they had restored their amicable relationship, agreeing that the "new program" was the best course of action and that the rebuttal should continue in the background. But internally there was skullduggery afoot. Dick Hall recalled that by April 1969 NICAP's "deterioration was pretty complete" and by autumn

> NICAP was literally falling apart and Don was unable or unwilling to take action. That was the point, after 11 years of strong loyalty, when I had to choose between NICAP and continuing to be an apologist for Keyhoe. With all that was at stake, I chose NICAP in the hope that Don could be let down gently and that the work he had fashioned could proceed to its culmination. That unavoidably involved working against him, in a sense, but really for him—as I rationalized it. We (Gordon and I) were going to try to activate the Board, as a last resort, to intervene and get things on the track.
>
> Unfortunately, what I didn't know at the time ... was that in the Last Days there were enough plotters and counter-plotters to people a comic spy story. The staff was by then in open revolt (which, in fact, had been building up for a year ...). Isabel [Davis] and Ted couldn't stand Gordon, and were engaged in their own private (and still not fully disclosed to me) plotting against him *and* Keyhoe. Gordon (with my help) was trying to keep a lid on the situation while quietly and discreetly plotting some kind of Board intervention. And Stuart, it turns out, was separately plotting with the Board without our knowledge, presumably with Isabel and Ted's knowledge .... So the right hand did not know what the left-hand was doing (we kept our activities quiet to avoid total disruption, and thinking that they were generally approved, which probably was a tactical error).[828]

In early autumn, another emergency appeal for money had gone out to members who once again sent contributions that saved the ship from sinking. Keyhoe thanked them for their help and admitted in the September-October *UFO Investigator* that it had been "embarrassing and an ordeal for Board and staff members" to issue another plea.[829] Even so, more money was urgently needed to keep things going, so he planned to issue another appeal. This proved to be the last straw for the Board.

In 1988 Dewey Fournet recalled that Hartranft, after talking with the Board, called to alert him that matters were now dire and it had been decided that the axe had to fall:

> Don was getting ready to put out another final appeal for funds, it was a very, very sad appeal, really, you could tell that the bottom could be dropping out if NICAP didn't get substantial contributions, and he [Hartranft] said we can't put up with this, we are losing members because of these constant appeals for additional funds besides the dues that they pay, and things are cluttering up ...[830]

Consequently, the September-October *UFO Investigator* was the last under Keyhoe's directorship. On December 3rd, the Board and Stuart Nixon, without Keyhoe's or Lore's knowledge, met "at the offices of Wald, Harkrader and Rockefeller in Washington, D.C."[831] Fournet could not attend because he "didn't have the time to go up there" to take part in discussions, so he authorized in writing his vote-by-proxy to be used as the Board saw fit. The meeting commenced at 10:30 am and took only four hours to bring to an end Donald Keyhoe's nearly thirteen-year tenure as head of NICAP.

The minutes of the meeting were blunt and decisive. Keyhoe's directorship was "terminated forthwith, and his active participation in the affairs of the corporation are hereby terminated at once [and he] shall be retired as an employee of NICAP as of December 31, 1969." If he wished, he could "retain indefinitely" the title of "emeritus" and his potential lump-sum severance pay "in no event shall ... exceed $1,600." As to Gordon Lore, the Board placed him "on an indefinite leave of absence (without pay)" and his arrears of pay, not to exceed $800, would be made if funds were available.

Before the meeting closed, Fournet was phoned and apprised of what had been decided, after which "he agreed to notify Major Keyhoe" of the Board's decision. He did so by telephone on December 5th—exactly a year after NICAP's "gripe session." Later, Fournet recalled:

> [S]ince I was the one that knew Don the best, they put the kiss of death on me to go ahead and call Don and tell him as gentle as I could that the Board had decided that he was

to become Director Emeritus, and that they get the acting directorship, and it fell on my lap to do that and that was one of the toughest things that I had to do in a long time, because I liked Don as a fellow, but Don got carried away on certain things.[832]

The axe struck Gordon within minutes of Fournet confirming to the Board that he had spoken to Don. Unlike Keyhoe, Lore was not given the courtesy of a "gentle" phone call, but received a curt telegram from Hartranft saying that "his services were no longer required." To make matters even worse, when he went to NICAP's office to collect his personal belongings, "he discovered that they had been searched, his desk had been rifled, and all the door locks had been changed by Stuart Nixon—by his own admission—allegedly under instructions from Mr. Hartranft."[833]

Gordon, still angry half a century later, remembered it vividly, as expressed personally to this author:

[Stuart] was directed by Colonel Joseph Bryan to crudely throw me out of my office in December 1969. He even demanded I immediately hand over the office keys to him and stuck out his grubby hand. I very nearly replied: "Open your lying mouth so I can throw it down your throat in the hope you will choke on it!" A bitter memory that five decades have not erased.[834]

It was all over.

Chapter 39:
After the Fall

It was perhaps symbolic that just six months after Keyhoe was ousted, NICAP's building was demolished to make way for the DuPont Circle subway station. The office was relocated further down Connecticut Avenue, at 1522, then by May 1971 was moved to 1730 Rhode Island Avenue, and by August 1972 had moved again, to 3535 University Boulevard W., Kensington, Maryland.

No less symbolic, only twelve days after Keyhoe and Lore's removal, the Air Force satisfied its long-held desire to get rid of the saucers. On December 17, 1969, "Secretary of the Air Force Robert C. Seamans, Jr., officially announced the termination of the Air Force's twenty-two-year study" and Blue Book was shut down. Dr. James McDonald called it "no great loss," though he feared that its closure would lead some to believe no problem existed.[835]

Coral Lorenzen was surprisingly phlegmatic about the collapse of her detested rival. She wrote to Rehn:

> The most recent news here is that NICAP has gone broke. One of the board members informs us that NICAP held a board meeting and when the board members found out what a financial mess they had, and how the membership records were so messed up, several of them resigned. Keyhoe was downgraded to "Director Emeritus", and Colonel Bryant [sic], an Ex-Air Force Colonel, has taken over as "President". This was bound to come; apparently those people never learned to manage money and that has been their problem. Although we have many differences, I hate to see it happen.[836]

On January 6, 1970, radio broadcaster Alan Douglas interviewed Keyhoe by phone in a broadcast titled "Have Flying Saucers Left?"[837] He was introduced as NICAP's Director of thirteen years, but it was almost exactly a month after he'd been ousted, so it's unclear whether this omission was erroneous or deliberate. Keyhoe made no direct reference to the cataclysm that had erupted in December, though his removal had been widely mentioned in the press. Even Jack Anderson's syndicated column, "Washington Merry-Go-Round," reported that "the world's largest group of believers, known as NICAP, is nearly bankrupt and leaderless."[838]

Keyhoe seemed evasive when he answered a phone-in question from a disgruntled NICAP member who queried a *New York Times* item of December 18th that named Col. Bryan as Acting Director. The caller wanted to know why members had not been informed of this change, and Keyhoe gave a somewhat nebulous response. He admitted there had been "some confusion" about this but said the fault lay with *The New York Times*, which had made an error in the titles of Bryan and also Lore. All this, he said, would "probably be clarified" in late January when there would be a Board meeting. Then he blurred the matter by adding that NICAP had been planning "reorganization, particularly in business procedures and so forth," and that "frankly, for a long time, I would like to get from under that and handle technical matters which I probably will do in future." He urged members to hang on for developments: "we've had some trouble but it looks now as though things are going to improve." This seemed to satisfy the caller, and it was not referred to again in the broadcast.

In this program, Keyhoe sounded very tired. He was seventy-two and had given the last twenty-two years of his life to the saucers, but the Air Force had emerged the victor in this long, attritional war, and worse yet he had been booted out of his own organization by his subordinates. Even so, he remained up for the fight and launched into a critique of the Condon Report, wholly optimistic that, any moment now, all would be revealed.

Moreover, he unwittingly confirmed what Richard Hall and Ted Bloecher had complained about—that he held documents outside of NICAP:

> I know some things that will break it and I've been trying independently of NICAP to get some of these things sprung open because in one case I know of—one case alone—would end this, would break it wide open if you could get the group involved to talk. Involves about 35 pilots and it's a case that's been suppressed for so long that practically no one will talk about it ...[839]

To which case he referred isn't known, but his on-air admission that he held such files was surely a red-flag for the intelligence agencies. Though it was true that NICAP's office files were open for inspection, this statement confirmed that Keyhoe secretly held others.

For a few months after the show, he seemed to keep a low profile, and during this period Hartranft et al. tried to create order. Strangely, financial matters suddenly improved when, after more than thirteen years of IRS refusal to allow tax-exempt status, it was granted without any argument or criticism about NICAP's policies, which it had previously used as grounds for denial.[840]

In May 1970, the first *UFO Investigator* under the new regime was issued, but it revealed nothing about the turmoil of recent months. In a few short paragraphs it said merely that Keyhoe had retired due to the "heavy administrative duties" that had kept him from "his writing and traveling interests." His title as Director had been retired with him, and he was now replaced by Col. Joseph Bryan III, wearing the newly created hat of President "pending election of a new President." On May 29th, the hat was passed to John Leland Acuff, a 37-year-old "businessman."

Little is found in public records about Acuff, but such as there is provides no clarity on how he made his living or with whom he associated. In 1948 he was a student at Bethesda's Chevy Chase High School, in 1950 his occupation is unknown, but when he married in 1953 he was recorded as a "student."[841]

In 1960, aged 28 and married for seven years, he was a student at American University and that same year was employed at Warren Teed, a pharmaceutical company. There he worked as a "detail manager," i.e., a sales rep pushing products to doctors.[842] In 1968 he was Executive Director at The Society of Photographic Scientists and Engineers (SPSE) in Washington and, by the time he joined NICAP, was head of his own management company, Acuff Associates.

Don, despite having been ousted from NICAP, became a member of its new Board in 1971. He represented to the Committee what the big names of his own Board had once done—prestige—but without him at the helm a great deal was lost that could not be regained. He did, though, keep an eye on its activities and would make his feelings about their plans or decisions known from time-to-time. His involvement was, of course, less than a shadow of what it had been, but his goal was unchanged. In October 1974 he wrote to Secretary of the Air Force John L. McLucas to inform him that "a startling UFO film ... prepared with Defense Department aid" was due to be released. It was *UFOs: Past, Present and Future* (re-released in 1976 and 1979 as *UFOs: It Has Begun*), produced by Adam F Sandler and Robert Emenegger. Don emphasized to McLucas that the film showed a fictionalized version of an actual landing at

Holloman AFB, which had been confirmed to him by a member of Sandler's staff as representing a genuine event. To bolster his case, he enclosed a three-page "suggested preparation plan and changes in the present AF operations," listing what action needed to be taken to end UFO secrecy.[843] He evidently had lost none of his fervor, nor his methodology.

NICAP staggered on for as long after Keyhoe's departure as it did under his directorship, and though it went through a relatively settled period— "marching to a new drum" under the new regime—it remained overall mired in uncertainty and difficulty, continuing to grapple with antagonism, hope, disappointment, suspicion, and managerial inadequacies.[844]

As to finances, things on the surface initially seemed to be improving. Members now, for the first time in NICAP's history, received their full quota of the *UFO Investigator* and no longer had to contend with the former incomprehensible renewal procedures or the frequent begging for funds. Moreover (though some NICAP veterans disagreed), the newsletter was well-written, wider-ranging, and had a more professional layout. Better yet, it was free of Keyhoe's interminable harangues about the Air Force, which often overwhelmed other UFO-related subjects that should have been covered.

But these much-needed improvements concealed yet more odd goings-on that eventually built up to another crisis for NICAP. Stuart Nixon, whom Dick Hall held "in very low esteem," had brought Acuff into the fold, who proved to be more interested in using NICAP to make money for his own management firm, Acuff Associates.[845] How he and Nixon became acquainted isn't known; both men had attended American University, though not at the same time, but no other connection between them is apparent. Acuff's own background is obscure—there were suspicions that he was a CIA plant—but whether or not that was the case, some believed he was using NICAP to line his own pockets.

The loyal Idabel Epperson hankered for the old regime. She wrote to Hartranft:

> For many years the name of Major Donald E Keyhoe and the word "NICAP" were synonymous. He had captured the hearts and won the confidence of the UFO minded public. Thousands joined NICAP—not because the name was NICAP—but because the name of Major Keyhoe was connected with it. Now the word NICAP stands alone without the prestige of Major Keyhoe's name. Now the various

news-media are less interested and so are prospective new members. It seems most unfortunate that some means of solving the financial crisis at NICAP could not have been worked out without the loss of Major Keyhoe.[846]

She didn't think much of the new management and, moreover, felt that something was amiss. She wrote to Keyhoe in March 1972 and expressed her disgust with Stuart Nixon and John Acuff:

> There is no need to tell you that NICAP is not the same … The heart of NICAP is missing—it seems now to be a mechanical robot—and a very heartless one, we have decided …We have been conscious of much intrigue going on here and there—but like the iceberg, we see only what is above the surface—but we know there is far more that is unseen.

Idabel pleaded with Keyhoe to write another book, which she and others thought "would sell like hot cakes," and in early October 1973 he obliged with *Aliens From Space*, the first of his UFO books to avoid the use of "Saucer" in the title.[847] In fact, Don had always disliked the term "flying saucers." In his early NICAP years, he said:

> I call 'em UFOs because even though you'll find the word flying saucers in the title of every book I've written that's er, because a lot of people don't know what UFOs are … it helps to make the subject a little more serious, it's a very, er, silly word - term - flying saucers, it's an unfortunate thing, if they'd have called 'em disks it would have helped or unidentified objects, but a lot of people hate to admit they believe in flying saucers just because of that name. Now I like to call 'em UFOs.[848]

Perhaps the title of his new book reflected a desire not only to ditch the term "flying saucers," but also to make the subject more encompassing. He told a reporter that "I've put everything on the line in this book … including my credibility."[849] *Aliens From Space* reiterated much of what had featured in his earlier books, including his perennial assertion that "The controversy now building up could finally lead to a showdown," but the later chapters considered what the aliens might look like and what might be their purpose for visiting Earth.[850] He suggested Operation Lure as a way to entice space visitors to make contact with humans, a plan that would involve using an isolated base with "unusual structures and novel displays" set up to attract the attention of aliens using "decoy discs." Though it sounded like something he might once have written for the pulps, it had first been suggested in the mid-sixties by NICAP special adviser Robert Spencer Carr and later expanded upon by Keyhoe and others.[851]

In *Aliens From Space*, he revealed that in late 1968 Operation Lure had been "far enough advanced" to merit a "confidential discussion with members of Congress," but by early October that year the plan was scuppered. Pentagon sources had told Keyhoe that the Condon Report was to be rushed through before the forthcoming election, because it was feared that if Richard Nixon won, his ear might be receptive to the "inside story" if given to him by the likes of McCormack, Goldwater, and Karth, leading to a delay in publishing the Condon Report.[852] Hence Operation Lure was dropped.

In the last few paragraphs of the book, Keyhoe was still optimistic and still banging his drum. From his position on NICAP's board, he was urging Acuff to take action—in effect to pick up where he had left off in 1969 and get back to "our original operating program and goals." His message was unchanged: NICAP must engage in an "all-out fight" to "end the cover-up," which of course, they never did.[853]

It might be inferred that Acuff/Nixon's passive, non-confrontational new order was approved of by the CIA. An undated, unreferenced document noted that NICAP

> Appears to be a fairly loose structure but rather efficient. Stuart Nixon (background in investigative journalism) [and] John Acuff ... (background unknown) make up ... the Editorial Review Board [which] relies heavily on both a loosely structured advisory group and a fairly well developed and well placed network of investigators.

As to the involvement of CIA and intelligence folks, the document reported that

> The advisory group ... also includes some ex-CIA and Defense Intelligence types who advise on investigative techniques and NICAP/Government relations. There does not seem to be any logical or systematic program by which these advisors are chosen, but rather the procedure seems to be to

simply offer one's services to the organization ... Often the advisors simply joined NICAP (a rather easy task since all it takes is a specified membership fee) ... The system of investigators is a good one.[854]

Acuff would remain as NICAP President until he resigned in October 1978, by which time it had become clear that he was using the Committee for his own financial gain by charging exorbitant "management fees" that were bleeding it dry. Gordon Lore later wrote:

> In the early 1970s, NICAP was operating on a budget of about $50,000 annually. Acuff Associates, however, took around $35,000 of this for "contracting services", and Acuff later indicated NICAP owed him approximately $20,000. Paltry sums—$76 one year, $20 the next—went into "general research."[855]

It's possible that Acuff's skimming of NICAP's funds and his eventual resignation was to some extent rooted in his own financial problems. In January 1976, Acuff Associates was listed under "Notice of Forfeiture of Charter of Delinquent Corporations" for non-payment of various taxes.[856] Perhaps, having milked NICAP dry, his debts eventually made it prudent for him to move on.

Dick Hall, still tangled with NICAP's interests, learned that Nixon had also worked for Acuff Associates but had been sacked from it some weeks prior to his leaving NICAP. He thought Nixon had been "plotting" with some of the Board against Acuff as a way to "worm his way back into power." Acuff himself, when questioned about Nixon's departure said the thing was "mutual."[857] Whatever the real story, Stuart was no longer cozy with Acuff and he quit (some say he was "sacked") on December 31, 1973. A few weeks later, he wrote to Dewey Fournet, who was by then on the Board of Governors, complaining that

> NICAP is now a one-man operation, with Jack filling all positions [though he] asked me to handle the newsletter on a free-lance basis for $100 a month, but since my former editorial assistant ... was getting $250 a month just to help me, I politely declined. Jack now receives that $250 plus all

lecture fees (which I never got) plus some other things ... I strongly believe there is a conflict of interest between Jack's role as President of NICAP (and a Board member) and his role as a contractor to NICAP. [H]e benefits financially and can continue to run NICAP as part of his own business. He is Executive Director of a medical society, which he also operates out of his office, and is involved in a dozen other ventures. NICAP provides enough money ... to underwrite all of this overhead.[858]

He added, "my credibility is not too good these days since I was the one (as you know) who proposed Jack's name."[859]

Gordon Lore last saw Keyhoe in 1973 at a press conference held to announce his new book *Aliens From Space*, and when the two got together later, it was no surprise that the subject of Nixon came up. He asked Don if he thought Nixon had been a CIA plant, to which he replied, "No. He's too dumb for that."[860] In reality, Keyhoe's almost permanent absence from the office during his tenure as Director had left him in no position to accurately make such a judgement, but others in NICAP who had worked with Nixon harbored deep suspicions and a strong dislike for him. Nonetheless, Hartranft still rated Stuart sufficiently to ask him to join the Board, but he replied that he wouldn't unless "other Board members feel the present situation is inconsistent with NICAP's best interests." The board would have to decide if it wanted "to be the 'hip-pocket' operation of a contractor.'"

Nixon's ambitions for NICAP—whatever they were—came to nothing.

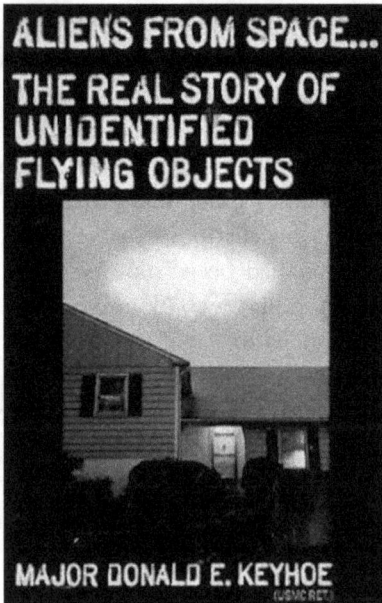

ALIENS FROM SPACE...
THE REAL STORY OF UNIDENTIFIED FLYING OBJECTS

MAJOR DONALD E. KEYHOE (USMC RET.)

Chapter 40: Aftermath

There can be no doubt that the Condon Report was the final nail in the coffin for both NICAP and for objective UFO research, but it's largely thanks to Keyhoe that the Colorado flimflam was exposed. Though neither he nor anyone else could overcome its effect, history has shown that his criticisms were entirely valid, and today the Condon Report is almost universally condemned as a travesty.

After its release, Robert Low's reputation was trashed, and perhaps as a result, he quietly left Colorado in 1970 to be vice-president of administration at Portland University in Oregon. In early 1974, he relinquished that position to take up part-time duties responsible for minority hiring.

Condon generally received less criticism than his sidekick, no doubt due to his illustrious academic track record, though "as a result of the *Look* article he was receiving phone threats and ... he'd had to ask the police for protection."[861]

In any case he retired in 1970, but as it turned out neither man lived long enough to see much of the devastating impact of their collaboration. Condon died on March 26, 1974, from "complications resulting from heart disease," and in November 1975, Low and his wife, flying from Red Bluff, California, died when their light aircraft spiraled out of the sky over wooded mountains near Myrtle Creek, Oregon.[862]

Dr. James E. McDonald, who continued to be critical of the Condon Report, attempted suicide by gunshot to the head on April 9, 1971, but succeeded only in blinding himself. On June 12th, he somehow convinced a taxi driver to leave him at a desert canyon a few miles from his home, where his body was found the next day; his second attempt to die by gunshot had been successful. *The UFO Investigator*, perhaps reflecting how remote the new regime was from NICAP's history, devoted only a short paragraph to McDonald's death, briefly acknowledging his UFO work but offering no praise or thanks for his support of NICAP, which he surely deserved. In unexpected contrast, the *APRO Bulletin* gave him a dignified and detailed tribute, describing him as APRO's "good friend and colleague and ... a brilliant, energetic supporter." If Coral Lorenzen felt any guilt about her years-long vindictiveness toward him, so vividly expressed to Gus Rehn, she kept it to herself. Now that he was dead she could afford to display a graciousness toward him that was entirely absent when he was alive. APRO itself came to an end when Coral died in April 1988, preceded by her husband's passing two years earlier.

In June 1972, Ken Purdy, the man who had pulled Keyhoe into UFO world, also died of a self-inflicted gunshot to the head, and ten years later, radio and TV presenter Dave Garroway, who'd been so supportive of Keyhoe and NICAP, died the same way.

* * *

In May 1969 while NICAP was in its death throes, a fledgling group, the Midwest UFO Network, was created, which by 1973 had become the Mutual UFO Network (MUFON). Today it is the best-known organization of its kind. Many of NICAP's old sweats and supporters joined the group, notably Dick Hall who served as International Coordinator and then as Editor of its journal.

In 1976, Walter H. Andrus, Jr., International Director of MUFON, invited Don to join the organization, but he declined. His reply to Andrus revealed that he was still actively working to end Air Force censorship. A recent bout of flu had slowed him down and prevented his "plans" from being "far enough along for me to discuss, at least confidentially." However,

> I can say this: The AF has gotten itself into a serious predic-
> ament, and there are some HQ members who are trying to
> figure a way out which won't set off another Watergate. (I
> don't want to be quoted on that yet, because the ones who
> are trying to end the cover-up could be in real trouble if cer-
> tain highups learned they have been secretly fighting the cen-
> sorship.) It is because of this critical situation that I shall have
> to hold off [joining] MUFON'S operations.

He pointed out to Andrus that becoming a member of MUFON at this time, when he was still on NICAP's board, "might add a little problem to my tricky situation there."

It's evident from this letter that he was still chafed at how he'd been ousted from his Directorship in 1969 and believed it was for some purpose other than bad management. He wrote:

> As you must know, the executive committee pulled a fast one

to get rid of me and my attacks on the AF and CIA cover-up. I could have disclosed how this was done to NICAP Sub-committees and it would have blown NICAP to bits. But I'd spent so much time I hated to destroy the organization, so I took the jolt (even though they owed me well over $20,000, money I'd let NICAP use instead of giving me my authorized pay.) They tried to get me off the Board, but I told them I'd blow them up if they took another step. I let them know I was staying so I could keep an eye on what they were doing, with the intention of getting NICAP back on the track if that's possible.

At this time, the board were trying to replace Acuff "because of complaints about Acuff's double role, director and also head of the company supposedly running NICAP," but he'd nonetheless asked Keyhoe to write an editorial for *The UFO Investigator*. Don told Andrus, "why, I don't know; maybe they think I'd go away and let it seem NICAP is doing a good job against the censorship."

He added, off the record, that he was "surprised to say the least" that APRO had approached him "with an offer of assistant to the research director, tied in with a plan to get NICAP back on track or blast it publicly." (At that time, APRO's research director was James A. Harder, PhD.) Coral Lorenzen, he said, "has been sore at me every [*sic*] since I became NICAP director; though I helped her build up her membership."[863]

Two years later, on July 29 and 30, 1978, MUFON held a symposium in Dayton, Ohio, former home of Blue Book, and Keyhoe was among the celebrated guest speakers. His talk—inevitably—was titled "Behind the UFO Secrecy." Here he met for the first time J. Allen Hynek, by now the most prominent name in saucer circles and head of the Center for UFO Studies (CUFOS), which he had founded in 1973. The two men shook hands, then shared the platform "on the same side of the UFO subject." Heartwarmingly, when Keyhoe was introduced, he received a "well-deserved ovation" from the audience. Now eighty-one, it had been three decades since he began to tackle UFO secrecy, yet despite repeated set-backs and defeats, his optimism was unchanged and he assured the gathering that "the pressure to end censorship is rapidly increasing."

Though hatchets were being buried and due respect given at this gathering, behind the scenes NICAP was entering another period of turmoil that would draw Dick Hall once more unto the fray. In August, he was alarmed to hear that Acuff was trying to sell off "the organizations' assets," thereby potentially placing its valuable files in jeopardy. Yet again he rolled up his sleeves and fought to prevent this calamity. He later wrote:

> For about five months, off and on, we negotiated with Hartranft, Richardson, and Charles Lombard, an acknowledged former CIA employee and aide to Senator Barry Goldwater. Also involved in the negotiations was Dr. J. Allen Hynek, Scientific Director of the Center for UFO Studies [CUFOS]. Richardson and Lombard at first seemed interested in reviving NICAP. In our view, however, other organizations (especially MUFON and CUFOS) were now the leaders in the field, and we were not in favor of perpetuating the NICAP organization, only in preserving its files.[864]

Among many options under consideration were affiliation with MUFON or CUFOS or "a combined umbrella group to pool the resources," but Hall remained doubtful about NICAP's existing Board. It seemed to display a "complete ignorance of UFO history, UFO groups, and prominent UFOlogists," and he "wondered if there were some hidden agenda behind their machinations."[865]

For a time, Dick's name was in the hat to become NICAP's new President, but he recalled with a hint of bitterness that after Acuff "was forced to resign," Lombard and another new Board member, John Fisher, who as "head of the American Security Council and Communication Corporation of America," opposed his candidacy in preference to the appointment of "some retired Government official."

This "official" was "a retired CIA employee," Alan N. Hall (no relation to Dick), who had supposedly taken up the position "as a post-retirement hobby [and] operated out of his home without access to the files," leaving NICAP to become "a hollow shell of its former self."[866]

The files, however, were salvaged:

> A short time later the Center for UFO Studies purchased the NICAP assets, the most important of which was the comprehensive sighting case investigative files which we had created with over 20 years of blood, sweat, and tears. Originally CUFOS intended to keep NICAP in existence as

a separate entity, but—in effect—NICAP was absorbed into CUFOS and ceased to exist as an organization. The NICAP sighting files have been preserved and remain an invaluable collection of significant data and historical information.[867]

According to Dick Hall in his 1994 account of NICAP's history, the organization closed in 1980, but in 1981 Keyhoe was still pursuing an end to UFO secrecy. He wrote to MUFON's Walt Andrus that, "off the record,"

> I'm writing a new book [which] reveals increasingly serious fears and tensions at the Pentagon which have been confidentially revealed to me by censors, members of AF Intelligence, and other important contacts I have made over the years. Even now, I am sometimes surprised at highly secret information these sources have entrusted to me. Their reason is growing fear that the almost incredible cover-up may be nearing the breaking point almost too late for the desperately needed preparation of the public ... I believe it will have a powerful effect on the public and the press, without causing a terrible panic. I've had a lot of private advice from my secret sources as to how the dangers can be carefully revealed along with things we can and should do in the line of defenses, if needed ... the public should be carefully prepared for whatever may come.[868]

The book was never written, leaving us to wonder today, what he had learned from his secret informants that had the potential to create "terrible panic" for which "defenses" might be needed for "whatever may come."

* * *

From January 1957 until December 1969, Keyhoe and NICAP were virtually one-and-the-same. After he was removed as Director, it slid into relative obscurity and continued to suffer from internal strife and financial woes. But without Don's vigor and unrelenting determination to overturn UFO secrecy, it could not hope—or perhaps did not intend—to be the internationally-renowned leader in objective UFO research. Keyhoe was, however, happy to see MUFON take up the torch. To Andrus he wrote:

> I'm very glad you have so many former NICAP members who gave me such valuable assistance and advice. As you say, they were really a great team for NICAP—and now they're a great team for you and MUFON.[869]

NICAP today is visible only as an old-style website, with many broken internal links and a near-impossible to navigate, incomplete database. Its "coordinator and archivist" is Francis Ridge, who maintains an up-to-date UFO news page on the site, but otherwise it is in a neglected and forlorn condition. Though it contains many documents of high value to researchers, only the most dedicated and patient can hope to find what they need.

Don has yet to receive the wider recognition his endeavors surely deserved, despite his unwavering aim to end government secrecy about UFOs. Even so, he probably could not have imagined that in the third decade of the 21st century, the "big break" he had been expecting since 1950, and for which he had endured so much in its pursuit, would still not have come.

Epilogue

Sixty years after Keyhoe's adventure with Charles Lindbergh, he was visited at his Luray home by Canadian author Michael Parfit, who was seeking material for his forthcoming 1988 book, *Chasing The Glory: Travels Across America*, which was an account of his own flight following the 1927 route taken by the Lone Eagle and Keyhoe. A frail, though smiling Don answered the door. When Parfit explained his purpose, the Major said he could tell him quite a few things about Lindbergh, but Helen then approached and asked the writer to return the next day, in part because her husband was unwell.

On Parfit's return, Keyhoe had forgotten that his visitor had come to talk about Lindbergh. Thinking the topic would be UFOs, he said "so much information kept pouring into me, and I knew darn well it wasn't all correct." Realizing he had strayed, Helen brought out a cherished photo of Don and Lindbergh to remind him of the subject matter. In spite of her decades of ill-health, she appeared much more robust and mentally alert than her husband, whose memory was now sketchy, interspersed with long silences.

Keyhoe's recollections of his tour and his friendship with Lindbergh were fragmentary but nonetheless still warm and close to his heart. He remembered him as "a great guy … a great pilot" who had "the happiest smile," but then he fell silent, lost in some other place. Helen tried to fill the void and told Parfit about the Peeping Tom at Lindbergh's window back in 1931. Contrary to what would later be written about this event, she said that Keyhoe had always since regretted not advising Slim that he should "have something on the windows to protect him."[870]

Parfit left, having learned little, but was nonetheless delighted to have spoken to the Major, even though he was evidently in a gentle decline.

By November 1988, Keyhoe, now aged ninety-one, was a patient at the Life Care Center in New Market, about twenty minutes away from his home in Virginia, where he died at 10 pm on the 29th from "possible pulmonary embolus" and "infirmities of age."

His death certificate cited his former occupation not as a writer, nor a

UFO researcher, but a US Marine.[871]

* * *

In the basement of Keyhoe's Luray home was a specially built, triple-locked room that was part of an "extensive security system" he had installed. It included external floodlights around the property and sensors inside the house leading to the basement, so he "could see when someone was walking up or down [the] steps." It was presumably in this room he kept the files withheld from NICAP and the names of his anonymous contacts, both inside and outside intelligence and the military. Soon after his death, this room was broken into by "agents" thought to be from the Secret Service who "carted out boxes of files." The door frame today still bears the scars of their forced entry.[872]

What Helen felt about this can only be imagined, but in her widowed years she cheerfully received visits from some of the old NICAP crew, including Dick Hall. He had by then put behind him the anger and angst that had blighted his relationship with Keyhoe, but it seems that Helen never told him or anyone else about the break-in and removal of the files. Evidently the "agents" hoped to find something that was not held in NICAP's now-preserved office files that, in any case, had always been open to serious researchers. They presumably also found the "highly secret information" Don intended to expose in his unfinished last book.

Helen survived her husband until April 1995, when she passed away age ninety-one at Montvue Nursing Home in Luray. Only thirteen months later, daughter Caroline, who had worked as a medical transcriber, died at the age of fifty-one, and the next month Keyhoe's son from his first marriage also died. Daughter Kathleen, as far as is known, still lives, though she does not respond to interview requests. Margaret, the first Mrs. Keyhoe, died a few days short of her 100th birthday, only a month after Helen. Don's sister, Katherine, never married and she died two months after him, in February 1989. None of Keyhoe's children had children of their own.

Donald and Helen Keyhoe rest together at Green Hill Cemetery in Luray, and from time-to-time visitors leave small tokens or miniature US flags at the grave as a mark of respect and remembrance for the man who, at great personal cost, battled for almost half his long life, against the odds, to end UFO secrecy.

Acknowledgements

I am grateful to many for assistance and/or permission to quote from their own work or personal collections. I am especially indebted to:

Michael Swords, Professor Emeritus, Western Michigan University for permitting use of his extensive NICAP archives, which have formed the spine of this work; to writer Daniel H. Mintz of New York who generously shared with me his research material for his own Keyhoe project: to Rob Swiatek of MUFON, who shared with me his collection of Ed Ruppelt's and Idabel Epperson's correspondence with Keyhoe; to Hakan Blomqvist of Sweden's *Archives For The Unexplained* (AFU), who provided me with valuable documents relating to Clara Colcord John, Thomas Townsend Brown, the Coral Lorenzen/K. Gosta Rehn correspondence, and some documentation on Meade Layne; and to the late Gordon Lore, former NICAP Assistant Director, whose helpfulness and enthusiasm for this book has been crucial.

My thanks also to: Tim Binnall, Bill Chalker, Jerome Clark, Wendy Connors and Rod Dyke (Archives for UFO Research), Antonio Huneeus, David Jacobs, Leslie Kean, Isaac Koi, Mark Pilkington, Fran Ridge, Alejandro Rojas, Paul Schatzkin, Doug Skinner, Jay Triche, Thomas Tulien, and the archivists at the US Naval Academy (Annapolis) and Pensacola Naval Air Station.

Endnotes

[1] Keyhoe, Donald E, *Flying with Lindbergh* (G P Putnam's Sons, 1928), p. 36.

[2] Ibid.

[3] Their claim has been disputed and continues to engender speculation.

[4] US Census: *1900*; Census Place: *Center, Wapello, Iowa*; Roll: 463; Page: 8; Enumeration District: 0124

[5] Waterman, Harrison L, History of Wapello County, Iowa, (The S J Clarke Publishing Company 1914), p. 275, https://archive.org/details/historyofwapello01inwate/page/244/mode/2up.

[6] *Ottumwa Tri-Weekly Courier* (Ottumwa, Iowa) Jan 12, 1909, p.5.

[7] *The Big Picture*, produced by The Army Audiovisual Center, National Archives and Records Administration, https://archive.org/details/gov.archives.arc.2569655.

[8] *Ottumwa Courier*, Sep 25, 1900, p. 7.

[9] Ibid., May 22, 1903, p. 5.

[10] Record of Patents, USA General Land Office Patent no: 145564, Jul 21, 1910.

[11] *McCoy's Ottumwa City Directory*, 1912.

[12] This school, built 1899, was closed in 1923 and replaced by the current high school.

[13] "Much to the surprise of …" See *OHS Yearbook* 1930. "Rare courtier …" See *Argus Yearbook* for years 1914 and 1915. In the latter, it is humorously implied that he was a political hot-head with respect to the ongoing conflict in Mexico.

[14] Carter's examination date was postponed.

[15] Reynolds, Clark G, *On the Warpath in the Pacific: Admiral Jocko Clark and the Fast Carriers,* Library of Naval Biography, 2013.

[16] Laning, Admiral Harris, *An Admiral's Yarn,* Naval War College Press, 1999.

[17] *The 1920 Lucky Bag: The Annual of the Regiment of Midshipmen, United States Naval Academy* by U.S. Naval Academy and M.O.J., 1919.

[18] Stevens, William O. and Carroll S. Alden, *A Guide to Annapolis and the Naval academy,* Lord Baltimore Press, Baltimore, MD.

[19] *Lucky Bag,* 1920.

[20] *Ottumwa Review,* Aug 18, 1916.

[21] Lucky Bag 1920 entry for Eugene Willard Kiefer (later Commander, captained

USS *Patoka* in WWII).

[22] *A Brief History of Marine Corps Aviation,* Historical Branch, G-3 Division, Headquarters, US Marine Corps, Washington, D.C.

[23] Ibid.

[24] Johnson, Lieutenant Colonel Edward C, USMC, *Marine Corps Aviation: The Early Years 1912-1940*, (1977).

[25] Keyhoe, Donald E, "Riding The Wind on a Gasbag," *Billings Gazette*, Nov 14, 1928.

[26] Naval Air Station Pensacola, Florida, (Naval History and Heritage Command), https://www.history.navy.mil/browse-by-topic/organization-and-administration/installations/naval-air-station-pensacola.html.

[27] Flying officers of the U.S.N. (Naval Aviation War Book Committee, Washington, D.C., 1919), https://archive.org/details/flyingofficersof00nava/mode/2up?ref=ol&view=theater.

[28] *Chronicle-Telegram* (Elyria, Ohio) Feb 8, 1929, p.1.

[29] *Billings Gazette* (Billings, Montana) Nov 4, 1928, pp. 1- 3.

[30] *Pensacola Journal* (Pensacola, Florida) Feb 27, 1920, p. 2.

[31] Ibid., Jan 2, 1921, p. 7.

[32] Johnson, Edward C., *Marine Corps Aviation: The Early Years 1912-1940*, 1977.

[33] Kaufman, Roxanne M., *100 Years of Marine Corps Aviation : An Illustrated History,* (Dept. of the Navy, 2011).

[34] *Annual Reports of the Navy Department for the Fiscal Year (Including Operations to November 15, 1922)*, United States Navy Dept, U.S. Government Printing Office, 1923, p. 33.

[35] *Colville Examiner* (Colville, Washington) Mar 19, 1921, p.1; *U.S., Marine Corps Muster Rolls, 1798-1958*, The National Archives, Washington, DC.

[36] *Annual Reports of the Navy Department for the Fiscal Year* (Including Operations to Nov 15, 1922).

[37] *Logansport-Pharos Tribune* (Logansport, Indiana) Nov 27, 1928, p. 7.

[38] Keyhoe was formally transferred from Quantico to Washington, D.C., on Nov 24, 1923.

[39] Vernal and Clara were married on Nov 21, 1922, in Washington, D.C.

[40] Research has not established if Keyhoe converted to Catholicism upon their marriage.

[41] No record was found of a relevant birth in 1923/24.

[42] Further details see SP 0004 Joseph E. Bishop collection, 1920s, https://www.dchistory.org/uploads/fa/sp0004.pdf.

[43] Military Pay Chart 1922-1942, https://www.navycs.com/charts/1922-officer-pay-chart.html; Report of The High School Visitor, University of Illinois for the year 1920-21, University of Illinois, Urbana, 1921, https://tinyurl.com/3fszte4n.

[44] Extensive research by this author did not find any earlier articles by Keyhoe.

[45] *Sunday Star* (Washington, D.C.) Nov 11, 1923.

[46] *Leatherneck* was first published on Nov 17, 1917. It became a magazine in 1925. Keyhoe's editorship was preceded by Lt. Harvey B. Alban.

[47] *The Leatherneck*, Vol 7, no 19 Apr 19, 1924. Also *Muster Roll of Officers and Enlisted Men of the US Marine Corps,* Marine Corps Institute Detachment, Marine Barracks, Washington, D.C., Jan. 1 to 31, 1925.

[48] Keyhoe's injury cut his ulnar nerve, which innervates the little and ring fingers. He would have difficulty using his little finger for typing thereafter.

[49] *Weird Tales* v5 #4, April 1925, p. 37.

[50] Sources for his appointment give different dates. The C&GS organization tree of October 1925 lists Keyhoe as Editor, but its *Bulletin* of Nov 1, 1925, lists him as probational Assistant Editor. The *Bulletin* of August 1926 records him as Assistant Editor. There are no surviving records relating to the date of his initial transfer to the C&GS.

[51] *Evening Star* (Washington, D.C.) Feb 23, 1929, p. 2.

[52] *Weird Tales* v7 #1, Jan 1926 p. 5.

[53] *Daniel Guggenheim Fund For The Promotion of Aeronautics,* Pamphlet Number One: Organization, p. 4.

[54] *Daniel Guggenheim Fund For The Promotion of Aeronautics,* Pamphlet Number Two (1928) p. 14.

[55] Keyhoe, Donald E., *Short Sketches of the Aeronautics Branch Personnel,* Aviation, July 13th, 1929 p. 142.

[56] The *Josephine Ford* had previously won the Ford Reliability Tour and had attained some speed records, within the US.

[57] *Annual Report of the Director, United States Coast and Geodetic Survey to the Secretary of Commerce for the Fiscal Year Ended June 30, 1927* (United States Government Printing Office, Washington, 1927).

[58] *Salt Lake Telegram* (Salt Lake City, Utah) Oct 31, 1926.

[59] Keyhoe, *Flying with Lindbergh*, p. 3.

[60] *Evening Star* (Washington, D.C.) Apr 18, 1927, p. 5

[61] Keyhoe, *Flying with Lindbergh,*, p. 4

[62] Ibid., 5.

[63] Ibid., 6.

[64] Ibid., 8.

[65] Today Hempstead House is a wedding venue.

[66] This anticipation caused the book to be sold in vast numbers, but readers were disappointed with the few pages he wrote about his trans-Atlantic flight.

[67] Keyhoe, *Flying with Lindbergh*, pp. 9-10.

[68] Ibid., 10.

[69] Ibid., 12.

[70] Because the fuel tanks were located ahead of the cockpit for safety in case of an accident, Lindbergh could not see directly in front, except by using a periscope on the left side or by turning the airplane and looking out a side window.

[71] Keyhoe, *Flying With Lindbergh*, p. 126.

[72] *Daily Dispatch* (Brainerd, Minnesota) Aug 30, 1927, p. 9.

[73] Very brief footage showing Lindbergh inspecting this model and also showing Keyhoe chatting to a small group under the wing of the Fairchild, while Lindbergh prepares to take off, is found at "Charles Lindbergh at Tucson, AZ, September 23-24, 1927," https://vimeo.com/331615015.

[74] Arrived Moundsville Aug 4, 1927 at 1:30 pm, see *West Virginia Archives and History*, https://images.wvculture.org/history/transportation/lindbergh01.html. Note that another source says Lindbergh inspected the plane in detail and the bottle had been cracked over it earlier by famous pilot James Doolittle when the plane was named "Lone Eagle," see *Charles Lindbergh, An American Aviator*, http://www.charleslindbergh.com/history/moundsville.asp.

[75] *Lincoln State Journal* (Lincoln, Nebraska) Aug 31, 1927, p. 8.

[76] This incident is told by Keyhoe in his book *Flying With Lindbergh*. However, in his article "Sky Tourists" (*Charleston Daily Mail,* Charleston, West Virginia, Jul 1929, p. 4), he writes that he and Phil Love buzzed the Indian camp at the same time as Lindbergh, in their own plane. It's not known why he gave this different account, though it was written with greater respect toward the native Americans than that which Lindbergh expressed to Keyhoe.

[77] Keyhoe, *Flying With Lindbergh*, p.49.

[78] Keyhoe, "Lindbergh Four Years After," *Saturday Evening Post*, May 30, 1931.

[79] Fairfield Daily *Ledger Journal* (Fairfield, Iowa) Aug 20, 1927.

[80] Nine people were allowed into the cockpit with Lindbergh during the tour. See *Charles Lindbergh, An American Aviator* for flight log: www.charleslindbergh.com/history/gugtour.asp.

[81] Lindbergh's extra 2,000 miles were due to his solo flying during the tour.

[82] Keyhoe, *Flying with Lindbergh*, p. 295.

[83] *Evening Star* (Washington, D.C) Feb 23, 1929.

[84] Found also mentioned as "Plucky Lindy." This author was unable to trace a copy of this book under either title.

[85] *Saturday Evening Post*, May 30, 1931.

[86] *Aviation Week*, Jul 13, 1929, pp. 143-145, http://archive.org/details/Aviation_Week_1929-07-13

[87] Helen is also recorded as Helen Wilson Gardner, and after marriage, as Helen Gardner Keyhoe.

[88] Wendy Connors and Roderick Dyke, "Profiles in Ufology," *Archives for UFO Research*, https://archive.org/details/ProfilesInUfologyMajorDonaldE.KeyhoeDr.JamesE.McDonaldFrankEdwardsGuide/18.mp3

[89] Friedman, David M., *The Immortalists: Charles Lindbergh, Dr Alexis Carrel, and Their Daring Quest to Live Forever*, Harper Collins, 2007, p. 40.

[90] *Morning World* (Monroe, Louisiana) Jan 3, 1932, p. 19.

[91] *Tenth census of the state of Florida, 1935*; (Microfilm series S 5, 30 reels); Record Group 001021; State Library and Archives of Florida, Tallahassee, Florida; *Washington DC City Directory*, 1937, p. 1679; *Evening Star*, Washington, D.C., Mar 23, 1935, p. B3.

[92] 1940; Census Place: Mount Vernon, Fairfax, Virginia; Roll: m-t0627-04261; Page: 2A; Enumeration District: 30-19A.

[93] Cantril, Hadley, *The Invasion from Mars: A Study in the Psychology of Panic*, with the assistance of Hazel Gaudet and Herta Herzog, with a new Introduction by Albert H. Cantril (Transaction Publishers, New Brunswick (USA) and London (UK) 2005), https://archive.org/details/invasionfrommars0000cant_g3i1/mode/2up.

[94] Keyhoe, Donald Edward, *If War Comes: M-Day — What Your Government Plans for YOU*, E. P. Dutton & Co, New York, 1940.

[95] *Cincinnati Post* (Cincinnati, Ohio) Jul 15, 1940, p. 6.

[96] *Evening Star* (Washington, D.C.) Jul 28, 1940, p. 65.

[97] Daly was a White House correspondent, according to Robin R. Cutler's 2017 article, "Cosmopolitan's 'Shocking Expose' of Real Spies and Intelligence in 1940" https://robinrcutler.com/2017/01/17/cosmopolitans-shocking-expose-of-real-spies-and-intelligence-in-1940/.

[98] "Traffic in Murder," *Cosmopolitan*, April 1940.

[99] *The Times Dispatch* (Richmond, Virginia) June 4, 1940.

[100] "Straight Up To Hell," *This Week Magazine,* supplement to *Evening Star* (Washington D.C), May 25, 1941, p. 4.

[101] *Evening Star,* Washington, D.C., Mar 6, 1943. Also see *Muster Roll of Officers and Enlisted Men of the US Marine Corps, Company 'C' Headquarters Battalion, 1 April to 30 April 1943.* The date of Keyhoe's promotion from 1st Lieutenant to Captain is not found in the records available to this author, but he was listed at that rank in *Muster Rolls* of Jan 1943.

[102] Confidential letter to NICAP staff, Feb 20, 1969, from The Archives of Professor Michael Swords. Other documentation available to this author gives no further insight on Keyhoe's activities in connection with policy decisions.

[103] The other writers were: Robert L. Taylor of *The New Yorker*; Roark Bradford, author of *All God's Children*; Jesse Stuart, author of *Taps for Private Tussie*; Hannibal Coons of *Colliers* magazine; Bernard Livingstone of Associated Press; William E. Buckley, a publishing executive; Robert Osborn, a freelance illustrator; and Ruth Oviatt, who worked in advertising.

[104] *Abilene Reporter-News,* Sep 22, 1946.

[105] The author is grateful to Daniel H. Mintz for directly confirming this with Warner Bros in Los Angeles.

[106] *Courier* (Ottumwa, Iowa) Sep 24, 1945.

[107] *Muster Roll of Officers and Enlisted Men of the US Marine Corps, Company 'C' Headquarters Battalion, 1 Oct to 31 Oct 1945.*

[108] As described in *National Military Establishment Office of Public Information: Memorandum to the Press,* released April 27, 1949. This was "a digest of preliminary studies."

[109] Keyhoe, Donald E. *The Flying Saucers Are Real,* Fawcett Publications, 1950.

[110] Summary of the Frank Edwards talk at the CSI New York meeting, Apr 28,1956, "Flying Saucers, in, on and off the air"(CUFOS).

[111] Keyhoe, *The Flying Saucers Are Real,* p.12.

[112] Ibid., 12.

[113] In May 1949, Keyhoe was aware that "it had been months since any important

sightings had been reported," so evidently he was keeping abreast of press reports. See *The Flying Saucers Are Real*, p. 13.

[114] Keyhoe, *The Flying Saucers Are Real*, p. 3; Lee Munsick interviewed by Daniel H. Mintz, Mar 2016.

[115] Lee Munsick, ibid.

[116] Dave Garroway Show, Apr 20, 1965, Wendy Connors and Roderick Dyke, "Profiles in Ufology," *Archives for UFO Research*, https://archive. org/details/ProfilesInUfologyMajorDonaldE.KeyhoeDr.JamesE. McDonaldFrankEdwardsGuide/13.mp3

[117] Keyhoe, Donald E, *Flying Saucers From Outer Space* (Tandem 1969 Reprint). p. 42.

[118] Ibid., 20.

[119] Ruppelt, Edward J., *The Report on Unidentified Flying Objects*, Doubleday & Company, Inc, Garden City, New York 1956, p. 61.

[120] *The Journal Herald* (Dayton, Ohio) Apr 2, 1951, p. 3

[121] Jim Bishop's obituary of Boal see *Oneonta Star* (Oneonta, New York), Jan 6, 1965, p. 4.

[122] On Sep 28, 1964, Boal died in a fire in his third floor New York apartment, due to having fallen asleep with a cigarette in his hand. "Fire Kills Diner's Club Editor in His Apartment in E. 57th St.; Sam Boal Wrote More Than 500 Articles in Journalistic Career That Began at 19," *The New York Times*, September 29, 1964, p. 18, https://www.nytimes.com/1964/09/29/archives/fire-kills-diners-club-editor-in-his-apartment-in-e-57-th-st-sam.html.

[123] Keyhoe, *Flying Saucers From Outer Space*, p. 41

[124] Ibid., 42.

[125] Ibid.

[126] Keyhoe, *The Flying Saucers Are Real*, p.108.

[127] Ibid., 109.

[128] Ibid.

[129] On Jan 2, 1950, Edwards' broadcasts, sponsored by the American Federation of Labour (AFL), were expanded to 38 states and 153 stations to be broadcast by the Mutual Broadcasting System: see *St. Joseph Union-Observer* (St. Joseph, Missouri), Dec 30, 1949. He was dismissed by Mutual in 1954, not because of his UFO reports but because he would not desist in mentioning the AFL's labor union rivals, see NICAP, http://www.nicap.org/bios/NICAP-Bios/Edwards.htm.

[130] Edwards, Frank, *My First 10,000,000 Sponsors*, Ballantine Books, 1956, p. 114.

[131] Keyhoe, *The Flying Saucers Are Real*, p. 111

[132] *Daily Telegraph* (Bluefield, West Virginia) Jan 6, 1950.

[133] Keyhoe, *The Flying Saucers Are Real*, p. 113.

[134] Ibid.

[135] Ibid.,115.

[136] *Green Bay Press-Gazette* (Green Bay, Wisconsin) p. 4.

[137] Ruppelt, *The Report on Unidentified Flying Objects*, p. 70.

[138] *Daily Republican Register* (Mount Carmel, Illinois) May 25, 1950.

[139] Jacobs, David Michael, *The UFO Controversy in America*, Indiana University Press, 1975, p. 51.

[140] Swords, Michael et al., *UFOs and Government*, Anomalist Books, 2012, p. 108, referenced as "Edward Ruppelt files," unpublished commentaries on military and scientific figures that he met during his tenure as UFO Project Blue Book chief. (This archive currently held for the Coalition for UFO Research by Michael Swords, Professor Emeritus, Western Michigan University, Kalamazoo, Michigan).

[141] Today there is largely agreement that Mantell saw a Skyhook balloon.

[142] For a more detailed account see "Project Blue Book 1951-1969" by Michael Hall, *NICAP*, https://www.nicap.org/bluebook/51-69.htm.

[143] His other decorations were five Battle Stars, one Theater Combat Ribbon, and the Air Medal.

[144] Ruppelt, Edward J, "What Our Air Force Found Out About UFOs," *True*, May 1954, *NICAP*, https://www.nicap.org/true-rup1.htm.

[145] Ibid.

[146] Ibid.

[147] Ibid.

[148] See "Project Blue Book 1951-1969" by Michael Hall, *NICAP*, https://www.nicap.org/bluebook/51-69.htm.

[149] Cooke, Charles, "Flying Saucers Again: Do You Believe in Them?" *Sunday Star*, Aug 7, 1966, http://www.project1947.com/articles/washstar66.htm; "college books" from Ruppelt, Edward J, "What Our Air Force Found Out About UFOs," *True*, May 1954, *NICAP*, https://www.nicap.org/true-rup1.htm.

[150] *Daily Herald* (Provo, Utah) May 21, 1952, p. 12.

[151] *The Gazette* (Montreal, Quebec, Canada) Jun 19, 1952.

[152] From interviews conducted by Daniel H. Mintz, March 2018, reproduced with

kind permission.

[153] Coral Lorenzen to Keyhoe, Nov 16, 1953, (Swords).

[154] Ruppelt, *The Report on Unidentified Flying Objects,* p. 132.

[155] Ed Ruppelt would later write that the Air Force's view was "all Menzel had was a couple of meaningless high school physics experiments." Moreover, Menzel had tried to "pull a deal with the Navy, only he was backing some kind of gun. He had decided that it was the salvation of the Navy and he had tried to put the pressure on them to back him [and] he offered to donate his time as a consultant in developing this gun." The Office of Naval Research (ONR) was interested and "Menzel strongly suggested that [the ONR bids]" be given to a "small outfit" he had named. "Since the bid was high, ONR did a little investigating and found out that Menzel was one of the prime backers of this 'non-profit research organization.' ONR canceled out on the whole thing." See *The Fifth Horseman of the Apocalypse,* NICAP, Sign Oral History Project, USAF, SOHP, UFO History, Loren Gross, Unidentified Flying Objects, UFO. Gross credits this quote from Professor Michael Swords files "Ruppelt's personal papers, Lot Il, Folder 29. Menzel File." http://sohp.us/collections/ufos-a-history/pdf/GROSS-1952-Jun-July-20-SN.pdf

[156] See *UFOs and Government,* p. 155, for Professor Michael Swords' recollection of an eyewitness account given to him in the 1980s. A "low ranking" officer and "several other Army and Air Force personnel," stationed at Andrews AFB, watched the objects through binoculars. They saw "moving balls of light" performing "impossibly fast" maneuvers. A report was made but was not found in Blue Book's files.

[157] Keyhoe, *Flying Saucers From Outer Space,* p. 78.

[158] Ruppelt, *The Report on Unidentified Flying Objects,* 1956, p. 166.

[159] The Bob Pratt files: Conversations with Major Donald Keyhoe (1977, 1978, 1979), https://tinyurl.com/54sm6nce.

[160] Sign Oral History Project (SOHP), Oral History Interview with Albert M. Chop, Nov 1999, interviewers: Thomas Tulien and Brad Sparks, https://sohp.us/interviews/pdf/Chop-Albert-1999.pdf.

[161] Ruppelt, *The Report on Unidentified Flying Objects,* p. 157. Note also that Coral Lorenzen quotes a prediction made to her by Ruppelt's assistant, Lt. Bob Olsson, of a "big flap this summer." It's unclear, however, whether this refers to the 1952 incidents. The quote is found in her letter to Keyhoe of Nov 16, 1953 (Swords). The prediction was made in the presence of Dr. J. Allen Hynek.

[162] Dr. Leon Davidson noted in his article, "ECM+CIA=UFO" in the Feb/Mar 1959 issue of *Saucer News,* the runway repairs at Andrews AFB. Al Chop in his 1999 SOHP interview said that the runways at Bolling AFB were also down at that time.

[163] Keyhoe, *Flying Saucers From Outer Space,* p. 90.

[164] Ibid., p. 91.

[165] Ruppelt, *The Report on Unidentified Flying Objects,* p. 168.

[166] Keyhoe, *Flying Saucers From Outer Space,* p. 92.

[167] Ibid., p. 93.

[168] SOHP, Interview with Albert M Chop, November 1999, https://sohp.us/interviews/pdf/Chop-Albert-1999.pdf.

[169] Keyhoe, *Flying Saucers From Outer Space,* p. 95.

[170] SOHP, "Interview with Albert M Chop," Nov 1999, https://sohp.us/interviews/pdf/Chop-Albert-1999.pdf.

[171] Huneeus, Antonio, "Interview with Blue Book liaison, Major Fournet," *Open Minds,* 1988, http:// www.openminds.tv/interview-major-fournet/438.

[172] SOHP: "Oral History Interview with Albert M Chop,"Nov 1999, https://sohp.us/interviews/pdf/Chop-Albert-1999.pdf.

[173] Keyhoe, *Flying Saucers From Outer Space,* p. 99.

[174] Ibid., 101.

[175] Ibid., 105.

[176] Ibid., 111.

[177] Ibid., 124-125.

[178] Ibid., 152.

[179] Ibid., p. 153.

[180] Memorandum to A. H. Belmont from V. P. Keay, Oct 27, 1952. Subject: Flying Saucers, https://tinyurl.com/5ephb8du.

[181] "'U.F.O.' Revisited, 'Unidentified Flying Objects,' 1956, Part Two: The Other Players," *NICAP,* reproduced from *Official UFO Magazine,* Feb 1977, second of two articles by Robert Barrow, https://www.nicap.org/ufochop2.htm.

[182] Huneeus, Antonio, "Interview with Blue Book liaison, Major Fournet," *OpenMinds,* 1988, http:// www.openminds.tv/interview-major-fournet/438.

[183] Fournet letter to John Keeling, documentary maker, *John Keeling Media,* Jan 20, 1997, https://johnkeelingmedia.files.wordpress.com/2017/06/dewey-fournet-pdf.pdf.

[184] SOHP: "Oral History Interview with Albert M Chop," Nov 1999, https://sohp.us/interviews/pdf/Chop-Albert-1999.pdf.

[185] Keyhoe, *Flying Saucers From Outer Space,* p. 242.

[186] In Keyhoe's *Aliens From Space* (Granada Publishing Limited (1975), first published by Doubleday & Company Inc, 1973), pp. 86-87, he writes of the Robertson Panel as if he had current knowledge of its existence, but this is likely due to conflation of events in his memory. He erroneously gives the start date of the meeting as Jan12th.

[187] Hynek, Dr J Allen, *The Hynek UFO Report,* Sphere Books Limited, London 1978, pp. 20-21.

[188] Jacobs, p. 80; *UFOs and Government,* pp. 170, 173.

[189] Ruppelt, *The Report on Unidentified Flying Objects*, p. 225.

[190] Coral to Keyhoe, Nov 16, 1953, (Swords).

[191] Druffel, Ann, *Firestorm: Dr. James E. McDonald's Fight For UFO Science*, Wild Flower Press, Columbus N.C., 2003, p. 270.

[192] Keyhoe, *Flying Saucer Conspiracy*, Henry Holt and Company, Inc, 1955, p. 230.

[193] Keyhoe, *Flying Saucers From Outer Space,* p. 243.

[194] This letter can be viewed at NICAP, www.nicap.org/images/Chop2let.jpg. Note that Keyhoe published this in *Flying Saucers From Outer Space* against the wishes of Chop, which led to some disagreement between them later.

[195] Keyhoe, *Flying Saucers From Outer Space* pp. 245-246.

[196] The order states that "Any person who makes an unauthorized transmission or disclosure of such a report may be liable to prosecution under the US Code, Chapter 37, or the Canadian Official Secrets Act, 1939, as amended." See JANAP 146, *NSA*, https://www.nsa.gov/portals/75/documents/news-features/declassified-documents/ufo/janap_146.pdf; for Letter of Promulgation dated Mar 10, 1954, see *CUFON*, http://cufon.org/cufon/janp146c.htm.

[197] *Wisconsin State Journal* (Madison, Wisconsin) Nov 25, 1953, p. 2.

[198] Air Force Regulation (AFR) 200-2, *CUFON*, https://www.cufon.org/cufon/afr200-2.htm.

[199] Jacobs, pp. 91-92.

[200] P. G. Strong, "Report on the Book Entitled 'Flying Saucers from Outer Space,'" Dec 8, 1953, *CIA*, https://www.cia.gov/readingroom/docs/DOC_0000015363.pdf.

[201] Ruppelt, "What Our Air Force Found Out About UFOs,*" True*, https://www.nicap.org/true-rup1.htm.

[202] Ibid.

[203] *The Times-News* (Twin Falls, Idaho) July 6, 1947; *Franklin County Times* (Russellville, Alabama) May 20, 1948; *The Tennessean* (Nashville, Tennessee) Dec 28, 1949.

[204] *UFOs The Secret History*, A film by David Cherniak, An All in One Films Production, 2008.

[205] O'Connell, Mark, *The Close Encounters Man: How One Man Made the World Believe in UFOs*, Harper Collins, New York, 2017, p. 359.

[206] Zeidman, Jenny, "I Remember Blue Book," *IUR*, March/April 1991, *NICAP*, www.nicap.org/articles/I_Remember_Blue_Book.pdf.

[207] Hynek, J Allen & Jaques Vallee, *Edge of Reality: A Progress Report on Unidentified Flying Objects* (Henry Regnery, Chicago, Illinois 1975) pp. 188/9. https://archive.org/details/dlscrib.com_hynek-and-vallee-the-edge-of-reality-1975_ocr_202012.

[208] Ibid.199.

[209] Ibid., 60, 61.

[210] SOHP: "Oral History Interview with Albert M Chop," Nov 1999, https://sohp.us/interviews/pdf/Chop-Albert-1999.pdf.

[211] "'U.F.O.' Revisited, 'Unidentified Flying Objects,' 1956, Part Two: The Other Players," *NICAP*, https://www.nicap.org/ufochop2.htm.

[212] Ruppelt, *The Report On Unidentified Flying Objects*. See also NICAP's *The UFO Evidence* (1964), which explains: "Ruppelt's assistants at various times during this period were Lt. Bob Olsson, Lt. Henry Metscher, Lt. Andy Flues, and Lt. Kerry Rothstien. From May to July 1953, Lt. Olsson was acting chief while Ruppelt was away on temporary duty. The position devolved on A/1C Max Futch briefly in July 1953, when Lt. Olsson was discharged."

[213] Memorandum For Record, Subject: Unidentified Flying Objects, *CIA*, Dec 9, 1952, https://tinyurl.com/mutwppw7.

[214] Ruppelt's job title from Northrop Memorandum to All Engineering Personnel, Mar 29, 1957 (Rob Swiatek Personal Collection).

[215] Jacobs p. 96.

[216] Keyhoe Letter to Ruppelt, Aug 15, 1954, (Swiatek).

[217] Census records are unclear as to his date of arrival in the US. The 1900 census gives the year 1895, but the 1910 census gives 1904.

[218] Hallett, Marc, with Richard W Heiden as Translator and Documentalist, *A Critical Appraisal of George Adamski: The Man Who Spoke to the Space Brothers*, Revised and Enlarged Edition, Internet Archive, July 2016, https://tinyurl.com/2ywdbbrh; 1920 US Census lists Marie and George Adamsky at Multnomah, Portland, Oregon.

[219] Halstead to Hall, Apr 24, 1965, (Swords).

[220] *Times-Advocate*, Escondido, California, June 4, 1948; Adamski had been a

cavalry private, which would have entitled him to benefit from the GI Bill of Rights (Adamski, George: Draft Registration "United States World War I Draft Registration Cards, 1917-1918," *FamilySearch,* https://www.familysearch.org/ark:/61903/1:1:K8QJ-86G.

[221] Shannon, Jean, *Feminine Reflections*, Desert Hot Springs, California Jan 5, 1950 refers to Adamski's talk the previous week.

[222] *Corona Daily Independent* (Corona, California) Apr 27, 1951, p.6.

[223] Keyhoe, *Flying Saucers From Outer Space,* p. 160.

[224] Handwritten note, undated, but post-Zamora incident, from recording made by Ray Stanford with request for his identity not to be released (Swords).

[225] Hallett, p. 204.

[226] *Los Angeles Evening Citizen News*, Apr 30, 1932.

[227] Lorenzen, Coral and Jim, *Flying Saucer Occupants,* Signet Books, 1967, p.36. The authors give no reference for Adamski's admission.

[228] Bielenberg, Kim, "Flying Saucers, Rolling Stones and Chat Show Punch-Ups," *Irish Independent*, Mar 3, 2001, Review section, p.3.

[229] FBI document (date unknown) ref: SD 100-8382, (Hallett, Appendix 3).

[230] Transcript of George Adamski Radio Interview, *Roth Mulholland Program*, Station WWI (950) broadcast 1:00 PM Tuesday Mar 23, 1954 (Swords).

[231] Arthur Campbell to Keyhoe, Feb 15, 1959 (Swords).

[232] Wallace Halsey died in a plane crash on Mar 27, 1963. His body and that of the pilot were missing until October 1976, when the wreckage and their remains were found in a forested area near St. George, Utah. Conspiracy theories arose in the interim. See *Los Angeles Times,* Nov 3, 1976.

[233] Barnes to Keyhoe (undated but stamped "Received,"July 24, 1959) (Swords).

[234] This Bill appears to be the one to which Barnes refers: HR 7843 – Authorize payment from the Employees' Life Insurance Fund of expenses incurred by the Civil Service Commission in assuming and maintaining the assets and liabilities of certain beneficial associations. Lankford (D Md.) – 5/29/57 – House Post Office and Civil Service.

[235] US Congress, Reports and Documents, 86th Congress 1st Session, House Documents no 89, Survey of Space Law, Staff Report of the Select Committee on Astronautics and Space Exploration, 1959.

[236] Adamski, George, *Inside the Space Ships,* Nelson, Foster and Scott Ltd, Canada, 1955.

[237] Ray E Barnes to Keyhoe, Jul 24, 1959 (Swords).

[238] Hallett, p.149.

[239] NICAP to Nicolaisen, Nov 17, 1965, *Archives For the Unexplained,* https://www. afu.se.

[240] *Flying Saucer Review,* Jan-Feb 1960, pp. 3-8, https://www.scribd.com/ doc/227605450/Flying-Saucer-Review-Jan-Feb-1960.

[241] Jacobs, p. 118.

[242] Keyhoe, *Flying Saucers From Outer Space,* p. 132

[243] Smith to Keyhoe, Aug 6, 1952 (Swords).

[244] For some, this memo supports the idea of the MJ-12 group, an alleged secret committee of scientists, military leaders, and government officials formed in 1947 by U.S. President Harry S. Truman to facilitate recovery and investigation of alien spacecraft.

[245] Smith to Keyhoe, Jan 7, 1954 (Swords).

[246] Smith to Keyhoe, Dec 11, 1955 (Swords).

[247] Wendy Connors and Roderick Dyke, "Project Blue Book Guide," *Archives for UFO Research,* Sep 6, 1957, https://archive.org/details/ProjectBlueBookGuide/84. mp3.

[248] McDonald to Wm T Sherwood, Feb 6, 1969 (Swords).

[249] "Disliked by ..." Coral to K. Gosta Rehn, Dec 18, 1959, *AFU.*

[250] Keyhoe, *Flying Saucers From Outer Space,* p. 107.

[251] Coral to Keyhoe, Oct 3, 1953 (Swords).

[252] Keyhoe, *Flying Saucer Conspiracy,* p. 55.

[253] Wendy Connors and Roderick Dyke, "Ufology Primer in Audio 1939-1959," *Archives for UFO Research,* broadcast Nov 16, 1953, https://archive.org/details/ UFOLOGYAPrimerInAudio19391959Guide/060.mp3

[254] Coral to Keyhoe, Oct 3, 1953 (Swords).

[255] *APRO Bulletin,* Jan, Mar, and Nov 1953, *Internet Archive,* https://archive.org/ search?query=apro+bulletin.

[256] *APRO Bulletin,* Nov 1953, p. 8, *Internet Archive,* https://archive.org/ search?query=apro+bulletin.

[257] *Crescent News* (Defiance, Ohio) Oct 8, 1953.

[258] Coral to Keyhoe, Jul 11, 1954.

[259] *APRO Bulletin,* Jan 1955, p. 6, *Internet Archive,* https://archive.org/ search?query=apro+bulletin.

[260] Keyhoe to Coral Jul 2, 1954; Keyhoe to Coral November 29, 1954 (Swords).

[261] Keyhoe to Coral Sep 22, 1952 (Swords). This letter is incomplete but appears to be a combined answer to her letters of August 19 and 29, 1954. His reply indicates that Coral's report to him of this sighting and the dog's reaction was mentioned in the missing page(s).

[262] Keyhoe, *Flying Saucer Conspiracy*, pp.122, 128.

[263] Gross, Loren, "The Fifth Horseman of The Apocalypse," *UFOs: A History* 1954 *Jan-May* p. 67, *SOHP*, http:// sohp.us/collections/ufos-a-history/pdf/GROSS-1954-Jan-May.pdf

[264] Halstead to Keyhoe, Aug 2, 1959 (Swords).

[265] Halstead to Hall, April 27, 1963 (Swords).

[266] Keyhoe to Ruppelt April 8, 1954 (Swiatek).

[267] It should be noted that this letter of April 11, 1954, was quoted by Keyhoe in the October 1961 *UFO Investigator*, https://archive.org/details/sim_u-f-o-investigator_1961-10_2_2/page/n5/mode/2up, in his item "The Captain Ruppelt Letters" but it differs from that available to, and quoted by, this author. In Keyhoe's version, Ed writes: "made it [the letter] formal, just so nobody in the Air Force will squawk that I'm being too friendly with you. Since it's all on record, I don't know why they should, but I want to hang onto my grapevine sources." (Swiatek).

[268] Keyhoe, *The Flying Saucer Conspiracy*, p. 121.

[269] James Phelan, a press correspondent from Long Beach, is thought to have partly ghostwritten the 1954 *True* article, "What Our Air Force Found Out about UFOs. " Phelan is described as Ruppelt's close friend in "The Forgotten Correspondence of Ed Ruppelt, by Michael Hall and Wendy Connors, " *NICAP*, http:// www.nicap. org/papers/ruppelt_forgotten.pdf; in 1952, D. S. (Dunham Sanford) Desvergers, a scoutmaster, claimed to have experienced physical contact with a landed alien craft, witnessed by his scout troop, but Ruppelt concluded the incident was a hoax.

[270] *APRO Bulletin*, May 1954, p. 8, *Internet Archive*, https://archive.org/search?query=apro+bulletin.

[271] Keyhoe to Ruppelt, May 11, 1954 (Swiatek).

[272] Ruppelt to Keyhoe extract from *UFO Investigator*, October 1961, p. 6, https:// archive.org/details/sim_u-f-o-investigator_1961-10_2_2/page/n5/mode/2up.

[273] Ibid.

[274] Ibid.

[275] Keyhoe to Ruppelt, Aug 15, 1954 (Swiatek).

[276] Stringfield, Leonard H., *Inside Saucer Post ... 3-0 Blue: Close Encounters of Many*

Kinds; CRIFO views the status quo: a summary report by Leonard H Stringfield.

[277] Ibid.

[278] Keyhoe to Eickhoff, Nov 30, 1954 (Swords).

[279] Keyhoe, *Flying Saucer Conspiracy*, p.231.

[280] Keyhoe to Eickhoff, Nov 30, 1954 (Swords).

[281] Keyhoe to Stringfield, Nov 30, 1954 (Swords).

[282] Keyhoe to Eickhoff Nov 30, 1954 (Swords).

[283] Keyhoe to Stringfield, Nov 30, 1954 (Swords).

[284] Keyhoe to Eickhoff, Dec 29, 1954 (Swords).

[285] Walton was a Senior Specialist in Education at the US Office of Education and authored several academic books. Clara's first husband was Ray Leslie, a traffic manager, who died in 1924.

[286] Clara says in her *LLP,* Feb 3, 1955, that she began publishing her newsletters in 1948. None of them prior to 1954 are known to have survived. Walton Colcord John *The Collected Issues of The Little Listening Post*, 2020; Clara to Edith C M Nicolaisen, Feb 15, 1957, *AFU*.

[287] See Schatzkin, Paul, *Defying Gravity: The Parallel Universe of T. Townsend Brown,* Tanglewood Books, (2008) for account given by Linda Brown, daughter of Thomas Townsend Brown. The Maryland property could not be located in the records available.

[288] Wile, Frederic William, *Emile Berliner: Maker of The Microphone,* Indianapolis, The Bobbs-Merrill Company (1926).

[289] Colcord, Doane B, B.S., M.D., Descendants of Edward Colcord of New Hampshire, 1630 to 1908, Mahlon J. Colcord, Coudersport, Pa, 1908, pp. 98-99, https://archive.org/details/colcordgenealogy1908colc.

[290] Walton Colcord John worked as a "check boy" in Battle Creek in 1897. Records suggest that Clara lived there at that time. She had many Colcord relatives in Battle Creek but records do not indicate that Clara and Walton were related; wedding announcement giving details of her career see *Battle Creek Enquirer,* Jan 10, 1930, p.6.

[291] *Little Listening Post,* Dec 1957, p. 2, Walton Colcord John, *The Collected Issues of The Little Listening Post,* 2020.

[292] *Cumberland News* (Cumberland, Maryland) May 13, 1953, p. 12.

[293] Girvan broadcast a surprisingly lucid talk on saucers in 1959 (date not known), but despite his belief in Adamski, he remarked that "to assert, without the support of evidence is a form of mental arrogance." He seems not to have realized that this

was precisely what Adamski and other contactees did (Wendy Connors and Roderick Dyke, "Ufology A Primer in Audio," *Archives for UFO Research*, https://archive.org/details/UFOLOGYAPrimerInAudio19391959Guide/098.mp3); sources usually claim that Clara was Adamski's ghostwriter. However, see Hallett who wrote that she compiled Adamski's material from various sources and organized it into book form.

294 *Granville Times* (Granville, Ohio) Jan 27, 1938.

295 *The Times Recorder* (Zanesville, Ohio) Nov 8, 1930.

296 *UFO Investigator*, October 1971, Special Edition, https://archive.org/details/sim_u-f-o-investigator_1971-10.

297 The source for Rose's salary is Morris K Jessup's letter to Gray Barker dated October 4, 1956, in which he says she gave up a "govt job" at that salary, which presumably refers to her employment with Van Zelm. If true, this was at the high end of the salary range for that period.

298 Jessup to Barker, October 4, 1955; May and Aug 1955 issues of *Little Listening Post* respectively, Walton Colcord John. *The Collected Issues of The Little Listening Post*, 2020.

299 *Maryland Saucer Mag*, Oct 1955, gives the minutes of the CRSM's first meeting on Sep 22, 1955, *NOUFORS*, https://tinyurl.com/35vsyp2y.

300 *Maryland Saucer Mag*, Nov 1955 for Adamski's reply to Rose, *NOUFORS*, https://tinyurl.com/35vsyp2y.

301 Ibid.

302 *Little Listening Post*, Dec 1955-Jan 1956, Walton Colcord John, *The Collected Issues of The Little Listening Post*, 2020. Don's book had been published in October, but Clara's newsletters were often compiled over a period of weeks before publication, which accounts for the delay in this information.

303 Rose Hackett Campbell to Clara John, Dec 3, 1957 (Swords).

304 Wendy Connors and Roderick Dyke, "Ufology A Primer in Audio," *Archives for UFO Research*, https://tinyurl.com/yeywyvp9.

305 Ruppelt to Keyhoe, Dec 8, 1954 (Swiatek).

306 Keyhoe to Ruppelt, June 28, 1954. Note that their letters are confusing with regard to the sequence of the advice asked and received. Ruppelt's "have been dickering with a publisher for a book" suggests the beginning of his enquiries, but this letter is from December 1954. Keyhoe was offering advice on this book as early as June 28, 1954, though in November that year, he wrote "Heard via the grapevine in NY you were writing a book." (Swiatek).

307 Keyhoe to Ruppelt, June 28, 1954 (Swiatek).

[308] Keyhoe to Ruppelt, July 11, 1954 (Swiatek).

[309] Ibid.

[310] Keyhoe, Major Donald E., *Flying Saucers Top Secret,* (G. P. Putnam's Sons, New York, 1960) p.74.

[311] "Conway"—source Lon Strickler, "Possible Methods of UFO Propulsion Examined - Part XVIII," *Phantoms and Monsters,* https://www.phantomsandmonsters.com/2020/12/possible-methods-of-ufo-propulsion_9.html; "Mysterious" - letter Robert G. Finlay to Jim [James] Phelan, Jun 20, 1954 (Swiatek).

[312] Phelan, ibid.

[313] Hall/Connors p. 11, *NICAP*, http://www.nicap.org/papers/ruppelt_forgotten.pdf.

[314] Ruppelt to Van Tassel, Mar 8, 1955 (Swiatek).

[315] Coral to Rehn, Aug 5, 1970 (AFU).

[316] Wendy Connors and Roderick Dyke, "Project Blue Book Guide," *Archives for UFO Research,* https://archive.org/details/ProjectBlueBookGuide/24.mp3.

[317] Transcription of telephone conversation between White and Ruppelt, Mar 28th, 1955. Ruppelt letters (Swiatek).

[318] Wendy Connors and Roderick Dyke, "Project Blue Book Guide," *Archives for UFO Research,* https://archive.org/details/ProjectBlueBookGuide/26.mp3.

[319] Northrop Aircraft, Inc, Memorandum, Mar 29, 1957 to All Engineering Personnel from Vice President and Chief Engineer (Swiatek).

[320] Project Blue Book Reference Notes, *The Black Vault,* http://documents.theblackvault.com/bluebookdesk/pbbreferencenotes.pdf.

[321] Clarke, A. C., Book Review, *Journal of the British Interplanetary Society,* Vol 15, no 5, No 72, September-October 1956, pp. 289-290.

[322] *Galveston News,* Jan 29, 1956, in Book Review by Stanley E. Babb; *Saturday Review,* Feb 25, 1956, by Siegfried Mandel as quoted in *Mirror-News,* Mar 12, 1956 by James Bassett.

[323] *APRO Bulletin,* Jul 15, 1956, *OpenMinds,* http://www.openminds.tv/pdf/apro/apro_july_1956.pdf.

[324] Stringfield to Keyhoe, Mar 8, 1956 (Swords).

[325] *UFO Investigator,* October 1961, p6, https://cufos.org/resources/nicap-publications-2/

[326] Keyhoe to Ruppelt, Apr 26, 1957 (Swiatek).

[327] Fry gave a talk to the Detroit Flying Saucer club in 1955, which is the only date

for a recording of him prior to Jan 1956 that could be located by this author.

[328] Clara to Brown, Feb 8, 1956 (Swords).

[329] The Scientific Notebooks of Thomas Townsend Brown Part 1, *Rexresearch*, http:// www.rexresearch.com/brown1/brown1.htm.

[330] Schatzkin.

[331] O'Riley was not his real name, according to Schatzkin.

[332] Schatzkin.

[333] Ibid.

[334] Ibid.

[335] Passenger list of SS *Liberte* arriving at New York from Southampton, England April 4, 1956, destination Leesburg, VA. The National Archives and Records Administration; Washington, D.C.; Passenger and Crew Lists of Vessels Arriving at and Departing from Ogdensburg, New York, 5/27/1948 - 11/28/1972; Microfilm Serial or NAID: T715, 1897-1957.

[336] Towt died in a car accident in 1962, age 39. Her service in the WAVES was Seaman 1st Class. Enlisted Nov 1944, discharged Nov 1945. Her date of employment at WPAFB isn't known, but her father worked there in 1952. At the time of her death, she was a secretary at a local real estate agency. There has been speculation that she was murdered, though press reports at the time and her death certificate confirm that she died in a vehicle crash. She died from heart syncope, traumatic shock, and brain trauma. The informant of death was Thomas Townsend Brown's wife, Josephine. Pennsylvania Historic and Museum Commission; Harrisburg, Pa; *Pennsylvania (State). Death Certificates, 1906-1968*; Certificate Number Range: 064351-067200.

[337] Keyhoe to Stringfield, Oct 10, 1956 (Swords).

[338] Neighbors interviewed Mar 2018 by Daniel Mintz of New York, kindly shared by email with this author.

[339] Ship's manifest *Ocean Monarch*. Don and Helen departed New York on Jul 28, 1956 and returned Aug 10th. The National Archives and Records Administration; Washington, D.C.; Passenger and Crew Lists of Vessels Arriving at and Departing from Ogdensburg, New York, 5/27/1948 - 11/28/1972; Microfilm Serial or NAID: T715, 1897-1957.

[340] "I am Linda Brown, the daughter of the physicist Thomas Townsend Brown AMA," *r/conspiracy*, 2014, https://tinyurl.com/5bhyxzaz.

[341] Wendy Connors and Roderick Dyke, "High Strangeness Guide," *Archives for UFO Research*, https://archive.org/details/HighStrangenessGuide/18.mp3. This recording was thought to have been made in 1955. However, Clara's reference

to a tape recorded interview with Jessup made "the other night," in her letter to Townsend Brown of Jul 14, 1956, is surely the one preserved by Connors.

342 Keyhoe, *Flying Saucers: Top Secret,* p. 38.

343 *Earth vs The Flying Saucers* was released to cinemas in July, but was showing at drive-ins in June.

344 Keyhoe to Coral Lorenzen, October 3, 1956.

345 SOHP: *Interview with Albert M Chop,* November 1999.

346 "Percentage"—letter Chop to Keyhoe, Oct 28, 1957 (Swords).

347 Keyhoe, *Flying Saucers: Top Secret,* pp. 138-139.

348 *APRO Bulletin*, September 1956, pg 13, *OpenMinds*, http://www.openminds.tv/pdf/apro/apro_sept_1956.pdf.

349 Keyhoe to Coral, Oct 3, 1956 (Swords).

350 NICAP, *The UFO Evidence,*1964, www.nicap.org/ufoe/UFO Evidence 1964.pdf.

351 Brown to Nixon, Oct 27, 1971 p. 2, *NICAP*, https://tinyurl.com/3rmcunnf.

352 *The UFO Investigator,* Special Commemorative Issue, October 1971, p 2, https://archive.org/details/sim_u-f-o-investigator_1971-10.

353 Wendy Connors and Roderick Dyke, "Ufology A Primer in Audio," *Archives for UFO Research*, https://tinyurl.com/yeywyvp9. Hastings interviewed by Long John Nebel, date not known.

354 Brown to Evan Evans of National Aviation Education Council, Jan 5, 1957, *CUFOS*, https://tinyurl.com/4f32vvmh.

355 *The UFO Investigator,* Special Commemorative Issue, October 1971, p 2, https://archive.org/details/sim_u-f-o-investigator_1971-10.

356 Undated, unaddressed note titled 'Sidelights—Gleaned from my correspondence' (Swords). The content is clearly in relation to the tentative prospectus.

357 Tentative Prospectus (Swords).

358 Projected figures not included in published prospectus, they were documented separately.

359 *The UFO Investigator*, May 1970, p. 4, https://archive.org/details/sim_u-f-o-investigator_1970-05.

360 Wendy Connors and Roderick Dyke, "Ufology A Primer in Audio," *Archives for UFO Research*, https://tinyurl.com/yeywyvp9.

361 John A. Kendrick to Fahrney, Nov 6, 1956, *CUFOS*, page 1 (https://tinyurl.com/mvuwpdvp) and page 2 (https://tinyurl.com/mscnb2nu).

362 Campbell is referred to as "a rich man" in Ivan Sanderson's undated notes, *CUFOS*, (pp. 1 (https://tinyurl.com/5d8wy75k), 2 (https://tinyurl.com/45ezpb4r), 3 (https://tinyurl.com/2vrtadzb) of his meeting with Brown.

363 See *Flying Saucers*, Civilian Saucer Investigation (NZ), Vol 5-No 1, 17th Quarterly issue, pp. 16-20, https://archive.org/details/Flying_Saucers_Vol_05_No_01_1957_07-09.

364 *The UFO Investigator*, Special Commemorative Issue, October 1971, p 2, https://archive.org/details/sim_u-f-o-investigator_1971-10.

365 From Garrett Rush's resumé in NICAP's files, *CUFOS*, https://tinyurl.com/2dpmdbwj.

366 *The UFO Investigator*, Special Commemorative Issue, October 1971, p 2, https://archive.org/details/sim_u-f-o-investigator_1971-10.

367 Keyhoe, *Flying Saucers: Top Secret*, p. 43.

368 Keyhoe to Coral Lorenzen, Oct 3, 1956 (Swords).

369 Coral to Brown, Oct 9, 1956 (Swords)

370 Brown to Ruppelt, Oct 18, 1956 (Swiatek).

371 Keyhoe to Stringfield, Oct 10, 1956 (Swords).

372 Anne Archbold had divorced her husband, Armar Dayrolles Saunderson, in the 1920s and thereafter reverted to her maiden name. She also legally changed the surnames of her children to Archbold.

373 Brown to Archbold, Oct 3, 1956 (Swords).

374 Keyhoe wrote to Mrs. Archbold, on Feb 7, 1957 and Apr 9, 1958, still hoping to interest her in NICAP (Swords).

375 Hall, Richard H. "The Quest For The Truth About UFOs: A Personal Perspective On The Role Of NICAP" *NICAP*, 1994, www.nicap.org/papers/hall-IUR1994.htm.

376 Occupation from US Census, Year: 1940; Census Place: Revere, Suffolk, Massachusetts; Roll: m-t0627-01643; Page: 15A; Enumeration District: 13-55; employer from Draft Card (undated) National Archives at St. Louis; St. Louis, Missouri; Draft Registration Cards For Massachusetts, 10/16/1940-03/31/1947; Record Group: Records of the Selective Service System, 147; Box: 150.

377 *Boston Globe*, Jan 24, 1944, p. 5, and *Nashville Journal*, April 4,1945, p.5.

378 *Belleville Daily Advocate*, May 19, 1945, p. 3.

379 *Evening Star* (Washington, D.C.) Jan 7, 1955, p. 2.

380 US Census, National Archives at Washington, DC; Washington, D.C.; *Seventeenth Census of the United States, 1950*; Year: *1950*; Census Place: *Washington,*

Washington, District of Columbia; Roll: *2528*; Page: *85*; Enumeration District: *1-1293.*

381 *Daily News-Miner* (Fairbanks, Alaska) Jan 11, 1971.

382 Progress Report 2, Board of Governors, Jan 7, 1957 (Swords).

383 *Albuquerque Tribune* (Albuquerque, New Mexico) Jun 17, 1954, p. 24.

384 See Bachrack, Stanley D., *The Committee of One Million : "China Lobby" Politics, 1953-1971* (Columbia University Press, New York 1976), https://tinyurl.com/bdn5vwy7; FBI file on Rochefort, May 1, 1956, *Keep and Share*, https://tinyurl.com/4xdjw7u9.

385 According to a short bio of Shreve in *The Baltimore Sun* of Sep 30, 1973, he was recruited because Chiang Kai Shek had personally requested him to draft a program for rural reconstruction.

386 Wolfe, Audra, "Project Troy: Ho Scientists Helped Cold War Psychological Warfare," *The Atlantic*, Dec. 2018, https://www.theatlantic.com/science/archive/2018/12/project-troy-science-cold-war-psychological-warfare/576847/. E. Howard Hunt of Watergate fame was employed by the ECA from June 1948 to February 1949: https://www.archives.gov/files/research/jfk/releases/104-10194-10023.pdf. In 1948, "spymaster" Richard Bissell became acting head (administrator) of the ECA until its closure in 1951 and in 1954 he joined the CIA. In 1959 he became the CIA's Deputy Director of Plans. See his memoir, *Reflections of a Cold Warrior: From Yalta to The Bay of Pigs.*

387 Amoss, Ulius Louis, 1895-1961, *SNAC*, https://snaccooperative.org/ark:/99166/w6rv38xt.

388 Ulius L. Amoss Papers 1941-1963, *Archives West,* http:// archiveswest.orbiscascade.org/ark:/80444/xv35579.

389 See bio of Ulius L. Amoss, *Spartacus Educational,* https://spartacus-educational.com/JFKamossU.htm.

390 Keyhoe to Ruppelt, Apr 26, 1957, Catron is listed as Board Member on NICAP letterhead (Swiatek).

391 Kobler, John, "He Runs a Private OSS," *Saturday Evening Post*, May 21, 1955, p. 31.

392 Ibid.,142.

393 *Baltimore Sun*, Nov 27, 1955, p. 40. The product was abandoned by Amoss when it was discovered to have toxic content, but it would later be revived and become a brand leader.

394 Layne lists himself as "spiritualist" in San Diego City Directories for 1950 and 1954.

[395] Hermann to Frank Edwards, Aug 1, 1954, *AFU*.

[396] *Daily News* (Los Angeles, California) Mar 17, 1952.

[397] *Daily Times* (New Philadelphia, Ohio) Feb 21, 1951.

[398] *Cosmopolitan*, Mar 1951.

[399] "Teacher," Year: *1940*; Census Place: *Chicago, Cook, Illinois*; Roll: *m-t0627-00929*; Page: *1A*; Enumeration District: 103-288.

[400] National Archives at Washington, DC; Washington, D.C.; *Seventeenth Census of the United States, 1950*; Year: *1950*; Census Place: *Los Angeles, Los Angeles, California*; Roll: *3672*; Page: *5*; Enumeration District: 66-447.

[401] Found in many classified press sections, but see *Daily News* (Los Angeles, California) Jan 21, 1951.

[402] *Daily News* (Los Angeles) Oct 14, 1952, p. 11.

[403] Edward W. Hermann to Gray Barker, Jan 29, 1955, *Thomas Townsend Brown*, http:// www.thomastownsendbrown.com/tpx/barker/l_hermann_1-29-55.jpg, 3rd letter.

[404] Note on Townsend from Edward Hermann, copied to Gray Barker and Meade Layne, Feb 16, 1955, *Thomas Townsend Brown*, http://www.thomastownsendbrown.com/tpx/barker/l_hermann_2-16-55.pdf

[405] *Arizona Republic* (Phoenix, Arizona) Feb 11 1942, p. 4.

[406] *Los Angeles Evening Citizen News*, Dec 16, 1960, p. 3.

[407] *Evening Vanguard* (Venice, California) Aug 30, 1963, p. 4.

[408] Hermann to Layne, Dec 23, 1954, *Thomas Townsend Brown*, http://www.thomastownsendbrown.com/tpx/barker/l_hermann_2-16-55.pdf, 2nd letter.

[409] Ibid., Townsend Brown was a client of Oscar W. B. Reed Jr, an expert on frequency allocation, who worked for Jansky and Bailey. Brown had submitted to Reed his Proposal for a Joint Services Research and Development Contract on behalf of The Townsend Brown Foundation in 1953. This was named Project Winterhaven, which was principally concerned with electro-graviitics.

[410] The Proposal shows "Issue 1: Oct 20 1952'"and "Issue 2: Jan 1 1953."

[411] Townsend Brown to Stuart Nixon Oct 27, 1971, p. 1, *NICAP*, https://tinyurl.com/3v44nuuu.

[412] Schatzkin, from FBI synopsis, May 29, 1953.

[413] Schatzkin speculates on the covert aspects of this activity at this time.

[414] Hermann's Notes on Townsend Brown as revealed in correspondence with Carl H Betz, Feb 16, 1955, *Thomas Townsend Brown*, http://www.thomastownsendbrown.

com/tpx/barker/l_hermann_2-16-55.pdf.

[415] Townsend Brown to Stuart Nixon, p. 2, Oct 27, 1971, *NICAP*, https://tinyurl.com/3ucw66t4.

[416] *Washington Daily News* (Washington, D.C.) October 23, 1956.

[417] The "Societé Nationale de Constructions Aeronautiques du Sud-Ouest in Paris" is listed in Townsend Brown's NICAP resumé, *NICAP*, https://tinyurl.com/365t6pj5.

[418] Memo on NICAP from Serling to Sanderson, *CUFOS*, https://tinyurl.com/52wdsaxr.

[419] The undated notes of Sanderson's meeting are unclear, apparently being written by a third party, but the most logical interpretation is that these were Keyhoe's comments to him about Clara during their lunch, rather than points raised during the meeting with Brown.

[420] Sanderson was accompanied at this meeting by "John" whose surname is not given, but this most likely was journalist John Daly, Keyhoe's long-time associate.

[421]Gross, Loren, *The Fifth Horseman of the Apocalypse, UFOs A History, November-December 1956*, SOHP, http://sohp.us/collections/ufos-a-history/pdf/GROSS-1956-Nov-Dec.pdf

[422] Sanderson could find no record of this company, but it was linked to Bahnson Labs of Winston-Salem, North Carolina. This company was headed by Agnew Bahnson Jr. and conducted experiments in gravity research. Bahnson and Brown were friends. Author Paul Schatzkin offers conflicting information as to the origin of the name "White Hall Rand." He credits it first to "wealthy industrialist" Albert "Loomis" who chose the name in admiration of Brown (with whom he was connected through Britain's Whitehall) and later credits Brown himself with creating the name, in honor of the same place.

[423] Jessup to Gray Barker, Oct 4, 1956 (Swords).

[424] Jessup to Barker, Dec 22, 1956 (Swords).

[425] Ibid.

[426] Ibid.

[427] *CSI-NY Newsletter*, Dec 1956.

[428] T.T. Brown Electrogravity Vacuum Experiments," *Richard Haider*, https://www.youtube.com/watch?v=Rp4hygoD3RU shows what is thought to be this experiment, being viewed by DeWitt. See also Schatzkin for additional information on this visit.

[429] "I am Linda Brown, the daughter of the physicist Thomas Townsend Brown AMA," *r/conspiracy*, 2014, https://tinyurl.com/5bhyxzaz

[430] *Saucer News*, Feb-Mar, 1957, pp. 5 and 16.

431 News article "Board Named to Probe Flying Saucer Reports," Nov 3, 1956, http://sohp.us/collections/ufos-a-history/pdf/GROSS-1956-Nov-Dec.pdf, page 4.

432 Note also that he is listed in HUAC Exhibit 58C with others under "List of Signers of Statement Defending the Communist Party." His counseling work was at the Pratt Clinic in Boston.

433 Halstead to Keyhoe, Feb 28, 1957 (Swords).

434 Jessup to Barker, Jan 24, 1957 (Swords).

435 Ibid.

436 Jessup to Barker, Nov 22, 1956 (Swords).

437 Keyhoe to Coral Lorenzen, Feb 1, 1957 (Swords).

438 Townsend Brown to Stuart Nixon, p. 3, Oct 27, 1971, *NICAP*, https://tinyurl.com/3ucw66t4.

439 Schatzkin.

440 Keyhoe interview on Long John Nebel show, date unknown, but likely early August 1958: Wendy Connors and Roderick Dyke, "Ufology A Primer in Audio," *Archives for UFO Research*, https://tinyurl.com/yeywyvp9.

441 Jessup to Barker, January 24, 1957 (Swords).

442 This figure quoted by Keyhoe with other financial details in *The UFO Investigator*, Aug-Sep 1958, p. 8, https://archive.org/details/sim_u-f-o-investigator_1958-09_1_5/page/n7/mode/2up.

443 The press carried an edited version of this statement, which is found complete in the North Jersey UFO Group's newsletter of April 1957. This appears to be an amended version of the press release held in NICAP's files.

444 *NICAP Confidential Report*, Feb 15, 1957 (Swords).

445 *The UFO Investigator*, Jul 1957, https://cufos.org/resources/nicap-publications-2/ The obituary for Campbell notes he had retired "in spring" that year.

446 Statement by Major Donald Keyhoe, *NICAP*, http://www.nicap.org/nicap/ Statements. His 4-page statement dated Mar 7, 1957.

447 Coral's letter to Brown "by hand" Oct 9, 1956, received at NICAP Oct 10th. Brown's annotation was followed by Rose's "mailed day of this request—11-20-56. Packet plus news release" (Swords).

448 *APRO Bulletin*, Jan 1957, *OpenMinds*, http://www.openminds.tv/pdf/apro/apro_jan_1957.pdf.

449 "This is cause for ..." ibid.; "We are now sure ..." *APRO Bulletin*, Mar 1957, *OpenMinds*, http://www.openminds.tv/pdf/apro/apro_mar_1957.pdf.

[450] Ibid.

[451] Coral to Keyhoe, July 29, 1957 (Swords).

[452] Bloecher to Keyhoe, Jan 28, 1957 (Swords).

[453] *Civilian Saucer Intelligence of New York*, May 1, 1957.

[454] Members were notified by special bulletin (see *The Fifth Horseman...*, https://sohp.us/collections/ufos-a-history/pdf/GROSS-1957-Mar-23-May-25.pdf). According to the *Washington Daily News*, Apr 10, 1957, Fahrney had resigned on Jan 23rd, but had agreed that no announcement would be made until a successor had been appointed. He had now requested that NICAP should make known his resignation. No mention of this is found in the documents available to this author.

[455] Keyhoe to Ruppelt, April 26, 1957 (Swiatek).

[456] *The Origin and Development of the CIA in the Administration of Harry S Truman: A Conference Report* (1994). Comment by R Jack Smith.

[457] United States. Department of State. (1996). *Emergence of the Intelligence Establishment.* Washington: U.S. G.P.O. pp. 746-756.

[458] *Report of the Dulles-Jackson-Correa Committee to the National Security Council.*

[459] Public Papers of the President of The United States: Harry S. Truman, January 1 to December 31, 1949, *Hathi Trust*, https://tinyurl.com/mr3999vu; Letter from Hillenkoetter to President Truman, Jul 6, 1948, https://tinyurl.com/tzbht9u3 explaining the reasons for the CIA's suggested date for Russia's A-bomb completion, adds: "This report, although prepared by the Central Intelligence Agency, was examined and concurred in by the intelligence agencies of the State, Army, Navy and Air Force Departments as well as by the Atomic Energy Commission."

[460] Allen, Robert S., *Yuma Sun*, Jul 24, 1950.

[461] Dulles to Hillenkoetter, Feb 16, 1953, https://tinyurl.com/4rnzx6bb.

[462] Hillenkoetter to Dulles, Jan 29, 1957, https://tinyurl.com/2n6p8fpu.

[463] Hall, Richard H. The Quest For The Truth About UFOs: A Personal Perspective On The Role Of NICAP, *NICAP*, http://www.nicap.org/papers/hall-IUR1994.htm.

[464] NICAP "Affiliate/Subcommittee Newsletter," Jun 25, 1956 (Swords).

[465] Munsick to Brown, Sep 8, 1956 (Swords). Munsick served at NICAP from April 24, 1957 to Sep 8, 1957.

[466] Keyhoe to Munsick, Feb 7, 1958 (Swords).

[467] Keyhoe to Ted Bloecher, April 25, 1957 (Swords).

[468] Wendy Connors and Roderick Dyke, "Ufology A Primer in Audio," *Archives for UFO Research*, https://tinyurl.com/yeywyvp9.

[469] Details of death in letter in NICAP files from Garrett C. Rush to Stuart Nixon, Nov 12, 1971, NICAP, https://tinyurl.com/2xccnema. Campbell died at 8615 Brandt Place, Bethesda, the same home he had shared with his first wife Irma. He is buried with her in Pennsylvania. He had published a booklet 'Truth and Flying Saucers' which Keyhoe hoped to republish but it appears he did not.

[470] Keyhoe to Harold H. Fulton, Jun 10, 1957 (Swords).

[471] *The UFO Investigator*, Jul 1957, p. 14, https://archive.org/details/sim_u-f-o-investigator_1957-07_1_1/page/14/mode/2up.

[472] Hynek, *UFO Report*, p.54. Note that Hynek said the "case itself was not spectacular" and was not confirmed by radar. NICAP, however, confirmed there had been radar sightings consistent with eyewitness accounts.

[473] *The UFO Investigator*, Jul 1957, p. 1, https://archive.org/details/sim_u-f-o-investigator_1957-07_1_1/mode/2up.

[474] Ibid, 6.

[475] The background to his withdrawal is unclear. *The UFO Investigator*, July 1957, reported that his name had been made public by "the former management," implying that was the reason for his departure, but Fahrney's January 1957 statement specifies that Wedemeyer would be NICAP's evaluator of UFO reports. Many press reports in July 1957 also mentioned Wedemeyer's role with NICAP.

[476] *The Item of Millburn and Short Hills* (Millburn, New Jersey) Jun 20, 1957.

[477] "I am Linda Brown, the daughter of the physicist Thomas Townsend Brown AMA," *r/conspiracy*, 2014, https://tinyurl.com/5bhyxzaz

[478] This anonymous donation was acknowledged in *The UFO Investigator*, Aug-Sep 1957. Don later learned that Rose was the donor.

[479] Keyhoe, *Flying Saucers Top Secret*, p.70.

[480] Ibid.

[481] Ibid., pp.76-78.

[482] *The UFO Investigator*, October 1961, p. 6, https://archive.org/details/sim_u-f-o-investigator_1961-10_2_2/page/n5/mode/2up.

[483] Keyhoe, *Flying Saucers: Top Secret*, p.79

[484] Keyhoe to Ruppelt, Jul 29, 1957 (Swiatek).

[485] Ruppelt to Keyhoe, Aug 3, 1957 (Swiatek).

[486] Wendy Connors and Roderick Dyke, "Ufology A Primer in Audio," *Archives for UFO Research*, https://tinyurl.com/yeywyvp9.

[487] "Stooge," *Muncie Evening Press*, Feb 4, 1958, p. 4.

[488] Keyhoe interview, Wendy Connors and Roderick Dyke, "Ufology A Primer in Audio," *Archives for UFO Research,* https://tinyurl.com/yeywyvp9.

[489] Ibid.

[490] Keyhoe, *Flying Saucers: Top Secret,* p. 157.

[491] Keyhoe to Munsick, Feb 7, 1958 (Swords).

[492] *The UFO Investigator,* October 1961, p. 6, https://archive.org/details/sim_u-f-o-investigator_1961-10_2_2/page/n5/mode/2up.

[493] Wendy Connors and Roderick Dyke, "Ufology A Primer in Audio," *Archives for UFO Research,* Long John Nebel program, Jan 1958, https://tinyurl.com/yeywyvp9.,

[494] Ibid.

[495] The Black Vault Documents, *The Black Vault,* http://documents.theblackvault.com/bluebookdesk/pbbreferencenotes.pdf.

[496] Gross, Loren E., *The Fifth Horseman of the Apocalypse, UFOs: A History January-February 1958,* https://sohp.us/collections/ufos-a-history/pdf/GROSS-1958-Jan-Feb.pdf.

[497] NICAP circular dated Jan 28, 1958 (Swords). The difference between this and the original statement as broadcast is likely due to Don relying on his memory of an ad-lib made under duress.

[498] Keyhoe to Bloecher, Jan 28, 1958 (Swords).

[499] Costello to Keyhoe, Jan 24, 1953 (Swords).

[500] Nash to Keyhoe, Jan 21,1958 (Swords). On July 14, 1952, Nash and co-pilot William H. Fortenberry sighted several flying objects "glowing like hot coals" in echelon formation maneuvering at extremely high speed over Chesapeake Bay. In 1959 Nash wrote to Dick Hall that some years earlier he had resigned from the Naval Reserve because the Air Force "got all over me" for "suggesting they had" some saucer hardware. He resigned because he "did not want to be under their control in any way," Nash to Hall, Jun 4, 1959 (Swords).

[501] Stringfield to Keyhoe, Jan 23, 1958 (Swords).

[502] Keyhoe Confidential Bulletin to members, Mar 5, 1958 (Swords).

[503] Keyhoe to Coral, Apr 9, 1958 (Swords).

[504] Gross, Loren E., *The Fifth Horseman of the Apocalypse, UFOs: A History, August-September 1958,* pp. 5, 7-12, https://sohp.us/collections/ufos-a-history/pdf/GROSS-1958-Aug-Sept.pdf

[505] *UFOs and Government,* pp. 277-279.

[506] Keyhoe to Otto Zausmer, Jan 29, 1958 (Swords).

[507] Keyhoe's "Notes for talk to Washington area NICAP Membership," Aug 27, 1958. (Swords).

[508] Announced in *NICAP Bulletin*, June 1958, p. 2. Expected date for removal was "on or about 1st June."

[509] Hall, Richard H. The Quest For The Truth About UFOs: A Personal Perspective On The Role Of NICAP, *NICAP*, http://www.nicap.org/papers/hall-IUR1994.htm.

[510] Keyhoe to Ruppelt, April 26, 1957 (Swiatek).

[511] Hall to Nash, August 11, 1958 (Swords).

[512] Adamski to Keyhoe, Jul 14, 1958 (Swords).

[513] *Saucers*, Vol VI - No 4, Winter 1958/59, p.7.

[514] Clara appears to have provided Don with the original for his appraisal and gave him her information about it by letter of Mar 26th, 1958 (Swords).

[515] *Saucers*, Vol VI - No 4, Winter 1958/59, p.7.

[516] Ibid., 2-6.

[517] Dove, Lonzo, *The "Straith" State Department Fraud*, (1958, revised 1959) Swords.

[518] Numerous sources cite 1984 as the year Moseley confessed to the prank.

[519] Letter Adamski to Gray Barker, Feb 17, 1958, reproduced in Barker's *The Saucerian Bulletin*, May 1, 1958, p5.

[520] Phyllis W Parrish to Keyhoe, April 22, 1958 (Swords).

[521] Keyhoe to Adamski, April 29, 1958 (Swords).

[522] Copy of *Cosmic Science* Series No 1, Part No 4 (Swords).

[523] Adamski to Keyhoe, Aug 15, 1958 (Swords); according to C. A. (Carol) Honey, McGinnis broke with Adamski in 1961, referred to in Honey's *SP Newsletter*, Apr 1964 (Swords).

[524] Honey broke with Adamski in 1963 in part because he had learned of a money-making scam by the latter, which offered "fortune telling" by post for $5. This talent, Adamski claimed, had been taught to him when he was "privileged to sit at the Council gathering (on Saturn) of our space brothers," *SP Newsletter*, Apr 1964 (Swords).

[525] This author also did not find any mentions of a "Committee" in newspaper reports of the time.

[526] Summary of conversation, phone, with W. B. Smith, March 30, 1960. Roosevelt Hotel. (Swords).

[527] Hackett to Fry, Feb 12, 1957 (Swords).

[528] NICAP to Fry, August 8, 1958 (Swords).

[529] *CSI Newsletter*, Jul 25, 1957, Mebane, Lex, *The Collected Issues of CSI News Letter: Civilian Saucer Intelligence Group*, 2020.

[530] Fry to NICAP, Aug 30, 1958; NICAP to Fry, Sep 4, 1958; Keyhoe to Nash, Sep 4, 1958; Fry to Hall, Sep 8, 1958 (Swords).

[531] NICAP to Fry, Sep 4, 1958 (Swords).

[532] David Jesus to Keyhoe, Jul 30, 1958 (Swords).

[533] Menger to Rose Campbell, received Jul 22, 1958; Keyhoe to Menger Aug 4 (Swords).

[534] *Valley Times* (North Hollywood, California) Jun 6, 1958, p.16.

[535] Epperson to Davis, Sep 16, 1958 (Swords).

[536] Rose Campbell to Lucy McGinnis, May 20, 1958. The misspelling "pround" may have meant to be either "proud" or, more likely, "profound."

[537] Keyhoe to Rose Campbell, Aug 15, 1958 (Swords).

[538] Don's own account of discovering Adamski's membership is given in *Flying Saucers: Top Secret*, p. 241. He said that Henry Brennard had phoned him immediately after Adamski's TV appearance, following which he'd checked NICAP's records and found the membership(s), but the timeline taken from his correspondence and his own accounts in *The UFO Investigator* suggest that he took no action until receipt of David Jesus' letter, on August 4th.

[539] Keyhoe to Rose Campbell, August 15, 1958 (Swords).

[540] *The UFO Investigator*, Aug-Sep 1958, p. 4, https://archive.org/details/sim_u-f-o-investigator_1958-09_1_5/page/n3/mode/2up.

[541] Keyhoe to Rose Campbell, August 15th, 1958 (Swords).

[542] *The UFO Investigator*, Aug-Sep 1958, p. 2, https://archive.org/details/sim_u-f-o-investigator_1958-09_1_5/page/n1/mode/2up.

[543] Kruckman to Smith, Sep 3, 1956 (Swords).

[544] Davis to Epperson, Sep 13, 1958 (Swords).

[545] Keyhoe to Munsick, Sep 26, 1958 (Swords).

[546] Munsick to Keyhoe, Feb 11, 1959 (Swords).

[547] *Journal of UFO History*, Jul-Aug 2004, Vol 1 no 3, for Jessup letter dated Sep 22, 1958.

[548] Pelley, William Dudley, "Seven Minutes in Eternity—Amazing Experience that Made Me Over," *The American Magazine*, Mar 1929, pp. 7-10, 140-144.

[549] *Report on Flying Saucers,* Ruppelt, 1956.

[550] Keyhoe to Coral Lorenzen, Nov 29, 1954 (Swords).

[551] Keyhoe to Munsick, Feb 7 1958 (Swords).

[552] Keyhoe to Ruppelt, Mar 13, 1958 (Swiatek).

[553] Keyhoe to Dulles, Mar 13, 1958 (Swords).

[554] Ruppelt to Keyhoe, Mar 31, 1958 (Swiatek).

[555] Hall, Michael and Wendy Connors, "The Forgotten Correspondence of Edward J. Ruppelt: The Story Behind Report On Unidentified Flying Objects,"p.17, *NICAP,* http://www.nicap.org/papers/ruppelt_forgotten.pdf.

[556] *The UFO Investigator,* June 1959, open letter Keyhoe to Ruppelt, pp 5-6, https://archive.org/details/sim_u-f-o-investigator_1959-06_1_8/page/n3/mode/2up.

[557] Ruppelt to Davidson, May 7, 1958 (complete version unavailable to this author, but referred to in detail by Davidson's reply of May 13th, 1958) (Swords).

[558] Tacker to Davidson, May 20, 1958, *CIA,* https://www.cia.gov/readingroom/docs/CIA-RDP80B01676R000700200015-9.pdf.

[559] Griffin to Ruppelt, Jul 12, 1958 (Swiatek).

[560] Ruppelt to Griffin, Jul 23, 1958 (Swiatek).

[561] Keyhoe to Coral, Jul 17, 1958 (Swords)

[562] Ruppelt to Keyhoe, Jul 30, 1958 (Swiatek).

[563] Keyhoe to Al Chop, Aug 21, 1958 (Swords).

[564] Coral to Keyhoe, April 14, 1958 (Swords).

[565] Coral to Keyhoe, June 9, 1958 (Swords).

[566] Keyhoe to Coral, May 16, 1958 (Swords).

[567] Keyhoe to Coral, Jul 17, 1958 (Swords).

[568] Druffel interview with Tim Binnall, Feb 22, 2009, *Binnall of America,* http://www.binnallofamerica.com/boaa2.22.9.html, reproduced here with kind permission.

[569] Friedman interview with Tim Binnall, Dec 23, 2006, *Binnall of America,* http://www.binnallofamerica.com/boaa12.23.6.html, reproduced here with kind permission.

[570] *The UFO Investigator,* Mar 1968, *CUFOS,* https://cufos.org/resources/nicap-publications-2/

[571] Rose Hackett Campbell to Coral, Jul 30, 1958; Keyhoe to Coral, Aug 4 1958 (Swords).

572 Coral to Keyhoe, Aug 9, 1958 (Swords).

573 Coral to Keyhoe, Aug 25, 1958 (Swords).

574 Jung to Keyhoe, Aug 16, 1958, reproduced in *The UFO Investigator,* Aug-Sep 1958, *CUFOS,* https://cufos.org/resources/nicap-publications-2/.

575 From Gordon Lore's collection, with permission.

576 Coral to Rehn, June 5, 1959 (AFU).

577 Coral to Rehn, June 29, 1959 (AFU).

578 Handwritten note Idabel Epperson to Isabel Davis, Dec 10, 1958 (Swords).

579 Epperson to McDonald, Jun 24, 1969, reproduced in Druffell's *Firestorm,* p. 572.

580 A. Scott Berg, *Lindbergh* (Simon & Schuster UK, 2013) pp 511-512.

581 Bob Pratt telephone interview with Keyhoe, Nov 26, 1979, "The Unreal World of UFOs" (The Bob Pratt Files), https://tinyurl.com/54sm6nce

582 Coral to Rehn, Jan 22, 1959 (AFU).

583 Coral to Rehn, Mar 26, 1959 (AFU).

584 Coral to Rehn, Sept 7, 1959 (AFU).

585 Rehn to Coral, Sept 14, 1959 (AFU).

586 Coral to Rehn, Sept 18, 1959 (AFU).

587 Undated note from Coral, but probably sent in Sept 1959 (Swords).

588 Keyhoe to Coral, Oct 2, 1959; Keyhoe to Moseley, Sept 29, 1959 (Swords).

589 Coral to Keyhoe, Oct 12, 1959 (Swords).

590 Coral to Rehn, Nov 4, 1959 (AFU).

591 Coral to Rehn, Oct 22, 1959 (AFU).

592 Coral to Rehn, Nov 4, 1959 (AFU).

593 Coral to Rehn, Nov 19, 1959 (AFU); First meeting with Fontes see *The APRO Bulletin,* May 1968, *OpenMinds,* http://www.openminds.tv/pdf/apro/apro_may_1968.pdf

594 Coral to Rehn, Nov 4, 1959 (AFU).

595 Rehn to Coral, Nov 13, 1959 (AFU).

596 Coral to Rehn, Nov 19, 1959 (AFU).

597 Rehn to Coral, Dec 13, 1959 (AFU).

598 Coral to Rehn, Dec 18, 1959, (AFU).

599 Coral to Rehn, Oct 30, 1959 (AFU).

600 Coral to Rehn, Nov 4, 1959 (AFU).

601 Death certificate for Jessup, Carlos Allende and his Philadelphia Experiment, https://windmill-slayer.tripod.com/aliascarlosallende/id6.html.

602 Mary Alice Jessup, born April 6, 1933, Iowa Delayed Births, 1856-1940. State Historical Society of Iowa, States Archives, Des Moines, Iowa.

603 Jessup, M. K., *The Case For the UFO* ("Varo Edition"), https://archive.org/details/THECASEFORTHEUFOVaroEditionM.K.Jessup/mode/2up.

604 Keel to Robert Goerman, August 10, 1983 in Goerman, Robert A., "Alias Carlos Allende," *Fate*, Dec. 1980, https://windmill-slayer.tripod.com/aliascarlosallende/.

605 Keyhoe to Moseley, Sep 29, 1959 (Swords).

606 Munsick to Hall, Oct 16, 1959 (Swords).

607 McDonald to Wm T. Sherwood, Feb 6, 1959 (Swords).

608 Hall to Arthur Campbell, Mar 20, 1959 (Swords).

609 *The UFO Investigator*, June 1959, *CUFOS*, pp. 1, 3, 4, https://cufos.org/resources/nicap-publications-2/

610 Hoffman to Tacker, memo, May 21, 1959 (Swiatek).

611 Ibid.

612 Sunderman to Ruppelt, Jul 17, 1959 (Swiatek).

613 Ruppelt's handwritten draft, date unknown, but likely early 1959 (Swiatek).

614 Flues to Ruppelt, May 12, 1959 (Swiatek).

615 *The UFO Investigator*, Dec-Jan 1960-1961, *CUFOS*, page, 8, https://cufos.org/resources/nicap-publications-2/

616 Hall to Sven Schalin, Nov 8, 1960 (Swords).

617 Munsick to Editor, *Air Force/Space Digest*, Feb 24, 1961 (Swords).

618 Bloecher to Tacker, Jan 25, 1961 (Swords).

619 *The UFO Investigator*, Jul-Aug 1960, *CUFOS*, p. 1, https://cufos.org/resources/nicap-publications-2/

620 Memo, Subject: Comments on Letters Dealing with UFOs, Apr 4, 1958 CIA, https://www.cia.gov/readingroom/docs/DOC_0005516043.pdf.

621 Clara John to Edith Nicolaisen, June 29, 1964 (AFU).

622 *The UFO Investigator*, Jul-Aug 1960, p.1, "AF Admits Keeping UFO Reports From Public," continued on pp. 2 & 3, https://cufos.org/resources/nicap-

publications-2/

[623] Salkin to NICAP, Jul 12, 1960 (Swords).

[624] Washington, District of Columbia, City Directory, 1960, listed as "Borsilleri."

[625] Townsend Brown to Stuart Nixon, Oct 27, 1971, *NICAP*, https://tinyurl.com/euyu2z8t.

[626] Ibid.

[627] Ibid.

[628] *The Little Listening Post*, Apr/May/Jun 1960, Walton Colcord John, *The Collected Issues of The Little Listening Post,* 2020.

"Krebiozen" p. 3; "Hastings" p 5. Krebiozen is a controversial and largely discredited drug for the treatment of cancer.

[629] There are six relevant documents relating to Mercury Enterprises and Keyhoe's alleged involvement upon which Druffel has drawn, but it should be noted that only the first, a memo dated June 24, 1960 (from/to redacted) is reproduced in the print version of *Firestorm,* p. 578). The Internet Archive version of *Firestorm* (https://archive.org/details/druffel_firestorm_james_mcdonald_fight_ufo_science) contains the other five which follow, unnumbered, after p. 578. The timeline and events described herein are constructed from these and other referenced documents.

[630] Tacker to Hoover, Aug 23, 1960 (Swords).

[631] Hoover to Tacker, Aug 31, 1960 (Swords).

[632] *Colorado Springs Gazette-Telegraph*, Jan 27, 1971.

[633] *The UFO Investigator,* Oct 1961, p. 7, *CUFOS*, https://cufos.org/resources/nicap-publications-2/.

[634] Kean, Leslie, *UFOs: Generals, Pilots, and Government Officials Go On the Record,* p. 109, (Three Rivers Press, 2010).

[635] Col. Coleman Case / Chases UFO At Low Altitude, *NICAP*, http://www.nicap.org/5507XXs_alabama_dir.htm.

[636] Wendy Connors and Roderick Dyke, "Profiles in Ufology: Major Donald E. Keyhoe, Dr. James E. Mc Donald & Frank Edwards Guide," *Archives for UFO Research,* https://tinyurl.com/4y6fucer.

[637] Lorenzen, *Flying Saucer Occupants,* p. 130.

[638] *The UFO Investigator*, Apr-May 1961, *CUFOS*, https://cufos.org/resources/nicap-publications-2/; Hall to Sven Schalin, April 19, 1961 (Swords).

[639] Hall to Michel, Jul 20, 1960 (Swords).

[640] Jacobs, p. 140.

[641] Ibid., 147.

[642] Ibid., 149.

[643] Ibid., 165

[644] *APRO Bulletin,* Mar 1961, pp. 3-7, *OpenMinds,* http://www.openminds.tv/pdf/apro/apro_mar_1961.pdf

[645] Coral to Karth, Jul 13, 1961 (Swords).

[646] Keyhoe to Brooks, Aug 11, 1961 (Swords).

[647] Karth to Keyhoe, Aug 28, 1961 (Swords).

[648] Karth to Keyhoe, Aug 28, 1961 (Swords).

[649] Ibid.

[650] *The UFO Investigator,* Aug-Sep, 1962, p. 8, *CUFOS,* https://cufos.org/resources/nicap-publications-2/.

[651] Note also that Don's account of Bethune's sighting differs in both these books and also from Bethune's own account given in the 1990s; George Brent was a well-known Hollywood actor, so it seems likely that Don had inadvertently used his name.

[652] Keyhoe, *Aliens From Space,* p. 97.

[653] Ibid. 101.

[654] Ibid. 102-103.

[655] Gross, Loren E., *The Fifth Horseman of the Apocalypse, UFOs: A History, Jul-Dec 1963,* pp.53-54, https://sohp.us/collections/ufos-a-history/pdf/GROSS-1963-July-Dec.pdf.

[656] *The UFO Investigator,* Aug-Sep, 1965, *CUFOS,* https://cufos.org/resources/nicap-publications-2/; Hillenkoetter to Menzel, see *Fifth Horseman,* ibid.

[657] Hall to Miller, Apr 27, 1962 (Swords).

[658] Hall to Munsick, Oct 17, 1962 (Swords).

[659] *The UFO Investigator,* Jan-Feb 1963, p.8, *CUFOS,* https://cufos.org/resources/nicap-publications-2/.

[660] *The Ottawa Citizen* (Ottawa, Ontario, Canada) p.28.

[661] *The UFO Investigator,* Mar-Apr 1963, p. 6, *CUFOS,* https://cufos.org/resources/nicap-publications-2/

[662] Ibid. 8.

[663] *The UFO Investigator,* Jun-Sep, 1963, *CUFOS,* https://cufos.org/resources/nicap-publications-2/

[664] Epperson to Sanderson, Jul 1, 1959 (Swords)

[665] Keyhoe to Green, telegram, Jul 6, 1959 (Swords).

[666] Hall to Green, May 15, 1962 (Swords).

[667] Miller to Hall, Jan 21, 1963 (Swords).

[668] Quintanilla, Hector, *UFO's An Air Force Dilemma*, available at *UFOs at Close Sight*, published 2001, https://ufologie.patrickgross.org/doc/quintanilla.pdf.

[669] Project Blue Book Reference Notes, *The Black Vault*, http://documents.theblackvault.com/bluebookdesk/pbbreferencenotes.pdf.

[670] Hynek & Vallee, *The Edge of Reality*, p. 194.

[671] Hynek, J. Allen, *The UFO Report*, p. 8. Hynek's comment that "many" reports were marked confidential or secret is at variance with his later remark in the same book (p. 61) that "very few" were marked this way.

[672] *The UFO Investigator*, Jun-Sep 1963, p. 3, *CUFOS*, https://cufos.org/resources/nicap-publications-2/

[673] *The Little Listening Post*, Jan-Feb 1964, p. 4, Walton Colcord John, *The Collected Issues of The Little Listening Post*, 2020.

[674] *The UFO Investigator*, Dec 1963 - Jan 1964, p. 2 *CUFOS*, https://cufos.org/resources/nicap-publications-2/

[675] *The UFO Investigator*, Jul-Aug, 1964 *CUFOS*, https://cufos.org/resources/nicap-publications-2/.

[676] Confidential Letter to NICAP Staff, Feb 20, 1969, p. 9 (Swords).

[677] *The UFO Investigator*, Jul-Aug, 1964, p. 3, *CUFOS*, https://cufos.org/resources/nicap-publications-2/.

[678] *The Little Listening Post*, Sep-Oct 1964, p.4, Walton Colcord John, *The Collected Issues of The Little Listening Post*, 2020.

[679] Hall to Munsick, Jan 12, 1960, "received a brief note and check of $50 for NICAP from Steve Allen yesterday ... Go, Steverino!" (Swords).

[680] *The Durham Sun* (Durham, North Carolina) Jan 27, 1965, p. 40.

[681] *The UFO Investigator*, Mar-Apr 1965, p.6, *CUFOS*, https://cufos.org/resources/nicap-publications-2/

[682] Munsick to Keyhoe, Jun 21, 1965 (Swords).

[683] *Kokomo Tribune* (Kokomo, Indiana) Apr 16, 1965, p. 5.

[684] *The UFO Investigator*, Mar 1968, p. 5, *CUFOS*, https://cufos.org/resources/nicap-publications-2/.

[685] *Press and Sun-Bulletin* (Binghamton, New York) Apr 12, 1965, p.6.

[686] Lore, Gordon, *Flying Saucers From Beyond The Earth* (Bear Manor Media) 2018, pp. xiii.

[687] Ibid., xvii

[688] Jaques and Janine Vallee, *Challenge To Science: The UFO Enigma* (Henry Regnery, Chicago 1966), p. 225.

[689] Rehn to Coral, Oct 11, 1967; Coral to Rehn, Oct 17, 1967 (AFU).

[690] *Charleston Evening Post,* Charleston, SC, Jul 15, 1965, reproduced in *The UFO Investigator,* Aug-Sep 1965, p. 4.

[691] Jacobs, pp. 171-173.

[692] Wendy Connors and Roderick Dyke, "Profiles in Ufology," *Archives for UFO Research*, https://archive.org/details/UFOLOGYAPrimerInAudio19471964Volume2Guide/49.mp3

[693] Wendy Connors and Roderick Dyke, "Profiles In Ufology Major Donald E. Keyhoe, Dr. James E. Mc Donald & Frank Edwards Guide," *Archives for UFO Research*, https://tinyurl.com/48v6xxd7.

[694] *Saturday Review,* Oct 2, 1965, pp. 10 & 16.

[695] *The UFO Investigator,* Jan-Feb, 1966, p. 5, *CUFOS*, https://cufos.org/resources/nicap-publications-2/

[696] Ibid., 8.

[697] For a detailed account of McDonald's interview with Rex Heflin, see Druffel, pp. 294-296; visit of McDonald to Epperson found in her hand-written notes of Jan 1966 (Swiatek); NICAP conclusion see *The UFO Evidence, Volume II: A Thirty Year Report,* Scarecrow Press, 2000.

[698] Hall's log, entries for Feb 17 and Mar 3, 1966 (Swords).

[699] LeBailly Memo, Sept 28, 1965, *NICAP*, http://www.nicap.org/docs/650928lebailly_docs.pdf.

[700] Wendy Connors and Roderick Dyke, "Project Blue Book Guide," *Archives for UFO Research*, https://archive.org/details/ProjectBlueBookGuide/56.mp3.

[701] Ford, Gerald R., News Release, March 25, 1966, *Ford Library Museum*, https://www.fordlibrarymuseum.gov/library/document/0054/4525586.pdf.

[702] Hynek & Vallee, *Edge of Reality,* p. 201

[703] Ibid., p. 200.

[704] Ford News Release, Apr 21,1966 (Swords).

705 "John Keel Visits NICAP," *John Keel*, re: Confidential report Keel to NICAP, APRO, Sanderson and Playboy, April 26, 1966, https://www.johnkeel.com/?p=4083.

706 "Keel and Sanderson Try to Write a Book (6)," *John Keel*, https://www.johnkeel.com/?p=1838.

707 "John Keel Visits Project Bluebook (2)," *John Keel*, https://www.johnkeel.com/?p=2468.

708 "John Keel Visits Project Bluebook (3)," *John Keel*, https://www.johnkeel.com/?p=2473.

709 This cannot have been true for every week. In 1965, according to *The UFO Investigator* of Jan-Feb 1966, NICAP received 40,000 letters in 1965; Richard H. Hall, "The Quest For The Truth About UFOs: A Personal Perspective On The Role Of NICAP," 1994, *NICAP*, http://www.nicap.org/papers/hall-IUR1994.htm.

710 NICAP Affiliate/Subcommittee Newsletter, Mar 9, 1966 (Swords).

711 "John Keel Visits Project Bluebook (3)," *John Keel*, https://www.johnkeel.com/?p=2473.

712 Jacobs, p. 183.

713 McDonald to Cerny, Jun 17, 1966 (Swords).

714 *Saga*, Sept 1966, pp. 23, 56, 58.

715 Keyhoe, *Aliens From Space*, p. 30.

716 Robert Low "Trick Would Be" Memo, Aug 9, 1966, *NICAP*, http://www.nicap.org/docs/660809lowmemo.htm; Ratchford, see Druffel p. 150.

717 Ibid.

718 Ibid.

719 A Letter from Lynn Catoe, April 9, 1968, *John Keel*, https://www.johnkeel.com/?s=catoe; also Druffel, p. 394 refers to McDonald's notes on this allegation.

720 Jacobs, p.185.

721 Ibid.

722 Swords et al., *UFOs and Government*, p. 309.

723 Lewis Branscomb, Apr 7, 1986, *American Institute of Physics*, https://www.aip.org/history-programs/niels-bohr-library/oral-histories/4531: "Ed Condon had hired me at the Bureau of Standards. I'd known him here. He of course is a figure in science policy. So he had a lot of influence"; "study at Duke" refers to experiments in parapsychology undertaken by Joseph Banks Rhine, at Duke University, NC, in the 1930s.

724 Robert Low "Trick Would Be" Memo, http://www.nicap.org/

docs/660809lowmemo.htm.

725 Vallee, *Challenge to Science*, p. 132.

726 Keyhoe, *Aliens From Space,* p. 130.

727 Ibid.

728 Ibid., 131

729 Ibid.

730 Jacobs, p. 201.

731 *UFOs and Government*, p. 310.

732 Hynek, *The UFO Report*, p. 281.

733 *UFO Investigator*, Oct-Nov, 1966, p.1, https://cufos.org/resources/nicap-publications-2/.

734 Fuller's description of McDonald, see *Look,* May 14, 1968, p. 58; *The UFO Investigator,* Oct-Nov 1966, p.1, *CUFOS*, https://cufos.org/resources/nicap-publications-2/.

735 *APRO Bulletin*, Sep-Oct, 1966, p. 2. *Open Minds*, http://www.openminds.tv/pdf/apro/apro_sep_1966.pdf. This refers to a remark made by McDonald reported in the *Daily News* of Oct 8, 1966, "Air Force Probe of UFOs Called "Scientific Scandal,'" *CIA*, https://tinyurl.com/bdhydz2k.

736 *The UFO Investigator,* Jan-Feb 1967, p.8, *CUFOS*, https://cufos.org/resources/nicap-publications-2/

737 Wendy Connors and Roderick Dyke, "Project Blue Book Guide," *Archives for UFO Research*, https://archive.org/details/ProjectBlueBookGuide/56.mp3.

738 *UFOs and Government*, pp. 313-4.

739 *The UFO Investigator,* Jan-Feb 1967, p.3, *CUFOS*, https://cufos.org/resources/nicap-publications-2/

740 *The UFO Investigator,* Mar-Apr, 1967, p. 2, *CUFOS*, https://cufos.org/resources/nicap-publications-2/

741 *APRO Bulletin*, Sep 1966, p.3, *OpenMinds*, http://www.openminds.tv/pdf/apro/apro_sep_1966.pdf.

742 *APRO Bulletin*, May 1967, p.6, *OpenMinds*, http://www.openminds.tv/pdf/apro/apro_may_1967.pdf.

743 Druffel, p. 19.

744 Ibid., p. 90.

745 Coral to Rehn, Sep 12, 1967.

[746] Coral to Rehn, Oct 3, 1967. (AFU).

[747] Coral to Rehn, Apr 10, 1970 (AFU).

[748] Druffel, p. 67.

[749] Druffel p. 147; for Hynek's own account see *The Edge of Reality,* p. 204.

[750] Druffel., p. 331.

[751] Coral to Rehn, Mar 11, 1967 (AFU).

[752] McDonald to Wm T. Sherwood, Feb 6, 1969 (Swords).

[753] Jacobs, p. 201.

[754] *The UFO Investigato*r, May-Jun 1967, *CUFOS,* https://cufos.org/resources/nicap-publications-2/

[755] UFO Briefing for Dr. Edward Condon, 5 May 1967, *CIA,* https://tinyurl.com/bdffn54x.

[756] *The UFO Investigator*, May-Jun 1967, *CUFOS,* https://cufos.org/resources/nicap-publications-2/.

[757] Keyhoe, *Aliens From Space,* p. 139.

[758] Coral to Rehn, Jun 12, 1967. (AFU).

[759] Lorenzen, Coral and Jim, *Flying Saucer Occupants,* pp. 157 and 158.

[760] Rehn to Coral, Sep 15,1967 (AFU).

[761] Coral to Rehn, Oct 3, 1967. (AFU).

[762] Hall to NICAP members, Dec 9, 1969, p.2 (Swords).

[763] Hall to Epperson, Feb 12, 1973, pp. 2 & 3 (Swords).

[764] Keyhoe, *Aliens From Space,* p. 146.

[765] Ibid., p. 148.

[766] Ibid., p. 150; See also pp. 177-178 re the CIA expressing the same concern in the presence of one of Keyhoe's informants.

[767] Special Notice to All Affiliates and Subcommittees, Jul 26, 1967 (Swords).

[768] Earley to Dick Hall, Jul 11, 1967 (Swords).

[769] *APRO Bulletin,* Sep-Oct 1967, p. 4, *OpenMinds,* http://www.openminds.tv/pdf/apro/apro_sep_1967.pdf.

[770] Coral to Rehn, Oct 17, 1967 (AFU).

[771] *The UFO Investigator,* Oct 1967, p.6, *CUFOS,* https://cufos.org/resources/nicap-publications-2/.

[772] *APRO Bulletin*, Sep -Oct 1967, p. 2, *OpenMinds*, http://www.openminds.tv/pdf/apro/apro_sep_1967.pdf.

[773] Epperson to Keyhoe, Nov 21, 1967 (Swiatek).

[774] Low to Ratchford, Jan 17, 1968, p. 1, *CIA*, https://www.cia.gov/readingroom/docs/CIA-RDP79B00752A000300100001-4.pdf.

[775] Druffel, p. 263.

[776] Ibid., p. 264; Jacobs, p. 204.

[777] Jacobs, p. 204

[778] Druffel, p. 273.

[779] Jacobs, p. 204; Note that Druffel says Mary Lou Armstrong was fired, p. 282.

[780] Ibid.

[781] Coral to Rehn, Feb 26, 1968, pp. 2-3 (AFU).

[782] Rehn to Coral, Mar 2, 1968 (AFU).

[783] Coral to Rehn, Mar 7, 1968 (AFU).

[784] *The UFO Investigator*, May-Jun, 1968, p. 5, *CUFOS*, https://cufos.org/resources/nicap-publications-2/

[785] Druffel, p. 344.

[786] Coral to Rehn, Mar 7, 1968 (AFU).

[787] *APRO Bulletin*, Mar 1968, p. 4, *OpenMinds*, http://www.openminds.tv/pdf/apro/apro_mar_1968.pdf.

[788] Lore to Keyhoe, Mar 21, 1968 (Swords).

[789] Druffel, p. 394.

[790] *UFO Investigator*, May-June 1968, p.6, https://cufos.org/resources/nicap-publications-2/.

[791] Keyhoe, *Aliens From Space*, p. 179.

[792] *The UFO Investigator*, May-Jun, 1968, p. 5, 6, *CUFOS*, https://cufos.org/resources/nicap-publications-2/.

[793] *The UFO Investigator*, Mar 1968, p. 2, *CUFOS*, https://cufos.org/resources/nicap-publications-2/

[794] Nicolaisen to Clara John, Sep 26, 1965 (AFU).

[795] District of Columbia, US Glenwood Cemetery Records, 1854-2013.

[796] *APRO Bulletin*, May-June 1968, pp. 2-3, *OpenMinds*, http://www.openminds.tv/pdf/apro/apro_may_1968.pdf.

[797] Keyhoe, *Aliens From Space*, p. 173

[798] Symposium on Unidentified Flying Objects: Hearings Before The Committee on Science and Astronautics, U.S. House of Representatives, Ninetieth Congress, Second Session, July 29, 1968, *NICAP*, http://www.nicap.org/books/1968Sym/1968_UFO_Symposium.pdf.

[799] Druffel, p. 241

[800] Keyhoe, *Aliens From Space*, p. 177.

[801] Jacobs, p. 207

[802] Keyhoe, *Aliens From Space* pp. 172-176; Lore, pp. 126-130.

[803] Druffel, p. 247.

[804] Hall to Epperson, Feb 12, 1973, p. 2 (Swiatek).

[805] *The UFO Investigator*, Sep-Oct 1968, p. 1, *CUFOS*, https://cufos.org/resources/nicap-publications-2/.

[806] Hall to Epperson, Feb 12, 1973 (Swiatek).

[807] Scientific Study of Unidentified Flying Objects Conducted by the University of Colorado Under contract No. 44620-67-C-0035 With the United States Air Force. Dr. Edward U. Condon, Scientific Director. Summary of The Study, Section II . *NCAS*, https://files.ncas.org/condon/text/sec-ii.htm. (Internet Edition Prepared by National Capital Area Skeptics(NCAS) District of Columbia-Maryland-Virginia USA; http://www.ncas.org.

[808] *UFO Investigator*, Jan/Feb 1969, *CUFOS*, https://cufos.org/resources/nicap-publications-2/.

[809] *The UFO Investigator,* Feb-Mar 1969, p. 8, *CUFOS*, https://cufos.org/resources/nicap-publications-2/.

[810] *The UFO Investigator*, Jan 1969, p. 3 *CUFOS*, https://cufos.org/resources/nicap-publications-2/.

[811] Tiede, *Guam News* (Agana Heighs, Guam) Feb 2, 1969, p. 18; Hines, *Courier-News* (Bridgewater, NJ) Jan 18, 1969, p. 15.

[812] Lore memo to Staff, Jan 27, 1969 (Swords).

[813] Hall to NICAP Board of Governors, Dec 3, 1969 (Swords).

[814] *APRO Bulletin*, Jan 1969, pp. 1 & 7, *OpenMinds*, http://www.openminds.tv/pdf/apro/apro_jan_1969.pdf.

[815] Ibid.

[816] Ibid.

[817] Rehn to the Lorenzens, Feb 28, 1969, (AFU).

[818] *The UFO Investigator*, Feb-Mar 1969, p. 1, *CUFOS*, https://cufos.org/resources/nicap-publications-2/.

[819] If such were issued, they are not found in the source material available to this author.

[820] Confidential letter to NICAP staff, Feb 20, 1969, p.2 (Swords).

[821] Ibid., p.3

[822] From personal interviews conducted in Luray by Daniel H. Mintz, kindly shared with this author by email Oct 2021.

[823] Email Daniel Mintz to author, Mar 18, 2018.

[824] Lore, p. 237.

[825] Hall to Epperson, Feb 12, 1973 (Swords).

[826] Bloecher to Fowler, Mar 17, 1969 (Swords).

[827] *The UFO Investigator*, May 1969, p. 6, *CUFOS*, https://cufos.org/resources/nicap-publications-2/.

[828] Hall to Epperson, Feb 12, 1973 (Swords),

[829] *The UFO Investigator*, Sep-Oct 1969, p. 2, *CUFOS*, https://cufos.org/resources/nicap-publications-2/.

[830] "Interview [1968] with Blue Book liaison, Major Fournet," *OpenMinds*, http://www.openminds.tv/interview-major-fournet/4381.

[831] For minutes of this meeting, see Druffel, p. 579, Appendix 17-B.

[832] "Interview [1968] with Blue Book liaison, Major Fournet," *OpenMinds*, http://www.openminds.tv/interview-major-fournet/4381.

[833] Hall to NICAP Board, Dec 9, 1969 (Swords).

[834] Email Lore to author, Aug 25, 2018.

[835] Jacobs, p.227.

[836] Coral to Rehn Dec 20, 1969 (Swords).

[837] Show listed in *Pittsburgh Post-Gazette*, Jan 6, 1970, p.25.

[838] *Sheboygan Press* (Sheboygan, Wisconsin) Dec 7, 1969,

[839] Wendy Connors and Roderick Dyke, "Profiles in Ufology: Major Donald E. Keyhoe, Dr. James E. Mc Donald & Frank Edwards Guide," *Archives for UFO Research*, https://tinyurl.com/4y6fucer.

[840] Internal Revenue Service to NICAP, Apr 16, 1970, p.1 (https://tinyurl.

com/5btc3zp9), p.2 (https://tinyurl.com/354xcbuk), *NICAP*

841 U.S., School Yearbooks, 1880-2012: Bethesda Chevy Chase High School; Year: 1948; United States of America, Bureau of the Census; Washington, D.C.; *Seventeenth Census of the United States, 1950*; Record Group: *Records of the Bureau of the Census, 1790-2007*; Record Group Number: *29*; Residence Date: *1950*; Home in 1950: *Bethesda, Montgomery, Maryland*; Roll: *2548*; Sheet Number: *1*; Enumeration District: *16-6*; Virginia Department of Health; Richmond, Virginia; *Virginia, Marriages, 1936-2014*; Roll: *101167949*.

842 Talon, *1960 American University Year Book,* Silver Spring, Maryland, City Directory 1960, https://archive.org/details/talon1960amer/page/n207/mode/2up?q=acuff ; Silver Spring, Maryland, *City Directory*, 1960.

843 Keyhoe to McLucas, October 27, 1974 (Swords). Note that in this letter, which precedes his 1976 debate with Col. William Coleman, he stated he'd been told that Coleman was "against the cover-up, in spite of his sometimes harsh ridicule of witnesses by AF orders, and that he was planning to help break the secrecy." See Mark Pilkington, *Mirage Men*, for his interview with Emenegger re: this film.

844 *The UFO Investigator,* May 1970, p.1, *CUFOS*, https://cufos.org/resources/nicap-publications-2/.

845 Hall to Epperson, Jun 23, 1972 (Swiatek).

846 Epperson to Hartranft, Jul 5, 1972 (Swords).

847 Epperson to Keyhoe, Mar 29, 1972 (Swiatek).

848 Keyhoe/Nebel Interview, Wendy Connors Collection, *Ufology A Primer In Audio*, https://tinyurl.com/yeywyvp9.

849 Robertson, Gary, "Ex-Marine Officer Still Battles To Tell 'Real Story of UFOs," *Richmond Times-Dispatch*, Jan 27, 1974 p C-7.

850 Keyhoe, *Aliens From Space,* p. 11.

851 Ibid., 270.

852 Ibid., 233.

853 Ibid., 283.

854 About NICAP, *CIA*, https://www.cia.gov/readingroom/docs/DOC_0000015455.pdf.

855 "NICAP and the CIA Connection," *UFO Research Newsletter,* Jun-Jul 1979, https://tinyurl.com/4ndybuty.

856 *The Daily Times* (Salisbury, Maryland) Jan 23, 1976, p.16.

857 Hall to Epperson, Feb 27, 1974, p.2 (Swiatek).

858 Stuart Nixon to Dewey Fournet, Mar 19, 1974, *NICAP*, https://tinyurl.com/yjtzeb29.

859 Ibid.

860 Lore, p. 245.

861 Druffel, p. 281.

862 *The Capital Journal* (Salem, Oregon) Dec 1, 1975, p. 22.

863 Keyhoe to Andrus, Apr 8, 1976 (Swords).

864 Hall, Richard H. "The Quest For The Truth About Ufos: A Personal Perspective On The Role Of NICAP," *NICAP*, http://www.nicap.org/papers/hall-IUR1994.htm.

865 Ibid.

866 Ibid.

867 Ibid.

868 Keyhoe to Andrus, Feb 18, 1981 (Swords).

869 Keyhoe to Andrus, Apr 8, 1976 (Swords).

870 Parfit, Michael, *Chasing The Glory*, Macmillan Publishing Company (New York), Collier Macmillan Canada Inc, 1988, pp. 207-209.

871 Virginia Department of Health; Richmond, Virginia; *Virginia Deaths, 1912-2014*, Death Certificate no: 1988042355.

872 Daniel H. Mintz interview with current owner, by email to author Oct 12, 2021.

SOURCES

PRIVATE ARCHIVES

(AFU) refers to "Archives for the Unexplained."

(Swiatek) refers to "Rob Swiatek's Personal Collection."

(Swords) refers to "The Archives of Professor Michael Swords."
(As this book was being published, CUFOS posted the Swords items at https://cufos.org/resources/nicap-documents/#Keyhoe.)

BOOKS

Adamski, George, *Inside the Space Ships*, Nelson, Foster and Scott Ltd. Canada, 1955.

Bachrack, D, *The Committee of One Million: "China Lobby" Politics, 1953-1971*, Columbia University Press, New York, 1976.

Bissell, Richard M., with Jonathan T. Lewis and Frances T. Pudlo, *Reflections of a Cold Warrior: From Yalta to the Bay of Pigs*, Yale University Press, 1996.

Bryson, Bill, *One Summer: America 1927*, Doubleday, 2013.

Colcord, Doane B, B.S., M.D., *Descendants of Edward Colcord of New Hampshire, 1630 to 1908*, Mahlon J. Colcord, Coudersport, Pa, 1908.

Dolan, Richard M., *UFOs and the National Security State: Chronology of a Cover-up 1941-1973*, Revised Edition, Hampton Roads Publishing Company, Inc., 2002.

Druffel, Ann, *Firestorm: Dr James E. McDonald's Fight For UFO Science*, Wild Flower Press, Columbus N.C., 2003.

Duffy, James P., *Lindbergh vs Roosevelt: The Rivalry That Divided America*, Regnery Publishing, 2010.

Edwards, Frank, *My First 10,000,000 Sponsors*, Ballantine Books, 1956.

Friedman, David M., *The Immortalists: Charles Lindbergh, Dr Alexis Carrel, and Their Daring Quest to Live Forever*, Harper Collins, 2007.

Gross, Loren E., *The Fifth Horseman of the Apocalypse: UFOs, a History*, 2000.

Hallett, Marc, with Richard W Heiden as Translator and Documentalist, *A Critical Appraisal of George Adamski: The Man Who Spoke to the Space Brothers*, Revised and Enlarged Edition, Internet July 2016.

Hynek, Dr J Allen, *The Hynek UFO Report*, Sphere Books Limited, London 1978.

Hynek, J. Allen & Jaques Vallee, *Edge of Reality: A Progress Report on Unidentified Flying Objects*, Henry Regnery, Chicago, Illinois 1975.

Jacobs, David Michael, *The UFO Controversy in America*, Signet, 1976.

John, Walton Colcord, *The Collected Issues of The Little Listening Post*, 2020.

Kean, Leslie, *UFOs: Generals, Pilots, and Government Officials Go On The Record*, Three Rivers Press, 2010.

Leslie, Desmond and George Adamski, *The Flying Saucers Have Landed*, Werner Laurie, London, 1953.

Keyhoe, Donald E, *Aliens From Space*, Granada Publishing Limited, 1975, first published by Doubleday & Company Inc, 1973.

Keyhoe, Donald E, *Flying Saucers From Outer Space,* Tandem 1969 Reprint.

Keyhoe, Donald E, *Flying Saucers: Top Secret*, G. P. Putnam's Sons, 1960.

Keyhoe, Donald E, *Flying with Lindbergh*, G P Putnam's Sons, 1928.

Keyhoe, Donald E, *The Flying Saucers Are Real*, Fawcett Publications, 1950.

Keyhoe, Donald E, *Flying Saucer Conspiracy*, Henry Holt and Company, 1955.

Keyhoe, Donald E, *M-day: If War Comes, What Your Government Plans for You*. New York: E. P. Dutton & Company, 1940.

Keyhoe, Donald E. and Gordon I. R. Lore, Jr., eds., *UFOs: A New Look*, NICAP, 1969.

Lore, Gordon, *Flying Saucers From Beyond The Earth*, Bear Manor Media, 2018.

Lorenzen, Coral and Jim, *Flying Saucer Occupants*, Signet Books, 1967.

Mebane, Lex, *The Collected Issues of CSI News Letter: Civilian Saucer Intelligence Group*, 2020.

O'Connell, Mark, *The Close Encounters Man: How One man Made the World Believe in UFOs*, Harper Collins, New York, 2017

Parfit, Michael, *Chasing The Glory*, Macmillan Publishing Company, New York, 1988.

Pilkington, Mark, *Mirage Men: A Journey in Disinformation, Paranoia and UFOs*, Constable, 2010.

Reynolds, Clark G, *On the Warpath in the Pacific: Admiral Jocko Clark and the Fast Carriers*, Naval Institute Press, Maryland, 2005.

Ruppelt, Edward J, *The Report on Unidentified Flying Objects*, Doubleday & Company, Garden City, New York 1956.

Schatzkin, Paul, *Defying Gravity: The Parallel Universe of T. Townsend Brown*, Tanglewood Books, 2008.

Serling, Ann, *As I Knew Him: My Dad, Rod Serling*, Kensington Publishing Corp. 2013.

Swords, Michael et al., *UFOs and Government*, Anomalist Books, 2012.

Wile, Frederic William, *Emile Berliner: Maker of The Microphone*, Indianapolis, Bobbs-Merrill Company, 1926.

REPORTS/JOURNALS

A Brief History of Marine Corps Aviation, Historical Branch, G-3 Division, Headquarters, US Marine Corps, Washington, D.C.

A History of US Naval Aviation, Capt. W H Sitz, USMC, United States Government Printing Office, Washington, 1930.

The Fairchild "All-Purpose" Cabin Monoplane. Aircraft Circulation No. 58, National Advisory Committee for Aeronautics, Washington, D.C., October 1937.

Aircraft Yearbook (1919 & 1922), Aeronautical Chamber of Commerce of America, Inc

Annual Report of the Director, United States Coast and Geodetic Survey to the Secretary of Commerce for the Fiscal Year Ended June 30, 1927, United States Government Printing Office, Washington, 1927.

Annual Report of the Secretary of Commerce, 1926, United States Government

Printing Office, Washington, 1927.

Annual Reports of the Navy Department for the Fiscal Year (Including Operations to November 15, 1922), United States Navy, U.S. Government Printing Office, 1923.

Arnold, Henry Harley, *Airmen And Aircraft: An Introduction to Aeronautics,* Ronald Press, 1926.

Brockett, Paul, *Bibliography of Aeronautics 1929,* Smithsonian Institution, 1930.

Catalog of The Public documents of the Congress and of all departments of the Government of the United States: the Comprehensive index provided for by the Act of Jan 12, 1895, Washington : U.S. G.P.O..

Cleveland, Reginald M. (Reginald McIntosh), *America Fledges Wings: the History of the Daniel Guggenheim Fund for the Promotion of Aeronautics.* Pitman Publishing Corporation, 1942.

Cloud, John, *Science on the Edge: The Story of the Coast and Geodetic Survey from 1867 - 1970,* NOAA Central Library.

Coast and Geodetic Survey Bulletin, US Coast and Geodetic Survey, Dept of Commerce, March 1926.

Fleming, Lt Col Charles A USMC, et al., *Quantico: Crossroads of the Marine Corps,* History and Museums Division Headquarters, US Marine Corps Washington, DC.

Flying Officers of the U.S.N. Naval aviation war book committee, Washington, D.C. [from old catalog] Washington, D.C., Naval aviation war book committee, [c1919].

Flying Officers of the US Navy 1917-1919, Naval Aviation War Book Committee, 1919.

Goldin, Claudia and Lawrence F. Katz. 2000. "Education and income in the early 20th century: Evidence from the prairies," *The Journal of Economic History* 60(3): 782-818.

Guam Newsletter (Mar/Apr/May 1921).

Historic American Engineering Record (Orote Airfield) National Park Service, Western Region, Department of the Interior, San Francisco (https://tile.loc.gov/storage-services/master/pnp/habshaer/gu/gu0000/gu0001/data/gu0001data.pdf)

History of Wapello County, Iowa, S J Clarke Publishing Co, Chicago, 1914.

Johnson, Lieutenant Colonel Edward C, USMC, *Marine Corps Aviation: The Early*

Sources

Years 1912-1940, History and Museums Division Headquarters, U.S. Marine Corps, Washington D.C. 1977.

Johnson, Thomas Lee, Roland Irvin Curtin, and United States Naval Academy. *Naval Ordnance: a Text-book Prepared for the Use of the Midshipmen of the United States Naval Academy*. Annapolis, Md.: The United States Naval Institute, 1915.

Journal of UFO Studies 95/96, The J. Allen Hynek Center for UFO Studies.

Kaufman, Roxanne M, and Laurie Schmidt. *100 Years of Marine Corps Aviation: an Illustrated History*. Washington, D.C.: U.S. Government Printing Office, 2011.

Keyhoe, Donald E. *M-day: If War Comes, What Your Government Plans for You*. New York: E. P. Dutton & Company, 1940.

Laning, Harris and Mark R Shulman, *HM 14: An Admiral's Yarn*, Naval War College Press, 1999.

Naval Ordnance: A Text-book Prepared for the Use of the Midshipmen of the United States Naval Academy, by Officers of the United States Navy, The United States Naval Institute, 1939.

Official register of the United States: persons in the civil, military, and naval service, exclusive of the Postal Service, Dept. of Commerce, Bureau of the Census

Oliver, William and Carroll S. Alden, *A Guide to Annapolis and the Naval Academy*, Wentworth Press, 2016.

Public Papers of the President of The United States: Harry S Truman January 1 to December 31, 1949, General Services Administration, National Archives and Records Service, Office of the Federal Register, 1999.

Regulations of the US Naval Academy Annapolis, Part I and Part II, 1911 (Revised to August 1, 1916).

Report of The High School Visitor, University of Illinois For the Year 1920-21, University of Illinois, Urbana, 1921.

Stevens, William Oliver, and Carroll Storrs Alden. *A Guide to Annapolis and the Naval Academy*, Lord Baltimore Press, 1910.

Talon American University Year Book, 1960.

Taylor, James C., *Ottumwa: 100 Years a City*, Ottumwa Chamber of Commerce,1948.

The 1920 Lucky Bag: The Annual of The Regiment of Midshipmen of The United States Naval Academy.

The Argus, Ottumwa High School Yearbooks 1915 & 1916.

The Aviation Industry: a Study of Underlying Trends, by Division of Commercial Research, Curtis Publishing Company, 1930.

The Type 'M' Kite Balloon Handbook, Navy Department Bureau of Construction and Repair, Oct 1919.

Thompson, Scott, *Flight Inspection History,* Sacramento Flight Inspection Office, 2008.

United National Association of Post Office Clerks (U.S.). *Post Office Clerk.* Washington, D.C.: United National Association of Post Office Clerks, 1909.

United States Naval Academy. *Naval Ordnance: a Text-book Prepared for the Use of the Midshipmen of the United States Naval Academy.* Annapolis, Md.: The United States Naval Institute, 1917.

United States Naval Academy. *Regulations of the United States Naval Academy.* Washington: G.P.O.

US Marine Corps Muster Rolls 1919-1958.

Widmer, Emil Joseph, *Military Observation Balloons (captive and free): A Complete Treatise on their Manufacture, Inspection, and Handling, with Special Instructions for the Training of a Field Balloon Company,* D. Van Nostrand Company, New York, 1917.

Woodhouse, Henry, 1884-1970. *Textbook of Naval Aeronautics,* New York: The Century Co., 1917.

RECORDINGS

Wendy Connors and Roderick Dyke, "High Strangeness Guide," *Archives for UFO Research,* https://archive.org/details/HighStrangenessGuide/18.mp3.

Wendy Connors and Roderick Dyke, "Project Blue Book Guide," *Archives for UFO Research,* https://archive.org/details/ProjectBlueBookGuide/84.mp3.

Wendy Connors and Roderick Dyke, "Profiles In Ufology Major Donald E. Keyhoe, Dr. James E. Mc Donald & Frank Edwards Guide," *Archives for UFO Research,*

https://archive.org/details/ProfilesInUfologyMajorDonaldE.KeyhoeDr.JamesE.
McDonaldFrankEdwardsGuide/18.mp3.

Wendy Connors and Roderick Dyke, "Ufology A Primer In Audio
1939 1959," *Archives for UFO Research*, https://archive.org/details/
UFOLOGYAPrimerInAudio19391959Guide/060.mp3.

Wendy Connors and Roderick Dyke, "Ufology A Primer In Audio, 1947-1964,"
Archives for UFO Research, https://tinyurl.com/yeywyvp9

NEWSPAPERS

Abilene Reporter-News (Abilene, TX)

Albuquerque Journal (Albuquerque, NM)

Appleton Post Crescent (Appleton, WI)

Authentic Science Fiction Monthly

Bee (Danville, VA)

Belvidere Daily Republican (Belividere, IL)

Bessemer Herald (Bessemer, MI)

Billings Gazette (Billings, MT)

Bridgeport Telegram (Bridgeport, CT)

Burlington Hawk Eye (Burlington, IA)

Cedar Rapids Gazette (Cedar Rapids, IA)

Charleroi Mail (Charleroi, PA)

Charleston Daily Mail (Charleston, West VA)

Chronicle-Telegram (Elyria, OH)

Davenport Democrat and Leader (Davenport, IA)

Dunkirk Evening Observer (Dunkirk, NY)

Escanaba Daily Press (Escanaba, MI)

Evening Capital and Maryland Gazette (Annapolis, MD)

Evening Star (Washington DC)

Evening State Journal (Lincoln, Nebraska)

Fort Madison Evening Democrat (Fort Madison, IA)

Frederick Post (Frederick, MD)

Helena Independent (Helena, MT)

Ironwood Daily Globe (Ironwood, MI)

Kingsport Times (Kingsport, Tennessee)

Lancaster Daily Gazette (Lancaster, OH)

Leatherneck

Lima News (Lima, OH)

Lincoln State Journal (Lincoln, Nebraska)

Logansport-Pharos Tribune (Logansport, IN)

Morning Herald (Hagerstown, MD)

Muncie Evening Press (Muncie, Indiana)

Nevada State Journal (Reno, NV)

Newark Advocate (Newark, OH)

New Castle News (New Castle, PA)

New York Times (NY)

New York Tribune (NY)

North Adams Transcript (North Adams, MA)

Oakland Tribune (Oakland, CA)

Ogden Standard Examiner (Ogden, UT)

Omaha Daily Bee (Omaha, NE)

Sources

Oshkosh Daily Northwestern (Oshkosh, WI)

Ottumwa Courier (Ottumwa, IA)

Ottumwa Semi-Weekly Courier (Ottumwa, IA)

Pensacola Journal (Pensacola, FL)

Press and Sun Bulletin (Binghamton, NY)

Register (Sandusky, OH)

Reno Evening Gazette (Reno, NV)

Richmond Palladium (Richmond, IN)

Salt Lake Tribune (Salt Lake, UT)

San Antonio Express (San Antonio, TX)

San Antonio Light (San Antonio, TX)

Sheboygan Press (Sheboygan, WI)

Stars and Stripes (Pacific Editions, 1945-1963)

Sunday Star (Washington D.C.)

Syracuse Herald Journal (Syracuse, NY)

Times Recorder (Zanesville, OH)

Valley Times (San Fernando Valley, CA)

Washington Daily News (Pamlico. Washington, NC)

Washington Post (Washington, D.C.)

Wisconsin State Journal (Madison, WI)

MAGAZINES

American Weekly

The American Magazine

Argosy

Aviation (1927)

Cosmopolitan (1937-1956)

Elks Magazine

Fantasy Science Fiction

Flying Aces (1930-1939)

Flying Stories

Leatherneck

Popular Mechanics (1914-1937)

Saga: The Magazine for Men

Saturday Evening Post

Sky Birds (1930-1933)

True: The Magazine for Men

Weird Tales (1925-1927)

INDEX

Wallace, Mike, 229-231, 233, 252-253, 292

War of the Worlds (radio), 52, 71

Warner, Jack, 59

Watkin, Lawrence E., 59

Watson, Harold E., 76, 79

Webb, Walter, 333

Wedemeyer, Albert C., 185, 203, 217

Weigle, John, 242, 244

Welles, Orson, 52-53, 61, 62, 68, 71, 76, 131, 261

Wells, H. G., 52, 62, 72, 80

Welsh, Bill, 237, 241

Werntz, Robert "Bobby" L., 7-8

Whedon, Spencer, 222, 224, 226, 254

Whitehall-Rand, 193

White, Betty, 135, 137, 140

White, Robert C., 136, 153, 158

White Sands Proving Grounds, 73, 142, 147

White, Thomas D., 290, 291

Whitted, John B., 62, 67, 72, 83, 219

Wile, Frederic W., 146

Williamson, George H., 116, 118, 141-142, 179

Williams, Alford J., 20

Williams, Donald A., 60

Wilson, Earnest A., 49

Wilson, Robert L., 104

Wilson, Woodrow, 31

Winchell, Walter, 69-70

Woodward, Bob, 98

Wortsman, Gene, 215

Wyman, Jane, 59

Zamora, Lonnie, 323-324, 363

Zausmer, Otto, 233

Zeidman, Jenny (*see also* Jenny Gluck), 108

Zuckert, Eugene M., 309

www.ingramcontent.com/pod-product-compliance
Lightning Source LLC
Chambersburg PA
CBHW050448270326
41927CB00009B/1649